FRENCH CRIME FICTION, 1945–2005

To Jacquie and George Oks, with love

French Crime Fiction, 1945–2005

Investigating World War II

MARGARET-ANNE HUTTON
University of St Andrews, UK

Routledge
Taylor & Francis Group

LONDON AND NEW YORK

First published 2013 by Ashgate Publishing

Published 2016 by Routledge

2 Park Square, Milton Park, Abingdon, Oxfordshire OX14 4RN

711 Third Avenue, New York, NY 10017, USA

First issued in paperback 2016

Routledge is an imprint of the Taylor & Francis Group, an informa business

British Library Cataloguing in Publication Data
Hutton, Margaret-Anne.
French crime fiction, 1945–2005: investigating World War II.
    1. World War, 1939–1945 – Literature and the war. 2. Detective and mystery stories, French – Themes, motives. 3. French fiction – 20th century – History and criticism.
    I. Title
    843.9'14093584053–dc23

Library of Congress Cataloging-in-Publication Data
Hutton, Margaret-Anne.
  French crime fiction, 1945–2005: investigating World War II / by Margaret-Anne Hutton.
    p. cm.
  Includes bibliographical references and index.
  ISBN 978-0-7546-6869-5 (hardcover: alk. paper)—ISBN 978-0-7546-9545-5 (ebook)
    1. French fiction—20th century—History and criticism. 2. World War, 1939–1945—France—Literature and the war. 3. Crime in literature. I. Title.

  PQ307.W4H88 2013
  843'.91409358—dc23
                                                                                    2012034454

ISBN 13: 978-1-138-27496-9 (pbk)
ISBN 13: 978-0-7546-6869-5 (hbk)

Contents

Acknowledgements   *vii*

Introduction   1

1   Reopening the Case of Georges Simenon   11

2   From Hybrid Whodunnit to Cyber-Sleuthing   45

3   Crimes, Criminals, and the Forces of Law and Order   81

4   Investigative Avatars   119

5   Criminal Continuities   157

Bibliography   *197*
Index   *215*

Acknowledgements

My thanks to friends and colleagues who read some of the chapters of the book at various stages of completion: Lucille Cairns; Máire Ní Fhlathúin; Lorna Milne; Claire Whitehead. Thanks also to Aimee Linekar who helped with some of the translations in Chapter 2. Finally, my thanks and love to Stephen for his support.

Introduction

Certainly none of the historians set out to play amateur detective.[1]

—Rousso

Genres are not to be mixed. / I will not mix genres. / I repeat: genres are not to be mixed. I will not mix them.

—Derrida[2]

Expressed in the most straightforward terms this book consists of analyses of a range of French-language works of crime fiction which represent World War II. Before teasing out these potentially tricky terms and phrases – the 'what?' and 'how?' of the matter – let me outline some answers to the question 'why?' First, the significance of the historical context, which in fact requires little explanation: shockingly swift French military defeat; political capitulation and collaboration; years of occupation; socio-political fragmentation and conflict ending in a period of regime change and transitional justice. Not to mention the theatre of war or the concentration and death camps beyond mainland France. That World War II has shaped France and the French is not really in question, so one answer to 'why this book?' is quite simply because it explores what some would call a national 'vector of memory',[3] in this case a corpus of works of fiction, which represents (and arguably reconstructs) those formative war years. Taken literally, which it often is not, the term 'memory' is in fact inapposite, given that many of the texts analyzed here were not written by individuals who lived through the war and few represent the real life experiences of their authors. Survivors of the war years are today small in number. Children of those first-hand witnesses or participants are likely to be grandparents themselves. Soon there will be no more memories of the war and no new testimonial or autobiographical accounts will be written or recorded. In the face of not just a generational, but an epistemological break with the past, fictional representations of the war are likely to gain increasing importance. As French historian Henry Rousso puts it, it may already be that for today's generation 'a film, history book, television programme, and newspaper

---

[1] Henry Rousso, *The Haunting Past. History, Memory, and Justice in Contemporary France* (U of Pennsylvania P, 2002), p. 62.

[2] Derrida, trans. by A. Ronell, 'The Law of Genre', *Glyph*, 7 (1980): 202–13, in David Duff, *Modern Genre Theory* (Longman, 2000), p. 220.

[3] The term 'vector of memory' is probably still most strongly associated with Henry Rousso's *Le Syndrome de Vichy* (Seuil, 1987), in which the author identifies official vectors (monuments, commemorations, etc.), those linked to associations (of deportees, soldiers, etc.), scholarly vectors (e.g., history books), and cultural vectors (literature, cinema, television). Rousso's limited discussion of the cultural vector focuses predominantly on film.

article can all have the same pedagogical impact when it comes to speaking of the past'.[4] To which list I would add, 'a work of crime fiction'.

Whilst there is an existing body of book-length publications on French literary representations of World War II – though considerably fewer works in this field, I think, than might be expected – these are of a quite different nature to what I propose here in terms of how both 'the war' and 'the literary' are defined. Earlier studies, for example Klein's *The Second World War in Fiction* (1984) or Harris's *Encounters with Darkness. French and German Writers on World War II* (1983), tend to focus on works produced between the war years and the 1950s, with only the occasional foray into the 1960s; both of these authors also extend their brief beyond prose fiction to other genres (drama, poetry, autobiographical writings).[5] Later comparatist works, largely inspired by the growing field of cultural memory studies, for instance Peitsch's *European Memories of the Second World War* (1999), typically move on to more recent texts, including those produced by a post-war generation, and again broaden the field of the literary to include a wide range of genres.[6] Alternatively, studies may look predominantly to the novel but concentrate on a few established figures, as is the case with Cloonan's *The Writing of War. French and German Fiction about World War II* (1999).[7] Other approaches, typified by Jones's *Journeys of Remembrance. Memories of the Second World War in French and German Literature, 1960–1980* (2007), are primarily concerned with representations of one specific aspect of the war, in this case the Holocaust, which remains the most extensively researched topic in the field.[8] Finally, works which focus entirely on French texts more often than not approach 'the war' primarily in terms of Resistance and collaboration, though these terms and the notion of their constituting a simple binary divide are duly unpicked. This applies, for instance, to Atack's *Literature and the French Resistance. Cultural politics and Narrative Forms, 1940–1950* (1989), Morris's *Collaboration and Resistance Reviewed. Writers and the Mode Rétro in Post-Gaullist France* (1992), and Lloyd's *Collaboration and Resistance in Occupied France* (2003).[9] None of the studies listed here, nor any other book-length English-language work, deals

---

[4]   Rousso, *The Haunting Past*, p. 15. Historian Richard Golsan has recently expressed a similar view, stating that 'it seems clear that the distinction between historical writing by historians and novelistic representations of the past by fiction writers is becoming increasingly blurred, certainly in the eyes of the general public': 'L'Affaire Karski: Fiction, History, Memory Unreconciled', *L'Esprit créateur*, 50.4 (2010): 81–96 [95].

[5]   Holger Klein (ed.), with J. Flower and E. Homberger, *The Second World War in Fiction* (Macmillan, 1984). Frederick J. Harris, *Encounters with Darkness. French and German Writers on World War II* (Oxford UP, 1983).

[6]   Helmut Peitsch, Charles Burdett, and Claire Gorrara, *European Memories of the Second World War* (Berghahn Books, 1999).

[7]   William Cloonan, *The Writing of War* (UP of Florida, 1999). Cloonan focuses on the work of French authors Camus, Sartre, Simon, Céline, and Tournier.

[8]   Kathryn N. Jones, *Journeys of Remembrance* (Legenda, 2007).

[9]   Margaret Atack, *Literature and the French Resistance* (Manchester UP, 1989); Christopher Lloyd, *Collaboration and Resistance in Occupied France* (Palgrave Macmillan,

with the representation of World War II in what might be called 'popular' genres such as crime fiction (nor indeed the saga or the romance, both of which would benefit from further research).[10] Two very short French-language works, *La Guerre dans le roman noir français* (1994) and *Le Polar français. Crime et histoire* (2002), discuss the representation of several different wars in French crime fiction, devoting only limited space to World War II, and consequently providing little in the way of analysis.[11] Unfortunately, Claire Gorrara's *French Crime Fiction and the Second World War: Past Crimes, Present Memories* (Manchester UP, 2012) was published too late in this book's production process to be included in this discussion.

In her diachronic study *Authoring War* McLoughlin briefly toys with the idea that 'each war has its own poesis, its "natural" way (or ways) of being represented', ascribing the epic novel to World War II.[12] Atack criticizes the author of *Encounters with Darkness. French and German Writers on World War II* for seeming to employ literary texts as 'empirical data' used to convey something of the experience of war.[13] Her own *Literature and the French Resistance* is divided into sections whose titles suggest a literary structuring principle: 'Literature of persuasion', 'Novels of unity', 'Novels of ambiguity'. Peitsch's *European Memories of the Second World War*, by contrast, appears to be structured around war-related categories, with sections entitled 'The German Soldier's Memory' and 'The Resistance Memory', though there is one literary-oriented header, 'The Media of Memory: May 1968 and Cinema'. All of these observations point to one of the key challenges facing those who write about literary representations of World War II: the need to balance, and ideally explore, the relationship between the historical and the literary.

As a genre which is usually regarded as highly codified, if not out-and-out formulaic, crime fiction is a useful test case for examining literary specificities. How might crime fiction in its various subgenres (more of which below) facilitate or skew the representation of World War II, or indeed offer new perspectives on it? Is the whodunnit more suited to the representation of certain aspects of the war than, say, the suspense novel? How, if at all, might crime fiction best go about

---

2003); Alan Morris, *Collaboration and Resistance Reviewed. Writers and the Mode Rétro in Post-Gaullist France* (Berg, 1992).

[10]   Lloyd remarks that 'It is a reasonable generalisation to state that most novels inspired by the Second World War tend to be either crude and violent adventure stories or wooden, sententious reconstructions', *Collaboration and Resistance*, p. 158. Although he acknowledges in a short discussion of Giovanni's *Mon ami le traître* that the latter has some 'historically persuasive commentary', this is deemed to be in spite of the fact that the thriller genre has a tendency to 'degenerate into formulaic plotting, stereotyped characterisation and tritely predictable cynicism', p. 191.

[11]   Emmanuel Jouvin and Laurence Ducousso, *La Guerre dans le roman noir français* (Médiatèque Louis Aragon, 1994); Elfriede Müller and Alexander Ruoff, *Le polar français. Crime et histoire* (La Fabrique, 2002).

[12]   Kate McLoughlin, *Authoring War. The Literary Representation of War from the* Iliad *to Iraq* (Cambridge UP, 2011), p. 10.

[13]   Atack, *Literature and the French Resistance*, p. 6.

representing Holocaust denial, and what might we mean by 'best go about' in this context? These are just some of the questions considered in the following chapters. But equally, how might the fact that works of crime fiction specifically represent World War II influence the type of investigator and his / her investigative methodology? Are there representations of crimes, criminals, and attitudes to each of these which are particular to these works of crime fiction precisely because the war years are represented? And the war, too, has its formulaic dimension: however much we may be aware of the rich stuff of history, the tendency to perceive that weave through familiar figures – member of the Resistance, collaborator, Jewish deportee, Gestapo officer, etc., – remains a strong one. The following chapters therefore also consider whether, and how, crime fiction may offer a new perspective on what have become almost stock figures of the war, or bring to the foreground entirely new protagonists and problematics. Crime fiction, finally, shares a wider concern with (the writing of) the history of World War II: the relationship between morality and legality; the potential difficulty in identifying clear-cut heroes and villains and the criteria by which to make such a judgment; the shifting nature of various links between past and present; how to uncover and represent 'the truth' about 'the past'. Reading crime fiction and its apparent constants (which turn out to be not quite so fixed) 'through' the narrative of World War II and its codified elements – and *vice versa* – results in a reappraisal of both.

Returning now to my opening description of this book as one which analyzes a range of French-language works of crime fiction representing World War II, some elaboration and explanation are in order. The adjectival 'French-language' rather than 'French' has been used because the work of two Belgian authors is discussed at some length: Chapter 1 consists of readings of texts by Georges Simenon, while Raymond Troye's *Meurtre dans un Oflag* (1946) is one of the four case studies which make up Chapter 2.[14] Two other examples might be spotted by the more pedantic: Stéphanie Benson, whose *Biblio-quête* (2001) is discussed in Chapter 5, is strictly speaking British but has lived in France since 1981 and writes in French; Maurice Dantec, whose *Les racines du mal* (1995) comes under scrutiny in Chapter 2, left France in 1998 and is now a naturalized Canadian. In all cases the works singled out for discussion have a strong French dimension: Simenon's four texts are set in France (or might be, in one indeterminate case), as are Benson's and Dantec's; my analysis of Troye's *Meurtre dans un Oflag* argues for a French / Belgian doubling or splitting in the narrating protagonist. A very small number of works – for instance Exbrayat's *Avanti la musica!* (1961) and Monsour's *Le Renard de la Forêt-Noire* (2002) – are neither set in France nor refer to any extent if at all to matters French. Texts such as these have been included in the bibliography but are not the subject of analysis. The less cumbersome but more ambiguous

---

[14]   These are the only two authors who are not French (or considered as French) and whose work is subject to substantive discussion. Others may be mentioned briefly in notes, e.g., Belgian Alain Berenboom (*Périls en ce royaume*), or Swiss Daniel Zufferey (*L'Étoile d'or*).

expression 'francophone [crime fiction]' has been avoided as the adjective still has connotations of an oppositional or at least differential construction in relation to metropolitan France.[15]

In terms of 'a range of' works of crime fiction, I have compiled and draw on a corpus of over 150 primary texts written by more than 90 authors and have aimed above all for inclusivity.[16] The texts are published between 1946 and 2008, allowing for diachronically shifting patterns of representation to be identified, either explicitly, or on the initiative of my readers. Less familiar names are included alongside established crime writers such as Amila, Aubert, Boileau-Narcejac, Daeninckx, Fajardie, Malet, and Vargas – to name just some. I have sought to recontextualize rather than rehearse the usual suspects: Modiano's *La Ronde de nuit* (1969), for instance, is discussed briefly in the light of a larger selection of texts set during the war years (Chapter 3); Daeninckx's *Meurtres pour mémoire* (1984) is referenced in Chapter 4 in the context of a broader discussion of the representation of historians as investigators and is mentioned again in the following chapter (but not analyzed) alongside other works linking the Algerian War with World War II. No gender policy has been in operation on my part, and I merely note that the corpus displays a not unexpected imbalance of approximately one female for every 10 male authors.

Moving on to more complex terminological territory, what do I mean by texts which 'represent World War II'? Atack's working definition of a war novel as 'one where the war is essential to the generation and resolution of the major conflicts and oppositions of the narrative' is a useful starting point which, whilst it has the disadvantage of potentially displacing the definitional exercise onto one of the other terms (what is meant by 'essential' or 'resolution'?), has the advantage of embracing plot, character, and thematic or symbolic development.[17] Atack's definition would not be far off the mark as a description of my own selection process, though for other reasons (notably my inclusion of texts published over a much more extended period and those set many years after the war) the end result in my case has been considerably broader. Works of crime fiction which represent World War II in the following chapters include those featuring any of the following (the list is far from exhaustive): nazis in various guises from 70-year-old submariners to those in hiding in 1960s' France or, indeed, clones; nazi hunters; black marketeering; wartime programmes of euthanasia and medical

---

[15] See for example Nina Sutherland's 'Trois continents, une guerre, un empire: Francophone Narratives of War and Occupation in the French Empire', *French Cultural Studies* 22.3 (2011): 187–96.

[16] Though the compilation process began before the Leeds-Durham FRAME database of French World War II narratives was made public, I did locate a small number of texts using this resource. There are, however, considerably more texts in the primary bibliography below than are identified under either 'crime' or 'detective' search terms in FRAME. The database can be accessed at: <http://www.frame.leeds.ac.uk/database/>.

[17] Atack, *Literature and the French Resistance*, p. 7.

experimentation; collaborationist journalists; Jewish deportees and survivors; French *gestapistes*; victims and perpetrators involved in the *épuration sauvage* (unofficial purges); wartime law enforcers of various hues. The corpus also displays a measure of geographical scope. The vast majority of texts are set in France, but not all: Amila's *Au balcon d'Hiroshima* (1985), for instance, unfolds for the most part in Japan; Couturier's *Sarah* (1997) takes us to an island in the Caribbean; Tabachnik's *Tango des assassins* (2000) is set in Argentina; and Las Vergnas's *Le Mystère Niagara* (1956) in the USA.

As will emerge, how, why, and to what effect the war is represented is inflected by the temporal texture of the texts. Some of the works included are set entirely during the war (though published across a span of over 60 years), from Malet's *120, rue de la gare* (1943) and Héléna's *Les Salauds ont la vie dure* (1949) to Manotti's *Le Corps noir* (2004) and Pécherot's *Boulevard des branques* (2005). Others are framed or multi-temporal narratives: Daeninckx's *La Mort n'oublie personne* (1989), for instance, moves between 1987, 1963, and 1944; d'Estienne d'Orves *Les Orphelins du mal* (2007) between the 2000s, the 1980s, and the war years. Many of the works are set wholly in the present (i.e., close to the date of publication) and represent World War II in various ways, from belated investigations into crimes committed during the war to unresolved legacies (literal and metaphorical) or Holocaust denial. Ultimately, what it means to say a text 'represents World War II' (which war, in whose eyes, when?) is part of what this book is all about, and each chapter, whether explicitly or implicitly, explores precisely this question. Chapter 1, for instance, considers the balance between historical specificity and temporally transcendent investigations into the human condition in Simenon's work. Chapter 2 looks to generic, synchronic, and diachronic variations in the representation of the war and takes us from symbolic readings of a whodunnit in a POW camp to ludic thrillers which seem to be more about language than war, to suspense novels which challenge Sartre's wartime vision, to a group of cyber serial killers playing 'Holocaust' in the 1990s. In Chapter 3 we see resistants, collaborators, and wartime criminality in a different light as new heroes and villains are foregrounded, whilst Chapter 4 investigates how the war is written into different discourses (e.g., historical, juridical, media) and how oedipal dramas come to represent transgenerational conflict centring on memories of the war. Finally, Chapter 5 examines some of the many ways in which the war continues to act upon the present.

Opening up new perspectives on the war and what it means to represent it is just part of the picture, however: this is also a book about 'works of crime fiction', another term which needs to be unpacked. Critical works on crime fiction or cognate terms such as 'detective fiction' ritually (I am tempted to say 'compulsively', since I find myself engaging in a similar, albeit metacritical, exercise here), open with a disclaimer to the effect that the subject matter of the book cannot be defined, before yielding to taxonomic temptation. Borges often comes to mind:

These ambiguities, redundancies, and deficiencies recall those attributed by Dr. Franz Kuhn to a certain Chinese encyclopedia called the *Heavenly Emporium of Benevolent Knowledge*. In its distant pages it is written that animals are divided into (a) those that belong to the emperor; (b) embalmed ones; (c) those that are trained; (d) suckling pigs; (e) mermaids; (f) fabulous ones; (g) stray dogs; (h) those that are included in this classification; (i) those that tremble as if they were mad; (j) innumerable ones; (k) those drawn with a very fine camel's-hair brush; (l) etcetera; (m) those that have just broken the flower vase; (n) those that at a distance resemble flies.[18]

Available categories for the sort of texts which critics of crime / detective fiction ponder are similarly profuse, if less absurd: hard-boiled; *néo-polar*; *polar*; police procedural; postmodern detective / crime novel; *roman à énigmes*; *roman jeu*; *roman noir*; *roman noir engagé*; *roman policier*; spy novel; suspense novel; thriller; whodu[n]nit.

This is not a comprehensive list. If I have included classificatory terms in two languages it is because cultural and linguistic factors are inevitably significant in a book written in English about French texts. Duff points out that Benedetto Croce saw little use for the concept of genre beyond that of 'arranging books on shelves', and when it comes to crime / detective fiction, shelving certainly seems to reflect a degree of generic uncertainty.[19] English-language critical works on crime / detective fiction are as likely to be shelved under the Library of Congress classmark PN (general literature) as under PR (English literature), whilst French-language works, which often focus partly or in some earlier cases entirely on Anglo-American fiction will nonetheless usually be located under PQ (French literature). There are no sub-classes for either 'crime fiction' or 'detective fiction'. Adding to classificatory ambiguities is a lack of critical engagement with terminology across national divides or, indeed, any genuinely comparative work. In 1929 Messac had recourse to an English term – *Le "Detective Novel" et l'influence de la pensée scientifique*; Gorrara repays the linguistic compliment with her *The Roman noir in post-war French culture* (2003).[20] Mine is not a comparative book nor do I undertake a linguistic analysis of French and English crime fiction terminology, though this is raised in the first chapter. I nonetheless flag the issue here as something of a caveat – is the *roman policier* the same as 'detective fiction' or is it perhaps more akin to 'crime fiction'?; do critics on both sides of the Channel mean the same thing when they refer to the *roman noir*? – and to note that there is scope for further research in this area.

---

[18] From Jorge Luis Borges, 'The Analytical Language of John Wilkins', in *Other Inquisitions, 1937–1952* (U of Texas P, 1975).

[19] David Duff, *Modern Genre Theory* (Longman, 2000), p. 25; Duff refers to Croce's 1902 *Aesthetic as Science of Expression and General Linguistic*.

[20] Claire Gorrara, *The Roman noir in post-war French culture* (Oxford UP, 2003); Régis Messac, *Le "Detective Novel" et l'influence de la pensée scientifique* (H. Champion, 1929).

My decision to use 'crime fiction' in my title and whenever I refer in general terms to my corpus of primary texts stems from the widely accepted nature of the term's inclusivity. Ascari notes that 'in the last thirty years crime fiction has become an umbrella term that includes the sub-category of detective fiction'; Porter describes the term 'crime literature' as 'the much larger and vaguer [i.e., than detective literature] category', whilst Knight sees 'the generally descriptive term "crime fiction"' as more useful since books [in the field which concern him] may often lack a detective or indeed a mystery but nearly always feature a crime or what appears to be one.[21] Horsley concurs, adding that 'the representation of *crime* without the reassuring presence of a detective is arguably the "parent" tradition'.[22] Of course things are never simple. Rezpka, for instance, feels bound to point out that some of the texts which might be considered examples of crime or detective fiction not only 'offer no mystery to be solved, but rather a difficulty to be overcome', but also 'do not, technically, involve crimes at all'. Priestman, similarly, observes that no 'technical crime' is committed in 15 of the Sherlock Holmes cases.[23] Objections such as these (and other potential terminological arguments) notwithstanding, in what follows when I use the term 'crime fiction' I do so to designate a genre, and one which subsumes all of the English-language categories listed above, which I refer to as subgenres (whodunnit, suspense novels, etc.).[24] Beyond these terminological explications, as was the case with the phrase 'representations of World War II', what is meant by both 'crime' and 'crime fiction' is the subject, explicit or implicit, of the rest of this book.

There remains one final categorizing complexity to acknowledge, and that is the relationship between crime fiction and fiction, or as some critics might see it, between 'popular' and 'high' literature. Attempting to solve this particular mystery would mean writing another book; the issue has intrigued critics for decades, and consensus on the subject is elusive. Todorov, for instance, notes that some types of crime fiction on the outer boundaries of the genre constitute an intermediary form between crime fiction ('roman policier') and fiction ('le roman tout court'),

---

[21] Maurizio Ascari, *A Counter-History of Crime Fiction* (Palgrave Macmillan, 2007), p. 6; Dennis Porter, *The Pursuit of Crime* (Yale UP, 1982), p. 11; Stephen Knight, *Crime Fiction 1800–2000: Detection, Death, Diversity* (Palgrave Macmillan 2004), p. xii.

[22] Lee Horsley, *Twentieth-Century Crime Fiction* (Oxford UP, 2005), p. 3. Uri Eisenzweig, by contrast, describes the classic whodunnit as 'l'*ur*-forme narrative policière', *Le Récit impossible* (Christian Bourgeois, 1986), p. 15.

[23] Charles Rezpka, *Detective Fiction* (Polity, 2005), p. 9; Martin Priestman, *Detective Fiction and Literature* (St Martin's P, 1991), p. 78.

[24] Needless to say critics cannot agree on the attribution of 'genre' and 'subgenre' labels. To select just one example, Palmer identifies the thriller as a genre (and one which encompasses spy stories and hard-boiled fiction) whilst Ascari refers to it as a subgenre of crime fiction. Jerry Palmer, *Thrillers. Genesis and Structure of a Popular Genre* (Edward Arnold, 1978); Maurizio Ascari, *A Counter-History of Crime Fiction* (Palgrave Macmillan, 2007).

though he rather unhelpfully does little to elaborate.[25] Porter, for his part, suggests that Hugo and Dickens wrote crime novels as opposed to detective novels, whilst Swirski, on the other hand, argues that it is still not the done thing to read a text like *Crime and Punishment* 'in genre terms'.[26] Priestman, meanwhile, elects to read 'detective' and 'literary' texts side by side in order to demonstrate how the former can be read 'as if' they were the latter.[27] I could go on. Criteria for differentiation between crime fiction and literary / 'high' fiction are often identified, and just as often invalidated: Swirski (amongst others) notes that forms of 'high' literature, for example the nineteenth-century novel, are arguably as repetitive and formulaic as works of crime fiction; Reuter (again amongst others) observes that the latter address the same sort of universal issues one might expect to find in 'high' literature.[28] Contrasting and conflicting views appear not just amongst critical works but in some cases within a single text: Lits, for example, here combining paratextual factors with notions of readerly competence, claims that works of crime fiction can be readily identified by their covers and the series they appear in, only to point out some pages later that works of crime fiction are increasingly being published in 'éditions blanches' (i.e., outwith any series: the epithet 'white' marks the contrast with the famous crime-oriented 'série noire').[29]

How we can differentiate crime fiction from adjective-free fiction is a question which is addressed explicitly at various stages of this book. Chapter 1, notably, asks not just whether Simenon's texts are about the war or not (and what this might mean) but also – and the two questions turn out to be linked – whether they are or are not works of crime fiction. The issue returns explicitly in the third chapter, where I suggest that it may be that all works of fiction set during World War II potentially fall into the crime fiction category. I have deliberately included in my corpus and discussion a small number of texts which are not marketed as works of crime fiction – which either lack any paratextual indicators designating them as such or which give out mixed signals – but which for various reasons can lay claim to that status. These include, in Chapter 3, Modiano's *La Ronde de nuit* (1969) and Daeninckx's *Itinéraire d'un salaud ordinaire* (2006); and in Chapter 4, Abécasssis's *L'Or et la cendre* (1997) and Modiano's *Dora Bruder* (1997). Other texts – for example Claude Courchay's *Retour à Malaveil* (1982) and Paul Guimard's *L'Ironie du sort* (1961) – which display significant similarities to works which are marked paratextually as examples of crime fiction, are mentioned in footnotes as points of comparison. Beyond my reading, or flagging up of, a number of works of fiction as examples of crime fiction, it may be that the reverse process

---

[25] Tzvetan Todorov, *Poétique de la prose* (Seuil, 1971), p. 65.

[26] Porter, *The Pursuit of Crime*, p. 24; Peter Swirski, *From Lowbrow to Nobrow* (McGill-Queen's UP, 2005), p. 28.

[27] Martin Priestman, *Detective Fiction and Literature*.

[28] Swirzki, *From Lowbrow to Nobrow*, p. 68; Yves Reuter, *Le Roman policier* (Armand Colin, 2005), p. 68.

[29] Marc Lits, *Le roman policier* (Éditions du Céfal, 1993), pp. 114 and 160.

takes place and that by the end of this book you have come to consider (at least some) works of crime fiction as more, or other, than their epithet suggests.

To close, some very brief comments on how this book has been put together and on pragmatic writing practices. Unless deemed by me to be essential to the comprehension of my argument, I have deliberately kept plot details to a minimum. That said, in many cases so-called 'spoilers' have been unavoidable. (I say 'so-called' because contrary to popular conceptions, and approached with a critical spirit, any work of crime fiction benefits from a second reading.) All translations are my own unless indicated otherwise. Working with close to 160 primary texts has allowed me to combine case studies of individual works with more synoptic analyses of patterns in, and recurring features of, the corpus as a whole. This perspectival shift between detailed analysis and a wider angle vision varies from chapter to chapter, and in some cases is combined within individual chapters. It is my intention, and hope, that the result not only provides an overview of what is an as yet largely unexplored corpus, but also offers some insight into both what a work of crime fiction is and does, and how the genre might allow us to see World War II differently.

Chapter 1
Reopening the Case of Georges Simenon

A good writer, of course, will always make us feel the gap between a mystery and its laying to rest.

—Hartman[1]

Such reactions convince me that, in my case at least, detective stories have nothing to do with works of art.

—Auden[2]

Acts of Criminal Categorizing

For many if not most readers, choosing 'a Simenon' almost certainly means selecting a detective novel starring the often eponymous inspector Maigret; but there is more to Simenon than his pipe-puffing sleuth. This opening chapter sets out to chart some of the fuzzy borderlines separating 'crime fiction' from 'fiction'. It also looks further into what it might mean to say that a novel 'represents World War II', and it does both of these things by turning to four of Simenon's texts which do *not* feature the pipe-smoking *commissaire*.

Simenon's work is typically divided into three broad categories. In an early phase of writing which took place primarily in the 1920s the author published some 190 books under many pseudonyms with various publishing houses (Éditions Arthème Fayard & Cie, Éditions J. Ferenczi & Fils, Éditions Jules Tallandier *inter alia*) in a range of popular collections. Such works are categorized by Alavoine as romances, light fiction, and adventure stories,[3] and described rather more judgmentally by Fabre as the 'partie "ignoble"' ['the "worthless" part'] of the author's output; 'les romans feuilletons alimentaires des débuts' ['the serialized potboilers he wrote at the start of his career'].[4] These works include, for instance, such tempting titles as *Le Gorille-Roi* (Tallandier, 1929) and *Les Nains des cataractes* (Tallandier, 1928), both appearing in the series 'Grandes Aventures et voyages excentriques' and written under the pseudonym Georges Sim, or, in the

---

[1] Geoffrey Hartman, 'Literature High and Low: The Case of the Mystery Story', in Glenn Most & William Stowe (eds), *The Poetics of Murder* (Harcourt Brace Jovanovich, 1983), pp. 210–29.

[2] Auden, 'The Guilty Vicarage', *Harpers*, May 1948, <http://harpers.org/archive/1948/05/0033206>. Accessed 2 December 2011.

[3] Bernard Alavoine, 'Roman populaire, roman policier et roman psychologique chez Georges Simenon: les trois facettes d'un auteur en quête de légitimation', in Jacques Migozzi (ed.), *Le roman populaire en question(s)* (PULIM, 1997), pp. 433–53 [435].

[4] Jean Fabre, *Enquête sur un enquêteur* (CERS, 1981), p. 7.

'Collection gauloise', written under the pseudonym Gom Gut, *Orgies bourgeoises* (Prima, 1926) and *l'Homme aux douze étreintes* (Prima, 1926). A second grouping comprises works published under Simenon's own name. Between 1931 and 1934 19 works featuring Maigret and nine without were published with Fayard. A move to N.R.F.-Gallimard led to the appearance of six further Maigret tales and 44 other novels between 1934 and 1947. Finally, with Presses de la Cité (1945–81), Simenon published 50 'Maigret' and a further 64 novels which did not feature the inspector. The four texts which form the case studies for this chapter, signed 'Simenon', belong to the final phase of production and are, in order of analysis: *La neige était sale* (1948), *Le Clan des Ostendais* (1947), *Les Autres* (1962), and *Le Train* (1961).

As the rather imprecise terminology – 'Maigret' and 'other novels' – used above indicates, ascribing labels to Simenon's work is not an easy task: just what *are* these four texts, and (how) can they be identified as examples of crime fiction? In 1934, by which time he had written 19 works featuring Maigret in under four years, Simenon stated 'J'en ai marre du personnage de Maigret. [...] Dorénavant, j'écrirai *des romans tout court*' (my emphasis) ['I'm fed up with the character Maigret. (...) From now on I'm going to write novels that are just novels'],[5] also referring to those of his later works which did not feature his increasingly popular police inspector as 'romans durs' (literally, hard, or tough novels). For Fabre, the latter constitute what he terms the 'partie "noble"' ['noble part'] of the Simenon corpus, the 'romans romans' ['novel novels'] or 'grands romans' ['great novels'], with those works starring Maigret relegated to mid-table status as the 'partie "demi-noble"' ['semi noble part'].[6] Already we can see various taxonomic principles, functions, and presuppositions at work: identifying, or more accurately constructing, discrete categories of the Simenon *œuvre* involves the date of production, the choice of publishers and series, the decision to publish pseudonymously or not, the inclusion or exclusion of the recurring character Maigret; into all of which categorizing strategies are embedded explicit or implicit value judgments. In what follows I hope to unpick what is perhaps the most common of the labelling manoeuvres: the splitting of the later corpus into 'Maigret' and 'not-Maigret' texts.

Designating a class of text by simple negation is not an uncommon enterprise when it comes to constructing literary categories. For Fredric Jameson, this process typifies syntactic or structural genre criticism (the contrary of 'comedy', for instance, becomes the 'non-comic'), deemed by him to be as unsatisfactory as the semantic model which functions by opposing one genre – or mode as he would have it – to another (comedy / tragedy).[7] Both approaches, Jameson points out,

---

[5]   Georges Simenon, *L'Âge du roman* (Complexe, 1988), pp. 58 and 60, cited by Alavoine, 'Roman populaire', p. 440.

[6]   Jean Fabre, *Enquête sur un enquêteur*, p. 7.

[7]   Fredric Jameson, 'Magical Narratives: On the Dialectical use of Genre Criticism', in David Duff (ed.), *Modern Genre Theory* (Longman, 2000), pp. 167–92 [169].

fail adequately to take historical considerations into account. Whilst this is not the place for a comprehensive analysis of the historical conditions of the ascription of genre categories to Simenon's work, certain questions should at least be asked. Is 'a Maigret' defined purely by the presence of a recurring literary character whose pipe-smoking silhouette has achieved iconic status? Platten affirms that by 1945 'Maigret (and his pipe) had become enshrined in the national consciousness'.[8] Can 'a Maigret' (1930s to 1970s) be of the same generic order as 'a Sherlock Holmes' (late 1890s) or, in the francophone context, 'a Nestor Burma' (predominantly 1950s) or 'a Poulpe' (1995 onwards)?[9] Dubois identifies other necessary brand features: 'lorsque nous disons "un Maigret", nous désignons par là, plus qu'un personnage, tout un univers fictionnel et tout un monde narratif' ['when we refer to "a Maigret", we are referring beyond just a character to a whole fictional universe and narrative world'].[10] Yet there is some doubt as to whether the 'fictional universe' and 'narrative world' of the Maigret texts are in fact so very different from those of the 'not-Maigret' novels. Narcejac, for instance, notes that the novels without the inspector 'are constructed on exactly the same lines as the novels with Maigret', with the latter's role simply being transferred to a protagonist who 'investigates' himself.[11] Boileau-Narcejac expand on the same point:

> Il n'est pas possible d'aller plus loin sans sortir du roman policier. Nous sommes sur la ligne de partage. Ajoutons Maigret à une histoire criminelle et nous avons un roman policier. Retranchons-le et nous avons un roman tout court. Dans les deux cas, le matériau est le même. La seule différence est que tantôt le coupable est le plus éclairé sur son compte par Maigret et tantôt il se révèle tout seul à lui-même […].[12]

> [It is impossible to go any further without leaving the realm of the detective novel. We are on the dividing line. Add Maigret to one of the criminal tales and it becomes a detective novel. Take Maigret away and it is just a novel. The material is the same in both cases. The only difference is that sometimes it is Maigret who casts light on the guilty party, and sometimes the latter comes to realize his guilt all by himself.]

Like all genre-related statements this too must be contextualized. Boileau-Narcejac state that a text which includes inspector Maigret is a 'roman policier', but what does this term with its reified epithet actually designate, and is it a

---

8   David Platten, 'Ceci n'est pas une pipe': shades of *noir* in Simenon', *Australian Journal of French Studies*, 43.1 (2006): 19–34 [19].

9   Nestor Burma is Léo Malet's recurring investigator; lone investigator Gabriel Lecouvreur, aka 'le Poulpe' features in the 'Poulpe' multi-authored series launched in 1995 by Jean-Bernard Pouy. For a brief discussion of the emergence and current state of the latter series see Platten, *The Pleasures of Crime* (Rodopi, 2011), 'The Age of the Octopus', pp. 203–11.

10   Jacques Dubois, *Le Roman policier ou la modernité* (Armand Colin, 2006), p. 171.

11   Thomas Narcejac, *The Art of Simenon* (Routledge & Kegan Paul, 1952), p. 16.

12   Boileau-Narcejac, *Le Roman policier* (PUF, 1975), p. 74.

category into which the Maigret texts can be slotted? Cawelti describes Simenon's Maigret texts as part of the classical detective novel tradition but also wonders why Simenon chose this form (or formula, as he describes it) 'to pursue ends that are close to those of the "serious" novel'.[13] Alavoine notes that Simenon may include the key 'roman policier' features of mystery and investigation as the framework for his Maigret novels, but he also points out that these novels diverge from the norm: 'Ou bien l'énigme n'en sera pas vraiment une parce que l'on connaît très tôt l'identité du criminel, ou bien l'enquête sera menée d'une façon très fantaisiste par Maigret, très loin des maîtres de la déduction' ['Either the mystery does not really qualify as such because the guilty party's identity is revealed very early on, or the investigation is carried out by Maigret in a very unorthodox manner, far removed from the methods of the masters of deduction'].[14] Dubois, taking a sample of 19 Maigret novels, enumerates six divergences from what he identifies as generic norms: there is no crime and no guilty party; the detective is not invited to lead the inquiry; the detective becomes personally involved in the inquiry; the detective does not lead the inquiry; the detective finds the guilty party but does not deliver him into the hands of the law; the detective is not innocent.[15] It is clear that both Dubois and Alavoine are basing their conception of the 'roman policier' on the classic detective novel or 'roman à énigmes'.

That Maigret is no Poirot or Miss Marple and that 'a with Maigret Simenon' cannot readily be likened to 'an Agatha Christie' or other classic detective novel seems to be generally accepted, so might a less problematic term of comparison than the classic whodunnit be found? Coming at things from another direction critics have sought to define Simenon's work as (proto-)*noir*, a term that has the benefits of flexibility which come with vagueness. It is also a term which some critics feel able to attribute to all of Simenon's work published under his own name. Unsurprisingly, given the pace at which criticism evolves – Breton notes that French critical work on crime fiction more or less ignores *noir* until the late 1970s[16] – the *noir* designation is favoured by anglo-saxon critics and more recent French critical works. Evrard, referring specifically to the Maigret novels, locates these texts astride the 'roman à énigmes' and 'noir' categories, noting the geographic scope of the works (no country mansions or cruise liners), the prospective drive of the narrative, and the emphasis on the psychology of the criminal.[17] Emmanuel similarly suggests that Simenon bridges the 'codified *roman à énigmes* of the early 1930s' and 'the splintering of the genre beginning with Léo Malet and the French

---

[13]   J.G. Cawelti, *Adventure, Mystery and Romance* (U of Chicago P, 1976).

[14]   Alavoine, 'Roman populaire', p. 439.

[15]   Dubois, *Le Roman policier ou la modernité*, pp. 177–8.

[16]   Jacques Breton, *Les collections policières en France* (Éditions du Cercle de la Librairie, 1992), 'Études et essais', pp. 241–78 [245].

[17]   Franck Evrard, *Lire le roman policier* (Dunod, 1996), p. 62.

roman noir in the early 1940s'.[18] Referring to 'the first great revolution in the crime novel' Mandel identifies Hammett and Chandler but also Simenon, Malet, and Ross MacDonald as participants: 'the tough, realistic detective novels of the Hammett / Chandler / Simenon / Ross MacDonald school were simply a transitional form between the drawing-room mystery and the world-wide adventure'.[19] Baronian, who focuses his attention here on the not-Maigret texts (which he terms 'romans durs'), hedges his bets and opts for grey rather than *noir*:

> J'ajoute que presque tous les romans durs de Georges Simenon s'inclinent, eux aussi, vers le gris […]. Ils formeraient de la sorte une espèce intermédiaire, à mi-chemin entre le roman de détection classique et le roman noir […].[20]

> [I should add that nearly all of Simenon's 'hard' novels also tend towards the grey (…). They thereby constitute a sort of intermediary category, midway between the classic whodunnit and the *noir* novel.]

Platten, finally, suggests that texts such as *La neige était sale* 'prefigured the "roman noir" of the late twentieth century'.[21] As long as we have *noir* in mind rather than the classic whodunnit, can we thus classify Simenon's Maigret and not-Maigret texts alike as examples of the 'roman policier'? Of course it all depends on what we mean when we use the term *noir*. If Simenon's novels are not described as fully *noir* but as precursors or transitional forms, it is at least partly because, as Platten points out, the term now tends to designate a text which is 'aggressively referential and often interventionist', a work which engages with socio-political – and, more recently, historical – issues.[22] The point to be stressed is that diachronic difference must be taken into account when attempting to designate generic categories: the meaning of 'roman policier' or 'roman noir' is not necessarily the same in 1930 and 2010, not to mention the fact that Simenon's own works will inevitably have modified, and not merely slotted into, these categories. As noted in the Introduction, cultural / linguistic terminological differences also impact on classificatory acts. Narcejac (above) uses the term 'histoire criminelle'; Fabre describes the texts without Maigret as 'romans du criminel'.[23] Although the adjective 'policier' in its primary sense indicates that which is relative to

---

[18]   Michelle Emmanuel, *From Surrealism to Less-Exquisite Cadavers* (Rodopi, 2006), p. 20.

[19]   Ernest Mandel, *Delightful Murder: a Social History of the Crime Story* (Pluto P, 1984), pp. 34–5 and p. 86.

[20]   Jean-Baptiste Baronian, *Simenon ou le roman gris. Neuf études sentimentales* (Textuel, 2002), p. 102.

[21]   Platten, 'Ceci n'est pas une pipe', p. 21.

[22]   Ibid., pp. 21–2. For a comparative study of degrees and types of socio-political engagement in crime fiction subgenres see Corcuff and Fleury, 'Profondeurs du social et critique politique: hypothèses comparatives sur Maigret et le néo-polar', *Mouvements*, 15/16 (2001): 28–34.

[23]   Fabre, *Enquête sur un enquêteur*, pp. 106–7.

the police, a more recent definition in the *Petit Robert* emphasizes criminality alongside investigation: 'Se dit des formes de littérature [...] qui concernent des activités criminelles plus ou moins mystérieuses qui font l'objet d'une enquête' ['Is said of types of literature (...) involving criminal activities of a more or less mysterious nature which are the subject of an investigation']. For an anglophone critic such as Malmgren, with a more inclusive label in his arsenal than his French counterparts, the categorization conundrum is easily resolved: Simenon wrote detective fiction (Maigret) and crime fiction (not-Maigret).[24]

So far, in terms of categorizing acts, I have suggested that *La neige était sale*, *Le Clan des Ostendais*, *Les Autres*, and *Le Train* may have affinities with aspects of *noir* fiction and, in terms of the terminology of anglophone criticism, may be examples of crime fiction. The next question is do the epithets 'noir' and 'crime' disqualify these texts as just 'novels'? Must a 'roman noir', for instance, be excluded from a category such as Fabre's tautological 'romans romans'? Part of the difficulty in classifying Simenon's work lies precisely in the dual nature of his output. In his work on paratext Genette suggests that eschewing pseudonyms usually plays to an author's advantage: the latter, or the publisher, uses the author's name and renown to promote sales ('This book is the work of the illustrious So-and So').[25] Genette further states that the author's name fulfills a contractual function whose importance in fiction is 'slight or non existent' (whereas in non fiction it can operate as a guarantee of authenticity and credibility).[26] When it comes to an author like Simenon, however, Genette's statements are less applicable. In the eyes of the reader for whom crime fiction is a devalued genre, any work with 'Simenon' on its cover may be similarly tainted. Alavoine, indeed, refers to the 'contamination' of Simenon's not-Maigret novels by those featuring the inspector.[27] He adds:

> Ce qui devient impossible – du moins en France – c'est de vouloir superposer deux carrières d'écrivain sous le même nom surtout quand on aborde un genre dévalorisé (le roman policier) et un genre jugé noble (le roman traditionnel, héritier du XIXème siècle).[28]

> [What becomes impossible – at least in France – is the attempt to build two separate careers as a writer using the same name, particularly when tackling one genre which lacks any prestige (the detective novel) and another judged to be of high literary status (the traditional novel, heir to the nineteenth century).]

Once again, context is all-important. Is the 'roman policier' still, as Alavoine suggested, a genre lacking any prestige? Certainly there have been changes

---

[24]   Carl Malmgren, *Anatomy of Murder* (Bowling Green U Popular P, 2001), p. 9.

[25]   Gérard Genette, *Paratexts: Thresholds of Interpretation*, trans. Jane E. Lewin, (Cambridge UP, 1997), p. 40.

[26]   Ibid., p. 41.

[27]   Alavoine, 'Roman populaire', p. 451.

[28]   Ibid., pp. 451–2. See also Boileau-Narcejac on readers' expectations with respect to detective novels and 'ordinary novels', *Le Roman policier*, p. 113.

in France. From being ignored in the academy to being discussed as an example of 'paralittérature', crime fiction, as Gorrara points out, now features on school curricula and has its own research infrastructure, as well as a specialist library, dedicated reviews, websites, prizes, and festivals.[29] This 'process of cultural legitimization' (Evrard similarly refers to a genre on the way to being legitimized)[30] certainly suggests acceptance at some level, but does it necessarily indicate a new-found faith in the aesthetic value of crime fiction? Would a 'roman policier' be accepted in France today without its epithet, i.e., as just 'a novel' or 'roman roman'? As a genre which fits neatly into the field of cultural studies, crime fiction was bound to make its way into the academy, but it is nonetheless often still regarded as an example of 'popular culture' rather than 'real', 'high' literature – in short, it is still often regarded as *crime* fiction rather than fiction.

In their discussion of the legitimization of crime fiction in France both Evrard and Gorrara record that since the 1990s most of the major publishing houses have established specialist 'fiction policière' collections.[31] Though this is almost certainly primarily indicative of marketing strategy rather than aesthetic judgment (not that the two are entirely separable), a brief glance at the publishing history of Simenon's 'romans romans' is certainly instructive. *Le Clan des Ostendais* (1947) was first published by Éditions N.R.F.-Gallimard; *La neige était sale* (1948), *Le Train* (1961), and *Les Autres* (1962) by Presses de la Cité. The 27 volume *Tout Simenon* (Paris: Presses de la Cité, 1988) brings together Maigret and not-Maigret texts (though a separate *Tout Maigret* is also available). Volume 3, for instance, includes *Les Vacances de Maigret* (1948), *La neige était sale* (1948), *Le fond de la bouteille* (1949), *La Première Enquête de Maigret* (1948), *Les Fantômes du chapelier* (1949), *Mon ami Maigret* (1949), *Les Quatre Jours du pauvre homme* (1949), and *Maigret chez le coroner* (1949).[32] Significantly, this combination of texts does not pass without comment: the editor clearly felt obliged to point out that the volumes comprise a mixture of 'Maigret' and 'novels' ('romans') whilst an index listing these in alphabetical order helpfully marks out the 'Maigret' texts with the letter 'M'. When the Pléiade edition was mooted, editor Jacques Dubois (describing Simenon – perhaps a little defensively – as 'un écrivain qui

---

[29]   Claire Gorrara, 'French Crime Fiction: from *genre mineur* to *patrimoine culturel*', *French Studies* 61.2 (2007): 209–14 [209–10]. Yves Reuter also suggests that the 'roman policier' has emerged from its semi-ghettoized position (his term), and is not longer subject to the sort of exclusion (he uses the term 'anathème') it faced in earlier decades, *Le Roman policier* (Armand Colin, 2005), p. 7. Marc Lits, using not dissimilar terminology, states that the 'roman policier' has finished its time in purgatory, *Le Roman policier* (Éd. Du Céfal, 1993), p. 155.

[30]   Evrard, *Lire le roman policier*, p. 28. See also Collovald and Neveu, *Lire le noir* (Centre Pompidou, 2004), a sociological study of the reception of crime fiction (in France) carried out in the light of what the authors refer to as the genre's newly acquired cultural legitimation (13).

[31]   Evrard, p. 28; Gorrara, 'French Crime Fiction', p. 209.

[32]   *Tout Simenon. Tome 3* (Paris: Omnibus, 2002).

vient un peu d'ailleurs que les écrivains les plus classiques' ['a writer who comes from a somewhat different place from the most classical writers'],[33] made his selection of texts according to two principal criteria: the volumes must showcase a representative sample of the author's work, and must include the 'great titles' (such as *La neige était sale*, described by Dubois as a pure masterpiece).[34] The first two volumes, *Romans* (2003), comprising 21 works, include five Maigret novels; volume III, *Pedigree et autres romans* (2009), has no Maigret texts. *La neige était sale* and *Le Train* appear in volume II; *Les Autres* in volume III.[35]

When I started writing this book, the four texts being discussed below thus seemed, in terms of their publishing history at least, potentially to have achieved the status of just 'romans', three of them receiving the ultimate institutional literary validation of a place in the Pléiade edition. I looked forward to the not-so-obvious task of parading them as examples of 'crime fiction'. All that changed in 2008 (I was not sure whether to be elated or horrified) when *Les Autres*, *Le Train*, and *La neige était sale* were signed up for the Livre de Poche 'Policier / Thriller' series, with *Le Clan des Ostendais* appearing in the Folio 'Policier' collection the following year. Even dedicated crime series, however, can keep classificatory boundaries a little blurred. The Livre de Poche collection, which includes translations of an extraordinarily eclectic range of Anglophone authors ranging from Elizabeth Peters to Ian Rankin to Ruth Rendell and Frederick Forsyth, is recognizable as such only by means of a black band on the front cover and the small image of a flaring match on the back. The words 'policier' or 'thriller' do not appear anywhere on or in the text. The editorial material on the inside page duly records that Simenon wrote 72 'Maigret' as well as what he was to call his 'novel novels' ('romans romans') or 'hard novels' ('romans durs'). The Folio 'policier' is clearly marked as such on the front cover, whilst the inside bio-bibliographical text states 'En 1931 le commissaire Maigret commence ses enquêtes ...' ['In 1931 inspector Maigret began his investigations ...'] but makes no mention of any other types of text produced by the author. The jury, it would seem, it still out.

The discussion thus far has, I hope, fulfilled its brief of exploring some of the classificatory boundaries between crime fiction and fiction with respect to Simenon's writing. No grand revelation, no definitive 'solution' regarding the generic status of Simenon's not-Maigret texts is offered here, partly because I do not believe that such clear-cut definition exists, and partly because the case studies below, and indeed the rest of this book, are intended to continue the process of investigation. Before moving on to these individual analyses, one last issue must be raised, and that is the presence of World War II in Simenon's work. Reading the critical material on the author, one might easily be persuaded that Simenon was not a promising choice of author to include in a book on the representation

---

[33]   Jacques Dubois, 'Simenon à la Pléiade', <http://laguinguette.com/lejournal/2003/07cult/>. Accessed 28 November 2010.

[34]   Ibid.

[35]   *Simenon, Romans, Tome I and Tome II*, ed. Jacques Dubois (Gallimard, 2003).

of the war years. Dubois, for instance, suggests that Simenon's Maigret texts have 'no historical markers';[36] Emmanuel states of the same texts that 'Simenon never alludes to either of the World Wars, much less to the occupation',[37] whilst Fabre asserts that Simenon's texts remain impervious to historical facts and never refer to World War II.[38] With respect specifically to Simenon's not-Maigret works Becker claims that 'Only two of Simenon's novels, *Le Train* and *Le Clan des Ostendais* […] are set against a background of war',[39] whilst Fabre suggests that some texts – including *Le Train*, *Le Clan des Ostendais*, and *La neige était sale* (*Les Autres*, strangely, is not mentioned) – evoke the Second World War.[40] Platten, finally, states that 'there are no dates, very few allusions to historical events', and registers the author's 'refusal to connive with any kind of historical narrative', adding 'Above all, politics, history and international affairs leave no impression on the "type Simenon", the small-time, suburban everyman who, in his multiple guises, populates his historical universe'.[41] As will become apparent in what follows, some of these statements are quite simply incorrect; all require further investigation.

La neige était sale: Proto-*Noir* Crime Fiction or (and) Coming-of-Age Novel?

Of the four selected texts it is *La neige était sale* which, at least on the face of it, has the strongest claim both to being a work of crime fiction and one which is 'about the war'. According to at least one critic 'it is difficult to imagine that the novel is set anywhere other than in France, or perhaps Belgium, in the early forties'.[42] Unlike the other three novels, *La neige* includes the commission of acts easily recognizable as crimes – a theft and two murders – and thus, one might suppose, a criminal, whilst also featuring at least three different investigating characters. Should anyone wish to label the text *noir* or proto-*noir*, they could readily select suitable generic traits identified by a range of critics: the text undoubtedly has its share of violence, action, and anxiety-inducing suspense (Boileau-Narcejac on the 'roman noir');[43] a narrative characterized primarily by prospective force but with a residual element of mystery, coupled with the representation of sordid crime and amoral characters (Todorov on the 'roman noir');[44] subjective point of view and

---

[36] Page Dubois, 'Oedipus as detective: Sophocles, Simenon, Robbe-Grillet', *Yale French Studies*, 108 (2005): 102–15 [109].

[37] Emmanuel, From Surrealism to Less-Exquisite Cadavers, p. 49.

[38] Fabre, *Enquête sur un enquêteur*, p. 28 and p. 121.

[39] Lucille Becker, *Georges Simenon Revisited* (Twayne Publishers, 1999), p. 31.

[40] Fabre, *Enquête sur un enquêteur*, p. 120.

[41] Platten, 'Ceci n'est pas une pipe', p. 22.

[42] Ibid., p. 26.

[43] Boileau-Narcejac, *Le Roman policier*, p. 85, citing Marcel Duhamel on the Série noire.

[44] Todorov, 'Typologie du roman policer', in his *Poétique de la prose* (Seuil, 1971).

a plot in which violence and death are ever-present (Reuter on the roman noir);[45] the depiction of an ill-fated relationship between the protagonist and society, with accompanying dominant themes of alienation and entrapment (Horsley on the *noir* thriller).[46] Having said all that, it could equally be argued that the investigators and indeed the investigation are not quite what might be expected of *noir*; that although there is a mystery, the hermeneutic code is dislocated from the crimes; that the latter are hard to define as such in the specific historical context we are likely to ascribe to the diegesis, and finally, that the protagonist does not believe himself to be a criminal. In fact, even arguing that the text specifically represents World War II is far from self-evident ....

La neige is unquestionably set during a period of war, and more particularly in a city under a regime of occupation. War is crucial to the plot to the extent that the protagonist, 19-year-old Frank Friedmaier, is arrested, apparently for his involvement with black market activities, and / or links to enemy agents, interrogated, and ultimately executed by representatives of the enemy forces. There is, however, nothing in the text which links it explicitly to World War II or indeed to any other specific conflict. Assouline suggests that Simenon left the location in *La neige* deliberately undefined in order 'to show that a man can be drawn into this kind of downward spiral in any country occupied by any army'.[47] Alongside his claim that readers are most likely to assume that the text is set in France or Belgium in the 1940s, Platten observes that 'Simenon dodges issues of memory and political bias that tend to bear on narratives of the Vichy years and forges ahead with an attempt to distill the evidence of occupied life'.[48] (The word 'dodges' here might be rendered less anachronistically as 'avoids'.) However, in spite of the indeterminate setting, as Assouline further notes, 'Since the German occupation was still very much in people's minds, many thought of the novel as taking place in northern or northeastern France', adding that Sven Nielson's publicity campaign suggested that the action unfolds in Belgium.[49] Stage and film versions of *La neige*, produced only a few years after the novel's publication, set the action during World War II and in occupied France, respectively.[50]

The fact that contemporary readers might have engaged with the text as a representation of the Second World War in a French setting is unsurprising (a comparison with *La Peste*, published a year earlier, might be made) given that potential links between the *La neige* and the 1940–44 German occupation range from the small- to the large-scale. The dual status of resistants as heroes and villains is emphasized: 'Hamling a dit *terroriste*, comme les occupants.

[45]   Yves Reuter, *Le Roman policier*.

[46]   Lee Horsley, *The Noir Thriller* (Palgrave, 2001).

[47]   Pierre Assouline, *Simenon* (Gallimard, 1996), p. 244.

[48]   Platten, 'Ceci n'est pas une pipe', p. 26.

[49]   Assouline, *Simenon*, p. 244.

[50]   Adapted by Frédéric Dard and directed by Raymond Rouleau, the play was staged in 1950. The film version was directed by Luis Saslavsky and released in 1953.

D'autres emploient le mot patriote' (44) ['Hamling said "terrorist", just like the occupiers. Others use the word patriot']. In several respects (see also below), the protagonist Frank is reminiscent of the eponymous young anti-hero in Louis Malle's *Lacombe Lucien*: like Lucien, Frank is represented as having been turned away from the Resistance: 'Il aurait pu être chef de réseau' (92) ['He could have led an underground network']; 'Il a tenté de s'engager, au début [...] et on l'a renvoyé à l'école' (92) ['He tried to join one early on (...) but he was sent back to school']. *La neige* represents black marketeering activities, food queues, and the population's reluctant ingestion of swedes (45). Denunciations are common. There is a curfew which the privileged (collaborating) few can circumvent if granted, as Frank is, a green card. The latter is told that conflicts exist between different factions of the occupying forces: rivalry between Abwehr and Gestapo representatives in occupied France is well-documented. Whilst each of these examples could arguably reflect other historical conflicts (or a generic situation of war and occupation), there can be no doubt that they served to nudge readers – both those contemporary with the 1948 publication and later readers familiar with World War II-related texts of all sorts – towards a reading of *La neige* as a work set in occupied France. The novel can, in other words, readily be interpreted as a text which represents 'the war' which is my concern here, but does that make it a text which is *primarily* 'about the war', as opposed to some other overarching theme? This question is best approached alongside a second key question: is this a 'novel' or a 'crime novel?'

Towards the start of the text Frank Friedmaier, a shiftless young man living in the brothel run by his mother and otherwise doing little beyond drinking in a local club, murders a soldier of the occupying forces with a knife. Not long after, prompted by his insalubrious acquaintance Kromer, he steals a collection of watches, intending to sell them to an occupying army general in exchange for cash and certain privileges. When he inadvertently reveals his face to the owner of the watches, the elderly Mlle Vilmos, who remembers him from his boyhood, he shoots her dead with the gun appropriated from the murdered soldier. Later in the text Frank tricks his 16-year-old neighbour, Sissy, into sleeping with Kromer (the girl believes she is with Frank). It may seem clear that Frank has engaged in both immoral and criminal acts, but how precisely do we define potential crimes if we choose to read the text as set in occupied France? Chapter 3 below explores just such complexities in some detail, so a brief outline will suffice here. Were a German soldier to have been murdered under the regime of Occupation in France the act might have fallen under the jurisdiction of the Vichy State as a common crime, but would more likely have been regarded as a military act and judged in a German field court. For many French citizens, of course, the murder would be regarded less as a crime and more as a patriotic act of resistance. The murder of a civilian (such as the fictional Mlle Vilmos) would not be of great interest to the occupying forces, but would come under the jurisdiction of the domestic government. Theft would come under the category of a common crime, but might equally in some contexts have been regarded in terms of black marketeering (usually but not always under the jurisdiction of the Vichy government, but equally an activity engaged in extensively by the occupying forces and their French collaborators, as Chapter 3 discusses). If the goods were sold to the occupying forces (as is the case with Frank and the watches), the act might well be regarded as one of collaboration, potentially punishable as a criminal act of treason in 1944. Defining crime, in other words, is far from straightforward in the context of a regime of occupation, and whilst it would be unduly pedantic to suggest that *La neige* is not a work of crime fiction because the 'crimes' cannot readily be defined as such, it is certainly the case that 'crime' is all too often taken as a given when it comes to theorizing crime fiction.

So far I have touched on some of the ways in which a phrase such as 'representing the war' and an apparently simple term such as 'crime' might be problematized. The next step is to ask whether we might regard both the war and the crimes represented in *La neige* as secondary concerns; means to a less historically or indeed less generically specific end. Can we read *La neige* not (merely) as a work of crime fiction about the war but (also? instead?) as a work of fiction dealing with broader, or just other, themes? In his discussion of the specificities of crime fiction Porter stresses the importance of what he terms the logico-temporal chain:

> The effect of the crime is revealed before the statement of its causes. This means that detective fiction is preoccupied with the closing of the logico-temporal gap that separates the present of the discovery of the crime from the past that prepared it.[51]

Although *La neige* is not a work of classic detective fiction (we know Frank dunnit) the need to close the logico-temporal gap, to uncover the past which 'prepares' the present, nonetheless remains when it comes to identifying motive: why does Frank kill the soldier? And is his act of theft motivated purely by greed and a desire to mitigate the rigours of the Occupation? Interestingly, Simenon's protagonist himself rejects any attempt to reason backwards from effect to cause:

> Il n'y a pas de *parce que* ... C'est un mot pour les imbéciles. Pour les gens du dehors, en tout cas. Avec les *parce que*, il n'y aurait rien d'étonnant à ce qu'on lui remette un jour une médaille qu'il n'a pas méritée, ou pour qu'on le décore à titre posthume. (215)

> [There is no *because* ... That's a word for idiots. For outsiders at any rate. With *becauses*, it wouldn't be at all surprising if one day he were given a medal he didn't deserve, or were decorated posthumously.]

Frank's reflections come in the context of his refusal to answer the questions of an officer of the occupying forces who interrogates, then tortures him. 'Les gens du dehors' ['outsiders'] might well – wrongly – ascribe Frank's murder of

---

[51]   Dennis Porter, *The Pursuit of Crime. Art and Ideology in Detective Fiction* (Yale UP, 1982), p. 29.

an enemy soldier and his subsequent silence under interrogation to his patriotic spirit. And yet, though access to the protagonist's point of view tells us that this reading is incorrect, the ultimate act of violence which is murder still requires an explanation. To make sense of the text the reader must seek beyond a war narrative of heroes and villains, but, must also, I would argue, reject Frank's denial of causality.

Frank's crimes, and his immoral, but probably not illegal, act regarding Sissy, are connected via various references to childhood and masculinity which provide an insight into possible (unconscious) motives for his acts. The reader learns that the theft of watches takes place in a house the protagonist frequented as a young boy, situated in the village where he was left by his mother with a wet-nurse, and where she visited him periodically accompanied by different men. Frank's unearthing of the hoard of watches can be read as an almost literal 'temps retrouvé', a return to childhood further suggested by potentially Proustian allusions to the cakes Mlle Vilmos had in the house when Frank was a child (76), and to the presence of uneven flagstones (77).[52] The triangular relationships of childhood (boy, unavailable mother, men) are echoed and repeated in Frank's conniving in what amounts to the rape of Sissy by a third party, an incident which is metaphorically tied once more to childhood via the temporal motif: 'Frank a monté ça comme un mouvement d'horlogerie, avec la minutie d'un enfant' (116) ['Frank had planned it all like clockwork, with all the attention to detail of a child'].[53] Oedipal motifs also mark the murder of the enemy soldier (tellingly nicknamed 'l'Eunuque', p. 15), an act likened more than once to a loss of virginity (9; 13). Various apparently passing observations emphasize Frank's insecurities. The protagonist's physical stature has in the past proven problematic: 'il lui est arrivé – mais c'est passé depuis longtemps – de porter de hauts talons, presque des talons de femme, pour se grandir' ['once – but it was a long time ago – he'd worn high heels, almost women's heels, to make himself taller'] (36). Standing in food queues like his neighbour Holst with his shopping bag in his hand would be too much of a potential indictment of Frank's masculinity: 'Frank ne l'a pas accepté. Pour rien au monde, il ne prendrait place dans une queue' (34) ['Frank refused to do it. Nothing in the world would make him stand in a queue'].[54] Frank kills the soldier at least in part in order to secure the latter's weapon, a transparently phallic symbol which appears again in almost comedic fashion when Frank takes Sissy

---

[52] Proust's 'madeleine' episode is well known. When Marcel steps on the uneven paving stones, thereby triggering a moment of intense joy and renewed confidence in his artistic abilities, he recalls not just the episode of the madeleine but also the spires of Martinville and the last works of Vinteuil (Proust, *Le temps retrouvé*, Gallimard 1954 edition, p. 222).

[53] For a discussion of the leitmotif of watches and clocks in Simenon see Assouline, *Simenon*, pp. 360–61. Assouline links this motif to an incident in Simenon's youth when his dying father gave him a watch which Simenon subsequently traded for time with a prostitute.

[54] The food queue also makes an appearance in Malle's *Lacombe Lucien* when Lucien, brandishing his German police card, allows France to skip the queue.

(itself an interesting choice of name which is altered to 'Suzy' in the film version) to the cinema. Frank is both pleased to see her and does indeed have a gun in his pocket: '– Sissy ... / – Oui ... / – Regarde ... / – Quoi? / – Dans ma main ... / C'est le revolver, qui luit faiblement dans le clair-obscur' (56–7) ['"Sissy ..." / "Yes ..." / "Look ..." / "What?" / "In my hand ..." / It was the gun, shining dully in the half light'].

Finally, frequent references, both literal and metaphorical, to eyes and specifically to damaged eyes, underscore the oedipal theme: Frank repeatedly recalls an incident from his childhood involving a blinded cat ('le chat avait un œil qui lui sortait de l'orbite', p. 124 ['the cat had one eye hanging out of its socket']; 'avec son œil hors de la tête', p. 132 ['with its eye hanging out of its head']); an acquaintance asks him for help in paying for an operation for his sister who will otherwise lose her sight (161); when beaten by the interrogating officer Frank feels as if he is losing an eye ('il avait l'impression que son œil gauche avait jailli de l'orbite', p. 222 ['he felt as though his left eye had jerked out of its socket', 179]). There can be little argument that an oedipal theme is present, and that it might serve to close Porter's 'logico-temporal gap' by casting light on the motive for Frank's acts. Given the far-reaching nature and connotations of an oedipal reading, might we not then eschew the 'crime fiction' label in favour of a reading of *La neige* as, for instance, a 'coming-of-age novel', and thus, perhaps, just as 'a novel'?[55] The answer has to be 'yes but'. If we are judging by this criterion – the oedipal theme present in the text – the two categories 'crime novel' and 'novel' are neither mutually exclusive nor positioned in a hierarchical relationship: as we will see in Chapter 4 below, oedipal motifs are, in fact, common in works of crime fiction and not merely the preserve of 'novel novels'.

So far the focus has been primarily on the representation of crime and criminality. To end this case study, attention must be turned to a staple presence in all detective fiction and a feature of some crime fiction: the investigator. *La neige* features at least three such figures: Kurt Hamling, a police inspector; an unnamed uniformed officer of the occupying forces; and a civilian-clad 'elderly gentleman' ('vieux monsieur') who belongs to another, unspecified, bureau of the occupying forces. As might be expected of a police inspector, Hamling turns up after each of Frank's misdemeanours. His status as investigator, however, is vestigial. Always on the point of questioning Frank he nonetheless stops short on each occasion: 'On croit toujours qu'il va dire quelque chose, poser une question' (41) ['You always feel he's going to say something, to ask a question']. As Chapter 3 will demonstrate, the domestic representatives of the forces of law and order have

---

[55] Readers following up on the crime/coming of age nexus could usefully read Pierre Magnan's *Un grison d'Arcadie* (Denoël, 1999) which opens with the murder of a former resistant, and ends with the double murder of those responsible for his killing, whilst focusing for the main in the intervening pages on the young first-person narrator's first sexual relationship, with an older woman. The text is not marketed or marked as a work of crime fiction.

reduced or compromised powers under a regime of occupation, and Hamling's curiously curtailed role may be a reflection of such a situation (Frank is never investigated for his murder of Mlle Vilmos, a crime the domestic police might have been expected to pursue). The police officer can also be viewed as a father figure in the oedipal drama of Frank's life – we are told that his relationship with Frank's mother dates back many years – or, indeed, as a self-conscious, metatextual gesture to the genre of crime fiction. The other investigating figures do interrogate Frank, each pursuing a distinct line of questioning: the uniformed officer investigates his dealings with the contraband watches, apparently in pursuit of the recipient of these stolen goods; the older gentleman shows interest only in Anna Loeb, a new addition to Frank's mother's brothel whom the interrogator believes to be a spy who gleans information from those members of the occupying forces who frequent the premises.

The two figures may investigate, or attempt to, but Frank, for his part, seems to be in another narrative altogether: his is not a role in a tale of crime and criminality. In his mind at least he is not in a real prison (185–6) and he is not a criminal: 'Ceux-là, ce sont des hommes qui ont été jugés, qui ont commis un crime, qu'on peut juger, inscrire dans les grands livres de la justice' (245) ['Those are men who have been tried, who have committed a crime, who can be judged and entered into the great ledgers of justice']. His reading of his situation transcends both criminal and war narratives. If he does not at first speak to either of his interrogators it is not for heroic or patriotic reasons but simply because he deems their questions, and indeed the entire context of crime and interrogation, to be irrelevant: 'le fait de parler ou de ne pas parler était sans importance' (217) ['Whether he talked or not did not matter']; 'Tout cela est sans importance' (155) ['None of that matters']. Here, as elsewhere, however, two interpretations are available, one of which reinforces the text as a war-centred crime narrative, and one which does not. Answering questions is 'sans importance' because Frank knows too much (the identity of the corrupt general to whom the watches were passed) so will never be allowed to live. Alternatively, answering questions is irrelevant because Frank is beyond the realm of crime and punishment, on a quest for a higher truth, or perhaps merely indifferent to truth. Similarly the proffered observation that 'tout le monde […] à quelque chose à se reprocher' (68) ['everyone has something on his conscience'] can be interpreted in the specific historical context of war and occupation (few people are blame free in such a situation), but may equally allude to the universal guilt of the human condition. Readers may be reminded of Meursault's utterances in *L'Étranger*: 'cela n'avait aucune importance' ['that didn't matter at all']; 'tout cela était sans importance réelle' ['none of it really mattered']; 'J'ai cru qu'il me reprochait quelque chose' ['I thought he was accusing me of something'].[56] Ironically, the theme of universal guilt also has links to crime fiction. As Auden suggested, 'the typical reader of detective stories is […] a person who suffers from a sense of sin'.[57]

---

[56]   Camus, *L'Étranger* (Folio, 1978) p. 11, p. 17, p. 69, and p. 35.

[57]   Auden, 'The Guilty Vicarage'.

The final element of the investigative process foregrounds Frank himself and indeed the reader in the role of investigator and centres on the character's fascination with his neighbour, father of Sissy, Gerhardt Holst. As mentioned above, the prospective pull of *La neige* (what will happen next; what will become of Frank?) is coupled with a specific mystery, an enigma waiting to be solved. While Frank's interrogators question him about thefts, murder, and possible spying, he remains preoccupied with Holst. Rhetorical questions both anticipate and goad the reader-investigator's curiosity: 'Pourquoi Holst? Il n'en sait rien' (93) ['Why Holst? He has no idea']. For Frank, and the reader, it is Holst who is 'un mystère, une énigme. Et, quand on se trouve dans la situation de Frank, on n'a pas le droit de se pencher sur les énigmes' (183) ['a mystery, an enigma. And when you find yourself in a situation like Frank's you have no right to focus on enigmas']. Where investigators traditionally seek solutions to criminal activities, 'comprendre', for Frank, seems to imply a higher order of knowledge and understanding: 'Comment avez-vous compris?' he asks Holst (266) ['How did you come to understand?']; 'Holst a compris!' (267) ['Holst has understood!']. Just what it is that Holst has grasped, the 'solution' to the mystery which runs parallel to the crime narrative which Frank steadfastly ignores, is never spelled out, but can be linked to Holst's tale of his own son, who died after he was caught stealing and jumped from a window in an attempt to escape. Not long before Frank dies, the mystery to which Holst holds the key is perhaps solved via the older man's utterance of the sybilline phrase: 'Le métier d'homme est difficile' (281) ['A man's lot is a hard one']. Solving the riddle means grasping the nature of the human condition.

As already stated, and as I hope this reading of *La neige était sale* has demonstrated, there are as many questions as there are answers when it comes to acts of criminal categorization – or criminal acts of categorization, as I have come to think of them. Is *La neige* 'about the war' (is it, to recall Atack, a narrative 'where the war is essential to the generation and resolution of the major conflicts and oppositions of the narrative'?).[58] Yes, if this means that a war which could be World War II plays a necessary role in the basic plot (Frank carries out certain acts, is arrested, interrogated, and executed). No, if war and Occupation are regarded as pretexts; if the historical setting is seen to be transcended by broader concerns. No, if, revisiting Assouline and Platten, above, p. 20, we believe that 'a man can be drawn into this kind of downward spiral' in many other settings, and that Simenon did not in fact seek to 'distill the evidence of occupied life'. Is *La neige était sale* a crime novel? Not if we accept the point of the view of the (doubtless unreliable) protagonist. Yes, if we strip the adjective 'crime' of any value-judgment and read it on exactly the same terms as we would the epithets 'oedipal' or 'coming-of-age'.

---

[58]　Margaret Atack, *Literature and the French Resistance: Cultural Politics and Narrative Forms 1940–1950*, (Manchester UP, 1989), p. 7.

Ellipsis and Anticlimax: *Le Clan des Ostendais* as *Noir* (Pseudo)-Thriller

Unlike *La neige était sale*, there is no doubting that *Le Clan des Ostendais* is set in France during World War II and that the war is the main driver of events. The text charts the quotidian activities of a large group of Flemish fishermen, led by Omer and his wife Maria, who have fled the German advance and headed by trawler for La Rochelle. Housed as refugees they integrate with some difficulty into the local population and continue fishing even when the Germans invade, before finally leaving for England. The text is temporally situated in the opening pages where we learn that it is May 1940 (13), with further dates or at least datable historical events punctuating the work thereafter: a reference to the capitulation of the Belgian king (100) places the action on May 28 1940; mention of German troops settled in Paris (130) to some time after June 14; the sinking of the *Champlain* (126; the ship was sunk in La Pallice harbour when hit by a mine) moves events on to June 17, and so forth. But what of *Le Clan* as a work of crime fiction? What might justify, or at least explain, its place in the Folio 'policier' series? The promotional text on the back cover hints at war-related acts of derring-do: 'avec un héroïsme certain, ces hommes vont résister. Ils en payeront le prix ...' ['with unquestionable heroism these men will resist. And they will pay the price ...']. The ellipsis is typical of the micro- and macro-narrative structures of the text. It is also, I suggest, typically misleading.

Although crimes may be hard to define in strictly legal terms in *La neige était sale* and may be interpreted as secondary to other thematic aspects of the work, they are at least identifiable in the concrete form of theft and murder. In *Le Clan* there is no perpetration of common crime, and the only deaths occur as the direct result of war: mines blow up three of the five Flemish trawlers killing several crew members including two of Omer's three sons. The only acts which might be designated criminal relate to possible cases of collaboration: two of the Flemish women are suspected of sleeping with the Germans; a question mark hangs over Omer's seemingly over-cordial dealings with the occupying forces, though nothing explicit is ever communicated and the text comes to a close without the issue being resolved. Hardly the stuff of crime fiction. Nonetheless, in spite of a distinct absence of criminal activity, elements of *noir* fiction and indeed of the thriller genre can be identified in *Le Clan* and may go some way towards accounting for the text's place in a 'policier' series. As Todorov states, forward thrust ('la prospection'), tension, and a feeling of unease characterize the 'roman noir'. Where the classic detective tale hinges primarily on 'mystère', *noir* is associated with curiosity, suspense, and an anticipation of what will happen next.[59] Horlsey associates the *noir* thriller with excess, sensation, suspense, the evocation of fear and anxiety, 'the creation of contrasts due to threatening eruptions in the normal', ambivalence, and vulnerability.[60] In spite of the decidedly un-thrilling nature of

---

[59] Todorov, *Poétique de la prose*, p. 60.
[60] Horsley, *The Noir Thriller*, p. 8.

the plot of *Le Clan*, which unfolds at a snail's pace under an un-*noir* beating sun in a distinctly un-*noir* rural setting, all of these generic descriptors do indeed feature in the text. They are, however, voided of all *noir*-related content; merely the narrative infrastructure remains. The text is constructed in such as way as to build up suspense and anticipation (rather like the melodramatic promotional text) only to fall away into bathos. This reiterative anticlimactic drive can be illustrated via three episodes.

The first incident takes place when the Flemish fishermen have just arrived in the village of Charron. Not without a measure of reluctance (these are after all 'foreigners') the locals have laid on a meal to welcome them. The chapter which relates this proairetic sequence opens with a typically anticipatory tease:

> Le fait qu'un des Ostendais était ivre fut évidemment la cause principale de ce qui arriva, il vaudrait mieux dire la cause immédiate, car, tôt ou tard, les mêmes faits ou des faits semblables ne se seraient-ils pas produits? (55)

> [The fact that one of the Ostenders was drunk was obviously the main cause of what happened, in fact it might be more accurate to say it was the immediate cause, since would the same events or similar ones not have occurred anyway, sooner or later?]

The rhetorical question and repetition of the word 'cause' stress that something is going to happen, but what? The text continues to toy with the reader by introducing Seppe, the drunken Flemish sailor, and by further cranking up the suspense with allusions to a forthcoming incident: 'Une autre cause, sans doute, moins directe mais peut-être plus profonde, c'était la question des kilomètres' (56) ['Without doubt another cause, less direct but maybe more significant, was the question of distance']; 'Et ce fut un détail futile qui déclencha l'incident' (63) ['It was a trivial detail which triggered the incident']. As with all narratives which create suspense delay is key: some 11 pages separate the initial 'Le fait que [...] fut évidemment la cause' and the final reveal of the long-anticipated end-point event. The latter, though, proves to be incommensurately trivial: irritated by what he perceives to be the local children's mocking of one of the Flemish elders, Seppe throws a fork which breaks a pane of glass, slightly injuring one of the children. The ensuing antagonism between guests and hosts rapidly fizzles out, and the narrative sequence comes to a close: 'Tel fut le premier soir des Ostendais à Charron' (67) ['Such was the first evening the Ostenders spend in Charron'].

The second slightly longer sequence is again characterized by a marked disproportion between build-up and outcome, and ties in this time more specifically to the context of war. Flavie and Mina, respectively the wife and daughter of trawlerman Pipke, are widely presumed to be engaging in 'horizontal collaboration' whilst Pipke is at sea. Omer's wife, Maria, advises him that Pipke and his family might best be instructed to leave on the next available refugee train to avoid further damaging the Flemish reputation. The narrative sequence opens once more with dramatic anticipatory force: 'Maria ne sut jamais ce qui s'était passé avec Pipke' (175) ['Maria never found out what had happened with Pipke'], closely followed by the sybilline 'Ce fut le jour où [...]' (175) ['It was the day that (...)']. In another long-drawn-out episode it is reported that Omer hesitated to broach the subject with Pipke whilst the men were out at sea, took him with him to deliver some of their catch to the local refugee centre but still said nothing, before finally informing Pipke of his decision to ask the family to leave as the two men sat in a local café. As with the episode of the thrown fork, the text hints repeatedly at catastrophic events to come. Expressions of hypothesis and the suggestion of withheld knowledge communicated via the use of impersonal pronouns serve to heighten readerly expectations: 'Ce qui se passa cette nuit-là [...] on n'en sut rien' (179) ['nobody knew anything about (...) what happened that night']; 'Pipke la suivit. Du moins le supposa-t-on' (180) ['Pipke followed her. At least that is what people assumed']. Just as such professed information lapses prompt the reader to assume that *something* has occurred, so an ellipsis as the narrative action cuts from night to the following morning leaves space for the reader's imagination. An ominous report about Pipke and his family is transmitted to Omer by another fisherman: 'C'est drôle ... Je n'ai pas vu ses femmes, ce matin ... Il a refermé la porte en partant et je crois qu'il a mis la clef dans sa poche ...' (180, Simenon's ellipses) ['It's strange ... I haven't seen the women this morning ... He locked the door as he left and I think he put the key in his pocket ...']. After a wait of some eight pages, during which Pipke is killed when his ship is blown up by a mine, the door to the locked room is finally opened to reveal ... not, as we doubtless assume by this time, the bloody corpses of either the two women or German soldiers, or both, but Pipke's family alive and well (though admittedly bruised). Both leave on the next refugee train. Instead of the anticipated murderous crime the text delivers the death of the putative perpetrator Pipke, making the point, perhaps, that war (or indeed life) consists of aleatory events; that telos is the stuff only of story books.

The third example comprises the macro-sequence beginning with the arrival of the Flemish fishermen and invasion of the Germans and concluding with the departure of the fishermen, and as such encompasses most of the text. Where the second sequence stoked up expectations regarding 'horizontal collaboration', in this case it is Omer's relations with the enemy which form the core of the suspense. Thanks in part to his ability to communicate with the Germans, Omer rapidly takes on the role of intermediary between the occupiers and the local population. He and the German commander are described as similar in nature; both are attributed mysterious qualities by Maria: 'il y avait dans sa voix la même gravité, le même mystère que dans celle d'Omer' (167–8) ['His voice had the same gravity, the same mysterious quality as Omer's']. Anticipation is built slowly but inexorably as the local population become increasingly hostile to Omer who is seen drinking with Germans and shaking hands with a German officer. A denunciatory letter describing the Flemish as traitors is dispatched to the German commander calling for their arrest, whilst, paradoxically, the fishermen are also described as 'Boches' by some of the locals (191). Maria, meanwhile, is increasingly disturbed by her husband's behaviour, and the reader shares her point of view. Why has Omer stopped playing with the children and digging his garden? Why does he no longer confide in her? What is the future which he alone seems to have foreseen?: 'dès le début de la guerre, il avait eu l'air de prévoir des choses que les autres ne soupçonnaient pas' (189) ['since the start of the war he had seemed to foresee events that others 'never even suspected']. Given the unremitting nature of the build-up and doubtless also the reader's expectation of common war narrative tropes of resistance and heroism – reinforced by the cover blurb – a cataclysmic denouement is expected. Again, expectation far outstrips delivery. Omer eventually tells Maria (but not the reader) of his cunning plan; she passes the information on to the other family members one by one (but still not to the reader). The text closes with the remaining Flemish families leaving under cover of night and sailing to England. No sabotage, no shoot-outs, no confrontations of any sort.

Read with certain generic expectations, *Le Clan des Ostendais* consists of a series of disappointing anticlimaxes. Everything about the text's paratext, structure, and narrative drive bills it as a wartime thriller, but Simenon's novel, far removed from high-octane action, seems to promise so much more than it delivers. War may quite simply be more or other than the reader expects. Adding to the bathos of a suspense narrative which is voided of dramatic climax, three more textual features introduce an ahistorical note to the work. First, a hint of the fantastic. The Flemish fishermen and their trawlers appear quite literally out of the blue: 'C'était presque irréel. Un matin clair et d'un calme absolu' (12) ['It was almost unreal. On a clear morning and a flat calm']; 'les bateaux étaient en quelque sorte arrivés là mystérieusement' (14) ['the boats had in a sense arrived there mysteriously']. An eerie silence prevails: 'Les ancres avaient glissé sans bruit' (14) ['anchors were dropped in silence']; 'Ils paraissaient faire partie d'un autre monde. Ils vivaient comme derrière un écran de verre. On ne les entendait pas' (26) ['They seemed to belong to a different world. It was as if they lived behind a glass screen. They did not make a sound']. And if these other-wordly echoes sound an atemporal note then so too do references to the natural cycle, set on each occasion against the historicity of war: 'Des paysans passaient sur la route, derrière leurs vaches, du même pas que tous les paysans du monde parce qu'il est rythmé sur celui des bêtes, du même pas que tous les autres jours de l'année, guerre ou pas guerre' (115) ['Peasants were passing by on the road, behind their cattle, walking like peasants do the world over, following the rhythm of the beasts, walking just as they did on any other day of the year, war or no war']; 'Le maire était malade. Il se mourrait. La guerre n'empêche pas les gens d'être malades, ni de mourir de maladie' (48) ['The mayor was ill. He was dying. Wars do not stop people from being ill, from dying of illnesses']. The tension between the historical and the ahistorical, already encountered in the readings of *La neige était sale* as atemporal oedipal drama or / and World War II crime novel, is further reflected in shifts of narrative point of view. Although the majority of the narrative is focalized via the principal characters – usually Omer or Maria – the text occasionally shifts abruptly into a parodically self-conscious omniscient mode. Chapter 5 opens as follows:

Un être qui, ce jour-là, eût observé d'en haut le village, à la façon d'un entomologiste penché sur des insectes, n'aurait sans doute rien enregistré d'anormal. Le comportement des humains, autour de leurs petites cases rangées le long des traits clairs des chemins, fut sensiblement leur comportement des autres jours. (102)

[A being who that day had looked down on the village from above, like an entomologist peering down at insects, would doubtless have registered nothing unusual. The behaviour of the human specimens, grouped around their little boxes lining the pale strips formed by the roads, was consistent with their normal everyday behaviour.]

The strange human creatures and their conflicts count for little from this point of view; once more the war narrative is if not eclipsed by, then at least set alongside, a (literally) higher order of existence. It is no coincidence that in its closing moments the text reiterates a phrase already encountered in *La neige était sale* as Omer reflects that 'il avait fait son métier d'homme' (218) ['He had done his duty as a man'].

Le Clan des Ostendais can be called into question as a war narrative, or may at the very least be read as an example which challenges the category's more dramatic avatars. Concomitantly, it has been demonstrated that the novel's status as a work of crime fiction ostensibly relates not so much to content but to the prospective drive of the narrative, which in fact topples into anticlimax with every sequence, making of the text something of a pseudo-thriller. Finally, as was the case with *La neige était sale*, the representation of the figure of the investigator in *Le Clan* adds to the profiling of the work's generic status. The text opens (symbolically?) with a description of the deserted *préfecture* of La Rochelle. The office of the 'préfet', we are told, 'perdait son prestige et son mystère d'être entrebâillée sur le vide de la pièce' (9) ['lost its prestige and mystery because the door was left ajar, opening onto the emptiness of the room']. The emptiness of the police premises is further stressed by insistent repetition: the streets of La Rochelle are 'aussi vides et sonores que les bureaux de la Préfecture' (10) ['as empty and echoing as the offices of the police station']. When the Flemish fishermen are housed in outlying villages the main family is moved to 'l'ancienne gendarmerie, désaffectée depuis longtemps' (60) ['the building, long since out of use, which formerly housed the local *gendarmes*'], another police building which is emphatically deserted: 'Elle était vide, complètement vide' (60) ['it was empty, completely empty']. The dysfunctionality of the police is evident, but what of the representation of law and order in more general terms?

In the classic whodunnit the socio-legal *status quo* is temporarily disrupted by a criminal element then restored thanks to the investigator's ratiocinative prowess. The police, who tend to represent a different social class in such texts, are often gently mocked. In *noir* fiction the official representatives of law and order are typically, though not inevitably, set against a non-aligned investigator (P.I., journalist, etc.) and may be portrayed as incompetent or corrupt agents of an equally corrupt state. Roth, using the term detective fiction very broadly, describes it as 'the story of a hero who counters transgressions against law and authority while repeatedly engaging in acts of transgression against law and authority'.[61] If we accept the wartime situation as an admittedly atypical manifestation of a transgression – or at least a disruption – of law and authority, then Omer, protagonist of *Le Clan*, can be regarded as a hero in Roth's terms. The imperative of compliance with the forces of law and order is stressed from the opening pages of the text when Omer is informed that his trawlers must be requisitioned: 'Les ordres sont formels' (14; repeated verbatim pp. 15 and 24) ['the orders are clear']. The Flemish fishermen, however, manifest what is described as a stubborn resistance to the established order (50) and Omer, as their leader, consistently and insistently ignores all directives: 'Il répond qu'il se moque du règlement' (19) ['He replied that he did not care about the regulations']; 'il ne ferait que ce qu'il voudrait' (45) ['He would act just as he pleased']. Disregarding the ineffectual French representatives of law and order and besting also the authority of the occupying forces by leaving under cover of night, Omer is, we might say, a law unto himself and as such, a typical *noir* protagonist in an atypical (pseudo)-thriller. The Flemish leader is also an inveterate pipe-smoker, and as such, is one of several figures in Simenon's fiction (we will encounter another in the analysis of *Le Train* below) who may be said to represent the writer himself: the ultimate figure of authority.

Les Autres as Pseudo-Whodunnit and Screen Narrative

With *Les Autres*, a short novel recounting the vicissitudes of the Huet family in the immediate aftermath of the death of patriarch Antoine Huet, we enter a different sort of textual territory. Most obviously the plot no longer unfolds during the war years: the action is predominantly contemporaneous with the date of publication (1962), though there are references to earlier periods. Rather than a third-person narrative of varying focalization, this is a first-person account which takes the form of a diary written by Blaise Huet, nephew of the deceased. As was the case with the previous text, no common law crimes are perpetrated, only war-related acts which could potentially be defined as criminal, specifically, the denunciation of a member of the Resistance. Strikingly, where *Le Clan des Ostendais* embraces typical features of *noir* fiction, *Les Autres* takes up classic elements of the whodunnit or 'roman à énigmes' and does so in an equally unexpected (and potentially subversive) manner.

Everything about this work sets it up as a classic detective story. As S.S. Van Dine insisted, a detective novel must be graced with a corpse (and the deader the better).[62] *Les Autres* ostensibly follows the rules of the game. The first line of the

---

[61] Marty Roth, *Foul and Fair Play. Reading Genre in Classic Detective Fiction* (U of Georgia P, 1995), p. 60.

[62] Rule 7 of Van Dine's 'Twenty rules for writing detective stories' (1928), in *The Art of the Mystery Story: A Collection of Critical Essays*, ed. H. Haycraft (Carroll & Graf, 1992), pp. 189–93.

text consists of the dramatic announcement that 'L'oncle Antoine est mort mardi, la veille de la Toussaint, vers onze heures du soir vraisemblablement. La même nuit, Colette a tenté de se jeter par la fenêtre' ['Uncle Antoine died on Tuesday, on Hallowe'en, probably at around 11 in the evening. That same night Colette tried to throw herself out of the window']. The trope of the sudden death of a relative is rapidly followed by another murder mystery favourite in the form of the unexpected return of the black sheep of the family (a nephew whom we learn in a passing comment has spent two years in a prison in England for procuring prostitutes): 'A peu près dans le même temps, on apprenait qu'Édouard était revenu et que plusieurs personnes l'avaient vu en ville' ['At about the same time it emerged that Edouard was back and that several people had seen him in town']. True to form (or genre) the novel also includes a large rambling house, an elderly retainer, highly disputatious family members, and a younger wife who is, almost inevitably, having an affair. Shortly after the corpse is discovered the standard figures of the police inspector, coroner, and lawyer enter the picture. As with many classic tales of detection, inheritance is central to the plot: to whom will the Huet fortune pass, given the competing claims of the deceased's wife, Colette, and his nephews Blaise, Lucien, and bad boy Édouard? Whereas *Le Clan* immersed the reader in a state of recurring anticipation (what calamity is about to unfold?), *Les Autres* insistently returns us to the retrospectively oriented questions of the mystery genre (who did what, how, and why?). As the narrator ponders how events might have turned out differently on the night of his uncle's death, a barrage of rhetorical questions and the potentially loaded word 'indice' (clue) encourage the reader to cast an equally interrogative glance at events:

> Que se serait-il passé si nous avions pris, ce soir-là, pour rentrer chez nous, le quai Notre-Dame? J'aurais certainement jeté un coup d'œil machinal à la maison de mon oncle. Y avait-il de la lumière, à minuit? Colette était-elle déjà rentrée? La voiture de Jean Floriau se trouvait-elle encore devant la porte? Un *indice* quelconque permettait-il de deviner, du dehors, qu'un drame venait de se passer et qu'un second drame allait se dénouer moins tragiquement? (13–14, my emphasis)

> [What would have happened that night if, to get home, we had gone via the Quai Notre-Dame? I would definitely have glanced up automatically at my uncle's house. Were the lights on, at midnight? Had Colette already come home? Was Jean Floriau's car still outside the front door? Was there some sort of clue that would reveal, to an outside observer, that a drama had just unfolded and that a second one was going to come to a less tragic conclusion?]

Various possible culprits are subsequently singled out by other characters. Blaise's mother, for instance, cannot resist mentioning Colette's thespian past, hinting that her apparent suicide attempt may have been a cover for – we are left to assume – a nefarious act of murder: 'Je ne sais pas si c'est de la comédie … quand elle était jeune, elle voulait faire du théâtre … Elle a suivi des cours …' (23) ['I don't know if it's an act … she wanted to be on the stage when she was young ... She went on some courses ...']. And if Colette is not guilty of the murder of her husband then suspicion directed at Édouard accrues as a result of over-determined references to the character's 'retour ahurissant' (10) ['extraordinary return']: 'Tu sais qui est en ville, depuis plusieurs jours, paraît-il? ... Ton cousin Édouard! ... Qu'est-ce que ça peut signifier? ...' (20) ['Do you know who has apparently been in town for several days? ... Your cousin Edward! What can it mean? ...']; 'Édouard ... qui avait mystérieusement réapparu' (21) ['Edward ... who had mysteriously reappeared']; 'Édouard qui venait de faire une réapparition inexplicable et inquiétante' (31) ['Edward who had just put in an inexplicable and troubling reappearance']. '[S]ignifier', 'mystérieusement', 'inexplicable': we are truly in the world of the detective story. Even when news emerges that Antoine died of an overdose presumed to be self-administered, the crime narrative reading is kept ajar: the attending police officer discretely pockets a bottle of sleeping tablets and a tumbler from the deceased's bedside table (35); it is suggested that Antoine had been treated for years for a non-existent heart condition (89).

It is not just the detective story tropes and finger-pointing issuing from various characters which invite – indeed urge – the reader to engage with *Les Autres* as a whodunnit: the text incorporates another classic feature of the detective novel. As Evrard points out: 'La recherche de la vérité, qui implique une enquête minutieuse et de nombreux interrogatoires, conduit l'auteur de roman policiers à privilégier la forme du dialogue' ['The search for the truth, which involves a detailed investigation and extensive questioning of suspects, is such that the writer of detective novels tends to favour dialogue'].[63] Veldman notes that scenes where suspects are questioned make up very large proportion of Simenon's 'Maigret' texts.[64] In the latter it is the police inspector himself who carries out the questioning; in *Les Autres* the investigative function is devolved to a range of characters. First and most fitting with respect to the classic detective mode, the police superintendent poses a series of rapid-fire questions to Colette's presumed lover, doctor Floriau, about the sleeping pills prescribed to the deceased (33ff). Although the police gradually lose interest in the case, the same pattern of interrogation is repeated on several subsequent occasions. Irène, the narrator's wife, for instance, directs over 15 consecutive questions at the character Nicolas Macherin (a rather obtrusively – some might say oedipally – close friend of the couple) in an attempt to discover the truth behind Antoine's death, be it murder or suicide: 'A cause de sa femme?' (50) ['Because of his wife?']; 'C'était une détraquée, non' (51) ['She was crazy wasn't she?']; 'En somme, elle se moquait de lui?' (51) ['So she was making a fool of him?']. Shortly thereafter, the narrator interrogates the dead man's butler-cum-chauffeur François in a similar fashion: 'Elle se montrait désagréable avec lui?' (57) ['Was she unpleasant to him?']; 'C'est vous qui avait servi le dîner?' (58) ['Was it you who served dinner?']; 'Comment était mon oncle?' (58) ['How was my uncle?']. However, although the narrator's questions are initially

---

63   Evrard, *Lire le roman policier*, p. 14.

64   Hendrik Veldman, *La Tentation de l'inaccessible* (Rodopi: 1981), p. 164.

akin to those which any criminal investigator might be expected to ask, the tenor of the exchange gradually shifts from the criminal to the existential, and when the narrator finally apologizes for his verbal volley – 'Il ne faut pas m'en vouloir de mes questions, François. Je cherche à comprendre ...' (59) ['You mustn't blame me for asking all these questions, François. I'm trying to understand ...'] – his apology is met with the sort of enigmatic response which might have come straight from Frank in *La neige était sale*: 'Tout le monde cherche à comprendre, monsieur Blaise' (59) ['Everyone's trying to understand, Monsieur Blaise']. Viewing his uncle's body sometime earlier the narrator had been surprised to detect an unfamiliar smile on the latter's lips (30). When Nicolas is asked by Irène why Antoine might kill himself he not only repeats the by-now familiar verb – 'vous ne pouvez pas comprendre' – but does so with an identical smile playing on his lips (50). Touching on the mysteries of the human condition, understanding has, it seems, once again passed into another realm, beyond a simple quest for the solution to a murder mystery.

Simenon uses the scaffolding of interrogation alongside other key traits of the whodunnit, but his text gradually drifts away from these tropes and structures: the mystery, it would seem, is not that of a murder at all, but rather that of life itself; the investigation is not into who killed Uncle Antoine, but rather into the very meaning of life. *Les Autres* can be described as a pseudo-whodunnit in the same manner as *Le Clan des Ostendais* is a pseudo-thriller: both use the architecture of crime fiction but void them of the anticipated criminal content. Just as there is no blood and thunder climax in *Le Clan* so there is no murder in this murder mystery. Even the inheritance turns out to be largely inconsequential. All three nephews inherit and Colette leaves for sunnier climes. The sum of money received will do little to alter the narrator's somewhat dreary life. As his wife points out: 'Pour nous, cela ne changera pas grand-chose' (151) ['It won't make much of a difference to us'].

So much for *Les Autres* as a work of crime fiction, but what of its status as a novel 'about the war'? The latter is not even alluded to until well over halfway through the text, at which point Édouard's wife, Marie, asks the narrator to facilitate his cousin's reintegration into the family. A wholly unexpected back-story is then provided. In the summer of 1943, we learn, 19-year-old Lucien (Blaise's brother) proposed to Marie, who at around the same time met and fell in love with Édouard. Lucien, who belonged to a resistance network, was arrested shortly thereafter and deported to Buchenwald. In his cousin's absence Édouard married Marie and started a family. Édouard then mysteriously vanished, and rumours emerged concerning his black marketeering activities as well as unspecified and uncorroborated acts of collaboration. Sometime after the Liberation, Lucien returned. The back-story ends with the information that a family friend sorting out German papers at the *Préfecture* had come across an anonymous letter denouncing Lucien, who, when shown the letter, immediately recognized the handwriting as that of Édouard. The eight page analeptic summary is certainly 'about the war', but how does this World War II narrative fragment fit into the broader economy of the text?

One answer to the question takes us back to *La neige était sale* and the gnomic utterance that 'everyone has something on their conscience' (68). The wartime back-story in *Les Autres* plays a key part in what is, under the whodunnit veneer, a work which is primarily concerned with 'big questions': life, death, and in this case, forgiveness. It is Édouard's wife who insists that 'On ne peut payer toute sa vie' (123) ['You can't go on paying all your life'], and by the close of the text the point seems to have been demonstrated: Antoine did include Édouard in his will; the errant cousin takes his place at the head of the family procession at the patriarch's funeral in the cathedral; as the text draws to a conclusion Lucien and Édouard have apparently overcome their differences and are jointly pursuing a project in journalism which they had initiated before the war. In this reading denunciation and deportation are a family affair and not part of a wider historical, ideological, picture. World War II is little more than a parenthesis. As the narrator puts it at the close of the text, life goes on (154). This interpretation substantiates those critical comments which stress Simenon's disengagement with the historical. As we have seen in the case of the previous two texts, however, historical war-related readings are not necessarily occluded by, but rather can exist in tension alongside, what I have tended to call ahistorical, even 'universalist' readings, just as correlatively the 'crime fiction' readings do not automatically preclude the works from being classified as 'novel novels'. Given this argument, I would like to conclude this case study by briefly sketching out an alternative reading of *Les Autres*.

In the opening pages of the text the narrator points out that he has a view of three edifices from his window: in the foreground, a urinal, in the middle distance, the roof of the Law Courts, and beyond that, the two towers of the cathedral (7–8). These three structures can be interpreted as symbolic of respectively the (less glorious aspects of the) human condition, human justice, and divine justice or Christian forgiveness. Strictly (legally) speaking Édouard's base denunciation of his cousin did not, in 1943, constitute a criminal act, but the immorality – in a religious framework, the sinfulness – of the deed is self-evident. By the close of the text Christian forgiveness has apparently prevailed, but can the same be said of human justice? Two fairly unobtrusive passages, both of which implicitly link the wartime fragment to the wider plot of *Les Autres*, indicate an answer in the negative. They also suggest that wartime events remain very much on the textual agenda, albeit in veiled form. When the narrator discusses Édouard's possible reintegration into the family with Lucien, the brothers joke about their cousin's past tendency to engage in philandering and hare-brained business schemes. Both are convinced that Édouard will not modify his behaviour. The narrator then asks a question – 'Qu'est-ce que nous pouvons y faire?' ['What can we do about it?'] – and immediately supplies his own, surprising, reply: 'Le tuer? Certes cela vaudrait mieux pour tout le monde …' (124) ['Kill him? That would certainly be better for everyone …']. In spite of the fact that the damning suggestion is mitigated by the narrator's disclaimer that he was being ironic, this remains a striking statement. Here, finally, is the missing murder, albeit only in virtual form. The death of Antoine and the pseudo-search for culprits and motives can be read as displacements of the true criminality in the text: an act of wartime denunciation avenged by murder (a not uncommon war narrative plot-line, as we will see in Chapter 5). *Les Autres* can, in other words, be read as a screen narrative behind (or through) which the trauma of World War II still lurks. It is perhaps no coincidence that another of the narrator's observations again links the death of Antoine with the war years. He notes of the funeral procession – headed by former denouncer and collaborator Édouard: 'Il y avait autant de monde, sur les trottoirs, que pour une manifestation patriotique' (140) ['There were as many people out on the streets as during a patriotic parade']. This time the irony is unflagged.

Le Train: Crime Fiction Symbols and Proleptic Intertextuality

A short text of some 150 pages, *Le Train* recounts how its first-person protagonist, husband, father, and radio repair-man Marcel Féron, temporarily escapes the hitherto incident-free mundanity of his existence. Faced with news of rapidly advancing German troops, Marcel and his pregnant wife and their four-year-old daughter leave their home and board an overcrowded refugee train. Obliged to settle in different carriages, the couple is then more dramatically divided when the train splits in two, leaving Marcel to take advantage of his unusual circumstances by engaging in a sexual relationship with Anna, a fellow-traveller. The affair continues when the pair arrive at the La Rochelle refugee centre, until such a time as Marcel (not with the greatest alacrity) tracks down his wife in a local hospital, where she has given birth to their son. Marcel's text – for it is revealed that it is he who writes the account we are reading – records a further fleeting encounter with Anna in December 1941, and his return to life as husband, father, and radio repair-man, albeit on a marginally larger scale. Unlike *La neige était sale* this text unfolds in a clearly designated geographical space as the titular train crosses France from Fumay on the Belgian border to La Rochelle, passing through Reims, Bourges, Auxerre, and Tour, amongst other cities. Although the bulk of the action takes place during the course of the train journey, thus in May 1940, the narrator's account spans most of the war, recording not only the later 1941 meeting with Anna but also the birth of the married couple's third child around the time of Liberation in 1944. With this text, however, the Livre de Poche 'Policier / Thriller' label becomes harder to explain. There is little or none of the anticipation or suspense of *Le Clan de Ostendais*; no whodunnit narrative shadowing as in *Les Autres*; no crimes and no potentially criminal war-related act such as collaboration. Even the cover blurb does little more than demonstrate that the most banal fragment of text can be made to sound portentous:

> Quand je me suis éveillé, les rideaux de toile écrue laissaient filtrer dans la chambre une lumière jaunâtre que je connaissais bien. Nos fenêtres, au premier étage, n'ont pas de volets. Il n'y en a à aucune maison de la rue. J'entendais, sur la table de nuit, le tic-tac du réveille-matin et, à côté de moi, la respiration

scandée de ma femme, presque aussi sonore que celle des patients, au cinéma, pendant une opération. Elle était alors enceinte de sept mois et demi.

[When I woke up, a familiar yellowish light was filtering into the bedroom through the linen curtains. Our windows, on the first floor, have no shutters. None of the houses on the street have any. I could hear, on the bedside table, the ticking of the alarm clock, and, beside me, the steady breathing of my wife, which was almost as deep as that of patients at the cinema, during an operation. She was seven and a half months pregnant at the time.]

Is there then anything at all about *Le Train* bar marketing strategy and / or the simple fact that it is a text set during the war years (the inevitable *noir* of the *années noires*?) which might justify its designation as a work of crime fiction, however loosely defined? In terms of common law crimes, the reader is informed, and indeed reminded on several occasions, that Anna had been in a women's prison, but the nature of her misdemeanour is neither pursued nor revealed. When she informs Marcel that she is Czech, has a Jewish mother, and no passport, the notion that she may be using him as cover crosses his mind, but is rapidly discarded. Certainly Anna has an unspecified criminal past and is something of a *femme fatale*, but given the brevity and the more or less non-existent consequences of her encounter with Marcel, she is not as *fatale* as might be expected of a true *noir* protagonist. Is Marcel himself then of a criminal disposition? Like Frank in *La neige état sale* he is self-confessedly apolitical: 'Ce n'était pas la France et l'Allemagne, ni la Pologne, l'Angleterre, Hitler, le nazisme ou le communisme qui, dans mon esprit, étaient en jeu. Je ne me suis jamais intéressé à la politique et je n'y connais rien' (14) ['It wasn't France and Germany, or Poland, Hitler, Nazism or Communism which, to my mind, were involved. I've never taken any interest in politics; it's something I know nothing about']. Perhaps this explains why when Anna approaches him in 1941 accompanied by an English airman, seeking a temporary hiding-place from the Gestapo, he refuses to help. Anna is shot a month later. The only 'crime', it would seem, is that of the narrator's wartime cowardice. Interestingly, the latter was expurgated from the text's screen adaptation a decade later.[65] Granier-Deferre's film demonstrates slightly greater ideological engagement and depicts a less pusillanimous protagonist. Czech Anna (Kupfer) of vaguely Jewish parentage is transmuted into German Jew Anna Schneider whose family is being held in a concentration camp. Marcel Féron's film avatar, Julien Maroyeur, insists that Anna be given an identity card in La Rochelle establishing her as his wife in order to protect her, and when she is captured some time later, he is interrogated by the police. Like his novelistic predecessor, Julien initially opts for cowardice, denying all knowledge of his erstwhile lover, but the film swerves in its closing moments: Julien embraces Anna and, we are left to assume, an imperilled future. This version may signify the triumph of love rather

---

[65]   The film version of the same name, directed by Pierre Granier-Deferre, was released in 1973.

than that of political commitment – war is primarily represented, as it was in the back-story of *Les Autres,* as a personal rather than an ideological matter – but the cowardice is expunged, and the post-war national image consequently emerges marginally more intact than in Simenon's original.

True to a pattern which should by now be familiar, *Le Train* is characterized by a tension between movement and stasis, the historically situated and the atemporal: the train may track across the country amidst bombs and terrified civilians but the enclosed spaces of the carriage and refugee centre represent a parenthetic escape from the protagonist's life story and, paradoxically, from history. War is a blip, albeit one which may facilitate soul-searching and a temporary respite from the quotidian. However, although the past, be it personal or historical, often appears to be repudiated in Simenon's texts, it also has a tendency to return. Oedipal motifs binding childhood to present patterns of behaviour were identified in *La neige était sale*, whilst one plot was seen to hide another in *Les Autres,* a pseudo-whodunnit screening the reality of a shameful historical episode of denunciation. A similar process can be traced in *Le Train* via the symbolism of spectacles.

Without his glasses the narrator-protagonist of *Le Train* cannot see clearly: 'sans mes verres, je suis aussi perdu qu'un homme dans la nuit, en tout cas dans un brouillard épais' (13–14) ['without my glasses, I'm as lost as a man in total darkness, or at least in thick fog']. Marcel suffers from such severe myopia that he has developed a nervous tic, repeatedly checking his left-hand pocket for his spare pair of spectacles. During his time with Anna, however, his eyesight undergoes a remarkable restoration, only to deteriorate once more upon his return to post-war ordinary life. What is to be made of this symbolism? As Platten notes, 'Ocular instruments – magnifying glasses, microscopes, and reading-glasses – are part of the folklore of detective fiction. For many, they symbolize the penetrating gaze of the great detective'.[66] That Marcel's eyesight improves during his parenthetic idyll with Anna may symbolize – in his eyes at least – a period of 'seeing clearly', an epiphany (we may be reminded of the recurring word 'comprendre' and its connotations in the Simenon *œuvre*) concerning what 'real life', what 'being a man' can and should signify: in this case something more exciting than having a wife, family, and career repairing radios. Read thus the symbol of the glasses links Marcel to the 'great detective' who, in this instance, attempts to investigate the meaning of his own life: 'si j'écris', he states, 'c'est surtout par besoin de découvrir une certaine vérité' (100) ['if I write, it is above all because of the need I have to uncover a certain truth']. But an alternative reading lends a psychoanalytic edge to the epistemological symbolism of spectacles, and undercuts the narrator's point of view. Marcel's inability to see can also be interpreted as symptomatic of a desire not to see. His condition, we learn, followed upon a series of illnesses which erupted after a specific incident in his childhood: the view of his mother returning to the house naked and with shaven head, followed by a crowd of jeering youngsters.

---

[66] David Platten, 'Reading-glasses, guns and robots: a history of science in French crime fiction', *French Cultural Studies*, 12 (2001): 253–70 [261].

The traumatic event took place in 1918 and is explictly linked to World War I: 'J'avais déjà vécu une guerre [...] j'avais six ans en 1914' (15) ['I had already lived through one war (...) I was six years old in 1914'], the narrator informs us just prior to his recounting of the maternal episode. Like Frank in *La neige était sale*, Marcel denies the existence of a causal link between past and present: 'ceci n'a sans doute rien à voir avec mes sentiments de 1939 ou de 1940' (15) ['all of which undoubtedly has no bearing on the feelings I had in 1939 or 1940'], but the reader need not of course accept the narrator's perspective. The oedipal motif of the sexualized mother is bound in to the historical wartime narrative. Why the mother's head was shaved is never explained, but for readers of *Le Train* the image would inevitably conjure up cultural memories of the next World War and the excesses of the *épuration sauvage* and the 'punishment' of those women who had slept with the enemy. As with *Les Autres*, the trauma of World War II returns to the text in unstated, spectral form.

Readers of a corpus of texts are not limited by the chronology of their publication, and my final reading of the spectacle symbolism in *Le Train* will engage very briefly in what I am going to term proleptic intertextuality: the reading of an earlier text through a later one. The text in question is another war narrative: Michel Tournier's *Le Roi des Aulnes* (1970).[67] First some minor, but nonetheless cumulative, points of commonality between the two texts can be identified. Tournier's protagonist, Abel Tiffauges is a garage mechanic; Marcel Féron repairs radios. Marcel's family keep domestic fowl, including a cockerel called Nestor (23), the name of a key character in *Le Roi des Aulnes*. Still on the avian theme, Marcel's father-in-law keeps racing pigeons, birds which feature at both a referential and symbolic level in Tournier's text. Both protagonists evince a desire to lay identity bare; to strip it of its social trappings. Tiffauges states: 'On rêve d'un bon tyran qui supprimerait d'un trait de plume état civil, carte d'identité, passeport [...], livrets de toutes sortes, cassier judiciaire' (*Le Roi*, 65) ['You dream of the benevolent tyrant who will at the stroke of a pen do away with civil status, identity cards, passports (...) official records of all sorts, police records']. Marcel, who (like Tournier's Tiffauges) relishes the approach of war for its liberating potential,[68] has no identificatory documents: 'à l'époque, elles [les cartes d'identité] n'étaient pas obligatoires en France. Je n'avais pas non plus de passeport' (110) ['at that time they were not compulsory in France. I did not have a passport either']. In the eyes of both Tiffauges and Marcel the war marks an important stage in their personal destiny: 'Cette guerre [...] c'était une affaire

---

67   Michel Tournier, *Le Roi des Aulnes* (Gallimard, 1970).

68   Tournier describes the not dissimilar attitude he experienced as a youth: 'J'avais fait des vœux ardents pour que la guerre éclatât, mettant fin à mes problèmes scolaires. J'étais dévorée par la soif de désordre et de catastrophe qui tourmente certains adolescents' ['I had desperately wished that war might break out and in so doing put an end to my problems at school. I was consumed by the sort of thirst for disorder and catastrophe that torments some adolescents'], *Le Vent paraclet* (Gallimard, 1977), p. 74.

personnelle entre le destin et moi' (*Le Train*, 14) ['This war (…) was a personal matter between me and Fate']; 'Personne n'avait autant que lui la conscience de son destin, un destin rectiligne, imperturbable, inflexible qui ordonnait à ses seules fins les événements mondiaux les plus grandioses' (*Le Roi*, 249) ['No one was as aware of his fate as he was, an imperturbable, inflexible fate which followed a perfectly straight line, and which moulded the greatest world events to his own ends']. And finally, the spectacles. Tiffauges suffers from 'une myopie gallopante, m'obligeant à porter des verres de plus en plus épais' (*Le Roi*, 109) ['terrible myopia which obliges me to wear glasses with ever-thicker lenses'], a condition which directly echoes that of his literary predecessor: 'j'ai besoin de verres de plus en plus épais' (*Le Train*, 152) ['I need glasses with increasingly thick lenses'].

There are further cross-overs linking the two texts, but this is not the place for comprehensive coverage. The point is rather to suggest that for the contemporary reader, Marcel and Tiffauges may become shadowy superimpositions. One character may screen another. Tiffauges's hypertrophic interpretation of signs blinds him to the nazi atrocities with which he becomes complicit, and although Marcel is a much tamer figure, his readings too result in an abnegation of responsibility: 'C'était comme si j'attendais un signe, comme si je voulais que le hasard décide pour moi' (18–19) ['It was as if I were waiting for a sign, as if I wanted Fate to decide for me']. Unlike the 'great detective', the short-sighted Tiffauges and Marcel ultimately prove themselves to be inadequate readers of signs. Interpreting *Le Train* via the proleptic intertext underscores the dangers of what Platten, referring to Tiffauges, calls 'an essentialist vision of a world which is ultimately tied to the will of the subject'.[69] Seen in this light – that of his successor Tiffauges's authoritarian blindness – Marcel's weakness seems all the more dangerous; his refusal to help the Jewish Anna resonating with Tiffauges's much greater myopic complicity with the nazi regime. In *Le Roi des Aulnes* it is a Jew, the young boy Éphraïm, who serves to reveal the truth of the camps to Tiffauges, reminding him of the raw referentiality of signs and symbols. The text hints at redemption in its apocalyptic closing pages when Tiffauge loses his glasses and, bearing Éphraïm on his back, surrenders control: 'Éphraïm, dit Tiffauges, je n'ai plus mes lunettes. Je ne vois presque plus rien. Guide-moi!' (*Le Roi*, 578) ['Éphraïm', said Tiffauges, 'I've lost my glasses. I can hardly see anything any more. Guide me!']. No such redemption is available to Tiffauges's more pedestrian predecessor whose crimes only foreshadow those of his successor.

Finally, one last link between Tournier's (Goncourt-winning, 'high' literary) text and Simenon's 'Policier / Thriller' is worth pursuing briefly: the use of first-person narrative forms. Tiffauges initially writes a diary as a means of escapism: 'pour échapper à ce garage, aux médiocres préoccupations qui m'y retiennent, et en un certain sens à moi-même' (*Le Roi*, 15) ['to escape from the garage, and all the mediocre preoccupations which bind me to it, and in a way to escape

---

[69]   David Platten, 'The Geist in the machine: Nazism in Tournier's *Le Roi des Aulnes*', *Romanic Review*, 84.2 (1993): 181–94 [184].

from myself']. Marcel, similarly, composes his retrospective account to show that for a short period he escaped his dull life and became 'un autre homme [...] capable d'une vraie passion' (152) ['a different man (...) capable of experiencing real passion']. Blaise, the writer-protagonist of *Les Autres*, is also a diarist (although the length and nature of the entries makes his more of a pseudo-diary), who chooses the form after a first literary project, a novel, is rejected by publishers (8). In all three texts the question of authority is paramount. Each of the first-person narrators is potentially unreliable. In the case of Tiffauges, the reader is provided with a heterodiegetic narrative as counter-balance to the highly personal and partial perspective of the narrator-protagonist's 'Écrits sinistres' (as his diary entries are somewhat pointedly entitled). Simenon's readers are afforded no such alternative narrative, but I would like to suggest that a figure of greater authority is surreptitiously introduced into both of his texts. An anonymous and well-informed individual pops up intermittently in *Le Train*: 'Comme d'habitude *l'homme à la pipe* était le mieux renseigné, d'abord à cause de sa position stratégique près de la porte, ensuite parce qu'il ne craignait pas de poser des questions' (91, my emphasis) ['As usual the man with the pipe was the best informed, first because of his strategic position near the door, and also because he wasn't afraid to ask questions']. In *Les Autres* Blaise, seeking literary validation, sends his novel to a writer acquaintance: 'le seul, des auteurs que j'ai lus, dont les personnages me donnent l'impression d'être des hommes comme moi, avec les mêmes problèmes, les mêmes préoccupations, la même façon de réagir' (8) ['the only one of the authors whose work I have read whose characters gave me the impression of being men like me, with the same problems, the same preoccupations, the same way of reacting']. Encoded as manifestations of Simenon himself,[70] both the writer offering literary advice and the pipe-smoker (the latter already present as police inspector Kurt Hamling in *La neige était sale*) not only challenge the writer-protagonists' perspective by alluding to a higher authority; they also introduce a highly self-reflexive element to both works. It is worth noting that the writer who reads Blaise's novel decrees damningly that 'on ne se sentait pas "en présence d'une œuvre littéraire à proprement parler"' (9) ['one did not feel that one was "in the presence of a literary work, in the true sense of the term"']. We have come full circle, back to the question of genre, and quality.

Closing Statement

At the start of this chapter *La neige était sale*, *Le Clan des Ostendais*, *Les Autres*, and *Le Train* were designated by a negative, oppositional, term as examples of Simenon's 'not-Maigret' works. The shortcomings of this descriptor and the

---

[70]　Read on a different level, the anonymous writerly acquaintance (interpreted by me here as Simenon) contacted by Blaise might also be linked to another literary mentor – Gide – who regularly read Simenon's own work. For a discussion of this literary relationship see Platten, *The Pleasures of Crime*, pp. 45–9.

various other labels ascribed to the texts – for instance 'novel novels', 'hard novels', 'grey novels' or precursors to *noir* – were discussed, and it was noted that terms such as 'roman policier' and 'roman noir' should not be considered as unchanging genre labels either in terms of characteristic traits or literary prestige. With respect to their marketing and publishing history, the four texts were seen currently to feature in both the Pléiade edition and as part of specialized crime series published by Livre de Poche and Folio, a combination which might, at least some years ago, have struck critics as unusual. Following on from the discussion of fiction and crime fiction labels, it was also observed that if critics' comments are anything to go by, Simenon may seem a perverse choice in a monograph involving novels concerned with World War II.

Taking the second of these issues first, what do these four texts have to tell us about representations of World War II and, more specifically, the Occupation? Although he kills a soldier of the occupying forces in *La neige était sale*, and subsequently remains silent when captured and interrogated, Frank is no heroic Resistance fighter,[71] and though he sells watches to the occupying forces in exchange for a green card, neither is he an altogether convincing collaborator. Simenon's anti-hero has little if any interest in the politics of the war. Not dissimilarly, *Le Clan des Ostendais* with its prospective force and building of suspense has all the elements of a wartime thriller with a potential Resistance hero (Omer) in place, yet the text repeatedly undercuts readerly expectations of dramatic action. The deported resistant (Lucien) and his collaborating denouncer (Édouard) in *Les Autres*, types who feature as key players in many World War II crime narratives, are relegated to a short, analeptic back-story in Simenon's take on the war, with the revenge narrative murder we might expect appearing only in virtual form as a throw-away quip. Finally, *Le Train* features the apolitical Marcel, who has an utterly inconsequential affair with, and later fails to hide, a woman who is subsequently executed by the nazis as a spy (the report of her death taking up a mere sentence in the tale). Only another virtual narrative – that constructed via a proleptic intertextual reading of Tournier's *Le Roi de Aulnes* – lends Simenon's anodine protagonist an edge as a significant figure in a war narrative.

In the light of many works of crime fiction which represent World War II, Simenon's texts can be said first and foremost to de-dramatize the war; indeed they could be read as subverting many texts which represent the war via (by now) familiar stereotypic characters such as resistant, collaborator, member of

---

[71] Frank's capture, interrogation by two factions, and execution might usefully be compared to that of the central figure in Paul Guimard's *L'Ironie du sort* (1961). Antoine too kills a German soldier and remains silent under questioning (in this case explicitly by the Gestapo and Wehrmacht), but does so to save a resistance network. Echoes of *L'Étranger* identified in *La neige était sale* are present here in the form of the priest who visits Antoine in his cell just prior to his execution. Guimard too, though in a very different way, undermines the resistance hero stereotype by stressing the role of fate, or chance, in all human lives. *L'Ironie du sort* is not marketed or marked out paratextually as an example of crime fiction.

the Gestapo, etc. Simenon's four novels certainly gesture towards such types, but the latter feature only as virtualities conjured up by a certain horizon of expectations. In all four texts the historical specificity of World War II – and the potential, shadowy but unwritten, stereotypical war narrative – is held in tension with an ahistorical narrative which explores the mysteries of the human condition, or perhaps, more specifically, what it means to be a man. This is a dialectical relationship: the nature of man cannot be fully explored without consideration of the historical specificities of the war, but neither, it is suggested, can the war be represented and comprehended without the broader picture of what it means to be human. Narratives which sever this tie, Simenon's texts remind us, represent an incomplete picture of both war and man.

In the case of all four texts the representation of the war cannot be separated from the other question which concerns us: are these works of crime fiction or just fiction? Strikingly, all four appear in dedicated crime fiction series, but apart from two murders and a theft in *La neige était sale* there are, strictly speaking, no crimes as such unless one counts collaboration, for the most part of a fairly minor kind (*Le Clan, Les Autres*, and *La neige*), failing to help someone who opposes the occupying forces (*Le Train*) or, approaching the matter of criminal activity from the point of view of the occupying forces, acts of Resistance or 'terrorism' (*Le Clan, Les Autres, Le Train*, and *La neige*, if one counts the murdered soldier as an unintended act of resistance). When investigation takes place typical investigative figures are often sidelined, and the focus of inquiry tends to the existential or metaphysical; 'comprendre' is extended beyond the resolving of a criminal mystery to an inherent human need to grasp the meaning (or meaninglessness) of existence. And yet, just as the war-related stereotypes remain, albeit in shadowy form, so too do the crime fiction devices, from the thriller-like narrative build-up of *Le Clan* to the whodunnit tropes and interrogative exchanges in *Les Autres*. Just as the texts call into question the stereotypical protagonists of war narratives so do they lay bare many of the norms of crime fiction. Again, this is a dialectic relationship: the crime novel is defined or constructed in relation to the novel novel (sic) and vice versa.

La neige était sale includes the curiously detached police inspector Hamling; *Le Clan des Ostendais* the trawlerman Omer who challenges the established order. In *Le Train* an unnamed character carefully observes the world from the open wagon doorway. All three, like inspector Maigret, but more importantly like Simenon himself, are pipe-smokers. In *Les Autres* an unnamed author judges Blaise's manuscript. The figure of authority, the writer, in other words, is inscribed in all four texts. Although it should have emerged by now that a case can be made for these texts as examples of both crime fiction and / or fiction *tout court* perhaps they can also be regarded as works of metafiction which explore not only the 'métier d'homme' or what it means to be a man, but also the 'métier d'écrivain', or what it means to be a writer, working in any genre.

Chapter 2
From Hybrid Whodunnit to Cyber-Sleuthing

'"[...] though he hadn't the shadow of a reason for taking the Diamond – he might have taken it, nevertheless, through natural depravity. Very well. Say he did. Why the devil—" / "I beg your pardon, Mr Bruff. If I hear the devil referred to in that manner, I must leave the room."'

—Wilkie Collins[1]

'But what does it matter? Even if Doctor Goebbels is deposed and Operation Dandelion is cancelled? They will still exist, the blackshirts, the Partei, the schemes if not in the Orient then somewhere else. On Mars and Venus.'

—Philip K. Dick[2]

The previous chapter explored the term 'crime fiction' as a category, and proposed both historically specific and more temporally transcendent readings of Simenon's (crime) novels. From this point on the designation 'crime fiction' and the fact that the texts discussed in some manner and to varying degrees represent World War II will no longer be the focal point of discussion. The aim in this chapter is rather to showcase the range and flexibility of both of these descriptors, and to this end four very different types of text have been selected. Raymond Troye's *Meurtre dans un oflag* (1946) presents as a straightforward whodunnit but can also be read as a text which casts an uncanny, gothic shadow. In sharp contrast, San-Antonio's self-reflexive and linguistically ludic *Laissez tomber la fille* (1950), *Les souris ont la peau tendre* (1951), and *Du plomb dans les tripes* (1953) romp their way through action sequences and quasi cartoon-strip adventures (the most recent cover artwork is, appropriately enough, designed by Georges Wolinski) in which the evil Germans invariably get their comeuppance. Boileau-Narcejac's suspense novels *Les Louves* (1955), *Maldonne* (1962), and *La Lèpre* (1976) turn the focus on the victim and bring a Sartrean twist to the war years via the themes of freedom and authenticity. Finally Maurice Dantec's *Les racines du mal* (1995) combines what McHale terms an epistemological with an ontological dominant by integrating crime and science fiction.[3] All of these texts are entirely or predominantly first-person narratives. Published over a period of five decades they should, if we are to believe Rousso's 'Vichy syndrome' pathology, reveal a mutating diagnosis of France's (and in one case Belgium's) relationship to its wartime past.

---

[1]   Wilkie Collins, *The Moonstone* (Oxford UP, 1999; first published 1868), p. 220.

[2]   Philip K. Dick, *The Man in the High Castle* (Penguin Books 1965; first published 1962), p. 236.

[3]   Brian McHale, *Constructing Postmodernism* (Routledge, 1992), especially pp. 146–7.

Troye's Hybrid Whodunnit

Raymond Troye, a lieutenant in the Belgian army, wrote *Meurtre dans un oflag* between 1942 and 1943 while he was being held first in Oflag VII in Eichstätt, Bavaria, and subsequently in Oflag II A, in Prenzlau.[4] The text is sparing with dates, but a reference to the capture of the first-person narrator Jules Francen on May 23 [1940] near Ghent, and an observation that he has been held prisoner in an Oflag for some 16 months, allow the narrative to be situated around November 1941. Whereas Simenon's *Les Autres* was described in the previous chapter as a pseudo-whodunnit which incorporated many of the tropes and narrative structures of the genre but did not, in fact, fulfill generic expectations, *Meurtre* delivers on all fronts, providing an enclosed setting, a murder victim, a restricted set of suspects, a detective, and a murderer. The plot thickens, however – or perhaps more appositely it is diffracted – thanks to the complexities and ambiguities of the first-person narrative.

Troye's decision to set his murder mystery in a POW officer camp clearly has an autobiographical dimension to it, but other authors of crime fiction too have been tempted by such circumscribed locations. The following brief overview is far from exhaustive but is intended to go some way towards contextualizing Troye's use of the Oflag setting within a broader body of crime fiction.[5] Set respectively in a fort on the Maginot line and an American repatriation camp, Nord's *Double crime sur la ligne Maginot* (1936) and Morris's *Assassin, mon frère* (1954) are both whodunnits. A German spy masquerading as a French officer is unmasked as the murderer in the first instance, and a *maquisard* in the second. Both texts are variants on the theme of the 'enemy within'. Enclosed claustrophobic spaces can also be put to the service of exploring and exploiting often murderous tensions between disparate social and political groupings. Amila's *Au balcon d'Hiroshima* (1985) throws together a heterogeneous mix of detainees in a Japanese camp, including common criminals passing themselves off as members of the Resistance. Delteil's *KZ retour vers l'enfer* (1987) focuses on communist deportees' plans to overcome their German captors and on the various political factions in an unnamed concentration camp. Readers may also be reminded of the presence of camps on French soil: Daeninckx's *La Route du Rom* (2003), for instance, highlights the existence of the Barenton internment camp and in so doing goes some way towards commemorating its Romani inmates.

Unsurprisingly given the sensitivity of the subject, texts do not tend to represent Jewish deportees in concentration or death camps, although such camps are referred to and can fulfil various functions: the plot of Jonquet's *Les Orpailleurs* (1993), for instance, pivots on the burial and theft of Jewish deportees' possessions

---

[4]   For further information relating to *Meurtre dans un oflag* see the website constructed and maintained by Troye's family at: <http://oflag.skynetblogs.be/>.

[5]   Texts may of course be set in different circumscribed locations (i.e., other than camps), such as a single house (e.g., Soulas's *Café sans tickets ...*, 1949), or on board a ship (e.g., Carraud's *Les poulets du Cristobal*, 1998, or Coatmeur's *On l'appelait Johnny*, 1979).

in Auschwitz;[6] Fontenau's *Otto* (1997) follows several generations of an East German family commercially involved in the construction of concentration and death camp crematoria; a growing number of texts mention such camps as part of a repudiation of Holocaust denial (see Chapter 5 below). Most commonly texts relating to the Shoah represent first generation Jewish deportee survivors or / and the impact of deportation on subsequent generations: in Monteilhet's *Le Retour des cendres* (1961) a returned Jewish deportee is embroiled in an inheritance scam; a former deportee murders one of the men responsible for her war-time arrest in Del Pappas's *Bleu sur la peau* (1998); in Bialot's *La Nuit du souvenir* (1990) the investigator is a former deportee who traces the motive of the criminal back to the theft of bread in the camps. Klotz's *Kobar* (1992) and Wagneur's *Homicide bon marché* (1996) both feature second-generation investigators who are, inevitably, compromised in their objectivity (see Chapter 4). Finally, texts may represent former nazis who worked in the camps: in Auclair's *Un Amour allemand* (1950), for instance, a French soldier falls in love with a German woman whose brother is revealed to have been in charge of a concentration camp; Boileau-Narcejac's *Maldonne* (1962) as we will see shortly, revolves around a former concentration camp commander's attempt to avoid death at the hands of nazi-hunters.

As this small but nonetheless representative sample of texts demonstrates, in the majority of cases camps of all sorts function as sites of at best French (or Belgian) internal division and conflict, and at worst, guilt, complicity in crime, or outright criminality. With the exception of texts focusing on nazi war criminals, Germans rarely feature, and when they do, strikingly, they tend to be represented as emotionally involved with, impersonated by, or impersonating French citizens. *Meurtre dans un oflag* is no exception in this. The German presence in the text is muted to the point of invisibility (we assume guards are present but they have no part to play), and the criminal is Belgian, with, as I will argue, an uncanny hint of Frenchness about him.

As would be expected of a classic whodunnit, Troye's text opens with a murder: lieutenant Jadin, in the chapel, with a blunt instrument (a hammer). The role of investigator falls to a fellow detainee, former police officer Ledru, who is aided in his task by another stock figure of the whodunnit, the intermediary, first-person narrator, Jules Francen. All the anticipated stages of an investigation duly unfold: potential suspects are questioned; Ledru and Francen discuss the case; an attempt is made on their life; the murder weapon is located and fingerprints lifted from it. At the close of the text Ledru gathers the officers together and utters words familiar to all aficionados of the mystery genre: 'le meurtrier d'Albert Jadin est

---

6   For discussions of Jonquet's *Les Orpailleurs* see Claire Gorrara, 'Reflections on Crime and Punishment: Memories of the Holocaust in Recent French Crime Fiction', *Yale French Studies*, 108 (2005): 131–45; and her 'Narratives of Protest and the Roman Noir in Post-1968 France', *French Studies*, 54.3 (2000): 313–25. Also Alan Morris, '*Roman noir, années noires*: the French Néo-Polar and the Occupation's Legacy of Violence', in David Gascoigne (ed.), *Violent Histories* (Peter Lang, 2007), pp. 131–54.

toujours en liberté, si l'on peut dire enfin […] car il se trouve parmi nous, entre ces barbelés […] Il est même présent dans cette salle' (158) ['The murderer of Albert Jadin is still at liberty, so to speak (…) for he is here amongst us, within these barbed wire fences (…) Indeed he is present in this very room']. The guilty party is identified as one lieutenant Van Damme and the whys and hows of the murder are explained (more of which shortly). Closure is provided when Van Damme dies attempting to escape from the camp. The final paragraph sees Ledru pronounce the sententious words which signal the generically dictated return to the status quo: 'Il a payé sa dette' (172) ['He's paid his dues'].

As I hope is becoming apparent, crime fiction is always potentially more or other than any one label might denote or connote, and this is only one way in which *Meurtre* can be read. In the Preface to the text dated April 1945, Prenzlau, lieutenant-general Michiels, Troye's senior officer and patron who undertook to have a copy of the author's manuscript bound and published in the camp, describes the work as 'beaucoup moins un roman policier qu'une étude de mœurs' (8) ['much more of a social document than a detective novel']. Troye's first-person narrator, who is explicitly writing the account we read ('qu'ai-je là écrit?', he asks at one point, p. 33 ['what have I just written?']; 'J'ai dû m'interrompre d'écrire', p. 35) ['I had to break off writing']), similarly refers to his text as 'un témoignage entre mille autres de notre vie captive!' (77) ['one amongst thousands of other accounts of our life in captivity']. Whilst the overlap between author and first-person narrator should not be exaggerated, both the paratextual and the intradiegetic observations foreground the contractual nature of reading genre; more specifically in this particular case, they underscore the fact that as readers we must decide whether to interpret segments of text as clues or (and) descriptive elements lending authenticity to what can be read as a testimonial account. At one point in the text Francen describes the officers leaving an amateur theatrical performance 'portant pour la plupart leur tabouret à califourchon sur les épaules. C'est la caractéristique de nos fêtes au camp: si l'on désire y être assis, il faut bien apporter son siège' (46) ['most of them carrying their stools on their shoulders. It's a typical part of our camp-life festivities: if you want to sit down you have to bring your own seat']. As commentators have observed, readers of crime fiction are paranoid; they see signs everywhere: 'Everything that is described or merely mentioned is significant because it has the status of a potential clue'.[7] But significant how? Is the carrying of stools a clue? Is one prisoner perhaps not carrying a stool for some as yet unspecified reason? And what should we make of the information that the prisoners all tend to walk around the perimeter fence in the same direction, that there are normally 32 officers to a hut, or that the edges of black-out materials are used to make counterfeit soup coupons? As Dubois points out of crime fiction, the most fleeting references or banal pieces of information are likely to be read as clues allowing us to solve the mystery in the end.[8] 'In the

---

7   Dennis Porter, *The Pursuit of Crime* (Yale UP, 1982), p. 43.

8   Jacques Dubois, *Le roman policier ou la modernité* (Armand Collin, 2006), pp. 131–2.

end' is the essential phrase here. It is a truism that hindsight creates clues, but it is also the case that it contributes to the construction of genre: until and unless the solution to the murder is revealed, all details in *Meurtre* may be clues (and thus part of a work of crime fiction), Barthean 'reality effects'[9] (belonging to a fictional testimonial account of life in an Oflag), or part of an autobiographical project (Troye's own testimonial account).[10]

As it turns out none of these details about life in the Oflag proves to be a clue, though it is easy enough to imagine a plot in which one would be. Two key passages provide the (or an) answer to whodunnit. First, over some three pages of back-story (101–3) it is revealed that Van Damme and the murder victim Jadin had both been in the military fort of Anceilles which, under Van Damme's command, was surrendered to the Germans even though some shells remained unused. Nothing further is made of this and the investigation moves on. Later, when the murder weapon is finger-printed, we learn that the wielder of the hammer was missing a digit: 'l'index de la main droite lui manque' (150) ['the index finger on his right hand is missing']. Very few readers would have picked up on the significance of an earlier description: 'Van Damme taquinait le doigtier qui lui protégeait l'un des doigts, de la main droite' (85) ['Van Damme was fiddling with the fingerstall that protected one of his fingers, on his right hand']. As Dubois puts it, '[i]ndices et effets de réel s'y [roman d'énigme] font interchangeables à volonté jusqu'à devenir indistincts' ['clues and reality effects in the whodunnit become interchangeable to the point of being indistinguishable'].[11] Van Damme has already been described as the amateur dramatic troupe's prop man, so the finger injury detail passes easily enough, though the especially paranoid reader might just question the phrase 'on his right hand', separated out as it is from the rest of the sentence by a redundant comma. Forensic evidence provides the final piece in the puzzle for Ledru, who accuses Van Damme of killing Jadin for fear that the latter would denounce him as a coward for capitulating before all ammunition supplies were exhausted. This makes of *Meurtre* a whodunnit with a strong message about the war: those who capitulate, especially prematurely, are criminals, and poetic justice dictates that they be punished by death. King Leopold's highly contentious decision to surrender Belgian troops to the Germans on 27 May 1940, against the wishes and advice of his government, echoes loud and clear in Troye's text.[12]

---

[9] Descriptive details apparently lacking function at the level of plot or character development can serve to create an illusion of 'reality' in the fictional work; see Barthes, 'L'Effet de réel', *Communications* no. 11 (1968): 84–9.

[10] See John Frow, *Genre* (Routledge, 2006) on the contractually temporal nature reading pp. 100–123.

[11] Dubois, *Le roman policier ou la modernité*, pp. 132–3.

[12] For another work of crime fiction which references King Leopold's decision and focuses on Belgian resistance and capitulation, see Alain Berenboom's *Périls en ce royaume* (2006), set shortly after the end of the war.

But what if Van Damme were not the (only) guilty party? Two other readings of *Meurtre* can be proposed, both of which establish the narrator Francen in the role of criminal. What I have yet to mention is the fact that Troye's first-person narrator suffers from amnesia and has no recollection of his movements on the night of the murder. He has, furthermore, personal motives for wishing the murder victim dead. This makes of Francen an atypical intermediary figure: such Watson-like characters whose role it is to stand between reader and detective are usually marked by their reliability, both morally and as narrators. It also adds a further virtual strand to the generic status of the text. Believing himself to be guilty (or claiming that he so believes), Francen insists that his text cannot function as a viable whodunnit – 'on connaît le coupable dès les premières pages' (98) ['we know who the guilty party is from the opening pages'] – and should rather be regarded as a form of confession (77). Reading the narrator as guilty, however, depends not on his explicit utterances but rather on the hyper-critical reader's interpretation of information and the manner in which it is presented. A lengthy analeptic foray into what is revealed to be Francen's and Jadin's shared childhood provides ample evidence of the narrator's hatred for the victim: acute class consciousness and a long-standing sense of social inferiority; Francen's inability to win academic plaudits whilst he and Jadin were in school together; Jadin's stealing Francen's girl. Add to this the information that Jadin has recently usurped the role of Figaro – another text about class – in the officers' drama production and Francen's motivation for murder is highly over-determined. For this very reason, however, we are likely to find him not-guilty and, like Ledru, continue our interrogative or paranoid reading. As Roth puts it: 'Obedient to the paradox of the obvious, a detective will deny meaning to the customarily meaningful fact, the piece of evidence';[13] indeed anything 'up-front' is mistrusted by both investigator and reader.

First-person narratives, especially those which engage in self-reflexive pronouncements about genre, inevitably precipitate a degree of interpretive ambiguity, and in *Meurtre* authorial double-bluff remains as a constant possibility. Readers may reject explicit signifiers of Francen's guilt, but what may be identified as more subtle clues tempt those who are seized by 'detective-fever'.[14] Do comments about class (which also contribute to the testimonial depiction of life in an Oflag), for instance, not indicate an on-going and un-self-diagnosed malaise on Francen's part? The narrator points out that his clothes are in rags but that the wealthy officers have of course bought new uniforms (78); the fact that officers should have to collect their own firewood is regarded by him as inappropriate (128). Unlike Oedipus, the most famous self-investigator, Francen believes himself to be guilty from the outset. Paradoxically, whilst readers discard

---

[13]   Roth, *Foul and Fair Play* (U of Georgia P, 1995), p. 185.

[14]   The expression is used by Mr Betteredge in Collins's *Moonstone* – another work of detective fiction featuring an amnesiac – to describe his growing fascination with, and involvement in, Sergeant Cuff's investigations.

that self-proclaimed guilt, possible oedipal motifs which are *not* bound in to any causal explanation encourage an imputation of guilt: Francen's symptoms include periods of temporary blindness (35); we learn that as he first came round from the head injury which caused the amnesia he hallucinated a large gelatinous eye (43); reading his own musings on his guilt he considers ripping a page from his notebook: 'Qu'elle me [la page] brûle les yeux!' (55) ['how it burns my eyes!'].

Oedipal motifs and unflagged allusions to motive such as those relating to class may thus prompt a reading which points to the narrator's guilt rather than Van Damme's. If the narrator were the guilty party then the war-related message would be diluted: as with Frank in Simenon's *La neige était sale* and Édouard in *Les Autres*, crime for Francen would be a purely personal matter. But this reading, like the differentiation of clues from 'innocent' descriptive passages, is a temporally dependent and thus a temporary affair. Competing epistemologies are at work in *Meurtre dans un oflag*: that of Ledru, that of the narrator, and our own as readers. Ledru combines what Platten has identified as two investigative heritages: the ratiocinative abstraction typical of the French detective fiction tradition, and the recourse to material evidence beloved of the English line.[15] Like Gaston Leroux's Rouletabille, Ledru appeals to a Cartesian-based epistemology.[16] His architectural image – 'L'édifice à construire s'appelle la vérité. [...] Partir sur une fausse piste équivaut à bâtir sur du sable' (99) ['The structure which must be erected is called truth. (...) Going off in the wrong direction is the equivalent of building on sand'] – echoes Descartes's *Discours de la méthode*.[17] To this he adds, as we have seen, a Holmesian belief in the importance of forensic evidence in the form of finger-printing. By the close of the text Ledru has designated Van Damme as the guilty party, and when another officer provides an alibi for Francen by pointing out that he was with him on the evening of the murder, the self-diagnosis of the investigator-narrator and our own reading of Francen as the guilty party seem to be invalidated; the little grey cells prevail over the damaged cells of the amnesiac (and those of the paranoid reader).

Roth suggests that it is precisely this type of closure and epistemological certainty which banishes the gothic from the whodunnit.[18] But need this be the case? After all, Roth also associates classic detective fiction with the uncanny:

---

[15]   David Platten, 'Reading-glasses, guns and robots: a history of science in French crime fiction', *French Cultural Studies*, 12 (2001): 253–70.

[16]   Master of deductive reasoning, Gaston Leroux's reporter-investigator, Joseph Joséphin, aka Rouletabille, made his first appearance in *Le Mystère de la chambre jaune* (1907). For humorous parodies of deductive reasoning see San-Antonio, *Laissez tomber la fille* (1975), pp. 180–81 and Pennac, *Au bonheur des ogres* (1988), pp. 232–3.

[17]   See Descartes, *Discours de la méthode* (1637), Part I for the image of palaces (of knowledge) build on sand, and Part III for that of the traveller (or seeker of knowledge) lost in the forest.

[18]   Roth, *Foul and Fair Play*, p. 36. For an extensive exploration of the hybrid zone between crime fiction and various forms of the supernatural (including the gothic) see Ascari, *A Counter-History of Crime* (Palgrave Macmillan, 2007).

'The act of murder generates a form of the uncanny called *suspicion*, an anxious atmosphere that renders the casual critical and the familiar strange.'[19] Dubois, for his part, describes the process of reading detective fiction as one which is '*hantée par la réponse attendue à la question initiale*' ['*haunted* by the anticipated answer to the question put at the outset'] (my emphasis).[20] To this I would add that clues too have something of the spectral about them; their status is temporally dependent (a clue usually only becomes a clue in the light of the solution to the mystery, revealed at the end of the reading process); they flicker in and out of existence, read as parts of the hermeneutic code or the purely descriptive, neither one thing nor another, just as Troye's work exists as both testimonial text and work of crime fiction. My last reading of *Meurtre* casts an uncanny shadow over the rational certainties of the text, by reinstating the narrator as murderer and suggesting that Van Damme can be read as his double.

To read Francen and Van Damme as two aspects of a single figure is to reject the rationality which the investigator Ledru and the classic whodunnit represent as the only means to the truth and to embrace the ontological instability of the text. It also means reading against the first-person narrator (and indeed possibly the author). Paradoxically, although this interpretation calls Ledru's rational epistemology into question (he finds Francen not guilty), the detective-reader nonetheless seeks, and finds, clues: this time those which signal the presence of the irrational. A gothic, uncanny fantastic is inscribed in the text's figurative language. The opening pages swarm with images of death and the demonic: 'fantastiques', 'grotesque', 'catafalques', and 'démonique' (11). The narrator fleetingly assumes vampiric qualities: 'je les mordrais' ['I could bite them'] (on the subject of colleagues talking endlessly about food, p. 14); 'Je m'assieds, ployant le cou pour ne point me cogner la tête au couvercle de mon cercueil' ['I sit down, bowing my head so as not to hit it on the lid of my coffin'] (on the bunk beds in the officers' hut, p. 14). Francen refers to exhuming and dissecting his hatred for Jadin (35). A recurrent headache is eerily (on second reading) described in terms of hammer blows (19). Later in the text a fellow officer asks Ledru if he still seeks the murderer, describing the latter as a 'fantôme' (134). The personal and the war-related come together in this reading, with shame as the common denominator. Francen's back-story is replete not only with hatred but also with self-recrimination: retrospectively, he realizes that he should have stood up to Jadin and been proud of his social class. Strikingly, his reflections on his childhood competition with the murder victim apply perfectly to Van Damme's wartime demeanour in the fort of Anceilles: 'je fus pusillanime. Refuser un combat perdu davance est une forme de courage; c'en est une de la lâcheté quand il reste un espoir de victoire' (41) ['I was spineless. Refusing to fight when the battle is lost from the outset is a form of courage; it is a sign of cowardice when hope of victory remains']. But if the narrator and Van Damme are read as one and the same person, then this is an impossible first-person

---

[19]   Ibid., p. 159.

[20]   Dubois, *Le roman policier ou la modernité*, p. 131.

narrative in which the narrator recounts his own demise. Or is the representation of Van Damme's death merely another bluff and does the murderer survive to tell his tale? Was Troye himself aware of the uncanny doubling in his own text? These are reasonable questions posed of an unreasonable text.

Van Damme as a name not also has devilish connotations – for Damme read 'damned' or 'damn me'[21] – it is also Flemish, and as such stands in contrast to Jules Francen – for which read 'France'. Bearing the uncanny reading in mind, is the deteriorating condition of the narrator's clothing in the camp not also a possible clue: 'Ma tenue, usée jusqu'à la corde, a été remplacée par un uniforme de soldat français' (78)? ['My outfit, which was threadbare, has been replaced by a French military uniform']. And given the testimonial reading, is the fact that Troye's mother was French and his father Belgian in any way relevant? Whatever the answers, reading Van Damme and France(n) as doubles means potentially extending the textual inscription of wartime shame and guilt: from Belgian capitulation to French military defeat and collaboration. However far we may wish to push the analogy, Troye's text reminds us that amnesia need not be just an individual pathology. *Meurtre dans un oflag* is marked by doubling or splitting: author and narrator; Ledru and Francen; Van Damme and Francen. To which could be added, extending the reading, not only Belgium and France, but also the scissions between King Leopold and his government in exile; Pétain and de Gaulle; collaborators and resistants.[22] Troye's text was written long before the war was over. Read as a narrative symptomatic of repressed shame or guilt which can be extended to a national level, it suggests that the psychological malaise diagnosed by Rousso may in fact predate his post-Liberation start-date.

San-Antonio: Self-Reflexivity, the Serial Hero, and the Comic War Thriller

San-Antonio, aka Frédéric Dard, had some things in common with his one-time mentor and friend Simenon.[23] Both men published their work under many pseudonyms especially in the early stages of their careers (Dard's magnificent alter egos include 'Kill Him', 'L'Ange noir', and 'Kaput'); both produced what some would regard as more 'highbrow' literature ('romans romans' or 'novel novels')

---

[21]   The expression is used in *The Moonstone*, for instance: 'There stands the house, and here stands Mr Franklin Blake – and, Damme, if one of them isn't turning his back on the other', p. 295 (the speaker is Mr Betteredge).

[22]   The notion of doubles and splitting might be taken further. Berenboom's *Périls en ce royaume*, for instance, includes a discussion of the Flemish / Francophone split and how, if at all, it can be superimposed onto a royalist / Republican split (192–3).

[23]   The two men fell out over the theatrical adaptation of *La neige était sale* when Simenon apparently took the credit for Dard's work. For a discussion of this relationship see Dominique Jeannerod, *San-Antonio et son double* (PUF, 2010), pp. 42–50 and pp. 86–7. Although Dard's texts featuring his first-person narrator San Antonio are written under the pseudonym San-Antonio, I will refer to Dard as the author in order to avoid any confusion.

alongside their crime fiction; both fashioned extraordinarily successful series featuring iconic investigators: *commissaires* San-Antonio and Maigret. Unlike Simenon, Dard's greatest success came not under his own name but that of his creation, San Antonio (later hyphenated), who was to feature in 175 titles published between 1949 and 2001 and whose adventures continue today under the authorship of Dard's son.[24] To varying degrees and with shifting emphases, World War II is represented throughout the San-Antonio series. The guide to the series written by Raymond Milési and appended in all the latest editions identifies two principal war-related themes: wartime or immediate post-war adventures and the hero's fight against former or neo-nazis.[25] The three texts discussed in what follows fall into the wartime tales category: *Laissez tomber la fille* (1950), set in Paris in October 1942; *Les souris ont la peau tendre* (1951), set in Belgium, 1943; and *Du plomb dans les tripes* (1953),[26] located in the Isère region of France subsequent to the action of the previous text. In all three works San-Antonio is working for the secret services. With positively burlesque plots, humour that would not always qualify as either subtle or politically correct, and a very particular writing style, San-Antonio texts are, quite literally, in a category of their own: having started out as part of the popular *Fleuve noir* 'Spécial Police' collection in 1949, they were given their own eponymous series in 1973.[27] A move from Troye to San-Antonio apparently signifies a shift from generic instability, narrative ambiguity, and the uncanny undertow of the gothic to surfeit, surface, and the self-evident. But what does the criminally up-front tell us about both genre and 1950s attitudes to the war years?

Laissez tomber la fille, *Les souris ont la peau tendre*, and *Du plomb dans les tripes* might be designated action or spy thrillers. They might equally be regarded as ludic, parodic versions of the same. All are characterized by frenetic action sequences involving fights, chases, captures, and escapes. Although characters – usually the bad guys – die, the violence is rarely gruesome, with hyperbole and humour off-setting any possibility of pathos. A typically murderous yet simultaneously ludic sequence with a seventeenth-century literary reference thrown in for good measure makes the point:

> Je lui mets pour cent sous de ferraille dans la poitrine et le voilà qui ouvre la bouche et tousse d'un air tout chose. Il ne pense pas plus à utiliser son feu que moi je ne pense à la marquise de Sévigné.

---

[24]   This includes posthumous publications (Dard died in 2000). Patrice Dard has taken over, publishing the 'Nouvelles aventures de San-Antonio' with Fayard. The first text, *Corrida pour une vache folle*, appeared in 2002.

[25]   Texts falling into the former category include: *Réglez-lui son compte* (1949); *Mes hommages à la donzelle* (1952); *Descendez-le à la prochaine* (1953); *Les doigts dans le nez* (1956); *La Tombola des voyous* (1957); and *San-Antonio renvoie la balle* (1960).

[26]   Henceforth indicated after cited material as LTF, SPT, and PT respectively.

[27]   See Breton, *Les collections policières en France* (Éditions du Cercle de la Librairie, 1992), pp. 379–81, and Jeannerod, *San-Antonio et son double*, pp. 78–84 on 'La collection "Spécial Police"'.

Il titube et s'écroule sur l'harmonium. Ça fait un drôle de concerto pour agonie, en do majeur.
Pendant que j'y suis, je donne de mes nouvelles à Ulrich.
Pan et pan! (SPT, 55)

[I stick a dime's worth of ammo in his chest and he opens his mouth and coughs like there's no tomorrow. He gives about as much thought to using his shooter as I do to the Marquise of Sévigné. He staggers and collapses onto the squeezebox. It produces a crazy kind of death-throe concerto in C major. While I'm at it I let Ulrich have it. Bang! Bang!]

In the closing pages of Troye's *Meurtre dans un oflag* inspector Ledru warns his gathered audience that unlike many detective stories the tale he is about to unravel will be both straightforward and banal (157). San-Antonio too feels compelled to point to the gap between reality and crime fiction: only in novels by authors such as Maurice Leblanc does one come across anything out of the ordinary, he insists; in real life the sensational is rare (LTF, 114). As always, disingenuous disclaimers of this sort are not to be taken at face value. The plots of *Laissez tomber*, *Les souris*, and *Du plomb* are indeed sensational, including, respectively, not just a stolen phial full of a gaseous substance used in the production of atomic energy, the hunting down of a spy in a Belgian resistance network, and a plot involving German prototypes for guided missiles, but also a murdered dwarf (to use the author's own term) hidden in a suitcase, codes written by Polish partisans on the undersides of tortoises, and all-important information relating to the manufacture of V10 missiles cunningly concealed in the form of a tattoo on the scalp of a scientist.[28]

This is a long way from the rather static criminal world of Simenon. But there is more to the San-Antonio texts than engagingly hectic action sequences. After all, San-Antonio, like Maigret, has been crafted as a character in such a manner as to make of him a hugely commercial and long-lived literary figure; the *commissaire* has even been described as a national hero.[29] The status of Dard's investigator as an iconic recurring character raises an important issue in the context of the present study, namely the tension between historical specificity and the atemporal, or between difference and sameness. A recurring character requires a recognizable, fixed set of characteristics. As Verdaguer puts it, San-Antonio represents 'cette

---

[28]   An element of fact lies beneath the baroque ornamentation in the last of these cases. Douglas Porch notes that intelligence provided by Resistance agents led to the early detection of plans to deploy V-1 and V-2 bombs: 'Reports by agents and *résistants* in several countries enabled London to begin to piece together from 1943 that the Germans were experimenting with guided bombs [...]. Much of this came through Polish and Alliance networks in France', *The French Secret Services* (Oxford UP, 1997), p. 249.

[29]   See Pierre Verdaguer, 'Le Héros national et ses dédoublements dans *San-Antonio* et *Astérix*', *The French Review*, 61.4 (1988): 605–16. Jeannerod notes that overall estimated sales for Dard's work fall between 200 and 290 million copies (p. 148); by 1973 the San Antonio series had sold approximately 115 million copies (Jeannerod, *San-Antonio et son double*, p. 150).

France éternelle de notre géographie mythique' ['that eternal France which is part of our mythical landscape'].[30] How is this fixity to be reconciled with plots set in a wide range of politico-historical contexts? What does being a (French) national hero signify in the specific diegetic context of World War II, and how might such a figure be received by 1950s readers and by their present-day homologues? A brief look at some of San-Antonio's character traits underlines the issues at stake.

Unlike James Bond, who first appeared around the same time (Ian Fleming's *Casino Royal* was published in 1953) San-Antonio is a populist as well as a popular hero, more likely to down a few glasses of wine swiftly followed by a triple brandy at the counter of his local bar than be served a cocktail – shaken or stirred – in a swanky hotel. In this he shares the hard-boiled tastes of FBI agent Lemmy Caution, a creation of Peter Cheyney, whose work is known to have influenced Dard.[31] San-Antonio, like both Bond (known as 'Mr Kiss Kiss Bang Bang') and the American *noir* heroes on which Caution is loosely modelled, also has something of an exaggerated appetite for women. Female characters may be given an active role in the story-lines, but they invariably succumb to the hero's charms.[32] Fleming brought us names such as Pussy Galore, Kissy Suzuki, and Honey Rider. For Lemmy Caution, women are 'dames', 'honeybelles', 'janes', 'mommas', 'honeylambs', 'hell-cats', 'honeybabes', and 'dolls';[33] for San-Antonio they are 'petites filles', 'filles-ruminants', 'gonzesses', 'souris', and 'poupées'. To say that women are objectified in San-Antonio texts would be something of an understatement: 'J'aperçois une jolie silhouette de femme et, malgré l'obscurité, j'ai l'impression que le visage qui l'agrémente doit être plus agréable à contempler qu'un kilo de pommes de terre' (SPT, 17) ['I spot the cute contours of a woman and, in spite of the darkness, I get the idea that the face topping it off must be kinder on the eye than a kilo of spuds']; 'Une infirmière, développée à bloc du côté des balconets' (SPT, 31) ['a nurse with all the right equipment up top'].

San-Antonio's attitude to alcohol and women may seem peripheral to the author's representation of World War II, but in fact it highlights the tension between the immutable traits of the recurring character (and mythical national hero) and the historical and potentially ideological specificity of the plots. The need to represent San-Antonio's penchant for women as a constant, for example, overrides or displaces historically specific ideological positioning: women are women, and whether they are in the Resistance or the Gestapo at some point they

---

[30]   Verdaguer, 'Le héros national', p. 608.

[31]   Evrard, *Lire le roman policier* (Dunod, 1996), p. 60. Jeannerod points out that Dard pastiches both Cheyney in particular and the *roman noir* more generally, *San-Antonio et son double*, p. 69 and pp. 126–7.

[32]   See Palmer's *Thrillers* (Edward Arnold, 1978), based in large part on the James Bond character, for a discussion of the typical / generic thriller hero and his attitude to women (pp. 29–39).

[33]   All terms are taken from Cheyney's *Your deal my lovely* (Collins, 1941) which is set in London during the war.

end up in the hero's embrace. In other words, the presence of a recurring hero with fixed characteristics inevitably detracts at least in part from a reading of the texts as representative or symptomatic of their era or indeed as realist representations of a given period. Rather than simply tell us about typical (or populist) attitudes to the war in the 1950s, these three San-Antonio texts also serve to formulate and consolidate the personality traits of a viable best-selling character.

San-Antonio's reflections on women may strike some readers as overly objectifying, but what if the examples chosen from Dard's texts were of a different order? Consider the following images: 'Dehors, il fait aussi sombre que dans le derche d'un nègre' (LTF, 103) ['Outside it's as dark as a nigger's asshole']; 'il fait plus noir là-dedans que dans la culotte d'un nègre en grand deuil' (LTF, 199) ['it's darker in there than in the pants of a nigger in full mourning']. Assuming that racism is not a fixed part of the national hero's character, then this is very much 'of its time'; it 'dates' the text in every sense of the word. Dard may be imitating the literary model of Cheyney's Lemmy Caution, who employs not dissimilar imagery: 'it is as plain to me as a negress on a white bedspread'; 'It is six o'clock when we get back to London. It is as black as a nigger but the rain has stopped'.[34] Either way, for the twenty-first-century reader expressions such as these cannot pass without comment, though they may well have done for the original readership. There are a number of possible responses to what we would now deem to be objectionable language and textual representations. Readers (or viewers) of Bond, for instance, may simply choose to set aside their partial discomfort: 'In an era of political correctness James Bond is a guilty pleasure of many academics'.[35] In his structuralist analysis of Fleming's texts Umberto Eco also gives the author the benefit of the doubt, concluding that 'a man who chooses to write this way is neither a Fascist nor a racist; he is only a cynic, an expert in tale engineering'.[36] The 1995 Bond film *Golden Eye* opts for an intradiegetic representation of potential viewers' objections as the new female 'M', played by Judi Dench, berates Bond as 'a sexist, misogynist dinosaur, a relic of the Cold War'.[37] Push sexist, and perhaps racist, representations far enough and Bond can be played for laughs, becoming a parody, and the same can be said of San-Antonio.

Not everything, however, can be attributed to parody or otherwise recuperated. I will be coming back to Dard's representation of World War II shortly, but conclude this part of the discussion with one last set of examples of potentially more controversial material: 'Si on m'enfermait dans un four crématoire, je me décarcasserais pour en sortir' (LTF, 134); 'nous n'avons pas plus de chances de nous tirer de là qu'un mec passé au four crématoire n'a de chances de mourir

---

[34] Cheyney, p. 76 and p. 192.

[35] Edward P. Comentale, Stephen Watt, and Skip Willman (eds), *Ian Fleming and James Bond. The Cultural Politics of 007* (Indiana UP, 2005), p. xvii.

[36] Umberto Eco, 'Narrative Structures in Flemming', in Christopher Lindner (ed.) *The James Bond Phenomenon* (Manchester UP, 2003), pp. 34–55 [46].

[37] Comentale *et al.*, *Ian Fleming and James Bond*, p. xvii.

de froid' (SPT, 107).[38] Such potentially offensive images may well indicate that the 1950s was an era not yet attuned to the realities of the Holocaust. They may equally suggest that a French populist national hero is characterized by political incorrectness. They also raise another key question: who speaks? Whilst some aspects of the San-Antonio texts can be put down to their being 'of their time' or as parodic, humour relating to the Holocaust pushes the possibility of such indulgent recuperative reading to its very limits. Dard has created a first-person narrator who is also an author (we learn in *Règlez-lui son compte* that the investigator San-Antonio is writing his memoirs), but there comes a point at which authors are answerable for the views articulated in their texts.

Of course the use of to say the very least highly original imagery is part of the San-Antonio brand which is known and admired for its zany humour, self-reflexivity, and sustained verbal play. All of these textual traits have an impact on both genre definition and the representation of World War II, indeed on any representational endeavour. If San-Antonio texts are primarily concerned with language rather than plot, then their generic status as thrillers may be called into question and the impact of their representation of, in this case, the war, may be diminished. If, as Gaudin puts it, all the San-Antonio texts are made up of the same ingredients, then the diegetic content becomes a mere vehicle for the exercise of the author's linguistic prowess.[39] According to Evrard, San-Antonio is 'un personnage inclassable qui n'entretient que des liens ténus avec le genre policier' ['an unclassifiable character with only tenuous links to the crime genre']. For Schweighaeuser too, Dard's stylistic games serve to exclude his works from the crime genre:

> La folie verbale, l'apostrophe au lecteur, les *mea culpa*, les jeux de mots insipides, les fausses 'notes de l'éditeur', les allusions à lui-même et à son passé, tout donne une œuvre qui finit par être à l'opposé du roman noir et même du roman policier en général.[40]

---

[38]   Translation is not straightforward, but the line could be rendered as 'If someone shut me in the ovens I'd do my damndest to get out'. The expression 'four crématoire' can mean a crematory furnace but is also used specifically to denote the ovens which burned the bodies of deportees in the World War II camps. The second passage could thus be rendered as: 'We've got about as much chance of getting out of there as a bloke in a concentration camp oven does of dying of cold.' The link between burning bodies and the camps is explicit in other San-Antonio texts. In his *Mes hommages à la donzelle* (Fleuve noir, 1973; 1952), a man disposing of a body in a boiler is met with the quip 'tu joues à Buchenwald?' ['Are you playing Buchenwald?'] (202). References to Jews in texts contemporary with Dard's also employ language offensive to today's reader: Piljean's *Passons la monnaie!* (1951), for instance, describes a character with 'une tranche de youpin' ['a Yid's mug'], the police inspector adding that 'Il avait tout du Cohen, si je me fais comprendre' ['He had Cohen written all over him, if you get my drift'] (22).

[39]   Nicolas Gaudin, 'Interventions digressives du narrateur, ou l'élaboration de San-Antonio', *French Review* 58 (1984): 58–67 [58].

[40]   Jean-Paul Schweighaeuser, *Le roman noir français* (PUF, 1984), p. 45. Warren Motte on the same topic seems undecided, stating in a single article that Dard's use of

[The verbal delirium, the apostrophes to the reader, the mea culpas, the bland word-play, the fake 'notes from the editor', the references to himself and to his past, all go to create a work which could not be further removed from the *roman noir* or even the crime novel in general.]

As we saw in the case of Simenon, generalizations of this sort need to be unpacked, depending as they do on genre definitions (how do Evrard and Schweighaeuser conceive the 'genre policier' or 'roman policier'?). More discrimination and specificity would be helpful. Verbal play and humour, for instance, have long been part of the 'roman noir' tradition. As Breton points out, early translations in the 'Série noire' collection were both edulcorated (some of the violence was felt to be too strong for a French readership) and verbally revitalized:

On aurait donc choisi d'en gommer la violence en faisant l'humour, en intercalant des commentaires qui étaient censés détendre l'atmosphère, en inventant des métaphores volontairement laborieuses et des jeux de mots approximatifs qui interpellaient le lecteur.[41]

[It was decided that the violence would be watered down by using humour, by interspersing the text with remarks which were meant to defuse the tension, by coming up with deliberately laboured metaphors and bad puns which drew the reader in.]

Some of the earliest of these translations were those carried out by 'Série noire' creator, Marcel Duhamel, whose 1949 translation of Cheney's *Your Deal, My Lovely, A toi de faire, ma mignonne*, includes light-hearted gnomic pronouncements and apostrophes to the reader: 'Votre mère vous a peut-être dit, un jour, qu'on ne doit pas trop penser au femmes? Si oui, elle avait tout ce qu'il y a de raison' (11); 'Si Geralda n'est pas dans la mouscaille, moi, je suis une princesse hindoue' (81).[42] Dard's use of slang, mixed register, apostrophe and puns is more extensive and more extreme, but is certainly not unique to him, dating back as it does not only to French translations and adaptations of American *noir* but also to home-grown francophone writers from the earliest days of the 'Série noire'. And this remained and remains an option for French crime writers. Frachet's *Comme dit ma grand-mère* (1967), for instance, includes pseudo-populist dictums – 'Mieux vaut recevoir un crochet du droit qu'une mauvaise nouvelle et mieux vaut apprendre l'hébreu chez Berlitz que la mort d'un homme qui vous doit de

---

crime fiction came to serve as something of a pretext for literary and linguistic play (195), then suggesting that in spite of play and parody most of the classic traits of the crime genre remain, before finally noting that an 'undercurrent of metaliterary discourse [...] tends to subvert generic tradition' (203), 'Introduction to San Antonio: du grand Dard', *French Forum*, 4 (1979): 195–205.

[41]   Breton, *Les collections policières en France*, pp. 44–5.

[42]   Cheyney's original reads: 'Maybe your mother told you it was wrong to get to thinkin' about women too much. O.K. Well, take it from me the old lady was right' (9); 'If little Geralda is not in a bad spot then I am an Indian Princess with the ague' (76).

l'argent' (71) ['It's better to be clobbered by a right hook than by bad news and it's better to learn Hebrew the Berlitz way than learn of the death of a man who owes you money'] – and a foreword situated on page 75 ('pour être sûr qu'on le lira' ['to be sure people read it']) complete with addresses to the reader concerning genre and the author's skills. Published some 40 years later Pécherot's *Boulevard des branques* (2005) continues the tradition; the following, for instance, are all taken from the first page: 'palpitant' ['ticker']; 'Mon pouls tressautait comme un lézard épileptique' ['My pulse was jumping about like an epileptic lizard']; 'sourdingue' ['mutt an' jeff']; 'mes esgourdes' (9) ['lugholes']. Many of the texts in the Poulpe series (all the titles of which are, in fact, puns) reveal similar stylistic characteristics. The following are taken from Kolaire's *Sur la ligne marginaux* (1999): 'Le ciel était bleu flic, et quelques rayons commençaient à matraquer le pavé' (41) ['The sky was cop-blue and a few rays of sun were just starting to club the pavement']; 'SherlockHolmser' (51) ['SherlockHolmsing']; 'pavlové à l'écran' (54) ['Pavlov-ed to the screen'].

Self-reflexivity too is an established part of the tradition. We have already seen, for instance, self-referential reflections on genre in Troye's *Meurtre dans un oflag* and this trend is common to a high proportion of crime fiction texts. Even a fairly dark work such as Merle's *Treize reste raide* (1997), to select just one example amongst many, includes a little self-reflexive repartee when investigator Laugier is told he should consider turning his hand to the writing of crime fiction: 'c'est la mode. Y a des types très lancés qui se sont mis au polar. Même Julia Kristeva ...' (17) ['it's all the rage. There are some proper intellectuals who've started writing crime novels. Even Julia Kristeva ...']; and, later in the same text:

> Je vous imagine écrire un polar de bonne compagnie. Écriture blanche pas si blanche, pas de psycho mais psycho quand même, du cul mais bon aloi, de la violence mais qui fait pas vraiment mal. Et Rouletabille le héros, témoin de l'injustice social. Et les recettes de cuisine, capital les recettes ... (166)

> [I can see you writing a respectable crime novel. Minimalist style, but not too minimalist, no psychologizing but psychological nonetheless, some sex but all in good taste, some violence, but the kind that doesn't really hurt. With Rouletabille as the hero, a witness to social justice. And there have to be recipes, recipes are crucial ...]

Finally, not all word-play in the San-Antonio texts is of the same order. A distinction can be drawn between those ludic linguistic elements which focus attention almost exclusively on the signifying system and the author-narrator as manipulator of language, and those which also have a direct bearing on the representational world. The former category of predominantly ludic interventions includes examples such as: 'Je ne peux pas vous le réciter en latin *because* je ne suis pas doué pour les language étrangères' (LTF, 20) ['I can't recite it to you in Latin *parce que* I'm no good at foreign languages']; 'laissez tomber vos préoccupations du moment – soyez tranquilles, elles ne se casseront pas' (LTF, 54) ['drop whatever's on your mind at the moment – don't worry – it won't break'] 'Les rues sont animées comme un dessin de Walt Disney' (PT, 144) ['The streets are animated like a Walt Disney cartoon']; 'Décidément ça se corse (chef-lieu Ajacio)' (SPT, 18) ['Things are getting curiouser and Corsica-er (capital: Ajacio)']. Other, more telling images, however, provide indirect comment on the war: 'mon corps ressemble à la photo aérienne d'une région bombardée' (LTF, 18) ['My body looks like the aerial photo of a bombsite']; 'Son crâne éclate comme une noisette dans le derche d'un soldat italien' (LTF, 90) ['His head exploded like a hazelnut in an Italian soldier's rear end']; 'En moins de temps qu'il n'en faut pour déclarer la guerre, nous sommes à l'horizontale' (LTF, 174–5) ['We hit the horizontal faster than it takes to declare war']; 'Ça [sable] craque sous les dents, comme de la pâtisserie d'occupation' (SPT, 11) ['It (sand) crunches between your teeth like Occupation cakes']; 'Cette fin de journée est plus triste qu'une carte de rationnement' (SPT, 11–12) ['This late afternoon's more dismal than a ration card']; 'un bruit de bottes retentit dans le silence. Ces bruits-là sont plus éloquents que des discours électoraux' (PT, 33) ['The sound of boots echoes in the silence. That kind of noise says more than any electoral speech']; 'Son visage est plus neutre que la Suisse' (PT, 35) ['His expression is more neutral than Switzerland']. Language play in these cases is also 'about the war'.

Linguistic verve, extravagant imagery, punning, self-reflexive comments, and apostrophes to the reader are not alien to works of crime fiction, and certainly need not automatically exclude a text from the crime genre. It is perhaps the sheer volume of such stylistic features which differentiates Dard from other crime writers (Platten, for instance, notes that at the time of his death San-Antonio's creator had been credited with some 20,000 neologisms).[43] And although the inscription of an authorial figure in the text is not atypical of crime fiction either, as the presence of 'l'homme à la pipe' in Simenon's works revealed, the creation of a first-person narrator-author whose name is adopted by the author as pseudonym does create something of a closed circuit of self-reflexivity. But for all their linguistic play – and in some cases, as we have seen, via that very play – and in spite of the fact that the existence of a recurring character dictates certain fixed patterns in the San-Antonio texts which may override ideological and historical specificity, a balance between the mimetic and the self-reflexive is inevitably maintained.[44] Though the scales arguably tip in favour of the latter, *Laissez tomber la fille*, *Les Souris ont la*

---

[43]   David Platten, 'Origins and Beginnings: the Emergence of Detective Fiction in France', in Claire Gorrara (ed.), *French Crime Fiction* (U of Wales P, 2009), p. 15. The authors of *Le Roman criminel* (L'Atalante, 1979) note that Dard was congratulated by the (then) President, Georges Pompidou, for his enrichment of the French language (p. 158). For a more scholarly discussion see P.-M. Gerin, 'San-Antonio fou de sa langue. Création lexicale dans un argot littéraire', *Initiales/Initials*, 5 (1985): 11–20.

[44]   Porter points out that 'As often as not detective novels are appreciated for their free motifs more than their bound ones', adding that 'it is important to realize that a successful novel is inconceivable without both', *The Pursuit of Crime*, p. 55. Amongst several examples he notes that Hammett's *Maltese Falcon* may be hard-boiled but includes an element of self-parody (60).

peau tendre, and *Du plomb dans les tripes* can of course still be read and analyzed in terms of their representation of the war years.

The three texts in question are marked by the era which they represent in one obvious way: San-Antonio has voluntarily suspended his position in the police force and operates as a secret agent engaged in counter-espionage. As Kitson points out, most wartime counter-espionage activity in France was initially directed at Allied as well as German spies, with agents tending to be associated with the Vichy government to varying degrees. The situation changed in November 1942 when the whole of France was invaded and Vichy's intelligence services were no longer allowed officially to operate.[45] Set during this post-invasion period, the three San-Antonio texts leave us in no doubt as to the hero's republican loyalties:

> San-Antonio est un mec règlo. Mon job a toujours été de bosser pour le gouvernement français. Je n'ai jamais travaillé à mon compte, ni pour le compte d'une boîte autre que celle dont la devise est: Liberté, Égalité, Fraternité. Quand je me suis aperçu que la pauvre Marianne l'avait dans le baigneur [...] je me suis retiré dans ma crèche' (LTF, 7)

> [San Antonio's straight up and down. I've always worked for the French government. I've never been a free agent, and I've never worked for anyone whose motto wasn't *Liberty, Equality, Fraternity*. When I realized that poor old Marianne was copping it (...) I decided to lie low in my pad.]

According to Kitson, memoirs written by former French agents have a tendency to stress links with the British and Americans in order to justify their authors' wartime credentials,[46] so Dard's decision to emphasize his investigator's links with the British government is worth noting. San-Antonio makes frequent reference to his connection with the (fictitious) head of the British secret services, Major Parkings, and especially relishes quips concerning British funding of his activities: 'c'est sa Gracieuse Majesté britannique qui régale' (SPT, 24) ['it's his Gracious British Majesty's treat']; 'c'est le roi d'Angleterre qui casque' (SPT, 162) ['it's the King of England who's footing the bill'].[47] Steering an uncontentious path, Dard mentions neither Vichy and Pétain nor de Gaulle and the Free French by name, and avoids any representation of the very real conflicts which existed in the secret services. The depiction of enemy agents is also telling. In the wartime world of San-Antonio the latter are German (or Austrian): in *Laissez tomber la fille*, for instance, French resistants Florence and Renard are unmasked as Germans Greta

---

[45]   Simon Kitson, *The Hunt for Nazi Spies* (U of Chicago P, 2008), p. 43.

[46]   Ibid., *The Hunt for Nazi Spies*, p. 78.

[47]   Such quips seem to have a basis in fact: Porch notes that the Free French were often short of resources: 'When in August 1940 the Deuxième Bureau shifted its two tables, one chair, and two benches to a tiny three-room suite in Free France's new headquarters at 4 Carlton Gardens, the officers had yet to receive their pay, much less any funds to carry out missions. "Go see the English", was de Gaulle's response to Passy's pleas for cash', *The French Secret Services*, p. 179.

and Karl; in *Les Souris ont la peau tendre* Thérèse turns out to be Elsa. Although spies masquerading as resistants were not uncommon during World War II, some 80 percent of them were in fact not German citizens but French nationals.[48] Dard represents an edulcorated version of events.

Does Dard similarly skew other aspects of French involvement in the war? Up to a point. French collaborators are represented in the texts and indeed one such character is killed by San-Antonio, though the act is carried out with a degree of reluctance: 'Oh merde! me dis-je en détournant la tête. Voilà qu'on est obligée de buter les vieux à c'te heure!' (PDT, 142) ['"Oh shit!" I said to myself, looking away. "Now we've even got to bump off OAPs!"']. The general tendency to passivity amongst the wartime French population is also noted, and attributed to fear rather than any sort of ideological commitment: 'ils ne remueraient pas le petit doigt pour venir voir ce qui se passe. En ces temps d'occupation, ils ont le trouillomètre au-dessous de zéro' (PDT, 16) ['They wouldn't lift their little finger to come and see what's going on. In these times of occupation, their shit-scaredometer's off the scale']. 'Horizontal collaboration' is treated with a similarly light touch: 'Y a une équipe de délurées dans les bonnes femmes, qui savent s'expliquer avec les fafiots de l'occupant. C'est une sorte de récupération, quoi!' (PDT, 100) ['There's a whole bunch of resourceful women who know how to get their mitts on the occupier's dosh. I'm telling you, it's a sort of redistribution!']. Like much populist literature San-Antonio expresses anti-war sentiments, occasionally communicated with some vehemence: 'Mais cette p … de guerre en a fait un héros à la noix, bien saignant, bien mort, auquel on refilera une médaille à titre posthume, plus tard, et que tout le monde oubliera' (SPT, 189) ['But this d … war made a pathetic hero of him, nice and bloody, nice and dead, who'll get a posthumous medal later on, and who'll be forgotten by everyone']. Although the Resistance features, the word itself is used sparingly, and most of the glory, as the series and recurring hero figure require, is devolved to San-Antonio himself. Bourgeois, leader of a Resistance network in *Les Souris ont la peau tendre*, for instance, may die fighting the enemy, but he cannot match the true hero's all-round prowess: 'Le Bourgeois, c'est peut-être un superman de la Résistance, mais question amour il a l'air aussi évolué qu'une portion de gruyère' (SPT, 128) ['Bourgeois may be a Resistance superman, but when it comes to love he's about as sophisticated as chunk of gruyère'].

To the extent that they are represented at all then, aspects of the civil conflict and the grey zone of ambiguous loyalties are afforded a degree of mitigation, with inglorious behaviour often explained or made light of, if not excused. Instead, the focus falls primarily on adversarial plots in which the Germans assume the role of enemy, and, as befits a series in which the hero must prevail, they always lose. Like women in these texts, the Germans are given various often humorous and deprecatory names (many familiar to the war generation) – 'Frizous', 'Frisés', 'Fritz', 'Chleuhs', 'verts-de gris', 'sulfatés', 'doryphores', 'les employés de M. Himmler' – and are the butt of numerous light-heated observations and comments:

---

[48] Kitson, *The Hunt for Nazi Spies*, p. 53 and p. 158.

'Ça parle teuton dans la cabane et c'est une langue qui me fatigue le tympan' (SP, 25) ['They're speaking Hun around here and it's a language that wears out my eardrums']; 'Je demande à Gertrude: – Connaissez-vous la recette du Führer en cocotte?' (PDT, 13) ['I asked Gertrude: "Do you know the recipe for casserole à la Hitler?"']; 'Félicie écarquille les châsses comme si on lui montrait la tête d'Adolf Hitler accommodée avec du persil' (166) ['Félicie gawps as if someone had just shown her Adolf Hitler's head, served up with parsley']. As with the potentially offensive imagery discussed above, verbal bravado of this type, which is a fixed component of the San-Antonio label, can on occasion jar with the historical context. When tortured by the Gestapo in *Laissez tomber la fille*, for instance, San-Antonio continues his banter with the voluptuous Greta, whose desire to inflict further pain on her prisoners is expressed in typically jocular, and some might doubtless say infelicitous, fashion: 'Employez les grands moyens, les super-grands moyens!' (LTF, 148) ['Bring out the big guns, the super big guns!']. San-Antonio's own attempt to extract information from the Gestapo agent succeeds not via the infliction of pain but when he threatens to shave her head like those held in what are euphemistically referred to as German 'internment camps': 'Tu a dû remarquer alors que tous les détenus, hommes ou femmes avaient les cheveux tondus? Je vais te déguiser en détenue …' (LTF, 188) ['You must have noticed that all the detainees, men and women, had their heads shaved? I'm going to turn you into a detainee']. The potentially inappropriate link between concentration camps and women's bodies appears in a different guise in *Les souris* via a punning allusion to former deportee David Rousset's *Univers concentrationnaire*: 'quand il y a une poupée dans mon univers concentrationnaire, je ne me sens plus!' (SPT, 89) ['when a doll enters my concentration(-camp) span, I'm happy as larry!'].[49]

Laissez tomber la fille, *Les souris ont la peau tendre*, and *Du plomb dans les tripes* offered the 1950s' reader a relatively uncomplicated retrospective vision of the war: some French citizens may have erred, but the true story lay in the defeat of the German enemy, largely at the hands of super-agent San-Antonio, avowed Republican, man of the people, womanizer, and wit. What can be made of Dard's representational choices? It could for instance be argued that the author's not especially hostile treatment of collaborators was aligned with the political climate of the time: January 1951 and August 1953, after all, witnessed the passing of two significant amnesty laws. Perhaps the intensification of the Cold War played its part. The allusion to David Rousset, an early critic of the Gulag, potentially heralds an awareness of not only nazi but also Soviet camps, and *Du Plomb dans les tripes* certainly acknowledges the post-war shift in alliances:

> Le monde, présentement, paraît partagé en deux blocs. Pourtant, le bloc vainqueur, ou du moins celui dont la victoire se dessine, c'est-à-dire celui des alliés, se craquelle déjà. Les alliés! Le mot contient les drames futurs. Une alliance est plus aisée à rompre qu'à sceller. (PDT, 187)

---

[49] David Rousset, *L'Univers concentrationnaire* (Éditions du Pavois, 1946).

[At present the world seems to be divided into two blocs. But the winning bloc, or at least the one whose victory is underway, in other words the Allied bloc, is already showing cracks. The Allies! The word speaks of drama to come. It's easier to break an alliance than it is to forge one.]

But there is more to it than this. '[N]ous ne sommes pas là pour épiloguer sur les errements de notre époque et l'inconscience de nos semblables ... Les hommes d'action ne sont pas des historiens' (PDT, 195) ['We're not here to hold forth on the waywardness of our times and the fecklessness of our fellow men ... Men of action aren't historians']. Dard's protagonist's observation serves to remind us that when analyzing literary responses to, and representations of, World War II, the conventions and requirements of genre must be taken into account. Dard's representation of the Germans as very bad and the French as not so awful says more about the hallmarks of the popular thriller genre than the political realignment of Germany in the 1950s, just as the downplaying of the Resistance may primarily serve the needs of the characterization of the eponymous recurring hero and 'homme d'action'. Significantly, the war-related texts published under Dard's own name – texts which were not envisaged (or initially marketed) as works of crime fiction, are written in standard French and do not, of course, feature San-Antonio – serve up a very different picture of the war.[50] *Équipe de l'ombre* (1941), for instance, which focuses on the German invasion and the subsequent exodus, includes a damning indictment of the French individualism and self-absorption which the narrator claims led to their defeat; *La Crève* (1946) closes with the execution of a French *milicien*; *Batailles sur la route* (1949) calls for a reassessment of black and white moralizing as a resistant questions his involvement in the 'épuration sauvage'; *Une gueule comme la mienne* (1958) charts the return to Paris of a collaborationist journalist. Dard's non-San-Antonio texts, in other words, represent a much less heroic vision of the war years, and one in which the Germans are all but occluded. The light-hearted San Antonio corpus is just one part of a complex synchronic picture even within the context of the work of a single author.

Boileau-Narcejac: Freedom and Authenticity in a Time of War

From San-Antonio's frenetic plots and prose we move to another form of crime fiction and another celebrated author – or authors, to be precise. Boileau-Narcejac is the pen-name adopted by Pierre Boileau and Thomas Narcejac (Pierre Ayraud), collaborators over a period of some 50 years in the production of crime novels, filmscripts, and children's literature as well as critical works on crime fiction. To many they are perhaps best known for the film adaptations of their novels, most notably *Les Diaboliques* (1955), Henri-Georges Clouzot's screen version of *Celle qui n'était plus* (1952), and Hitchcock's *Vertigo* (1958), an adaptation of

---

50   Jeannerod makes a similar point, *San-Antonio et son double*, p. 59.

D'entre les morts (1954). Boileau-Narcejac are above all regarded as exponents of the 'roman à suspense', a mode of crime fiction characterized by its espousal of the victim's point of view (hence the alternative label 'roman de la victime'),[51] and a build-up of tension as a trap inexorably closes on the protagonist. One of the above readings of Troye's *Meurtre dans un oflag* saw the text partially undermine the forces of logic and reason via a foray into the uncanny. San-Antonio's texts can be described as comic or light-hearted thrillers. The final section of this chapter will address Maurice Dantec's combination of crime and science fiction. For Boileau-Narcejac, the 'roman à suspense' has links to all of these modes:

> s'il [le suspense] développe un climat trop envoûtant, il se constitue en roman fantastique et l'explication finale, alors, devient décevante. Elle est de trop. Le suspense doit se tenir entre *thriller* et science-fiction.

> [If the suspense novel builds too intense an atmosphere, it can become a novel of the fantastic and the final explanation is a disappointment. It is redundant. The suspense novel must navigate a path between the *thriller* and science-fiction.][52]

The following discussion traces the development of recurring themes in three texts published over a period of some 20 years. Set in Lyon towards the end of the war, *Les Louves* (1955) recounts the travails of escaped POW Gervais who assumes the identity of his dead colleague, Bernard, in order to benefit from the easy life offered by the latter's 'marraine de guerre',[53] Hélène, and her sister Agnès. Trapped by his lies and the women's machinations, Gervais increasingly struggles to maintain his false identity. The text closes with the revelation that Hélène, now his wife, has been using him from the outset, and is poisoning him in order to lay her hands on an inheritance. *Maldonne* (1962), set around the time of its publication, features failing musician Jacques Christen who is paid to play the part of the deceased Paul de Baer in order that the latter's wife, Gilberte, can claim an inheritance. Unsurprisingly, all is not as it seems and Christen, who has in fact been hired to stand in for Gilberte's real husband, nazi war criminal Martin von Klaus, finally dies at the hands of nazi hunters. Lastly, *La Lèpre* (1976) takes the form of a letter written in 1957 by aspiring politician Marc Pradier to his adopted son Christophe, in which he attempts to explain his conduct during the war and his unmerited reputation as a resistance hero.

Les Louves, *Maldonne*, and *La Lèpre* have at their core a thematic interplay of freedom / imprisonment and authenticity / role-play, with the war assuming a different, and indeed evolving, function from one text to the next. The protagonist Gervais is knowingly playing a part in *Les Louves* – that of his fellow-soldier

---

[51] Boileau-Narcejac, *Le roman policier* (PUF, 1975), p. 89. Reuter discusses the specificities of the 'roman à suspense' in his *Le Roman policier*, pp. 74–90.

[52] Ibid., p. 103.

[53] These were usually young women who 'adopted' soldiers, writing to them and sending them parcels.

Bernard – but he is also deceiving himself. As a recently escaped POW he is familiar with literal imprisonment, and up to a point is indeed trapped in the flat of Hélène and Agnès by the increasingly menacing presence of German troops on the streets of Lyon. In a more figurative sense, it is due to the deceit he perpetrates that the flat becomes for him a 'champ clos' (110) – literally a circumscribed space but also a combat zone – to such an extent that he misses his former literal incarceration, stating that the Stalag was an enclosed space which suited him (148), and comes to regard his current hosts as part of a long line of jailers: 'Ma mère, ma femme, le stalag et Bernard, maintenant Hélène et Agnès, toujours des prisons et des geôliers' (45) ['My mother, my wife, the stalag, and Bernard, and now Hélène and Agnès, endless prisons and jailers']. Tellingly, the English translation of the text is entitled 'The Prisoner'.[54]

Literal and figurative prisons have already featured to a lesser extent in this and the previous chapter: in Simenon's *La neige était sale* the protagonist Frank insisted that he was not in a real prison and sought to differentiate himself and his case from that of other detainees; Troye's narrator verbally signals his awareness of the play between literal and metaphorical freedom: 'le meurtrier d'Albert Jadin est toujours en liberté, *si l'on peut dire enfin ...*' (158, my emphasis) ['Albert Jadin's killer is at liberty, *so to speak*']; the Oflag prisoners remain lively and animated 'pour affirmer leurs droits imprescriptibles d'hommes libres (*sic*)' (112, author's parenthesis) ['to affirm their inalienable rights as free men (*sic*)']. It is, however, the wartime pronouncement made by another author that perhaps has the greatest resonance with the themes which emerge in these three Boileau-Narcejac texts: 'Jamais nous n'avons été plus libres que sous l'occupation allemande' ['Never were we more free than during the German occupation'].[55] Sartre's provocative paradox arises from the extreme context of war and especially Occupation which, he claimed, was such that individuals had to endure 'sans fard et sans voile, cette situation déchirée, insoutenable qu'on appelle la condition humaine' ['without pretence and quite transparently, this harrowing, unbearable situation which we call the human condition'].[56] Confrontation at every moment with the 'réalité d'homme' (Simenon's 'métier d'homme' comes to mind)[57] meant being faced with the radical freedom to choose: 'le choix que chacun faisait de lui-même était authentique puisqu'il se faisait en présence de la mort' ['the choice that each individual made of his life was an authentic choice because it was made

---

54   *The Prisoner*, trans. Geoffrey Sainsbury (Hutchinson, 1957).

55   Sartre, 'La République du silence', in *Situations III* (Gallimard, 1949), pp. 11–14 [11].

56   Ibid., p. 12.

57   Sartre uses the phrase 'métier d'homme' in 'Qu'est-ce qu'un collaborateur?': '[...] le métier d'homme – ce métier têtu et borné qui consiste à dire oui ou non selon des principes, à "entreprendre sans espérer, à persévérer sans réussir"' ['man's calling – this obdurate and stubborn calling which consists of saying yes or no according to certain principles, of "embarking on projects without hope, of persevering without succeeding"'], *Situations III*, p. 53.

in the face of death'].[58] Extreme situations precipitate extreme knowledge – 'la connaissance la plus profonde que l'homme peut avoir de lui-même' ['the most profound understanding that man can have of himself'] – as individuals defined themselves and others: 'en se choisissant lui-même dans sa liberté, [il] choisissait la liberté de tous' ['in the act of choosing himself in his freedom, he chose freedom for all'].[59]

Both a philosophical and a highly rhetorical propagandist text,[60] 'La République du silence' represents the Occupation as an opportunity or catalyst for the recognition of radical freedom. But what role does the war play in Boileau-Narcejac's suspense novel? On the one hand, it facilitates both the premise and aspects of the development of the novel's plot: the introduction of a complete stranger into the women's flat via the 'marraine de guerre' system passes as plausible; when Bernard's sister, Julia, turns up unexpectedly and risks exposing Gervais as a fraud she is conveniently killed by German soldiers on the streets; Gervais's physical deterioration due to the poison administered by Hélène is disregarded by his doctor, who puts it down to the debilitating period the protagonist spent in a Stalag. Beyond that, however, the Occupation is explicitly represented as very much secondary to individual concerns. Gervais points out that the metaphorical war raging amongst the three characters matters considerably more than the 'véritable bataille rangée' ['out and out pitched battle'] being waged simultaneously in Lyon: 'notre petite jungle individuelle nous suffisait; la grande, autour de nous, avec ses massacres, ses fusillades, ses crimes de toutes sortes, nous l'avions presque oubliée' (128) ['our own little jungle was enough for us; we'd almost forgotten the large one which was all around us, with its massacres and gunfire and all sorts of crime']. The former POW's total lack of interest in any further engagement in the war is coupled to his refusal to accept responsibility for his own acts and thus for his own 'self'. Gervais is a master of bad faith, either blaming others or his essential nature for his shortcomings: 'Les vraies passions, les vraies douleurs, les vrais crimes, les vrais sacrifices, m'avaient été refusés. Je n'y pouvais rien. J'étais un infirme du cœur' (140) ['Real passion, real pain, real crimes and real sacrifices: all of these had been closed off to me. I couldn't do a thing about it. I was an emotional invalid']; 'Un petit coup de pouce, un rien de plus, et j'aurais été un grand bonhomme' (92) ['A helping hand, just a little bit more, and I would have been a great man'].

The 'nous' in Sartre's essay primarily embraces resistants, though it stretches at one point to include 'tous les Français qui [...] ont dit *non*' ['All the French people who said *no*'].[61] However, like many in France during the war, one suspects,

---

58   Sartre, 'La République du silence', p. 12.

59   'La République du silence', pp. 12–13 and p. 14.

60   As Susan Suleiman notes: '[...] the interest of this text is not factual. Its power is rhetorical, even at the expense of facts', *Crises of Memory and the Second World War* (Harvard UP, 2006), p. 20.

61   'La République du silence', p. 12. See Suleiman, *Crises of Memory*, for further comments on Sartre's use of pronouns and what she calls his 'unanimist rhetoric', pp. 18–21.

Boileau-Narcejac's protagonist falls into neither category. For the narrator of 'La République du silence', the heightened awareness of mortality occasioned by the Occupation meant an increased perception of the nature of freedom. For the crime fiction writers Boileau-Narcejac and their protagonist Gervais, it is an opportunity for the murderer Hélène to end the latter's life more easily: as he puts it, 'en ce moment que vaut une vie humaine?' (183) ['what's a human life worth these days?']. Gervais is a man who refuses to face the consequences of his freedom, literal or figurative, Occupation or no Occupation. In 'La République' Sartre asserts that 'le secret d'un homme, ce n'est pas son complexe d'Oedipe ou d'infériorité, c'est la limite même de sa liberté' ['the secret of a man is not his Oedipus complex or his inferiority complex, it is the limit of his own freedom'].[62] A very different take on the subject can be read in *Les Louves*. Gervais, we learn, had passively watched his wife drown in a boating accident. Years later he allows Julia to be shot on the streets of Lyon by German soldiers, sheltering in a courtyard as she hammers helplessly on the door 'comme un noyé qui se débat encore un peu' (134) ['like a drowning man still struggling a little']. The repetition of Gervais's act (or non-act) is underscored by the imagery. Combined with details of the protagonist's troubled relations with his mother – to whom, we learn, he felt inferior – and with the triangular relationship of the principal characters of *Les Louves*, such repetition is highly suggestive of precisely those unconscious forces Sartre's essay discards. Gervais in fact explicitly alludes to 'tout ce que je m'efforçais de refouler derrière les portes closes de ma mémoire ...' (70) ['everything I tried to hide away behind the closed doors of my memory']. The textual repetition of the choice not to act – once during a boating incident and again in the wartime context of Occupation – both chimes with Sartre's notion of the extreme situation which brings with it an awareness of mortality precipitating radical choice, but also reminds us that war is not the only context in which such awareness may arise. *Les Louves* has much to say about bad faith, the nature of the 'self' and figurative imprisonments, but World War II ultimately functions as a useful, rather than altogether necessary, context or pre-text.

The representation of the war and the manner and extent of its connection to the exploration of the concepts of freedom and authenticity changes with *Maldonne*. As with *Les Louves* role-play, lies, and imprisonment feature in various guises, both literal and figurative: Jacques Christen agrees to take on the role of his (apparent) double Paul de Baer; Gilberte's supposed brother Martin is really her husband; Gilberte herself is playing the part of the innocent wife whose amnesiac husband de Baer has returned to her. The consciously adopted roles and sustained deceit makes of the house the sort of Sartrean 'huis clos' which ideally suits the suspense novel. Like Gervais, Christen styles himself a sort of prisoner on parole (143) and soon comes to regard his newly constituted 'family' as jailers. In contrast to *Les Louves*, however, the war is thematically imbricated in this text to a considerably greater extent. Published in 1962 *Maldonne* was being

---

[62]   Sartre, 'La République du silence', p. 13.

written, we can assume, during the period of Adolf Eichmann's capture (1960), trial and execution (1961), and indeed Eichmann is mentioned briefly in the text. Whereas in *Les Louves* one French escaped POW adopted the identity of another, here the French civilian Christen unknowingly stands in for former nazi and war criminal Martin von Klaus. The principal crimes in *Les Louves* are the murders of Agnès and Gervais, with the war serving as a useful backdrop; in *Maldonne* the protagonist's figurative double, von Klaus, is wanted for crimes against humanity. Allusions to concentration camps and war crimes inevitably invite comparisons: what is a victim in a crime story compared to the victims of the Shoah? How are we to compare 'ordinary' murder for monetary gain with crimes against humanity?

In *Les Louves* the past and repressing that past were represented as personal concerns in the form of Gervais's putting aside of difficult maternal and personal relationships. In *Maldonne* the past is bound up with the war. Christen fakes amnesia in order to be able to account for any gaps in his knowledge about the man whose role he has adopted, but his observation that this is not so unrealistic a scenario – 'Le cas est fréquent d'individus qui oublient ce qui est, pour eux, une cause d'angoisse' (152) ['It is often the case that individuals forget something that causes them anxiety'] – actually applies to Gilberte and, potentially, beyond. Amnesia for Gilberte is an act of bad faith, akin to a willed forgetting. Like Gervais ('tout ce que je m'efforçais de refouler derrière les portes closes de ma mémoire ...', *Les Louves* p. 70) she sets aside potentially guilt-inducing memories: her rejection of news of the existence of concentration camps ('c'était si bizarre, si impensable!', p. 189) ['it was so odd, so unimaginable!']; her willingness to believe her husband's claims that charges against him were greatly exaggerated; not wishing to know precisely what he was accused of; denying that she was in any way complicit. Boileau-Narcejac's referencing of the Holocaust keeps the emphasis very much on the guilty party, and although that guilty party is German, it is also the case that he is married to a French woman, passes as French, and has a French stand-in who dies in his place.[63] The significance of the French connection is open to interpretation. The implication may be that the French are metaphorically wedded to German guilt.[64] Or, perhaps, that they can be substituted for the Germans, either in the sense of being equally guilty, or alternatively, in the sense of acting as scapegoats. Whatever the interpretation, and however indirectly, French involvement in the war has entered the picture. The third and final text considered here, *La Lèpre* (1976) addresses the issue rather more directly.

---

[63] For further discussion of the representation of characters of mixed French/German nationality see below, Chapter 5, p. 149 and pp. 152–3.

[64] Sartre in 'Qu'est-ce qu'un collaborateur' points out that the work of collaborationist writers often figures France in feminized form vis-à-vis Germany: 'On relèvera partout dans les articles de Chateaubriant, de Drieu, de Brazillach de curieuses métaphores qui présentent les relations de la France et de l'Allemagne sous l'aspect d'une union sexuelle où la France joue le rôle de la femme' ['Throughout the work of Chateaubriant, of Drieu, of Brazillach you can find strange metaphors which represent Franco-German relations as a sexual union in which France plays the part of the woman'], p. 58.

The performance of roles is once again key in *La Lèpre*, this time in the form of the choices made by first-person protagonist Marc Pradier during the Occupation: will he be part of the first-person plural 'nous' in Sartre's 'République du silence', choosing the path of resistance represented in the text by the Gaullist Armande, or will he take the side of suspected collaborator Pléaux? In fact, the text undermines the notion of such black and white choices and identities: this is less a case of saying 'no' to the Germans and more of a 'yes, no, maybe'. If Pradier initially agrees to help Armande it is not, as he states with a measure of bad faith, the result of any choice – 'Ainsi, je pénétrais pas à pas dans la clandestinité. Je n'avais rien voulu, rien décidé' (72) ['So it was that step by step I entered this underground world. I hadn't wanted this, I hadn't made any choice'] – but rather because of his growing feelings for her and his fear of losing face: 'J'étais son prisonnier' (94) he states of the woman he is to marry. Pradier, who has also befriended Pléaux, finds himself in the unenviable role of double agent: assigned to kill the collaborator, he in fact ends up facilitating his escape to South America. When he is stopped in Pléaux's car by the *milice*, Pradier is imprisoned as the vanished collaborator's killer, but freed shortly thereafter when a group of *maquisards* rescue one of their number being held in the same location. Pradier's false identity is born: henceforth he embraces his role as resistance hero, killer of a notorious collaborator. Pradier lies by omission, and having once publically accepted his heroic resistance identity he is obliged to choose it again and again as his political career accelerates under the post-war regime. As he puts it (with a telling disculpating shift to the impersonal): 'On ne peut revenir en arrière. On est condamné à se taire, encore et encore' (126) ['You cannot go back. You are condemned to remain silent, again and again']. This offers us a rather different take on the notion of a 'Republic of Silence.' Boileau-Narcejac's text flags up the unsaid stuff of history.

Although *La Lèpre* (published in 1976) belongs in purely chronological terms to the final post-1974 'obsessive' phase of Rousso's Vichy syndrome, it in fact illustrates perfectly the preceding 1971–74 'return of the repressed' category of cultural vectors. As well as reminding its audience of the ambivalence of many French citizens during the war, Boileau-Narcejac's text challenges the notion of a unified and heroic French nation via its representation of memory and the past. Gervais (*Les Louves*) and Gilberte (*Maldonne*) repressed difficult memories; Pradier finds himself suffering from unwanted anamnesia: 'A la vérité, nous voulions oublier. Moi, surtout! Mais je découvre que ma mémoire, bien trop fidèle à mon gré, a tout enregistré, tout retenu' (11) ['Truth to tell, we wanted to forget. I did especially! But I'm discovering that my memory, which is far too reliable for my liking, has recorded everything, stored everything']. Some 13 years on Pradier cannot shake off memories of the collaborator Pléaux who alone can reveal the truth of Pradier's actions during the war and who thereby comes to embody all of the protagonist's – and by extension France's, I would suggest – wartime guilt: 'La vérité, c'est que Pléaux me hantait' (131) ['The truth is that Pléaux was haunting me']. Like a literal, embodied manifestation of the return of the repressed, Pléaux, the revenant (195), reminiscent here of Balzac's Colonel Chabert (another man of contested identity at the cusp of a changing political regime)[65] comes back to France from South America where he has been 'refoulé loin des vivants' (199).[66] From this moment on Pradier lives with the fear that his false heroism may be revealed.

And it is not just aspects of the Occupation years which stage a disruptive return. Just as Pléaux the collaborator returns to haunt the complicit Pradier 13 years after the war, so the 1976 reader of *La Lèpre* was confronted with an evocation of the Algerian War over a decade after Algerian independence. In fact, legacies of colonialism feature to some degree in all three of Boileau-Narcejac's texts. In *Les Louves* inheritance is related to personal gain: Hélène discovers that Bernard's uncle has left his nephew a considerable fortune in the form of a plantation on the Ivory Coast, but the status of the latter as a French colony has little if any further significance in the text. In *Maldonne* an uncle bequeathing a fortune to Gilberte's husband is invented to justify the need for Christen's act of impersonation, whilst legacies of a more figurative historical variety are evoked by von Klaus, who in an attempt to convince his wife of his innocence, compares the treatment of Jews as slave labourers to the deaths of those who built the Burma Road and Panama Canal (189). It is left to the reader to pass judgment on this piece of self-serving comparison. *La Lèpre* dispenses with the plot device of literal inheritance and focuses instead on the legacy of war handed from father to (adopted) son. Pléaux returns, and Pradier writes the letter we are reading to Christophe, at the height of the Algerian War. The text invites the reader to consider possible links between the two wars: speaking to Christophe who is on leave from the Algerian conflict, Pradier claims to be reminded of this own time as a resistant (219), whilst simultaneously fearing that Christophe may endanger his life by seeking to emulate his father's (false) heroic past. Pradier's letter is ultimately both an act of self-justification and a confession in which he symbolically seeks judgment from the next generation. In Boileau-Narcejac's scheme of things, that second generation is pragmatic rather than traumatized: Pléaux is killed with little after-thought by Christophe, who simply wishes to put his parents' mind at ease when he learns of the problem the returning collaborator poses. As we will see in Chapter 5 below, this early representation of the Algerian conflict and its links to the Second World War serves as a useful point of comparison and contrast with later works of crime fiction.

Discussion of Dard's work pointed to the synchronic variation resulting from genre choice. Boileau-Narcejac's three texts demonstrate the diachronic evolution

---

[65]   Pléaux's words to Pradier about Armande – 'Elle a beau être orgueilleuse, il y a des cas où il faut bien transiger' (185) ['It's all good and well for her to be so proud, there are times when you have to compromise'], echo those addressed to Chabert by his solicitor, Derville, on the subject of his wife: '– Il faudra peut-être transiger, dit l'avoué. / – Transiger, répéta le colonel Chabert. Suis-je mort ou suis-je vivant?' ['"You may have to compromise", said the solicitor. "Compromise", repeated Colonel Chabert, "Am I dead or am I alive?"'], Balzac, *Le Colonel Chabert* (Gallimard, 1974), p. 58.

[66]   Although this can be rendered as 'hidden away far from the living', 'refoulé' also has psychoanalytic connotations of repression.

of representations of World War II in an author's (or in this case authors') work: from a convenient period setting which primarily smooths the way for both plot and thematic development (*Les Louves*), to a text which centres on the impersonation of a wanted nazi war criminal by a French substitute (*Maldonne*), to an exploration of the difficult path trodden between resistance and collaboration and the legacy of war passed from one generation to the next (*La Lèpre*). Reading Sartre's 'La République du silence' in the light of Boileau-Narcejac's texts, and vice versa, demonstrates the potential for bringing together different genres – in this case crime fiction and the philosophical / rhetorical / political essay. Analysis of representation of the war years should mean not only synchronic and diachronic analyses of specific genres but comparative studies of different genres: crime fiction need not be discussed in critical isolation.

Serial Killers and the Final Solution: Dantec's Cyber-Sleuthing

From the *huis clos* of suspense we move to genre-busting futuristic realities. Psychotic serial killer Andreas Schaltzmann is arrested and given a life sentence for his crimes (though he commits suicide soon after). A small interdisciplinary group of scientists led by Arthur Darquandier, an expert in cognitive neuroscience, believes that another cell of killers, responsible for over one hundred murders, remains at large and is responsible for some of the murders attributed to Schaltzmann. After lengthy cyber-investigations involving journeys in virtual space and the downloading of prodigious quantities of data – including Schaltzmann's personality, complete with his unconscious – into Darquandier's investigative 'neuromatrix', and as the turn of the millennium approaches, the killers are tracked down and eradicated. The text we read – *Les racines du mal* – is a reconstruction of these events authored by first-person narrator Darquandier in Cape York in the year 2020, the narrator having left a France facing constitutional collapse, with the world apparently on the brink of apocalyptic disaster.

   Like his narrator, the novelist, essayist, (post-)punk rock musician, and controversial public figure Maurice G. Dantec left France, adopting Canadian nationality in 1998, some three years after the publication of his second highly successful novel, *Les racines du mal* (1995). Variously described as an example of the 'extreme contemporary', a 'neuro-polar', a work of 'cyber-*noir*' or 'cyber-punk',[67] this 750-page sf-*noir* combination would require considerably more space than is available here to do it justice with respect to its innovative take on genre. For that reason what follows will focus primarily on the text's articulation of

---

[67]   Dantec's texts as examples of the 'extreme contemporary' are discussed by Lawrence Schehr, 'Dantec's Inferno', in *Novels of the Contemporary Extreme* (Continnum: 2006), pp. 89–99. The labels 'neuro-polar' and 'cyber-noir' both feature in Virgile Jouanneau and Sandra Gabbai's, 'Entretien avec Maurice G. Dantec', March 1996, <http://www.les-ours. com/novel/dantec/dantec1.htm>. Accessed 30 November 2011.

World War II topoi. Performing (and of course thereby modulating) both crime and science fiction genres, *Les racines du mal* should, following McHale, combine two overarching principles or dominants:

> SF [...], like postmodernist fiction, is governed by an *ontological dominant*, by contrast with modernist fiction or, among the genres of 'genre' fiction, detective fiction, both of which raise and explore issues of epistemology and thus are governed by an *epistemological dominant* (my emphases).[68]

In fact, epistemological concerns are not so readily disconnected from the ontological (how does one arrive at an ontology without an epistemology?) and McHale does not explore the viable integration of different or competing 'dominants'. In the case of *Les racines du mal* the ontological and the epistemological are brought together in an ethical nexus of allusions to World War II, though this is not 'a novel about the war' in the same sense as any of the texts previously discussed. These have either been set during the war or, if unfolding post-war (such as *Maldonne*, *La Lèpre*, and Simenon's *Les Autres*), have nonetheless represented first-generation participants in the conflict. Born in 1959 and thus very much a post-war author, Dantec references the Occupation and Holocaust rather differently, and does so in three principal contexts: as one of a number of role-playing games engaged in by a group of serial killers; as part of the psychotic universe of the solo serial killer Schaltzmann; as a key component in the narrator's view of the human species and the nature of evil.

The principal prospective thrust of *Les racines du mal* consists of the tracking down of the 'Club des Ténèbres', a cell of five serial killers eventually located by Darquandier and his neuromatrix. This is an investigation which mobilizes both the epistemological and the ontological dimension of the text. The killers are found thanks to technology which is not (yet) of our world: the neuromatrix not only has an infallible memory and endless capacity for acquiring and collating new data (a form of super-detective or indeed super-reader); it also integrates the biological with complex IT circuitry. This futuristic vision is, however, coupled with a turn to the past, for it is from World War II that the killers seek inspiration. The 'final solution' is the latest in a series of increasingly violent role-playing scenarios, all of them variations on the theme of murder. In the lead-up to the turn of the millennium the serial killers are playing Holocaust. True to this latest 'theme', their victims are found to have died from lethal injection; the group's mobile home contains nazi paraphernalia and Holocaust denial texts and is equipped with a system for gassing victims with a substance similar in composition to Zyklon B; an on-board 'four crématoire' contains human ashes: as Darquandier puts it, theirs is 'un vrai Luna Park nazi' (637) ['a real nazi theme park'].[69]

---

[68]   McHale, *Constructing Postmodernism*, p. 247.

[69]   Given that Dantec's serial killers are not ideologically motivated, his text is not of the same order as those discussed below in Chapter 5, which includes an analysis of texts which represent French neo-nazis and Holocaust deniers.

Dantec's referencing of the Holocaust in this context displays an element of incongruity or contradiction, and in this it is perhaps typical of late twentieth-century attitudes. The Final Solution is both potentially trivialized by being reduced to the status of a game (admittedly in the minds of killers) whilst simultaneously being held up as (still) the ultimate example of evil; the Holocaust is both potential simulacrum and very real ethical touchstone. However, the text only toys with ontological instability in this case: the killers may be 'playing' at Nazis but they are actually killing their victims. Paradoxically, this game is for real. Furthermore, although Dantec's represented 'final solution' maintains the perpetrators as purveyors of evil, the 'solution' is not that of a Jewish 'question' or 'problem'; indeed the link between perpetrators and victims is decoupled: these criminals kill only to assuage their boredom:

> Mais lorsque la vie tout entière n'est plus qu'un vaste 'espace de loisirs', sans but ni direction, neutre et sans affect, 'média froid' où les séries télé s'enchaînent aux jeux stupides, au déluge publicitaire et à l'ennui, le nombre des solutions se restreint au fur et à mesure que s'empilent les frustrations. (434)

> [But when life is nothing more than a vast 'leisure park', with no goal or direction, neutral and devoid of affect, an example of 'cold media' where TV series blend into mindless games and endless advertising and boredom, the number of solutions dwindles as frustrations mount.]

This is not to say that contemporary society necessarily makes murderers of us all. Dantec mitigates this suggestion by providing back-stories of extreme dysfunction for his serial killers: these are damaged, depersonalized extremes. The critique of society nonetheless stands, and carries over to a second set of World War II allusions, linked this time to the lone killer Andreas Schaltzmann.

The serial killer group play 'final solution' in an attempt to alleviate their *ennui* and do so in full knowledge of their actions. By contrast, when Andreas Schaltzmann carries out his murders and engages in blood-thirsty rituals involving small mammals and a food blender (not for nothing is he dubbed 'the Vampire of Vitry-sur-Seine') he is not operating in a reality commensurate with our own. He is, to use a popular locution, on another planet: 'la Planète du mal' (743) ['Planet evil']. Schaltzmann's is an alternative reality controlled by alienazi [sic] dictatorship (80). In his psychotic universe of alternative history World War II was won by the nazis in alliance with extraterrestrials from the planet Vega. According to this revisioned past Operation Overlord failed and a 'mythe du 6 juin' was created (123), though these truths are kept hidden from the general public. In this paranoid parallel reality Schaltzmann is being hunted by the Gestapo and their alien allies: if he kills, it is in pre-emptive self-defence, indeed something of a heroic gesture. Dantec presents us with a killer who represents not just resistance but the Resistance: Schaltzmann claims to have been in a concentration camp (Paris is full of such camps disguised as high rise estates and halfway houses, p. 18) and believes he runs the risk of being returned to one; he listens to 'Radio Londres' (82) and fears torture and death at the hands of a Barbie, a Touvier, or a Heydrich Alien (106).

One group of serial killers thus take on the role of nazis in *Les racines du mal* whilst another killer assumes the part of Jew / resistant (in itself a potentially controversial representation). In both cases the war and its key 'protagonists' serve as symbols – of evil in the former case and of resistance to evil – and notably *not* victim – in the latter. The ontological and epistemological are inextricably linked in both contexts: via the futuristic investigative neuromatrix in one case, and the embedded parallel world of Schaltzmann in the other. Dantec's alternative history of nazi victory is of course far from new – Philip K Dick's *The Man in the High Castle* (1962), Eric Norden's *The Ultimate Solution* (1973), and Robert Harris's *Fatherland* (1992) are just a small sample of the many texts which play out a similar scenario[70] – but there are differences. This alternative history exists only in the mind of the delusional Schaltzmann. References to alien life-forms in alliance with the nazis both add a note of rather black humour (encapsulated for instance in the notion of 'un Heydrich Alien') and suggest that evil is 'out there' rather than within humanity – a notion which is countered by the killer cell and, as we will see, by Darquandier's own views. Although Schaltzmann is a criminal, his self-perception as a representative of resistance (indeed the putative founder of a resistance movement) frames a further attack on a society. The killer's dystopic vision is of a totalitarian society of absolute media control in which all citizens are manipulated by the alienazi media machine (116). After several generations of propaganda the present population has become complicit, actively supporting or at the very least no longer questioning the society in which they live. Drawing parallels between the 1930s and the 1990s, Dantec uses the nazi era and (French) cultural memory of invasion and collaboration as a wake-up call to face the dystopic reality of contemporary France. In a criminal world the psychotic and paranoid criminal killer is also a prescient seer of truth.

The third referencing of the war comes not in the guise of characters' performance of war-time roles (nazis, Jews, resistants) but rather of the first-person narrator's disquisitions on the nature of humanity. For Darquandier man is an inherently bellicose animal and evil an inevitable part of evolutionary life: 'le mal, c'est-à-dire la mort, la violence, l'agressivité et l'instinct de destruction, formait une composante essentielle de la vie' (279) ['evil, in other words death, violence, aggression, and the destructive instinct, are an essential part of life']. Darquandier's reflections in *Les racines du mal* echo Dantec's own expressed beliefs: 'Je crois que l'homme est cruel et que ça fait partie de son programme parce que c'est un prédateur et qu'il a besoin de son instinct de tuer pour pouvoir survivre' ['I think that man is cruel and that that's part of his programming because he is a predator and needs his killer instinct in order to survive'].[71] The nazis, both author and narrator go on to suggest, were (are) part of us and what we can be.

---

[70]   Robert Harris, *Fatherland* (Hutchinson, 1992); Eric Norden, *The Ultimate Solution* (Warner Paperback Library, 1973). See also Len Deighton *SS-GB* (Cape, 1978), and more recently Stephen Fry, *Making History* (Hutchinson, 1996).

[71]   Jouanneau & Gabbai, 'Entretien avec Maurice G. Dantec'.

Usually heavily based on forensic science and the police procedural, serial crime novels nonetheless often introduce a gothic cadence; indeed for Horsley, '[a]t their most symbolic, such texts elaborate the myth of the solving rational intellect pitted against the myth of the inhuman monster'.[72] In *Les racines du mal* a belief in the all too humanly monstrous is conveyed not just via the narrator's Darwinian musings but via a process of doubling. Darquandier idly fantasizes about a psychiatrist with whom he disagrees becoming one of Schaltzmann's victims; later, he discovers that the school reports of one of the band of killers closely matches his own. Not for nothing is the investigator and scientist nicknamed 'Dark'.

Although Dantec's *Les racines du mal* is set some 50 years after World War II, and its futuristic narration some 20 years after that, the events of the past continue to play their part, with nazis and resistants assuming a complex symbolic role. Taken metaphorically, the war in *Les racines du mal* unfolded not just in the past; it continues, albeit in a different form, today. To conclude this section we might consider another text which treads a not dissimilar path. Amélie Nothomb's *Acide sulphurique* (2005) is not labelled a work of crime fiction (although it could be). The text unfolds on the set of a programme entitled 'Concentration', in which kapos and prisoners, in the style of Big Brother (or its French equivalent, 'Loft Story'), are filmed 24 hours a day for the entertainment of a rapt TV audience. As the programme becomes increasingly interactive, the audience come to 'select' those prisoners who are to die. And in this bleak dystopia these weakest links do really die. As with *Les racines du mal* Nothomb's short work critiques what is perceived as an all-pervasive and invasive media, and a complicit population (viewing figures for 'Concentration' eventually include 100 percent of the population). Nazis are once more the chosen symbols of ultimate evil and state control. But there is one key difference. At the close of the text Zdena, a kapo who at the outset revelled in her role – 'je suis du côté des forts' (16) ['I'm on the side of the fittest'] she states in pseudo-Darwinian language Dantec's narrator would be proud of – puts a definitive end to the programme by threatening to torch the set. Even if they do not all live happily ever after, they all live. Nothomb's is a more redemptive vision of humanity.

Closing Statement

A whodunnit, ludic thrillers featuring a recurring character, suspense novels, and a *noir* sci-fi / crime combination: what can these very different types of text tell us about 'crime fiction representing the war'? First, genre ascriptions have been revealed to be more complex and labile than is often suspected, whether this be in terms of preconceptions regarding individual types of text (the whodunnit, etc.) or the relationship between crime fiction and other types of narrative. Troye's *Meurtre*

---

[72]   Lee Horsley, *Twentieth-Century Crime Fiction* (Oxford UP, 2005), p. 139. Dantec acknowledges the gothic roots of [his] crime fiction in his 'La Fiction comme laboratoire anthropologique expérimental', *Les Temps modernes* 595 (1997): 263–81.

dans un oflag yielded up the expected ingredients – a murder, a rational detective, and a restricted set of suspects, for instance – but it was also open to a darker, irrational, reading which debunked ratiocinative and forensic processes as well as the generic norm of the reliable narrator recounting the tale of the investigator's prowess. Simultaneously – or perhaps more accurately, consecutively, or intermittently – the text functioned as a testimonial account of life in a POW camp: details need not always be clues. Analysis of Dard's San-Antonio texts reminded us that, contrary to some critical views, crime fiction can retain, indeed has a long tradition of, self-reflexivity, linguistic play, and humour. Just as *Meurtre dans un oflag* may be read in terms of two or more genres (it is generically unstable), so the San-Antonio works are, to paraphrase Jean Ricardou, adventures in writing, in *both* senses of that phrase. As examples of the suspense novel *Les Louves*, *Maldonne*, and *La Lèpre* revealed a generically typical thematic emphasis on freedom, entrapment, and role-playing. Read alongside 'La République du Silence', they also displayed their potential as texts which complement, even contest, other narratives of the war, in this case Sartre's philosophical vision of human freedom and authenticity. Finally, Dantec's *Les racines du mal* demonstrates both that genres which are often considered as distinct may come together (a synchronous hybrid), and that far from being static, 'crime fiction' continues to develop and mutate (a diachronous evolution).

The case studies above also show that different types of crime fiction may inflect representations of the war differently; genres, or subgenres, both restrict and facilitate types of representation. Set in a circumscribed location, the whodunnit suits explorations of difference within apparent sameness – the friend who is in fact foe, the patriot who is a coward, etc., – rather than representing an overtly adversarial world of, say, Germans versus Allies. With inevitably limited action sequences, emphasis will tend to fall on the cerebral or psychological, whether in the form of the investigator's strategizing or the suspects' motives. Troye's text thereby proved suited to exploring cowardice, shame, and guilt, with the doubling, or splitting, of Van Damme and Francen combining personal and political motives for murder. As a text written in captivity and during the war, *Meurtre dans un oflag*, unsurprisingly, does not include any of the typical war narrative figures (collaborator, resistant, black marketeer etc.), reminding us to look beyond these typologies. It also demonstrates that 'symptoms' can be found in texts which predate Rousso's post-Liberation starting point: here the shame of an individual also represents that of capitulating nations. Finally, as a Belgian francophone text, Troye's whodunnit points to the potential for comparative work on representations of the war years across national literatures.

Where the whodunnit is limited in terms of action sequences and eschews the representation of the explicitly adversarial, the light-hearted thriller provides both in abundance. What San-Antonio's texts also demonstrate is that genre can be as limiting as it is facilitating: the representation of, for instance, members of the Resistance, is inflected by the need to perpetuate the characteristics of the recurring hero San-Antonio, who must stand out as the most heroic figure in the textual economy. The need to maintain recognizable traits in the hero, such as his enthusiastic womanizing, means that gender trumps the ally / enemy divide: nazis or not, German women are fair game. The degree to which specific aspects of these texts are representative of their time – sexism and racism, for instance, but also puns and jokes about concentration camps – and how far these are dictated by genre, may be hard to ascertain. What is important is that any analysis of representations of the war must both factor in the strictures and specificities of genre, and be sensitive to inevitable differences in the reception of texts with the passing of time.

Like the whodunnit the suspense novel tends to be character- rather than plot-centered so favours the exploration of complex psychological states. With the focus very much on the victim, these texts can be used to manipulate the reader's expectations and preconceptions: do we, for instance, side with the protagonist of *La Lèpre*, whose ideological fence-sitting comes back to haunt him? Or the escaped POW who chooses to play no further part in the real war? Published over three decades, Boileau-Narcejac's texts also showed how representations of the war may evolve within a single authorial corpus, revealing specific concerns and preoccupations – literary as well as socio-political – in each case. War and Occupation in *Les Louves* provide a useful period setting, but beyond that they also facilitate a complex play of metaphor relating to the themes of freedom, combat, and imprisonment. Texts need not of course respond punctually to events: whereas *Maldonne* represents a nazi war criminal at a time when eyes would have been on the Eichmann trial, *La Lèpre* raises the ghost of Algeria years, if not decades, before the unnamed war entered the public domain.

Although only one is set during the war years, all three of Boileau-Narcejac's texts represent participants in the war: a POW; a nazi war criminal and his complicit wife; a collaborating resistant. 'Representing the war' in these cases in part means inviting readers to reassess their views of the war years and those who took part or stood aside, though of course more timeless concerns – freedom, guilt, memory and forgetting – are also thereby represented. With Dantec we move into very different territory: *Les racines du mal* strips the war of politics, ideological or national affiliations and defamiliarizes war narrative figures. The nazis in this text are French serial killers acting out their own Holocaust through sheer boredom and with indifference to the status of their victims. Jews and resistants are represented by a serial killer who inhabits an alternative reality in which nazis and aliens work together. Dantec references the war in order to attack the mind-numbing nature of contemporary society which seems to strip individuals of the capacity for critical thought: fail to engage with the world around you, he seems to suggest, and the evil in mankind will out. 'Representing the war' in *Les racines du mal* is primarily a means to an end, where that end is critiquing the present. The types of text which draw on readers' familiarity with the wartime past and the various ways in which past, present, and future interact will be discussed again in Chapter 4 and, especially, Chapter 5. The next chapter, by contrast, sets out to reveal something of the complexities of concepts of criminality and law and order during the war years.

Chapter 3
Crimes, Criminals, and the Forces of Law and Order

Les fous furieux embrigadés dans l'idéal c'est tout de même un spectacle qu'il vaut mieux admirer de loin.

—Alphonse Boudard[1]

How are we to distinguish between the force of law of a legitimate power and the supposedly originary violence that must have established this authority and that could not itself have been authorized by any anterior legitimacy, so that, in this initial moment, it is neither legal nor illegal – or, others would quickly say, neither just nor unjust?

—Derrida[2]

Mon ami le traître (1977), José Giovanni's tale of a common criminal turned wartime collaborator, describes the inmates of a French jail in the aftermath of the war:

La prison Saint-Pierre en cette fin d'été 1946 rassemblait des droit commun et des collabos. Avec la particularité suivante: parmi les droit commun il y avait d'authentiques résistants qui comptaient des amis parmi les collabos. Des amis d'avant guerre. Des relations de cambriole ou d'agression. Et la politique et les tendances n'étaient pas parvenues à les séparer.[3]

[In the late summer of 1946, Saint-Pierre prison held both common criminals and collaborators. With the following distinctive characteristic: amongst the common criminals were genuine resistants who regarded some of the collaborators as friends. Friends from before the war. Fellow burglars or muggers. And neither politics nor factions had managed to drive a wedge between them.]

---

[1]   Alphonse Boudard, *L'Étrange Monsieur Joseph* (Robert Laffont: 1998), p. 26.

[2]   Jacques Derrida 'Force de loi: le "fondement mystique de l'autorité"', *Cardozo Law Review*, 11 (1989–90): 920–1045, in parallel text, trans. Mary Quaintance.

[3]   José Giovanni, *Mon ami le traître* (Gallimard, 1977), p. 183. A similar description of Fresnes prison can be found in Boudard's *L'Étrange Monsieur Joseph*: 'Ça se balançait des vannes, quolibets, insultes entre les voleurs, les assassins et les enfants du Maréchal. "Pourris! Ordures! Fumiers! Traîtres! Boches!" xétéra …, puis ça se calmait, s'échangeaient alors des tuyaux, des nouvelles' (21) ['thieves, murderers, and followers of Pétain hurled jibes, jeers, and insults back and forth. "Bent bastards! Scum! Traitors! Hun!" etc …., then things calmed down news and information were exchanged'].

Giovanni's laconic outline calls attention to the existence of two different socio-legal orders: a pre-war Republican state with an established code of law, and a wartime regime of occupation and civil conflict operating under a highly complex *de facto* legal system. These two socio-legal orders can be linked to two narratives featuring familiar actors: that of 'normal' criminality in which law enforcers come up against criminals (we might call this the regular crime fiction narrative); that of wartime legal and social deregulation in which the key actors are most commonly identified as resistants, collaborators, and members of the occupying forces (say narratives of World War II or of Occupied France). Common criminals such as bank robbers or murderers condemned within one narrative might be Resistance heroes within another. Further potential complexity is added by a temporal aspect: collaborators who acted with legal impunity throughout the Occupation might be defined retrospectively as criminals in the name of (restored, if ever suspended) Republican law.[4] Giovanni's *Mon ami le traître* is just one of many works of crime fiction which bring attention to these criminal complexities. Other works demonstrate how the motive behind a criminal act carried out during the Occupation may be disguised by the perpetrator or interpreted by law enforcers as either personal or political; the personal may, in fact, be politicized by the precarious socio-legal context. Those responsible for the maintaining of law and order, meanwhile, appear in various guises – a *gendarme*, for instance; a member of the *brigades spéciales* or a *milicien*; a German soldier or officer in the Gestapo – each in all probability espousing different views regarding the nature and legitimacy of the 'law' and the 'order' they are expected to uphold.

All of this serves as a reminder that crime, criminals, and the putative forces of law and order are constructed in and by historical and socio-political context, a simple enough fact which is brought into sharp relief by a corpus of crime fiction texts, but all too often disregarded or at least underemphasized by theorists of the genre. Thus, *pace* the majority of the latter, the criminal who features in a classic detective story or whodunnit, for instance, is likely to be a member of a clearly designated (usually middle- or upper-class) social group and not a professional criminal. The crime – most often murder – constitutes the temporary disruption of a largely cohesive social order which is restored, and thereby reinforced, by the close of the text thanks to the extirpation of the criminal from the group. This is, in other words, described as a reactive genre which interrogates neither the dominant social order nor the law.[5] Broadly speaking, the shift to *noir* is said to bring a greater equilibrium between what we might call the criminal individual and

---

[4]   An edict promulgated on 9 August 1944 by the Provisional Government of the French Republic declared the Vichy regime illegal and its constitutional edicts nul and void; Vichy henceforth became known as the 'de facto' but not 'de jure' government (see Fraser, *Law after Auschwitz*, Carolina Academic P, 2005, pp. 153–4). My thanks to Professor David Fraser of Nottingham University for his email replies to some of my legal queries.

[5]   Scaggs, *Crime Fiction* (Routledge, 2005), p. 44; Porter, *The Pursuit of Crime* (Yale UP, 1982), p. 125; Evrard, *Lire le roman policier* (Dunod, 1996), pp. 95–9.

criminal society: the representation of crime is often accompanied by a questioning of the judiciary and the dominant social order; police officers may be depicted as corrupt; a gap opens up between morality and legality ('le Bien' and 'la Loi').[6] In spite of its subversive trappings crime fiction of this sort may nonetheless remain conservative at its core: although Evrard, for instance, associates French *noir* with revolt against the social order,[7] for Porter, American hardboiled crime upholds 'established societal order', whilst Mandel regards Chandler and his ilk as challenging local, but not national, power structures.[8] There is, however, general agreement that socio-political critique in crime fiction is directly proportional to the degree of state criminality identified.

This simplified but I think not misleading digest prompts two observations. Firstly, theorists of crime fiction are predominantly driven by genre (e.g., classic whodunnit or 'roman noir') in their analyses – or, more usually, typologies – of criminals and criminality. Secondly, two key concepts, that of 'social order' and that of 'the law', subtend most theoretical expositions. Both of these predominantly ahistorical tendencies have their limitations. Consider a small sample of propositions: 'a crime is by definition an anti-social act committed by one member of a human group against the group as a whole or another member of the group';[9] 'It [the crime] always depends on a legal definition and the law [...] is a key element of the superstructure in ensuring the reproduction of the existing power relations in a society'.[10] Or: 'The murder is the act of disruption by which innocence is lost, and the individual and the law become opposed to each other'.[11] Whilst there is of course an element of truth to these observations, the rest of this chapter will reveal the extent to which they are nonetheless problematized by crime fiction which is set in a context of war and, especially, a regime of Occupation. In this case both 'the law' and 'social order' are disrupted to such an extent that definitions of criminals and crimes – and thus potentially of crime fiction – have to be reappraised.

In what follows priority is given to works of crime fiction set during the Occupation, though a number of texts set after the war which explicitly raise the issue of potentially competing narratives – war vs post- or pre-war; 'normal' society vs regime of Occupation – or the complexities of the social and legislative orders in occupied France, are also included. Unlike the previous two chapters the aim here is not to provide readings of individual texts but rather to convey a synoptic impression of thematic constants and significant variants in the corpus of texts on which this study is based. A first section explores representations of the

---

6   Evrard, *Lire le roman policier*, pp. 95–6.

7   Ibid., p. 101.

8   Porter, *The Pursuit of Crime*, p. 125; Mandel, *Delightful Murder* (Pluto P, 1984), p. 36.

9   Porter, *The Pursuit of Crime*, p. 120.

10   Ibid.

11   Auden, 'The Guilty Vicarage', *Harpers*, May 1948, available at: <http://harpers. org/archive/1948/05/0033206>. Accessed 2 December 2011.

relationships between common crime and political crime, personal and political motives, and some of the tensions which arise between morality and legality. The portrayal of common criminals, from the petty crook apparently or actually turned patriotic resistant to the French *gestapiste* wielding a German police pass is the focus of a second section, whilst a third explores the depiction of various representatives of the forces of law and order (but which law, and which order?). The chapter concludes by briefly revisiting Patrick Modiano with a view to establishing a more nuanced sense of his place in both the field of crime fiction and that of fictional representations of Occupied France than is evidenced in appraisals which lack the contextualization offered by familiarity with an extensive corpus of crime fiction.

Definitional and Jurisdictional Boundaries: Political, Common, and State Crime

Set in Paris and Lyon in 1941, Malet's *120, rue de la gare* (1943) is constructed around two murders: that of Bob Colomer, colleague of the private investigator protagonist Nestor Burma, and that of gangster George Parry *aka* Jo Tour Eiffel. The criminals turn out to be apparently respectable members of society: Montbrison, a lawyer, kills Colomer in cahoots with *commissaire* Bernier; Dorcière, a surgeon, murders Parry. The motive in both cases is personal: greed in the first instance (Montbrison and Bernier are after the gangster's stash); sexual jealousy in the second (Parry steals Dorcière's mistress). At face value there is nothing specifically war related about the crimes or indeed the criminals. This is fairly standard *noir*, from the corrupt police officer and judge to the sanctioning of rough justice by Burma, who pronounces that given his criminal profile, the victim Parry got his just deserts (if not due legal process) (212). As Gorrara points out, however, bombing raids, movement across the demarcation line, and the rare blond tobacco smoked by Montbrison all play their part in the plot, whilst Malet's P.I. Burma can be interpreted in terms of a symbolic reassertion of French mastery and identity in the face of defeat at the hands of the Germans.[12]

Gorrara also registers Malet's representation of the disordered nature of society under Occupation, and although she does not go on specifically to connect this condition of social disruption to perceptions and constructions of crime and criminality, the connection can be made. The motive for the murder of Colomer may be greed, but it can be interpreted as an avarice which is bound in with the very particular nature of the socio-legal situation. As *commissaire* Bernier points out, society has been turned on its head as a result of black marketeering: 'nous vivons à une curieuse époque ... Je connais [...] d'ex-traîne-savates qui sont maintenant des roule-carrosses' (94) ['we're living in strange times ... I know (...) some former low-lifes who are now living it up to the nines']. As we shall see below,

---

[12]   Claire Gorrara, 'Malheurs et ténèbres: narratives of social disorder in Léo Malet's *120, rue de la gare, French Cultural Studies*, 12.3 (2001): 271–83.

many individuals who operated in the black market were in effect participating in a system of organized crime and were granted *de facto* legal immunity by the occupying forces with whom they openly collaborated. A police officer such as Bernier, or a judge such as Montbrison, would have been powerless in the face of the new breed of law enforcers (actually flouters of the law), i.e., German occupiers and in some cases convicted French criminals. Looked at in this light, *120, rue de la gare* is less of a typical 'roman noir' 'revolt against the social order', to reprise Evrard, and more of a demonstration of how in a time of war there is no stable social-legal order.

Beyond its flagging up of social and legal disruption Malet's text also reminds us of the potential collision of pre-war criminal narratives and those subsequently formed around conventional (not to say stereotypical) wartime categories such as 'resistant', 'collaborator', etc. As Burma points out in his indictment of the lawyer Montbrison, during the Occupation common murderers were not necessarily the dominant concern of the French police, some of whom at least were more intent on locating political 'terrorists' (aka resistants):

> Comment soupçonner une personalité dans votre genre d'être l'auteur d'une fusillade? Surtout que, obnubilés par la hantise du crime politique, ces bons bougres [the police] devaient écarquiller les yeux à la recherche d'un type à la barbe en brousaille et au couteau entre les dents. (202)

> [How would anyone suspect your sort of type of being responsible for a shooting? Especially since the police, poor devils, obsessed as they are by the spectre of political crime, must have been searching high and low for someone with a shaggy beard and a knife clamped between his teeth.]

Political crime is merely alluded to in Malet's text,[13] but the complexities relating to both the circumscription of political and common law crime and the jurisidictional territories at stake – who will seek to enforce which law – are recurring motifs in crime fiction set during or shortly after the Occupation. Meckert's *Nous avons les mains rouges* (1947) brings crime and war narratives together as one of his characters attempts to dispel any qualms amongst his colleagues over the killing of police officers: 'Les Allemands qu'on a tués sont morts en faisant leur devoir. On a descendu les soldats d'Hitler. On descendra maintenant les soldats de Saint-Plouc [i.e., the police]. C'est l'ennemi. Qu'est-ce qu'il y a de différent là-dedans?' (103) ['The Germans we killed died doing their duty. We offed Hitler's soldiers. Now we'll off these country bumpkin cops. They're the enemy. What's the difference?']. A good question, and one which many texts explore. Siniac's *Sous l'aile noire des rapaces* (1975) also presents us with the act of murder (or perhaps more accurately, 'killing') inscribed in two, superimposed narratives. When German soldiers block the route of a truck bearing gold bullion being

---

[13]   As Gorrara notes, minimal political references are to be expected 'of a text published in 1943 in Paris when strict controls over every aspect of publication militated against any openly anti-German or anti-Vichy statements', 'Malheurs et ténèbres', p. 276.

evacuated from Paris to Bordeaux,[14] escaped criminal Sambionetti whose aim it is to seize the loot has no hesitation in gunning them down. As the mildly ironic post-killing assessment suggests, this is no political act; the German soldiers die 'tués par un truand en rogne, comme de vulgaire flicards, c'était plus tout à fait *la guerre*, mais du banal *fait divers*' (196, my emphases) ['killed by an angry crook, like common cops, it wasn't really war any more, just a run-of-the-mill murder']. The same two narratives (war and crime) are invoked later in the text when a group of apolitical criminals are encouraged to kill German soldiers by imagining themselves in a context of common law 'normality': 'Préparez-vous à tirer à mort, les mecs! lança-t-il. Vous n'avez qu'à fermer les yeux et penser à des poulets!' (201) ['Get ready to shoot until you drop guys! Just close your eyes and think of cops!'].

Murder or (and) terrorism / patriotism? A single physical act is open to a threefold interpretation. In Héléna's *Les salauds ont la vie dure* (1949)[15] protagonist and common criminal Maurice shoots dead his unfaithful girlfriend, the German soldier with whom she has betrayed him, and a member of the Gestapo present on the scene. Maurice's colleague Jimmy sums up likely responses to the killings on the part of various law enforcers:

> Si ce n'était que les boches, les flics s'en foutraient. Mais il y a la tordue. Elle est française, elle. Et d'autre part, s'il n'y avait qu'elle, les Allemands laisseraient choir. Avec tes salades, tu t'es foutu tout le monde sur le dos. (34)

> [If it was just Jerry, the cops wouldn't give a damn. But there's that silly cow as well. And she's French. On the other hand, if it was just her, the Germans would let it drop. With all your shenanigans you're got everyone breathing down your neck.]

The French police concur when they subsequently point out that the murder of the girlfriend falls under the jurisdiction of French law (39), but nonetheless let Maurice go free: after all, he has also eradicated two members of the occupying forces. For these particular law enforcers one killing is an unlawful murder whilst the other two are patriotic acts of resistance – albeit not intended as such – which trump the first. Héléna's text reflects the legal complexities of the time. After the signing of the armistice on 22 June 1940, although the German occupiers exercised *de facto* power, under the Hague Convention *de jure* power returned to the domestic (Vichy) government.[16] Whilst the latter thus kept criminal

---

[14]   The Banque de France evacuated its considerable store of gold bullion and currency between 17 May and 23 June 1940. When these were repatriated from various locations in 1946, surprisingly, only a small proportion was unaccounted for. See Tristan Gaston-Breton's *Sauvez l'or de la Banque de France* (le cherche midi, 2002).

[15]   Material quoted from *Les salauds* is hereafter marked as 'SVD' where necessary. For a complementary discussion of Héléna's work, see Platten, *The Pleasure of Crime* (Rodopi, 2011), pp. 77–92.

[16]   For a detailed analysis of the justice system(s) in operation in France between 1940 and 1944 see Clément Million, *Occupation allemande et justice française: les droits de la*

jurisdiction over common law crimes under the Penal Code the occupier had the right to legislate to maintain public order:

> The authority of the legitimate power having in fact passed into the hands of the occupant, the latter shall take all the measures in his power to restore, and ensure, as far as possible, public order and safety, while respecting, unless absolutely prevented, the laws in force in the country.[17]

Under this system certain acts, such as murder, would usually fall under French jurisdiction, but attacks on German soldiers would most likely be dealt with by *Feldkriegsgerichte*, German military courts administering German law.[18] When not unofficially sanctioned by the occupying forces, black marketeers might be tried in a French court or a German military court. We are a long way from straightforward notions of 'social order' and 'law': the former is dominated by an enemy presence, fractured internally by competing French interest groups, and subject to hierarchical disruption and inversions of power and status; the latter is interpreted and imposed variously by different forces in the name of competing ideologies.

Crime fiction theory, as discussed above, is frequently unable to accommodate ambiguous or politicized demarcations of criminality. This corpus of crime fiction, however, returns time and again to precisely such historically situated complexities, suggesting that criminal acts perpetrated under the regime of Occupied France were dislocated from codified definitions, becoming subject to either pragmatically or ideologically motivated interpretation by both perpetrators and different group of law enforcers. In *Le Festival des macchabées* (1951),[19] Héléna's sequel to *Les salauds ont la vie dure*, the French police offer advice should Maurice and his colleague be stopped by Germans: 'Si on vous demande quelque chose [...] répondez que vous êtes des truands, des braqueurs [...]. N'essayez jamais de leur dire que vous faites de la politique' (FM, 76) ['If they ask you anything (...) say you're crooks or gangsters (...). Don't ever tell them you're acting out of political conviction']. Although protagonist Maurice's killing of the German soldier (above) is motivated by jealousy, he jokingly suggests to the French police that

---

puissance occupante sur la justice judiciaire 1940–1944 (Dalloz, 2011). Million states that the original terms of the Armistice were, in fact, soon superseded (17), and that as early as 1941 had indeed become more or less null and void (392). By 1943–44, he suggests, the French judicial system could operate only if and when its decisions served the interests of the Occupying forces (393).

[17] Annex to the Hague Convention of 1907, 'Regulations Respecting the Laws and Customs of War on Land', Section III. 'Military Authority over the Territory of the Hostile State', Article 43.

[18] See G. Eismann 'L'escalade d'une répression à visage légale. Les pratiques judiciaires des tribunaux du Militärbefehlshaber in Frankreich, 1940–1944', in *Occupation et répression militaire allemandes: 1939–1945. La Politique du 'maintien de l'ordre' en Europe occupée* dir. G Eismann and S. Martens, (Éditions Autrement, 2007), pp. 127–68.

[19] Material quoted from *Festival* is hereafter marked as 'FM' where necessary.

it was a political hit (SVD, 38). German officials, for their part, elect deliberately to define the act as politically motivated in order to justify their own subsequent killings as reprisals (SVD, p. 50).[20] Concrete examples such as these are a constant in works of crime fiction from the late 1940s onwards. Beyond highlighting the dislocation of criminal acts from common law definitions, they also demonstrate the degree to which motive and intentionality can be manipulated. Often, they are linked to a debunking of the myth of the disinterested, politically driven resistant. In Daeninckx's *La Mort n'oublie personne* (1989), for instance, the apparently political murder of a printer by a member of the FTP is later revealed to have been motivated by envy and greed; Ouvard's *Le plongeon du frère Boileau*, written 25 years earlier, culminates in the revelation that Resistance leader and present-day trawler skipper Le Darec's wartime execution of his neighbour, Scaer, as a collaborator, was no more than a move to get his hands on Scaer's lucrative lands, oyster beds – and wife.

Killing becomes (even more) ethically and legally complex in times of war. Although in texts set during the Occupation eliminating Germans is not usually represented as a criminal act, at least in the eyes of French law enforcers, the morality of the deed may nonetheless be called into question. A face-off between a German soldier and a resistant in Héléna's *Les Clients du Central Hôtel* (1959) is represented as an inherently hopeless situation: 'seuls au bord de leur vie perdue, de leur existence gâchée, et tous les deux avaient vingt ans' (143) ['embarked alone on their wasted lives, their ruined existence, and both of them just 20 years old'], though the soldier is killed nonetheless. When it is a Franco-French affair, killing becomes yet more complicated. To what extent, and under what specific circumstances, can acts and their perpetrators be considered to be decriminalized by war? Many texts flag up the issue of (dis)continuities between pre-, post-, and wartime definitions of crime, especially murder, and indeed the words 'assassin' and 'assassinat' are located at the thematic centre of several works. In the case of French citizens killing each other, it is the treacherous *milicien* who is represented as the most acceptable target, but even in such cases, hesitation may be expressed. When a resistant sets out to kill a member of the *milice* in Héléna's *Les Clients*, for instance, the morality of the act is called into question as the narrator reflects upon the apparent freedom war offers individuals to commit acts normally regarded as illegal, describing the situation as an anarchy of murder (115). The killing of a *gendarme* who betrayed members of the Resistance to the Germans in *Les salauds ont la vie dure* is stripped of its criminal associations by the perpetrators: 'Nous ne sommes pas des assassins' (SVD, 381) ['We're not murderers']; 'Ce n'était plus

---

[20]   In his study of the police under the Occupation Jean-Marc Berlière notes of the murder of Germans by French citizens that the essential issue was whether the Vichy regime decided to qualify such crimes as political or criminal. In the early days of the regime, he states, the tendency was to describe such murders as common crimes, thereby undermining potential patriotic claims and reducing the perpetrators to the status of 'de vulgaires assassins' ['common murderers'], Berlière, *Policiers français sous l'Occupation*, (Perrin, 2001), p. 154.

un crime, c'était une exécution' (SVD, 385) ['It was no longer a crime, it was an execution'].[21] Morris's *Assassin, mon frère* (1954) takes a slightly different tack, distinguishing between anonymous acts of war which are nonetheless still labelled crimes – '[C]rimes absurdes, crimes aveugles tels qu'il s'en commet des millions en temps de guerre' ['Absurd, indiscriminate crimes of the sort committed by the million in times of war'] – and acts involving direct and deliberate engagement with the victim: 'L'homme qui avait tué Raoul Milaud savait qu'il le tuait. La guerre n'était plus là pour excuser son acte. Il n'était, devant Dieu et devant les hommes, que le plus bas des assassins' (42–3) ['The man who'd killed Raoul Milaud knew he was killing him. There was no longer a war to excuse his act. He was, before God and man, no more than the most despicable of murderers'].

Both Héléna's and Morris's texts express the struggle to reconcile the apparent legality of killing (or at least its legitimation) during times of war with the morality of such acts. Daeninckx's *La Mort n'oublie personne* follows a similar line, emphasizing the issue of the (dis)continuity of the legal order by looking forward to the immediate post-war period. Acting in the name of the Resistance, a naïve young recruit to the FTP joins his leader Camblain on a mission to shoot dead two Frenchmen, one accused of sending letters of denunciation to the Gestapo, the other a member of the LVF (*Légion des volontaires français contre le bolchevisme*). Although Ricouart does not actually pull the trigger (largely due to his ineptitude) both he and Camblain are arrested in 1947 and found guilty of murder. Daeninck's text is set in May 1944, late enough for *Comités départementaux de la libération* to have been set up by the *Comité français de libération nationale* and thus for certain acts against 'enemy forces' to be legitimized. However, as Bourdrel points out in his *L'Épuration sauvage*, there was no way of stopping individuals or groups from acting on their own motivations whilst invoking the name of the Resistance.[22] Represented as having been tortured by the *milice* and deported, Ricouart in fact figures in the textual economy as at worst an innocent victim and at best a Resistance patriot. The *post factum* charge of murder propels the character – and the reader – from one narrative into another: 'Le mot "assassinat" me heurta. J'eus envie de réagir mais le juge ne m'en laissa pas le temps' (144) ['The word "murder" shocked me. I wanted to react but the judge didn't give me time to']. From a war narrative of patriots we have abruptly moved into the world of common criminality. One might also consider Héléna's *Le Goût du sang* (1953) in which protagonist Jacques Vallon starts out killing *miliciens* for the Resistance but continues his murder of collaborators after the war, thereby becoming the object of a police murder inquiry.

So far the focus has fallen on an act – that of killing – which is, broadly speaking, recognized as a crime in one socio-legal order or narrative (pre-war;

---

[21]   See also the conclusion to Alain Demouzon's *Agence Melchior* (2006) in which the eponymous P.I.'s father posthumously confesses to having killed a man (a collaborator) but to thereby being neither an upholder of the law / dispenser of justice ['justicier'] nor a murderer (430).

[22]   Philippe Bourdrel, *L'Épuration sauvage* (Perrin, 2002), p. 56.

post-war; crime fiction) but may not be in another (wartime; war narrative), and it has emerged that in bringing these two narratives into collision the crime fiction corpus both interrogates definitions of criminality, legality, and morality, and casts new light on wartime categories – representing, for instance, the resistant patriot as common criminal, or the murdered *milicien* as victim of an immoral act. Fiction set during the years of Occupation also explores acts and activities particular to that historical context, such as black marketeering, denunciation, and collaboration of other hues, asking once more what criteria one might bring to bear in adjudging such acts criminal.

Set in Créteil shortly after the end of the war, Blond's *L'Ange de la rivière morte* (1946) follows an investigation into multiple murders, revealing at the close that the murderer killed to cover up his theft of large sums of money hoarded by his victims: all former black marketeers. Blond's plot and choice of victim and killer invite consideration of the criminality or otherwise of black marketeering, an activity of somewhat ambiguous legal and ethical status during the Occupation years. Blond's killer himself passes from black marketeering during the war to theft after (302), before moving beyond the pale by committing murder. But we are also reminded that his victims hide their loot to avoid paying taxes: arguably theft by another name. The forces of law and order as represented by Blond do little. A local police officer acknowledges with utter indifference the vast sums of money made by illegal trafficking (28), whilst the *commissaire* wearily acknowledges the shift from pre-war crime to the deregulated 'social chaos' (86) that prevails in 1946. Before the war, he points out, criminals could be readily identified and categorized; by 1944 half the population is living not merely on the margins of legality, but in a state of blissful disregard for it (87). The Vichy government was granted legal power to regulate affairs under the special circumstances of the Occupation, including taking measures against black marketeers, and as historian Fabrice Grenard points out, many citizens fell foul of the new economic legislation, with more than a million cases concerning possible breaches of the law being processed between 1940 and 1944.[23] By 1942, however, a blind eye was being turned in many cases. As Paul Sanders states, at a time when rules were imposed by the Occupying forces, breaking the law need not be seen as wrong-doing;[24] trafficking might be considered in some cases as a patriotic act of resistance.[25] The German authorities, for their part, often set out to protect their own financial interests.[26]

Defining crime in this case is partly a matter of scale. Vichy legislation of 15 March 1942 differentiated between what Sanders refers to as small-scale black market activity engaged in to help feed one's family (often referred to as the 'grey

---

[23]   Fabrice Grenard, *La France du marché noir (1940–1949)* (Payot, 2008), p. 7.

[24]   Paul Sanders, *Histoire du marché noir 1940–1946* (Perrin, 2001), p. 8.

[25]   Grenard comments on the concept of a '"marché noir patriotique"' ['patriotic black marketeering'] which emerged especially post 1943, *La France du marché noir*, p. 185.

[26]   See Million, *Occupation allemande et justice française*, p. 302.

market') and large scale fraud.[27] Though the police in *L'Ange de la rivière morte* are represented as showing little concern with black market criminality, the text flags up rather more intransigent post-war attitudes directed towards those large-scale operatives whose activities descended into collaboration: a passing reference informs us that as newspapers analyze de Gaulle's latest speech, a Minister (unnamed but potentially identifiable as *ministre du Ravitaillement* Yves Frage) broadcasts a call for the death penalty to be pronounced on all 'rois du marché noir' (228) ['black market bosses'].[28] Blond does not indicate which category his trafficking victims fall into, though the large sums of money they possess after Liberation may be regarded as damning. Unsurprisingly, given its early date of publication, *L'Ange de la rivière morte* goes no further in its exploration of the post-Liberation socio-legal situation, but Manotti's much later *Le Corps noir* (2004) does. Bourseul, one of the central characters in the text, is a large-scale black marketeer and industrial spy who socializes and collaborates openly with the occupying forces. Where *L'Ange de la rivière morte* arguably metes out a form of rough justice via the deaths of the traffickers, Manotti's big-time black marketeer survives the war by offering his services in the post-war economic reconstruction. Represented as canny enough to have had a toe, if not a foot, in the camp of the victors, and financially well-connected, Manotti's criminal does not face due process for his acts, though he is textually 'punished' by the death of his son (ironically, a member of the Resistance). Manotti's fiction reminds us of the post-war pragmatism that often prevailed over any penal, or indeed moral, code. The restored Republic quite simply could not function if all collaborators working in the public sphere and commercial infrastructure of the country were purged. Manotti's fictional law-breaker is represented as contributing to the establishment of a new social order.[29]

Le Corps noir broaches, but does not pursue, the issue of the legal complexities relating to post-war (re)criminalization of collaboration. As early as 26 June 1944 de Gaulle's Provisional Government had effectively declared the Vichy administration (or *de facto* authority calling itself a government) illegitimate and set the legislative clock back to 16 June 1940. Collaborators were now

---

[27]   Sanders, *Histoire du marché noir*, p. 49.

[28]   Farge's announcement that large-scale traffickers would face the death penalty was made amidst much publicity. The law was adopted on 14 August 1946 and passed on 2 October 1946: see Grenard, *La France du marché noir*, p. 276.

[29]   Set just after the war Noël Simsolo's *Exterminateurs* (2001) can usefully be read as a companion piece to *Le Corps noir*, exploring as it does the various possible fates of different 'types' in the new political climate, from economic collaborators to *miliciens*, resistants to black marketeering common criminals. Fajardie's *Sous le regard des élégantes* (1997) mentions in passing that whilst collaborationist writers and journalists were to fare badly at the end of the war, economic collaborators would have an easier time of it (103 and 105). Henri Amouroux makes the same point in his *Grande histoire des Français sous l'Occupation* (Robert Laffont, 1988), contrasting what he calls 'collaborationnistes d'affaires' and 'collaborationnistes d'idées' (515–16).

criminals who, if found guilty of *intelligence avec l'ennemi*, faced the death penalty (whether or not they had believed that Vichy represented the legitimate government of France). Giovanni chooses as the protagonist of his *Mon ami le traître* (1977) a common criminal jailed for assault and robbery, subsequently released from jail by the occupying forces with whom he then collaborates. The text opens with George Galtieri on the run: 'C'est l'article 75 ... intelligence avec l'ennemi ... douze balles à l'aube' (27) ['It's Article 75 ... relations with the enemy forces ... execution at dawn']. Giovanni's text conveys a cynicism vis-à-vis post-war justice which is common to many texts. Galtieri betrays his country, but is exonerated for his (non-violent) collaborative crimes by Commandant Adrien Rove, head of the *Service de Renseignement*, whom he provides with invaluable information about the Germans and their allies. The text closes, however, with Galtieri betrayed by Rove, who denies any knowledge of the deal struck and watches the former collaborator die at the hands of a firing squad. Too late, the law enforcer has a change of heart, describing the execution as 'a murder' (207). A not dissimilar point is made in Meckert's chilling *Nous sommes tous des assassins* (1952) when an illiterate and apolitical young man René le Guen awaits his execution in jail. The naïve Le Guen (described at one point as simple-minded) is guilty of murder, but has been manipulated by resistance leaders. In this text too the death penalty is condemned as a crime carried out in cold blood (207).

'Trahir ... C'est drôle comme les hommes paraissent attirés par ce mot qu'il emploient indifféremment pour les défections guerrières et leurs infortunes conjugales' ['Betrayal ... It's funny how men seem drawn to this word which they use indiscriminately to refer to wartime defections or their conjugal misfortunes'].[30] Mazarin's *Collabo-Song* (1981) is also structured around the theme of betrayal, both personal and political, focusing specifically on the act of denunciation. The text charts the downfall of protagonist Laure Santenac who betrays her philandering husband by planting resistance tracts in his desk and denouncing him to French *gestapistes*. Trapped into working for the SS to avoid being denounced as a denouncer, Laure is planning by the close of the text to flee France via an escape network. Manotti's text points to the weighty repercussions of denunciation: Laure's apolitical act of betrayal is said to amount to murder by proxy (108), and indeed her husband, actually a Gaullist agent, commits suicide when arrested. The post-war legal position regarding denunciation was somewhat murky. David Fraser notes that although such acts were criminalized, these legal measures 'smacked of *ex post facto* penal law',[31] and as Peter Novick points out, 'The principle [...] that laws enacted after the crime which they set out to punish

---

[30] Mazarin, *Collabo-Song* (Zulma, 1998), p. 112.

[31] David Fraser, *Law after Auschwitz* (Carolina Academic P, 2005), p. 180. See also Thomas Mertens, 'Continuity or Discontinuity of Law? – David Fraser's *Law after Auschwitz: Towards a Jurisprudence of the Holocaust*', German Law Journal, 08.05 (2005): 533–46.

are worse than no laws at all, is one common to all systems of jurisprudence'.[32] How then does Mazarin choose to punish his protagonist? In fact, he does not extend his text into the post-war period of transitional justice, opting instead to remark at the close that his protagonist's escape is to be facilitated by a certain 'docteur Eugène', aka Marcel Petiot.[33] Mazarin's 'solution' is reminiscent of the murder of black marketeers in *L'Ange de la rivière morte* and the death of trafficker Boursel's son in *Le Corps noir*. In the face of the inevitable conflicts between legality and morality engendered by the context of Occupation and the transition to a post-war socio-legal regime, crime fiction, it would seem, frequently opts for a model of closure available only to the writers of fiction: that of poetic justice.

This section opened with Malet's *102, rue de la gare* (1943), so it is fitting that it should close with a text written over six decades later which can be read as a response to Malet's Nestor Burma series: Pécherot's *Boulevard des branques* (2005), set in 1940 and featuring P.I. Nestor Bohman. Malet brought the notion of wartime socio-legal deregulation to the fore by selecting his criminal from the legal profession. The lawyer Montbrison kills for personal gain, arguably prompted to do so by the destabilizing inversion of social categories and hierarchies caused by war and Occupation. Safe from the fear of censorship, writing with all the perspective afforded by distance, and doubtless aware of accusations of racism and possibly anti-Semitism levelled at Malet,[34] Pécherot takes the concept of deregulation in a different direction. The plot of *Boulevard des branques* need not be rehearsed here. It is enough to note that the text hinges on the investigator's – and reader's – lack of certainty regarding the motive behind an act of murder: was it committed for personal monetary gain (an attempt to secure apparently hidden Spanish Republican gold), or did the killer strike to cover up a state-endorsed programme of euthanasia? Pécherot's text, which includes references to French eugenicist Alexis Carrel (164), and provides an epigraph stating that an estimated 40,000 patients held in French psychiatric hospitals died between 1940

---

[32] Peter Novick, *The Resistance Versus Vichy: The Purge of Collaborators in Liberated France* (Columbia UP, 1968), cited in *Transitional Justice. How Emerging Democracies Reckon with Former Regimes*, vol. II., ed. Neil J. Kritz (United States Institute of Peace P, 1995), p. 86.

[33] Marcel Petiot, living and practising in Paris under the name of Dr Eugène, most (in)famously set up a fake escape route for Jews and others fleeing France in 1943. The supposed escapees never saw South America but were instead killed by Petiot who in 1946 was tried, found guilty of, and condemned to death for, multiple murders.

[34] Emmanuel describes Burma as an anti-hero who is attractive to readers in spite of being racist, sexist, and arrogant, *From Surrealism*, p. 83, adding that 'Malet, although a racist, was neither a collaborationist nor an overt anti-Semite', p. 91. Malet's representation of Jews is, however, certainly open to criticism, as David Fraser rightly points out in his 'Polarcauste: law, justice and the Shoah in French detective fiction', *International Journal of Law in Context*, 1.3 (2005), pp. 237–59, 'Léo Malet: his tales of Paris and his dangerous Holocaust narrative', pp. 249–53.

and 1945, juxtaposes common and state crime. How, if at all, are governments held accountable for the crimes they perpetrate? Can the State function as an actor in a crime narrative? Amila's *Au balcon d'Hiroshima* (1985) carries out a not dissimilar comparative exercise by juxtaposing the victims of a bank robbery (two criminals and a police officer) with the deaths caused by the devastating allied fire-bombing of Tokyo in 1944–45: 'Qu'étaient donc les trois morts [...] devant cet Apocalypse?' (20) ['How significant were the three dead men next to this Apocalypse?']. Amila's text closes with the perpetrators of the hold-up escaping from a Japanese camp only to walk into what is revealed to be the city of Hiroshima, unaware of what is now their own fate.[35]

This is not the place to discuss the relative (il)legality and (im)morality of armed robbery, fire-bombing civilians, euthanasia programmes, or the dropping of atomic bombs, though reading war-based works of crime fiction certainly prompts such comparisons. Related to at least one of these potentially criminal acts – that of the implementation of a state-endorsed euthanasia programme – is the notion of 'lawless law', and it is with this concept that the current section will end. Like Malet's Burma, Pécherot's private investigator Bohman stresses the socio-legal deregulation precipitated by the war: 'La guerre a vraiment tout chamboulé. Me voilà du côté de l'ordre' (38) ['The war really has turned everything on its head. Here's me on the side of order'], he remarks with a measure of irony to a *préfet de police*; whilst police officer Bailly notes in throw-away style 'Le désordre, en ce moment ...' (257) ['Oh you know, disorder today ...']. Where for Malet, however, crime was something perpetrated by an avaricious individual, Pécherot's text stresses the immorality or injustice of Vichy legislation. *Boulevard des branques* ends with the enforced closure of Bohman's agency, branded 'ENTREPRISE JUIVE', and the arrest of the Bohman, whose father is revealed to have been a Jew.[36] In his referencing of anti-semitic legislation Pécherot touches on the question of what in 1946 Gustav Radbruch termed 'statutory lawlessness'. Recoiling before the horrors of the Nazi regime, Radbruch insisted that legal positivism must cede to natural law in certain contexts: 'Preference is given to the positive law [...] unless its conflict with justice reaches so intolerable a level that the statute becomes, in effect, *unrichtiges Recht* (false law) and must therefore yield to justice'.[37] Radbruch was writing about Nazi Germany, but as Pécherot's text reminds us, Vichy France enacted its fair share of unjust law. Interestingly, the question of

---

[35] For a different take on the bombing of Hiroshima – and its consequences decades later – see Jean-Marie Villemot's *L'œil mort* (1999).

[36] One might compare this with Malet's *Nestor Burma contre CQFD* (1945), in which Nestor Burma only jokes that he is a Jew (71).

[37] Gustav Radbruch, 'Gesetzliches Unrecht und übergesetzliches Recht', first published in the *Süddeutsche Juristen-Zeitung* 1 (1946): 105–8. Available in translation as 'Statutory Lawlessness and Supra-Statutory Law, trans. B. Litschewski & S.L. Paulson, *Oxford Journal of Legal Studies*, 26.1 (2006): 1–11.

whether Vichy legislation was, in fact, *unrichtiges Recht* in radical discontinuity with the past is one that is addressed by David Fraser and answered by him in the negative.[38] Fraser's argument that many lawyers remained in place after the Occupation, and that it was precisely these lawyers who were responsible for 'creating a category of persons [Jews] that could be exterminated but not murdered',[39] affords us a wholly different perspective on Malet's fictional lawyer, Montbrison.[40] Returning to Gorrara's critique of Malet's text, in which, as stated above, Malet's Burma is interpreted in terms of a symbolic reassertion of French mastery and identity in the face of defeat by the Nazis, one is also left questioning both the cost of that apparent 'mastery' and the potentially exclusive nature of 'French identity'.

Good and Bad Criminals: Redrawing Moral Boundaries

Where the previous section demonstrated how crime fiction stages different ethico-legal constructions of common, political, and state crime, the perspective now shifts specifically to the representation of criminals in the corpus, where 'criminal' in this case means as defined by pre-war French law. What happens, in other words, when common law criminals are written into a war / Occupation narrative? Usually represented as working class, and doubly marginalized by their extra-legal status, how do such characters 'fit' in a fictional world usually dominated by heroes and traitors? Is their marginality such that they shun patriotism? To what, if any, moral codes do common criminals subscribe in a context of radical socio-legal deregulation? Is the Occupation context represented as a catalyst for change (for better or worse, however these may be defined)? A first group of criminals will be seen to (dis)engage to varying degrees with war and patriotism whilst nonetheless stopping short of collaboration. It will then be suggested that a second, contrastive group of collaborating criminals turned *gestapistes* set the benchmark for a new moral code.

---

[38] Fraser, *Law after Auschwitz*. See also Thomas Mertens, 'But was it Law?', *German Law Journal*, 7.02 (2006): 191–8.

[39] Fraser notes that the vast majority of lawyers 'continued to operate on a daily basis as if they were in fact living under a system of law that was continuous with the system of law under which they had always worked' *Law after Auschwitz*, p. 152.

[40] See also the judge represented in Héléna's *Le Goût du sang* (E. Vinay, 1953): 'il avait toujours cru à l'autorité. [...] C'est ainsi qu'ayant, à l'origine de sa carrière, prêté d'abord serment à la République, il n'avait pas hésité, comme beaucoup de ses collègues, à prêter serment à Pétain, sans que sa conscience en fût le moins du monde chargée' (39) ['he had always believed in authority. (...) So it was that having at the start of his career sworn an oath of loyalty to the Republic, like many of his colleague he did not hesitate to swear an oath of loyalty to Pétain, without his conscience being in the least bit troubled']. The issue of legal (dis)continuity in Belgium is also raised by a lawyer in Berenboom's *Périls en ce royaume* (B. Pacuito, 2006), pp. 104–5.

'Good' Criminals

At one end of what can be identified as a representational spectrum, common criminals are depicted as being oblivious to, or actively repudiating, ideological engagement with the war, whether this be in the form of military combat or participation in Resistance activities. Criminal elements in the majority of texts are drawn from the working classes – what one of Siniac's characters graphically describes as 'les paumés, les lèche-crottes, les privés de tout' (*Sous l'aile*, 303) ['the marginal, the gutter dwellers, those deprived of everything'] – and anti-war sentiments are typically couched in terms of populist, class-driven antipathies. Héléna's protagonist, for instance, directs his wrath at officers: 'c'est comme ça qu'ils gagnent les batailles, avec la peau des autres' (*Le Festival des macchabées*, 241) ['that's how they win battles, with other people's lives'].[41] Siniac's ex-criminal legionnaire, fighting in Tunisia, targets the politicians: 'La sueur de mon front? Elle est sur ce champ de bataille ... et les politicards vont la foutre en bouteille pour la revendre à leur profit!' (*Les Morfalous*, 51) ['The sweat of my brow? I left it on the battlefield ... and the bloody politicos are going to bottle it and sell it at a profit!']. The object of contempt may remain unspecified, as when a dying criminal urges his colleague to make the most of the social upheaval occasioned by the war: 'Profite de leur guerre de merde' (*Sous l'aile*, 103) ['Make the most of their shitty war']. In all of these cases the enemy is displaced from outwith to within the social order: class conflict and social inequality are represented as being of greater significance to the common criminal than German occupiers.

Partial or comprehensive disengagement from the war extends beyond the battlefield to the context of Occupation where it often takes the form of an unequivocal rejection of patriotism by criminal characters: 'le patriotisme, je m'en fous. Mon pays, c'est mon portefeuille et ma police c'est mon Colt' (SVD, 21) ['I couldn't give a toss about patriotism. My country's my wallet and my police is my Colt']; 'ma patrie, c'est ma peau' (SVD, 120) ['my country, it's my own skin']; 'Mon pays, mon pote, il est là-dedans' ['a strong-box full of gold]' (*Sous l'aile*, 304) ['My country, mate, is right in there']. For most, the Occupation is represented as amounting to nothing more, or less, than an opportunity to pursue and indeed intensify criminal activities engaged in prior to the outbreak of war. As one character puts it, 'La loi, c'est fini' (*Sous l'aile*, 158) ['the Law's had it']; occupied Paris has become a land of opportunity where everything is possible (*Le Corps noir*, 38). Such swaggering assertions usually coincide with at the very least mockery, and as often instrumentalization, of the Resistance. Asked if he is part of the *maquis* as he forces a local at gun-point to supply him with petrol, Héléna's criminal protagonist opts for gentle irony: 'Oui, mon gros, je fais mon

---

[41]   For a discussion on this and other 1950s' texts which undermine the Resistance myth and 'portray French society during the Occupation as a battleground of cruelly competing interests', see Margaret Atack, 'Representing the Occupation in the Novel of the 1950s: *Ne jugez pas*', *Cincinnati Romance Review*, 29 (2010): 76–88 [81].

petit maquis tout seul, moi, je n'ai pas l'esprit grégaire' (SVD, 127) ['Absolutely mate, I'm resisting all by myself, I'm not the sociable type']. The leader of the Free French, de Gaulle, is demoted from iconic patriot to figure of fun: 'ç'avait été la Libération, avec un mec du genre grande asperge qu'on baladait partout' (*Au balcon*, 11) ['then it was the Liberation and a long thin beanpole of a bloke they paraded about everywhere']. Proclaimed indifference to the war may take the form of reducing its antagonists to the status of interchangeable actors, as when Héléna's narrator off-handedly considers a colleague's current occupation: 'Peut-être qu'il faisait partie d'un service allemand? A moins que ce ne soit le contraire et qu'il ne soit enrôlé dans la Résistance?' (SVD, 20) ['Maybe he was part of a German department. Unless it was the other way round and he'd joined the Resistance?']. Amila's crooks adopt an expedient approach by assuming different identities as the situation dictates: decorated resistant for some, and SS lieutenant for others (*Au balcon*, 77).[42] Being 'in the Resistance' may be represented as merely one of several options, a temporary role performed according to the fluid demands of changing circumstances: 'maquisard un jour, trimard le lendemain [...] patriote couci-couça, démerdard par vocation' (*L'Orchestre d'acier*, 23) ['in the *maquis* one day and on the road the next (...) sometimes patriotic, sometimes not, always looking after number one']. Masquerading as resistants may indeed facilitate further criminal activity. The bank-robbers at the centre of Amila's *Au Balcon d'Hiroshima* convince the local Resistance group of their patriotic credentials before stealing from and where necessary killing members of the local population. Taking sides is often purely for monetary gain: a trio of apolitical crooks and deserters in Siniac's *Les Sauveurs suprêmes* set out to rescue an important figure in the Italian resistance being held by the Germans in exchange for cash, duly killing members of the Allied forces who threaten to ruin their plan.

From what we have seen so far common criminals are for the most part represented as indifferent or hostile to the war or (and) in some instances, as self-conscious performers of roles drawn from the war narrative; these are characters who lack political conviction or any sense of national loyalty. But although this is the default narrative position, it is only part of the story. War and Occupation are also on occasion represented as contexts which precipitate either a re-evaluation of criminal morality, or, in some cases, a change of attitude. This pattern is typified by Héléna's wayward criminal, Maurice. Initially, the latter's code of practice and of honour transcends wartime categories:

---

[42]   In Fajardie's *Après la pluie* (1998), set in 1947, brothel doorman Maurice le Sourd, a former criminal, tellingly equates the two categories, much to the narrator's despair: 'fallait bien quelqu'un pour garder la boutique des fois que les fifis ou les fumiers de la Gestap' auraient eu des idées malsaines. / F.F.I., Gestapo: il avait beau être un brave type, il mettait tout dans le même sac' ['someone had to be there to keep an eye on things in case the Resistance or Gestapo filth got ideas. / Resistance, Gestapo: he may have been a good bloke but he lumped everything in together'], p. 74.

Je n'ai jamais fait de politique et tout ça me laisse complètement indifférent. Je n'aime pas qu'on me cherche d'histoires, c'est tout. Que ce soit truand, flic ou allemand, le premier qui m'embête, je lui rentre dedans [...]. (SVD, 120)

[I've never been into politics, the whole thing leaves me cold. I just don't like people hassling me. Whether it's a crook or a cop or a German, anyone who crosses me, I'll lay into him.]

Acting with honour means adhering to a pre-existing criminal value system which dictates, for example, that you do not kill the weak (SVD, 264), do not shoot people in the back (SVD, 165), and owe a debt to those who assist you. Morality, such as it is, is linked to a timeless, decontextualized construction of masculinity: forget the code of honour, and you are not a real man (SVD, 82). As Héléna's diptych unfolds, however, a change occurs. War appears to induce a process of ethical self-reflection: 'J'en arrivais à essayer de me définir, de me cataloguer moi-même, comme l'exige la morale bourgeoise' (SVD, 114) ['I got to the point where I was trying to define who I was, what type of person, as bourgeois morality dictates']. As *Les salauds ont la vie dure* moves towards its conclusion, Maurice develops distinct signs of patriotic spirit: 'je commençais à me convertir à une nouvelle morale et surtout à trouver un nouvel idéal, un idéal mêlé de haine et d'amour, un idéal de mort et d'espoir' (297) ['I began to convert to a new moral code and especially to find a new set of ideals, ideals where love and hatred met, ideals linked to death and hope']. The close of the text sees the former criminal join the *maquis*, don a tricolour armband, and scrawl '*République française*' over official notices referring to the '*État français*' (385). Patriotism meets populism as Maurice heads for the local bistrot because, as he puts it, that's how stories always end in France (385).

Héléna's representation of patriotic transformation is a knowing one which teeters on the edge of, without ever entirely toppling into, the satirical and parodic, and indeed the second volume of the diptych sees his protagonist reject what he calls Resistance zealots (FM, 242) in favour of a number of undercover missions. Maurice's attack of patriotism, as he comes to call it (FM, 242), can be compared to Siniac's indubitably 'harder', more cynical *noir* vision of criminality. Compare Héléna's writing of patriotism to, for instance, an ex-brothel mistress's proud assertion in Siniac's *L'Orchestre d'acier*: 'Je suis une patriote! [...] J'ai comme qui dirait une drapeau tricolore entre les gambettes!' (40) ['I'm a patriot! (...) You might say I've got the tricolour between my legs']. Or the last words of one of the criminal protagonists in *Au Balcon d'Hiroshima*, who dies 'dans l'ultime angoisse des existences ratées, minables petits artisans, simples "droits communs". – On aurait dû se faire patriotes, mec!' (172) ['suffering the ultimate anguish of those who have wasted their lives, wretched small-timers, simple common criminals – "Mate, we should have become patriots!"']. In all cases being or becoming a patriot – we could say moving from a crime to a war narrative – is represented as at best an ambiguous and ambivalent venture. What does emerge quite clearly, however, is the notion that war and Occupation can afford an opportunity to shift from the margins of society and assume a previously unacknowledged identity. Even Siniac's cynical protagonists make a clear distinction between criminals and French citizens: a crook must be distinguished from 'a real Frenchman' (*Sous l'aile*, 226). Indeed common criminals are on occasion described as quite simply not French: 'Pas des Français, des truands, des voyous. C'est pas tout à fait pareil. On est un peu d'un royaume à part, si tu préfères' (*Sous l'aile*, 305) ['Not Frenchmen, gangsters, crooks. It's not quite the same thing. Put it another way, we're kind of from a different world']. When Héléna's Maurice shoots a collaborating *gendarme* he is transformed in his own eyes from a hold-up merchant and common criminal to a French citizen (FM, 97).

As doubly marginalized characters, working-class criminals do not sit comfortably in a narrative favouring protagonists battling to defend their nation. Consequently, most of the common criminals represented in crime fiction set during the war and Occupation at best perform the role of resistant, and as often deride or instrumentalize a patriotic outlook. There are, however, exceptions, as typified by Héléna's protagonist Maurice, who turns into what crime critic Mandel might refer to as an 'outlaw hero' or 'poacher turned gamekeeper', both types the representation of which he correlates to 'growing scepticism about law and order, and the state'.[43] Mandel's theorizing of the 'good criminal' can be supplemented by a figure drawn from French popular – and populist – fiction: the 'mauvais garçon', or, literally, 'bad boy'. A small-time crook living on the margins of law and order, the 'mauvais garçon' embraces anti-bourgeois values; he is, in the words of Michel Rolland, symbolic of opposition to the mainstream moral codes.[44] But what does such an opposition constitute in the representational context of Occupied France? According to Rolland, it was precisely the war and Occupation which occasioned the demise of the 'mauvais garçon' in the 1950s:

> On ne peut, dans la recherche des causes de la disparition progressive du type, éviter le renvoi aux référents de l'époque récente: les voyous de la réalité qui avaient œuvré sous l'Occupation aux côtés de la Gestapo, ne permettaient guère que l'on réinscrivit sans inventaire le type dans la mythologie populaire.[45]

> [When investigating the causes of the gradual disappearance of the [mauvais garçon] type, one cannot avoid consideration of real cases from the recent past: the real crooks who worked alongside the Gestapo under the Occupation meant that the type simply could not automatically be reinscribed into popular mythology.]

Rolland, I think, overstates his case. Not all common criminals collaborated, and crime texts often represent both criminals who do and those who do not.

---

[43] Mandel, *Delightful Murder*, p. 132.

[44] Michel Rolland, 'Construction et métamorphose d'un type populaire dans la culture médiatique: le mauvais garçon', in Migozzi, *Le Roman populaire en question(s)*, 1997), pp. 37–45 [39].

[45] Ibid., p. 45.

Mandel links a possible return of the representation of the criminal as an 'object of sympathy' to perceptions of an increasingly corrupt State and a growing symbiosis between criminals and the police.[46] Let us transpose this to the context of Occupied France. In *Le Festival des macchabées* Maurice pronounces the following judgment just before killing a fellow criminal: 'Avant la guerre déjà, tu en croquais à la Préfecture. [...] Mais que tu sois passé au rang d'espion allemand, je l'aurais quand même pas cru' (FM, 165) ['Before the war you were a grass for the police. (...) But I'd never have believed you'd go so far as to become a spy for the Germans']. Maurice expresses what can be identified across a broad range of crime texts as a new moral code which serves to differentiate 'good' from 'bad' criminals. Although they do not necessarily quite achieve the status of Mandel's 'objects of sympathy', 'good criminals' – those who may be indifferent or hostile to the war and indeed to the Resistance, but who nonetheless stop short of collaboration – are certainly to be differentiated from their 'bad' counterparts. Writing on the criminal *milieu* of the war years, historian Grégory Auda objects to what he identifies as idealized representations of common criminals, stating that too many authors try to represent criminal codes of honour as if these 'virtues' alone earned criminals some kind of redemption.[47] As the following observations demonstrate, this does not usually apply to crime fiction's representations of 'bad' criminals.

'Bad' Criminals

> Les hommes du service pratiquaient le vol dans la plus pure tradition de leur milieu, à cette différence près que, bien qu'agissant en criminels – nous entendons par là sans approbation directe des autorités d'occupation –, ils étaient néanmoins couverts par leur carte du service et le soutien de Lafont.[48]

> [The men who worked in the department were thieves after the purest tradition of their background, with just one difference i.e. although they acted like criminals – and by that we mean without the direct approval of the occupying authorities – they were nonetheless covered by their official papers and by Lafont's support.]

Shortly after the armistice was signed the occupying forces, initially in the form of the *Abwehr* and subsequently under the auspices of the *Sipo-SD*, set about accumulating both material goods and information. 'Bureaux d'achats' – literally purchasing offices – were established as commercial fronts for what amounted to large-scale black marketeering (the 'marché brun' or brown market, so named after the colour of the German uniforms), counter-espionnage and counter-terrorism (i.e., counter-resistance) activities. The best-known of these was the

---

[46]   Mandel, *Delightful Murder*, p. 129.

[47]   Grégory Auda, *Les belles années du "milieu" 1940–1944* (Éditions Michalon, 2002), p. 206.

[48]   Ibid., p. 129.

'Bureau d'achat Otto' put in place by Herman ('Otto') Brandl and soon headed up by common criminal Henri Lafont (aka Henri Chamberlin aka Henri Normand), whose life had hitherto been dominated by a series of prison sentences. Not long after being introduced to Brandl, Lafont, who had recently escaped imprisonment thanks to a chaotic mid-exodus transfer, was deemed to be one of the most powerful men in Paris, gathering around him growing numbers of criminals whose release from jail he himself often secured. Based at 93, rue Lauriston, Paris, the *Carlingue* or 'bande Bonny-Lafont', so named after revoked police officer Pierre Bonny was engaged to run the administrative side of the 'business', prospered, progressively taking on the status of a parallel police organization (torture and assassination were not uncommon) before finally beginning to disintegrate in the early summer of 1944.[49] On 26 December 1944 Henri Lafont and Pierre Bonny were both found guilty of treason and executed. Theirs was just one example, albeit the most powerful, of several similar collaborating organizations out of which French *gestapistes*, many of them former common criminals, operated.[50]

Héléna's tepidly patriotically engaged character Maurice could be said to stand at one end of a moral scale of 'good' to 'bad' common criminals established within crime fiction set during the Occupation. Siniac and Amila, for the most part, represent more cynical, altogether antipathetic criminals, who for all their sustained rejection of patriotism are nonetheless clearly differentiated in the narratives from those criminals who collaborate. Other authors opt for the portrayal of those at the opposite end of the scale – common criminals turned French *gestapistes* – representing both fictitious and historically 'real' characters, most frequently Henri Lafont. In the majority of cases such criminals characters are placed in a Parisian setting, though common criminals turned *gestapistes* could be found throughout France (Del Pappas's *Bleu sur la peau* and Robert Merle's *Treize reste raide*, both set in Marseilles, for instance, are exceptions).[51] In many cases textual references to Lafont and his ilk are no more than fleeting. When Burma's secretary urges him to press ahead with a knotty case involving a certain fictional character Bramovici, Malet's P.I. retorts 'Pourquoi pas Joanovici, aussi?' (*Du rebecca rue des Rosiers*, 33), alluding to another notorious *gestapiste* and colleague of Lafont. One of the criminals in Manchette's *Que d'os!* is described as 'branché sur la rue Lauriston' (74); another, in Siniac's *Les mals lunés*, has similarly bad references: 'les méthodes de la Gestapo, ça le connaît. Pendant l'Occupation, il a trempé un

---

[49] For a biographical account of Pierre Bonny see Jacques Bonny's *Mon père, l'inspecteur Bonny* (Laffont, 1975).

[50] In his *2 sous d'amour* (subtitled '*une biographie du Milieu français sous l'occupation allemande*'), Auguste le Breton laments the fact that the pre-war criminal *milieu* was infiltrated by traffickers and collaborators such as Lafont; individuals who, he states, did not share the same code of honour as their pre-war counterparts and recognized only one law: that of money (12–13).

[51] For discussion of the French Gestapo operating in the provinces, see Jean Cathelin and Gabrielle Gray, *Crimes et trafics de la Gestapo française* (Historama, 1972), Tome I, Part 2 'La Province au pillage', continued into Tome 2.

peu dans la rue Lauriston ...' (40) ['he's familiar with the methods of the Gestapo. He got involved in the rue Lauriston during the Occupation ...'].[52] The 'la bande à Bonny' (61) is name-checked in Siniac's *Ferdinaud Céline*, and features as the 'carlingue' in Fajardie's *Querelleur* (126). In the case of allusions such as these, which function as a form of shorthand for extreme collaboration, the reader's historical knowledge seems to be taken as a given. More often, the interplay of fiction and history in texts which represent or refer to the 'bande Bonny-Lafont' proves to be revealingly complex.

Embodying most of the extremes of French collaboration, the 'bande Bonny-Lafont' has both assumed, and projects onto the host work in which it appears, a hybrid identity, situated somewhere in the generic hinterland between history, fiction, and myth. *Crimes et trafics de la Gestapo française*, for instance, may be presented as a historical work, but a chapter on Lafont and his group opens dramatically *in medias res*:

> 'Max, il faut me trouver des gens qui achètent à n'importe quel prix et nous vendent à n'importe quel prix toutes les marchandises de ce pays.'
> – 'Quels gens?'
> – 'N'importe qui, peu importe.'
> Tel fut le dialogue entre Otto Brandl et Max Stocklin, agent suisse de l'Abwehr [...].[53]

> ['Max, I need to get hold of people who'll buy anything this country's got for sale at any price and sell on to us at any price.'
> 'What sort of people?'
> 'Anyone, it doesn't matter who.'
> Such was the dialogue which took place between Otto Brandl and Max Stocklin, the *Abwehr's* Swiss agent (...).]

This in spite of an introduction subtitled 'In search of the truth' in which the authors insist that even very recent history must be treated like any other historical research.[54] In his *Les Belles Années du "milieu", 1940–1944*, a work of better (historical) pedigree, Auda on more than one occasion communicates an unease generated by the nature of his primary material. Lafont's (historically recorded) securing of the release of criminals from Fresnes prison on July 16, 1940, for instance, is described by the author as a hallucinatory scene of a sort more suited to a bad work of crime fiction.[55]

---

[52] See also Siniac's *Le Tourbillon* (1976), a complex tale of crooks and revenge which moves between the present (1970s) and the war years, and includes several characters who for various reasons found a place, if only a temporary one, in the bande Bonny-Lafont, 93, rue Lauriston.

[53] Cathelin and Gray, *Crimes et trafics*, p. 65.

[54] Auda, *Les belles années*, p. 17.

[55] Ibid., p. 59.

Other works featuring major French *gestapistes* also defy simple genre categorization: (crime) fiction or non-fiction? Roger Borniche's *Le Gang* (1975), which tells the tale of former members of the *Carlingue* (notably Pierrot le Fou, aka Pierre Loutrel), originates in an interview with Loutrel's sister and a police file (Borniche was himself a police officer), but the facts are presented in the form of fiction, with no paratextual flagging up of the historically real status of the author's chosen protagonists. Serge Jacquemard's *La bande Bonny-Lafont* (1992), published respectively by *Fleuve noir* and *Éditions Scènes de crimes*, is prefaced by the author's thanking those who provided accurate information without romanticizing ('romancer', a term which can also suggest 'making into a novel') or misrepresenting the facts. The text adheres to the chronology of Lafont's biography and to historical fact, whilst sounding different generic notes:

> Ainsi s'achève dans ce décor sordide, par ce sombre matin d'hiver, l'épopée d'une bande de malfrats et de dévoyés que n'avaient pas émus les malheurs de la patrie, et que l'esprit de lucre avait entraînés aux pires extrémités de l'horreur et de la trahison (174).

> [Here, in this sordid setting, on a grim winter's morning, concludes the epic tale of a group of thugs and delinquents who remained untouched by their country's suffering, and who were led by a base desire for wealth into the worst excesses of horror and treachery.]

Collaborating criminals appear as epic (anti-)heroes: Borniche echoes Jacquemard's choice of words when he refers to 'la triste épopée de l'un des hommes les plus dangereux de notre époque' (11) ['the dismal epic tale of one of the most dangerous men of our time']. Manifesting a further unfixity of genre boundaries Alphonse Boudard's *L'Étrange Monsieur Joseph* (1998), which traces Joanovici's wartime biography, is labelled a 'récit' or 'account' (whether fictional or historical is left unspecified). The back cover states that Alphonse Boudard carries out an inquiry into one of the most enigmatic of characters ('personnages'). These are interesting ambiguities: the 'inquiry' is both that of the historian and the writer of crime fiction; 'un personnage' can signify either a high-profile public figure or a fictional character. Lafont, Joanovici, and company are 'larger than life' figures whose biographies constantly threaten to exceed the frame of historical narratives: as Auda notes, their exploits seem to belong more properly to the world of crime fiction. How then do crime writers choose to represent them? Five texts written over a 40-year period reveal consistencies in two areas: Lafont and other renowned *gestapistes* are used as a yardstick against which to judge other criminals and crimes; historical and fictional discourses are collapsed or forced into collision.

Siniac introduces the historical figure of the big-time *gestapiste* into *Sous l'aile noire des rapaces* just as the crime narrative is drawing to its conclusion. Labeyrie, one of the fictional perpetrators involved in the attempted theft of gold bullion, leaves Paris for La Rochelle to locate his former colleague in crime, Torgier, and proceeds to laud his new boss: Henri Lafont. Compared to the sheer scale of the latter's organization, the criminal activity detailed up to this point is regarded as trifling indeed: 'les vols comme on a tenté d'en faire [...] c'est de la connerie. Par contre, tu vois, avec Lafont, eh bien ...' (346) ['the kind of jobs we've been trying to pull (...) are just bullshit. With Lafont though, let me tell you ...']. The ellipsis speaks for an already near-mythical status. Siniac, who entitles this chapter 'Le collabo', elaborates a clear moral divide: Torgier expresses disgust rather than admiration for his former colleague's latest activities ('Alors tu travailles pour les Chleuhs', p. 343) ['So you're working for the Hun']; the author disposes of his 'bad criminal' – we are told in perfunctory manner on the penultimate page that Labeyrie is executed at the Liberation – whilst sparing Torgier. Written four decades later, Pécherot's *Boulevard des branques* establishes the same distinction. Riton, the murderer in the crime narrative we read, warns P.I. Nestor Bohman and police officer Bailly of darker criminal times to come: 'C'est que le début. [...] Y'a plus de prison assez balaise pour eux. [...] C'est l'heure des truands' (275–6) ['It's only the beginning. (...) There's no prison secure enough to hold them (...). It's time for the gangsters to rule']. The era of the common criminal has given way to that of the criminal turned *gestapiste*. In the new criminal economy characters such as Riton and Torgier are demoted (or promoted?) to the status of almost amiable amateurs.

Mazarin's *Collabo-Song*, which features members of both Lafont's gang and that of Georges Delfanne (aka Christian Masuy), also represents the moral bankruptcy and unprecedented nature of this new breed of criminal, in this case via the downfall of the protagonist, who initially at least has no concept of French *gestapistes* and their powers. As Auda points out, the expression 'French Gestapo' has the potential to shock.[56] Unlike Siniac and Pécherot, Mazarin chooses to represent and not merely allude to Lafont, Masuy, and several members of Lafont's band (including Abel Danos, Adrien le Basque, and Nez-de-braise), balancing extensive dialogue with historically accurate information. Fictionalized exchanges such as '– Abel Danos. / Mes amis m'appelent le Mammouth' ['Abel Danos. My friends call me Mammoth'], or 'Danos devient sérieux. / – Pourquoi tu viens pas avec nous chez Lafont?' (130–31) ['Danos grew serious. "Why don't you come with us to Lafont's?"'], sit alongside informative comments passed on to the naïve protagonist – and the reader: '– Edmond [the protagonist's husband] a été arrêté par un service parallèle de la Gestapo qui opère sous couvert d'un bureau d'achat de l'Abwehr' (93) ['Edmond's been arrested by an unofficial Gestapo section operating under cover of one of the *Abwehr's* purchasing offices']. There is, however, no paratextual material to indicate where fiction starts and stops. Just as with the works written by Borniche, Boudard, and Jacquemard, crime fiction representing Lafont and the *gestapistes* typically conflates – in the case of readers unfamiliar with Lafont and others – fiction and history.

---

56   Auda, *Les belles années*, p. 23.

Siniac's *Sous l'aile* is punctuated by a timeline of historical events which is set apart from the diegesis and serves to contextualize the fiction: for instance, '20 juin 1940 / Bombardement de Bordeaux. / La défaite est presque totale. / Les Allemands entrent en Gironde' (293) ['20 June 1940 / Bombing of Bordeaux. / Defeat is almost total. / The Germans are entering the Gironde']. In spite of this chronicling gesture towards history there is no indication anywhere in the text that Lafont is anything but a fictional character; many readers will assume that that is precisely what he is. Compare this to Manotti's *Le Corps noir* which represents Lafont and several of his fellow *gestapistes* alongside an entirely fictitious rival gang. Like Siniac, Manotti introduces a differentiated element of historical discourse into her work: each chapter is prefaced by a date (the text runs from 6 June 1944 to 25 August 1944) followed by a short italicized account of key wartime events. Some two thirds into the text Lafont, having hitherto appeared on the same footing as the fictional characters, appears in the italicized text, doubtless to the surprise of a fair handful of readers: 'Mercredi 2 août. *A Paris, Lafont brûle les archives de la Carlingue, rue Lauriston. [...] A l'est, sur le front nord, les troupes soviétiques prennent Kaunas [...]*' (210) ['Wednesday 2 August. *In Paris Lafont is burning the archives of the Carlingue at rue Lauriston. (...) In the East, on the northern front, Soviet troops are taking Kaunas*']. Lafont the 'personnage' – real historical figure and / or fictional character.

Adding to the layer of historical discourse which takes the form of dates and key historical incidents in *Le Corps noir* is a paratextual note from the editor on the historical context of the novel which closes with a reminder of the scale of criminal collaboration in Occupied France: 'En 1944, il y a en France 1,800 Allemands membres de la Gestapo et 30,000 auxiliaires gestapistes français' (8) ['In France in 1944 there were 1,800 German members of the Gestapo and 30,000 Gestapo auxiliaries of French nationality']. Compare this to Pécherot, who unlike Manotti, elects not to represent or even refer explicitly to Lafont in his *Boulevard des branques*, though an unusually well-informed reader might take note when P.I. Bohman is informed that Maillebeau, a key suspect, has unexpectedly been released from jail (290). [57] The text does, however, come complete with an epilogue which ostensibly complements the fiction in the form of historical information: the existence of the *Carlingue* is mentioned; it is stated that Henri Lafont was responsible for the release of the criminal Maillebeau (this should, historically speaking, read as 'Maillebuaux'), and that Lafont and Bonny were both executed (295–6). Again, we have a shift from fiction to history: for most readers this will be the first indication that Maillebeau is anything but a 'personnage' in the purely literary sense, and probably the first time too that they grasp the historical reality of the power of some common criminals during the Occupation. Like all good crime fiction writers, Pécherot introduces a twist in the very last lines of his paratext. Having provided his historical material in suitably pedagogic manner, he

---

[57]   Maillebuaux is described by Auda as one of the pillars of Lafont's band, *Les belles années*, p. 64.

closes with a conflation of discourses: 'Emprisonné à la Santé, Nestor en sortit un mois plus tard. […] Envoyé au stalag, il s'en évada en mai 1941, mais cela est une autre histoire' (296) ['Jailed in *La Santé*, Nestor left the prison a month later. (…) Sent to a *Stalag* he escaped in May 1941, but that's another story']. And indeed it is, since Malet's *102, rue de la gare* opens with Nestor Burma's escape from a stalag; *Boulevard des branques* is thus established as a prequel. Histoire (history) and histoire (story) collide.

This section has suggested that crime fiction set during the Occupation is consistent in establishing a moral scale of criminality calibrated not in terms of the perpetration of varying types or degrees of codified common crimes but rather in relation to values drawn from a war or Occupation narrative: the 'bad' criminal is defined not by his (and it is invariably his) breaking of the law or disruption of the social order but rather by his collaboration with the occupying powers. 'Good' criminals, who may be murderers and thieves, regain some of the moral high ground to the extent that they maintain some remnant of national – if not quite patriotic – loyalty. The corpus also shows that a certain group of historically 'real' criminals, most often members of the *Carlingue*, are often used to represent the 'bad criminal' born of the Occupation, and that the nature of their (real) wartime activities is such that it can be inserted into a work of crime fiction with little, if any, fabulation. As historian Auda notes almost apologetically at the very start of his work on the French *gestapistes*: 'tous les ingrédients du roman noir sont ici rassemblés' ['all the ingredients of the crime novel can be found here']; 'la vie même des protagonistes s'apparente par bien des aspects aux plus sombres polars: pouvoir et trahison, histoires de sang et d'argent' ['the protagonists' lives are in many respects similar to those of the darkest of crime novels: power and betrayal, tales of blood and money'].[58]

The Occupation generated a social-legal order in which French criminals might knock on doors uttering the words 'Police allemande' or walk into the *Préfecture* demanding the release of fellow criminals. Set in 1946, Fajardie's *Après la pluie* (1998) follows an investigation into wartime economic collaboration and features two central fictional characters: Henri Sarcey, a *gestapiste* who operates out of the rue Lauriston and *commissaire principal* Darrigaud, who passes information to the Germans during the war. One criminal individual and one with police powers, but which is which? And who, in this crime fiction, is the baddie of the piece? In a moment of ironic self-abasement – 'Le mauvais Français que j'ai été et tout ça …' ['The bad Frenchman that I was blah blah'] – Sarcey mocks Darrigaud's (false) Resistance credentials and undermines his self-proclaimed status as 'un flic d'élite, un patriote vrai de vrai' (63) ['An elite cop, a patriot through and through']. As the next section will show, as was the case with crimes and criminals, representations of the French police under the Occupation inevitably show some departures from the 'norms' of crime fiction.

---

[58]   Auda, *Les belles années*, p. 12.

The Forces of Law and Order

Historian Jean-Marc Berlière is sanguine about (what should have been) the moral conflict faced by the French police serving in Occupied France:

> Servir l'État français, obéir à ses instructions, faire respecter ses lois – comme les y engageait toute leur culture professionnelle – va amener les policiers – tout en servant les intérêts de l'occupant – à transgresser clairement tout ce qui avait fait l'objet de leur mission pendant plusieurs décennies de démocracie.[59]
>
> [Serving the French State, following orders, enforcing the law – as everything about their professional culture engaged them to do – was to lead the police blatantly to go against what had been their brief for several decades of democracy whilst simultaneously serving the interests of the Occupying forces.]

Or, as a bit-part *inspecteur* puts it rather more laconically in San Antonio's *Laissez tomber la fille*: 'tout est déréglé. [...] Ce n'est pas drôle d'exercer un métier comme le nôtre à notre époque (41) ['everything's all over the place (...). It's no fun at all having a job like ours today'].[60] Representatives of the police in crime fiction usually fulfil certain functions, all of which relate in some manner to their position as representatives of the State and their consequent duty to enforce law and order. In broad terms, they fall somewhere between two poles: they may be positive moral figures opposed in the textual economy to the criminal elements (usually in the more conservative of texts); they may alternatively be flawed or corrupt to varying degrees and thereby contribute towards a critique of the prevailing socio-political order, in which case they often act as foils to a morally superior investigator figure, or morally ambiguous criminal. All of these roles are complicated in crime fiction which is subtended by the presence of more than one State and more than one legal system: does the police element represent – in both senses of the term – the (illegal in the eyes of some) Vichy government or the (illegal in the eyes of others) exiled Republic? Perhaps, indeed, the State in question is that of the Third Reich. Partly but not wholly correlative to the question of 'which state' is that of 'which police'. It might be a French *gendarme* rejecting Vichy: 'Je m'en tamponne. Il [le gouvernement de Vichy] m'a assez cassé les pieds. Je suis aux ordres du gouvernement légal. Je suis Français, non?' (*Le Festival de macchabées*, 227) ['I don't give a toss. Vichy's already done my

---

[59] Berlière, *Policiers français*, pp. 23–4.

[60] Harlay's *Le Sel de la guerre* (2008) comments on several occasions on the state of the police during the war: 'Tout le monde marchait sur des œufs. On ne comptait plus les mutations et les licenciements. La police judiciaire avait été rebaptisée police de sûreté, Darnand remplaçait Bousquet [...]. Même les Allemands avaient placé les pouvoirs de police entre de nouvelles mains. Un foutoir permanent. ['Everyone was tip-toeing about. There were endless transfers and sackings. The criminal investigation department had been renamed the department of security, Darnand replaced Bousquet (...). Even the Germans had placed police powers in new hands. It was a permanent bloody shambles'] (30).

head in enough. I serve the legal government. I'm French aren't I?']. Or a French *milicien* shooting French 'terrorists'. Perhaps, indeed, an officer of the *Abwehr* or the SS. In these works of crime fiction the 'forces of law and order' or indeed the 'police' can refer to several, often ideologically opposed, official or semi-official bodies (such as the French *gestapistes* already discussed). Assuming a degree of historical accuracy, fictional representations of the relationship between police(s) and State(s) also depend to some considerable extent on when during the Occupation texts are set. Works of crime fiction may represent relations under the terms of the armistice, or those which prevailed subsequent to the Bousquet-Oberg agreement of August 1942 which saw apparently greater autonomy granted to the French police but at the cost of an increased repression of 'terrorists'.[61] They may be set before or after the occupation of the southern zone in November 1942. By the time Darnand's *milice* took over in late December 1943 legal and social deregulation had reached an apogee; no legal constraints seemed to remain, with some areas of France operating more and more like a police state.[62] Clearly there is considerable scope for the representation of 'the' forces of law and order, but certain patterns in works of crime fiction can be identified.

First, members of the police who support the (superseded or suspended) Republican State or those who merely attempt to carry out their duties but do so without heeding the changing circumstances are nearly always represented as moral figures – the 'good cop' – though ineffectual in the new order, and consequently often dead by the close of the text. Even in the skewed ideological fictional world of San Antonio, a democratically inclined police officer cannot express his views, serve the (former) state, and emerge unscathed: as we saw in Chapter 2, the protagonist San Antonio turns instead to the secret services. More typical of the 'good cop' is a figure such as Bailly in Pécherot's *Boulevard des branques*, largely disempowered by French *gestapistes* (see above). Siniac's *Sous l'aile noire des rapaces* features police officer Buranty, steadfast in his desire to defend the gold bullion belonging to the Bank of France, but finally disposed off peremptorily by the author in the closing pages, shot without a second thought by one of Lafont's men, having survived for months in the company of 'ordinary' criminals. Buranty's failure to grasp the fact that a new socio-legal order prevails – he displays no political affiliations – makes of him a flawed hero whose only reward is to receive a posthumous medal (356). Police officers largely stripped of their status as upholders of law and order also featured in Chapter 1 above, whether in the form of the passive *inspecteur* Kurt Hamling in Simenon's *La neige était sale* or by means of the symbolically deserted *préfecture* and *gendarmerie* in *Le Clan des Ostendais*.

---

[61] See Henri Longuechaud *Conformément à l'ordre de nos chefs. Le drame des forces de police sous l'Occupation* (Plon, 1985), p. 96.

[62] Berlière, *Policiers français*, p. 41.

The abrupt demise and posthumous be-medalling of Siniac's police officer is narrated from the point of view of a criminal character, albeit a 'good' criminal. Buranty's status as an honest and dutiful police officer might have been expected to set him up as the criminal's opponent in the textual economy, but in the corpus this place is now taken by the 'bad criminal' or collaborator. Héléna's diptych, narrated in the first person by increasingly good criminal Maurice, depicts a wide range of representatives of the forces of law and order including pro- and anti-Vichy *policiers* and *gendarmes* as well as *miliciens*. Apart from the character of the *milicien*, Héléna, like many other authors, does not attempt to name or differentiate between branches of the police specific to the Occupation context such as the 'brigades spéciales', or 'gardes mobiles': most often, as would be expected of a crime narrative, his protagonist refers merely to 'flics' or 'poulets' ['cops']. When it comes to encoding morality, however, as with Siniac's good criminal, Maurice's sympathies ultimately lie with the democrats: an anti-Vichy cop trumps a collaborating criminal; the Occupation narrative prevails over the crime tale norms.

The third and final common feature of crime fiction texts relates to an absence rather than a presence, and that is the relationship between the police and Jews. Although the latter are mentioned in some of the works which have been discussed so far in this chapter, these texts do not stage any extensive interactions between the French police and Jewish characters; there are no round-ups, nor do any members of, for instance, the specially created 'police aux questions juives' make an appearance. This notable absence can be explained in large part by publication dates: most of the texts set during the Occupation were published pre-1980, an era which preceded the awakening and cultural expression of Jewish memory in France. It is thus unsurprising that it is the most recently published text, Pécherot's *Boulevard des branques*, with its judaicized Nestor Burma / Bohman, which stages a brief encounter between French police and a Jew. As P.I. Nestor Bohman is led away by German soldiers the leader of the accompanying French police can only signal his impotence, shrugging to indicate that he can do nothing to help (294). Although it is outwith the remit of this chapter, it is important to note that later texts often acknowledge the by-now notorious role played by French police in the persecution and deportation of Jews. Thus, to give just a few examples, Abécassis's *L'Or et la cendre* (1997) includes a character named Maurice Crétel who is loosely based on René Bousquet; Bialot's *Babel-Ville*, like many other works set after the war, emphasizes the tainted legacy of the French police via a character's response to their latter-day avatars: 'Réaction conditionnelle. Depuis l'Occupation, mon grand-père a une réaction immédiate dès qu'il entend le mot "Police". Cela déclenche un réflexe irrésistible, il se cache' (139) ['Pavlovian reaction. Since the Occupation my grandfather reacts the second he hears the word "Police". It triggers an uncontrollable reflex: he hides']. As we will see in Chapter 5, a great many texts portray the police on the (extreme) political right and point to a continuity from the Vichy years through to the present day.

Finally, in this consideration of the representation of the forces of law and order, two almost contemporaneous texts stand out owing to their sustained focus on the French police(s) under the Occupation: one, already mentioned, is Manotti's *Le Corps noir* (2004); the other is Daeninckx's *Itinéraire d'un salaud ordinaire* (2006). Title notwithstanding – the 'corps noir' refers to the SS – Manotti's text represents a whole gamut of law and order enforcers, from the occupying forces and their French *gestapiste* auxiliaries to police officers working in the Parisian *Renseignements généraux* and the *Mondaine*. Manotti's text covers a short span of time (6 June to 25 August 1944) as the Occupation neared its end. By contrast, Daeninckx's *Itinéraire* follows the career of a single police officer, Clément Duprest, over a 40-year period from 1942 to 1981. Both texts raise questions about the French police and regime change, political engagement, individual responsibility ('I was only following orders'), and, lastly, genre.

Police officers serve the State, but what happens when a new, undemocratic regime is installed? Daeninckx's text is divided into two parts: 'Au service de l'État' and 'Au service de la République', and the blandness of the anaphoric titling is echoed in the author's dull protagonist who passes heedlessly from one regime to another, starting his career in the specially created anti-'terrorist' *Brigades spéciales II* in 1942,[63] before hunting down Communists post-war, members of the *Front de libération nationale* during the Algerian War, then May 1968 protestors.[64] The final words of the text serve to emphasize continuity in the eyes of the protagonist: 'Dans le taxi qui l'emportait vers l'inactivité, il se dit que s'il avait servi l'État puis la République, l'âge le mettait à l'abri d'avoir à servir la gauche' (386) ['In the taxi which carried him towards a life of leisure he told himself that he had served the French State then the French Republic, age at least saved him from having to serve the Left']. This is, specifically, represented as a continuity of the political right: Duprest leaves public office just before Mitterrand becomes President. Given the short time span which it represents, Manotti's *Le Corps noir* would not seem to be concerned with continuity, but the issue is addressed both intradiegetically and paratextually. For Manotti, the traceable line of descent from Vichy does not in fact stop at 1981 but rather continues into and indeed subtends Mitterrand's period in office: the generation in power right up until 1990, she suggests, was born of the legacies of the Resistance and

---

[63] Berlière, *Policiers français*, pp. 167–208.

[64] Daeninckx may have found his inspiration for Duprest's career trajectory in Maurice Rajsfus's *La Police de Vichy* (le cherche midi, 1995). Rajsfus ponders the hypothetical career of a police officer involved in wartime Jewish round-ups, the uprising of the Paris *préfecture*, the anti-miners' strikes of 1947 and 1948, the round-up of Algerians during the demonstration of 17 October 1961, and police charges against students during May 68. He concludes: 'À cinquante-cinq ans, cet honorable représentant de l'ordre pourra enfin prendre une retraite bien méritée après un vin d'honneur dans son commissariat, persuadé d'avoir été, durant plus de trente ans, un bon serviteur de son pays' (32): an ending very close indeed to that afforded to Daeninckx's protagonist ['Aged 55 this honorable representative of the forces of law and order will finally be in a position to take up a well-deserved retirement after a reception at the police station, convinced that he has served his country well for more than 30 years'].

the Occupation.[65] In Manotti's eyes, Daeninckx's protagonist would doubtless have thrived under the so-called left: the legacy of Vichy underwrote the Mitterrand *septennats*. It is worth noting that in fact, the final page of *Itinéraire* sees Duprest recognize René Bousquet heading into the newly elected Mitterrand's garden-party: the Vichy connection remains unstated but echoes loud and clear.

The capacity of the French police to serve the Vichy State is represented – and condemned – by both authors. According to Domecq, a Gaullist agent masquerading as a police officer and Manotti's hero (inasmuch as she has one), the French police will function under any government; continuity of service is assured by an inculcated frame of mind: 'Poids de la hiérarchie, culture de l'obéissance [...] Une culture propre à l'institution policière. Un très fort respect du gouvernement légal' (194) ['The weight of hierarchy, a culture of obedience (...) A strong respect for the legal government']. Serving the Vichy State, though, has its drawbacks. The police do not fare well in Manotti's crime fiction. 'Good cop' Ricout, one of two brothers, fails to grasp the realities of the new order and is killed by *gestapistes* in whose commercial affairs he attempts to intervene. As Domecq puts it, Ricout's earnest determination to do his job counts for nothing in a world where such an attitude has become utterly redundant (111). The 'bad' Ricout sibling, who like Daeninckx's protagonist is a member of the *Brigades spéciales*, and who stands by his political convictions to the end, is also written out of Manotti's script, thrown by unknown hands from a window of the Paris *Préfecture* in the course of the Paris police insurrection. In the *noir* world of Occupied France it is usually the pragmatists, those whose identity is suitably labile, who survive. Tellingly, the only significant character representing some form of law and order left standing by the close of Manotti's text is the *false* police officer, Domecq.

'Je suis un policier ... Je ne fais pas de politique, mon boulot, c'est de faire respecter la loi ...' (69) ['I'm a police officer ... I'm not interested in politics, my job is to enforce the law']. So speaks Daeninckx's Duprest, but at what point does the law and order enforcer become a criminal in carrying out his duty to the State? When Duprest is tried as a collaborator he disclaims all personal responsibility: the law recognizes the fact that a crime is not committed when immoral actions are carried out on the instructions of a legitimate authority (151–2). Once more we are back to a conflict between legality and morality, grist to the crime fiction mill, but more usually played out between a representative of the State and another, maverick character (usually an investigator figure of some sort). In 'real life', Duprest's involvement in certain wartime activities would have had more complex legal repercussions than the character proclaims. According to Article 3 of an *ordonnance* of 28 November 1944, a crime was not deemed to have been

---

[65]   See the interview at: <http://www.bibliosurf.com/Rencontre-avec-Dominique-Manotti> and F. Frommer and M. Oberti, 'Dominique Manotti: du militantisme à l'écriture tout en parlant politique', *Mouvements* 15/16 (2001): 41–7. Continuities between the war years and Mitterrand's presidency are also represented in Manotti's *Nos fantastiques années frics* (2001).

committed by a police officer (in this case) whose acts were strictly in compliance with, and did not exceed, orders received. However, as Berlière points out, Article 3 goes on to state that acts of collaboration, for instance, could not be justified if those in question had the capacity and opportunity to avoid carrying them out and if this refusal would have served the country.[66]

This of course raises further questions, and Daeninckx chooses to let his protagonist off the hook in order to make his point. Duprest, in his blind obedience, exemplifies Domecq's claim in *Le Corps noir* that there is no room in the police for critical thought or individual initiative (194). The protagonist's unthinking trajectory, communicated all the more forcefully by a third person narrative which rarely, if ever, affords the reader access to Duprest's thoughts (Manotti, by contrast, slips in and out of her protagonists' point of view), is reminiscent of what Hannah Arendt referred to as another famous law enforcer's 'thoughtlessness':[67] Adolf Eichmann, an SS *Obersturmbahnführer* and Clément Duprest, a (fictitious) French police officer; one embodying the 'banality of evil', the other a 'salaud ordinaire': both condemned, in different discursive contexts, as criminals.

Manotti and Daeninckx incorporate historical figures in their fiction: Lafont, but also, for instance, *préfet de police* Bussière in *Le Corps noir; commissaires* David and Tissot, René Bousquet, and Coluche in *Itinéraire*. Daeninckx demonstrates his close attention to historical detail – note, for example, his reference to a monthly bonus of 1,000 francs' danger money awarded to members of the *Brigades spéciales* (128) – whilst Manotti acknowledges the input of historian Berlière in her paratext. Both authors are writing well-informed historical fiction, but are they writing crime fiction? After all, we have already noted that the real-life exploits of many 'characters' from the Occupation years slot unaltered into works of so-called crime fiction. Questions can and have been posed in relation to the genre of both these texts. Daeninckx is known primarily as a writer of crime fiction but *Itinéraire* is published in Gallimard's 'blanche' edition. The cover blurb, in a bet-hedging move, describes the work as 'un roman psychologique noir'. For her part Manotti has stated that she did not think of *Le Corps noir* as a crime novel as there was neither an investigation nor any suspense. More a novel than a crime novel, she offered the text to Seuil publishers. Later, she realized she had been wrong in her genre analysis.[68] The cover of the *Points* edition bears the infamous SS insignia and is labelled 'Thriller'. These and indeed many other texts set during the Occupation introduce an additional factor to any attempt to define crime fiction. Although *Collabo-Song* – to take just one more example –

---

[66] Berlière, *Policiers français*, p. 55.

[67] Hannah Arendt, *Eichmann in Jerusalem. A Report on the Banality of Evil* (Penguin Books, 1994). For a discussion of Arendt's *Eichmann* in relation to a work featuring an SS officer (of mixed French/German parentage) and, indeed, two detectives, see my 'Jonathan Littell's *Les Bienveillantes*: Ethics, Aesthetics and the Subject of Judgment', *Modern and Contemporary France*, 18.1 (2010): pp. 1–15.

[68] <http://www.bibliosurf.com/Rencontre-avec-Dominique-Manotti>.

was first published by *Fleuve noire* in its *Spécial police* series, and won the *Grand prix de la littérature policière* in 1983, this is, arguably, a work which does not represent a single criminal act: denunciation and collaboration were not, at the time, crimes; Petiot's multiple murders are mentioned only in an epilogue. 'C'est un film policier!', exclaims one of the characters in Héléna's *Les salauds ont la vie dure*, to be met with the unperturbed reply, 'Oh! Vous savez, on en voit comme ça tous les jours. Nous traversons une drôle d'époque' (SVD, 279) ['It's like being in a crime movie!'; 'Oh, you know, things like that happen every day. We're living in pretty strange times']. Can texts which represent a historical period 'où la moitié du pays fait partie de la police tandis que l'autre moitié est résolument hors-la-loi' (*Les salauds ont la vie dure*, 76) ['where half the country are part of the police and the other half are operating outside the law'] be anything *but* works of crime fiction? Are all texts set during the *années noires* inevitably *noir*? Maybe, but as I hope to have demonstrated, the collision of two narratives – crime story and tale of war / Occupation – also produces a specific sort of fiction which interrogates the very categories on which it is usually grounded: crime, criminal, law and order, but also resistant, collaborator, black marketeer.

Recontextualizing Modiano: A First Step

Many of Patrick Modiano's texts would sit comfortably – and productively – in each if not every chapter of this book. Given the author's already extensive critical exposure, discussion of his work will, however, be limited to a brief discussion of *Dora Bruder* in the next chapter and, in what follows, *La Ronde de nuit* (1969).

La Ronde de nuit is a fragmented, hallucinatory first-person account of an unnamed young man's simultaneous involvement in both a Resistance network (though the word 'Resistance' is never used) and a group of French *gestapistes* (the word 'collaborator' is also studiously avoided). Formal fracturing and hyperbolic representation notwithstanding, there are obvious similarities with many of the other works of crime fiction discussed in this chapter. First, the *gestapistes*. Modiano is probably the first writer of fiction to represent the 'bande Bonny-Lafont', appearing here in the guise of *inspecteur* Pierre Philibert (= Bonny) and 'le Khédive', also know as Monsieur Henri Normand (104) (= Lafont). Amidst nightmarish images and grotesque freeze-frames Modiano inserts some informative elements, describing the group's function as that of a police service operating out of a 'bureau d'achat' (103) and those in it as one of the most formidable of the French Gestapo groups (152). More than any other text in the corpus (*Collabo-Song* would come closest) Modiano engages in sustained dramatization of his historical-fictional characters ('personnages'), from extensive dialogue to the eventual shooting of 'Lafont' by the narrator. As with other texts in the corpus, Modiano smudges the fiction / history boundary: there are no paratextual indications that these are historical characters and since it is the narrator, and not the author, who claims that he has invented nothing and that all the characters he mentions existed (133), the statement is unlikely to be taken at face value. Although *La Ronde de nuit* eschews the representation of police officers common to other texts, the narrator does point to the *gestapistes'* ability to act with impunity. We learn, for instance that Monsieur Philibert maintained working relations with former police officers such as Rothé [sic], David, Jalby, Jurgens, Santoni, Permilleux, Sadowsky [sic], François, and Detmar' (91). The author makes no attempt to bring to the reader's attention the fact that these are all historical figures, the majority associated with anti-Jewish measures, several of them executed after the war.

Modiano's representation of 'bad criminals', as I have called Lafont and his fictitious equivalents, may share some of the features found in the many other works of crime fiction, but the function of these characters in *La Ronde* differs. I have argued that in most other texts the *gestapistes*, whether real or fictional, serve as moral touchstones against which other characters can be judged: comparisons are invited, for instance, between the *gestapiste* and the 'good' (non-collaborating) criminal or the 'good cop'. In nearly all cases the *gestapiste* represents one of the worst examples of French collaboration and signals an unprecedented upheaval in the socio-legal order. The function of the *gestapistes* in *La Ronde* must be considered in relation to the narrator's position as 'double agent'. As in other texts discussed in this chapter, the Resistance is the subject of irony and mockery. According to the narrator the network's leader, the *lieutenant*, belongs to the burdensome race of heroes (71); his pompous patriotic speeches are undermined in the text by upper-case emphases (he speaks of Good, and Freedom). Héléna's Maurice (above) could not quite recall whether his friend had joined the Resistance or a German service (SVD, 20). Modiano's narrator moves not dissimilarly between *gestapistes* and resistants, wondering at one point whether the Khedive (Lafont) and the Resistance leader are not one and the same person (73). The narrator's almost aphasic indifference to the parts he plays seems to be summed up in a reprised phrase: 'un phare indiquait que nous étions à proximité de la côte. [...] Aucune importance' (120) ['A lighthouse showed that we were near the coast. (...) No matter']; 'Aucune importance. Je passais au milieu de cette agitation, raide comme un somnambule' (139) ['No matter. I wandered through all this upheaval like a sleepwalker']; 'Cette situation précaire m'empêchait de dormir. Aucune importance' (140) ['This precarious situation was stopping me from sleeping. No matter']; the refrain, however, is not particular to Modiano. In Chapter 1 we witnessed Simenon's criminal protagonist expressing not dissimilar sentiments. Many other texts echo the same words (what follows is merely a small sample): 'Ils avaient vécu une époque désespérée, une époque où rien ne paraissait avoir d'importance' (*Assassin, mon frère*, 122–3) ['They'd lived in desperate times, times when nothing seemed to matter']; 'Pour lui non plus, maintenant, les choses n'avaient pas beaucoup d'importance' (*Les Clients du Central Hôtel*, 72) ['For him too now nothing mattered any more']; 'Quelle importance?' ['What does it matter?'], 'Ça n'a pas d'importance' (*Les Clients*, 77 and 153) ['It doesn't matter']; 'Tout cela lui semblait sans aucune importance' ['From what he could see it mattered not a jot']; 'Tout ça n'a plus beaucoup d'importance' (51) ['None of that matters much any more']; 'Rien n'avait d'importance' (*Au balcon*, 23, 51, 164) ['Nothing mattered'].[69]

All this should seem very familiar, from the mockery of the idealism of the Resistance to the putative equivalence of resistants and collaborators to the taking on of different Occupation narrative roles. But there is one crucial difference. In the rest of the corpus it is the common criminal who assumes the role of the marginalized cynic for whom the war and patriotism have little meaning. In Modiano's case it is a well brought up young man (55), a individual who, as critics have long noted of Modiano's work, is a representative of the author himself. *La Ronde de nuit* may be set during the Occupation, but rather like *The Usual Suspects*, it is also an imaginative reconstruction at two removes. If Modiano's first-person narrator moves to and fro between the Resistance and the 'bande Bonny-Lafont' whilst engaging ideologically with neither it is not because of social marginalization (the working-class criminal) but what we might call diachronic marginalization: that of the uncomprehending second generation whom Modiano and his narrator represents. The common criminal in the corpus was, as noted above, regarded as 'not French', so it is perhaps unsurprising that Modiano's narrator should carry only a Nansen passport (140). In this textual economy the narrator-author *is* a criminal of sorts, guilty of betraying his nation via his inability to inhabit its constitutive Occupation narrative with its heroes and villains.

Finally, and very briefly indeed, how, generically, should we categorize *La Ronde de nuit*? Two popular critical guides on the text completely bypass its possible status as a work of crime fiction.[70] It is published in the Gallimard 'blanche' series, although in terms of 'content' alone it is no less a work of crime fiction that *Collabo-Song* (indeed it even offers up a P.I. agency as an added crime narrative feature). Perhaps we should call it postmodern crime fiction, anti-detective fiction, or metaphysical detective fiction.[71] Perhaps. As long as two points are taken into account.

---

[69]   Alan Morris comments on what he calls this leitmotif in *La Ronde de nuit*, noting that it also appears in several other of Modiano's works, *Patrick Modiano* (Berg, 1996), p. 92.

[70]   Bruno Doucey, *La ronde de nuit de Patrick Modiano* (Hatier, 2001); Denise Cima, *Étude sur La Ronde de nuit, Modiano* (Ellipses, 2000).

[71]   For readings of Modiano's texts as parodic or anti-detective or meta-detective fiction, see, for instance: Jeanne Ewert, 'Lost in the Hermeneutic Funhouse: Patrick Modiano's Postmodern Detective', in R.G. Walker and J.M. Frazer, *The Cunning Craft: Original Essays on Detective Fiction and Contemporary Literary Theory* (Western Illinois UP, 1990), pp. 166–73; Martine Guyot-Bender, *Mémoire en dérive: poétique et politique de l'ambiguïté chez Patrick Modiano* (Minard, 1999), especially 'Dérapage policier/dérapage historique', pp. 49–73; Akane Kawakami, 'Patrick Modiano's Unreliable Detectives', in Anne Mullen and Emer O'Beirne *Crime Scenes* (Rodopi, 2000), pp. 195–204; Kawakami, *A Self-Conscious Art. Patrick Modiano's Postmodern Fictions* (Liverpool UP, 2000), especially 'Being Serious: Modiano's Use of History', pp. 69–88 and 'Being Playful: Parody and Disappointment', pp. 89–108. For a more general discussion of parodic or metatextual crime fiction and closure (based on works by Robbe-Grillet, Butor, Perec, and Echenoz), see Simon Kemp's *Defective Inspectors* (Legenda, 2006), especially Chapter 3, 'Completing'.

Claims that the text is parodic or subversive of crime fiction should be, but often are not, based on an awareness of the breadth of crime fiction: a lack of closure or of a teleological plot, for instance, are not unusual in *noir* crime fiction. Suggestions that the text displays postmodern (or metaphysical) themes and is thus an example of postmodern crime fiction can be dangerous: self-consciousness and the disruption of historical and fictional boundaries, for instance, are not uncommon to crime fiction; a concern with false or multiple identity is typical of much crime fiction and especially likely to find a place in crime fiction set during the Occupation, a period when such metaphors of postmodernity tended to be literalized. Categorizing crime fiction once again proves to be far from straightforward. Furthermore, as I hope this brief (re)contextualization of a much discussed text demonstrates, expanding the critical field beyond the work of a single author can yield up new perspectives on familiar works.

Closing Statement

The primary aim of this chapter has been to reveal features common to a corpus of crime fiction texts which are set during the war, or more precisely, which represent life under the Occupation. Whether explicitly or implicitly all such texts highlight in various ways some of the legal and moral definitions and implications of acts perpetrated either during the regime of Occupation or at time of regime change or what might today be called transitional justice. The acts represented may be specific to the historico-legal context, such as collaboration, denunciation, or black marketeering, or more generic, most obviously, killing, and may or may not be designated as crimes. Putting it another way, the chapter examines what happens when a crime narrative of cops and robbers, or law enforcers and criminals, intersects with a war narrative of Resistance patriots, collaborators, nazi occupiers etc. in a setting marked by extreme legal and social deregulation.

What happens is that both narratives are called into question. A common criminal in a pre- or post-war world of Republican law and order may feature as a Resistance hero in a wartime narrative. He may equally reject or merely play such a part for the sake of expediency. Murder can become a patriotic act, and an apparently patriotic act can conversely be revealed to be motivated by self-interest. Upholding law and order for some means collaborating; for others, killing. The State itself may be regarded as criminal, its laws simply too immoral to be deemed lawful. Law and order, in any event, become problematic terms subject to multiple political points of view and conflicting legal codes. The same act can change status depending not only on either the perpetrator or the judging onlooker (for example, German soldier, pro- or anti-Vichy French police officer, member of the Resistance) but on the date of perpetration: denunciation and collaboration may retroactively become criminal acts of treason; an execution in the name of patriotism may revert to being plain murder. Already key to much *noir* crime fiction, the relationship between the legal and the moral is problematized further during the Occupation regime: is killing a German soldier less reprehensible than gunning down a collaborating Frenchman? Does the latter constitute murder? In times of war values have to be recalibrated: in comparison with the French *gestapistes*, the common crook can become something of a positive figure even if he rejects patriotism.

These representations of crimes, criminals, and those who seek to enforce laws remind us of something we already know but may, along with some critics and theorists of crime fiction, too readily forget: categories such as 'crime', 'criminal', 'law', and 'order' cannot and should not be reified; they are dependent on context, and to the extent that crime writers write realist fiction, they mould their literary creations to the specific social, political, historical, and legal specificities of the period. As we have seen, a particular context – in this instance that of the Occupied France of World War II and its immediate aftermath – will generate crime fiction with its own particular brand of cops and robbers, heroes and villains, legal and moral conflicts.

Chapter 4
Investigative Avatars

I, knowing nothing, put the Sphinx to flight,
Thanks to my wit – no thanks to divination!

—Sophocles, *Oedipus the King*[1]

Je ne suis pas, moi, un rédacteur de chiens écrasés, déclara le jeune Rouletabille dont la lèvre inférieure exprimait alors un mépris infini pour la littérature des 'faits diversiers.'

—Leroux, *Le Mystère de la chambre jaune*[2]

In Fred Vargas's *Un peu plus loin sur la droite* (1996) medieval historian Marc Vandoosler, who has been co-opted into the search for a putative murderer by the text's principal investigator, comes across an elaborate machine-sculpture. A firm cranking of the handle sets the engineered parts in motion and results in the ejection of messages printed on small pieces of paper: 'Vous brûlez!' (156) ['You're burning!']; 'Pourquoi non?' (156) ['Why not?']. Like all good historians – and crime fiction investigators – Marc recognizes the importance of directed enquiry: in order to profit from this mechanical Pythia he must first ask of it specific questions, though when he does, he is disappointed by the indeterminateness of the proffered answers. Towards the close of the text it is revealed that the divinatory contraption was erected not in the spirit of engineering enterprise, nor indeed as a means of harmless entertainment, but rather by the murderer, to cover the grave of one of his victims. Vargas's sybilline machine invites interpretation as a symbol of epistemological methodology and inquiry, and it is to the representation of the seekers of answers that we now turn. The previous chapter focused on the depiction of crime, criminals, and the different modalities of law and order during the war years. Discussion now shifts from perpetration to investigation and those enquiring figures who like Oedipus (though usually with less self-injurious consequences) eschew the prophetic in favour of hard graft and (supposedly) hard facts.

Some indication of the potential wartime particularities of the figure of the investigator have already come to light in previous chapters, most obviously in the context of the exploration of representations of the police under the regime of Occupation. We have also encountered, amongst other investigative figures, an uncanny (self)-investigating POW in Troye's *Meurtre dans un Olfag*, the eponymous

---

[1]   Sophocles, *Antigone; Oedipus the King; Electra* (Oxford UP, 1994), trans. H.D.F. Kitto, ll. 397–8.

[2]   Gaston Leroux, *Le Mystère de la chambre jaune* (Livre de Poche, 1960; first published 1908), p. 27.

commissaire San Antonio obliged temporarily to leave a compromised police force under Vichy in favour of secret service duties, and the creation of a Jewish version of Malet's P.I. Nestor Burma in Pécherot's *Boulevard des branques*. In this chapter attention is turned to *post-war* investigators caught up in war-related cases. Representations of the distrust aimed at the contemporary police force, regarded by some as besmirched by a wartime legacy of collaboration and anti-Semitism, have already been mentioned in the previous chapter. There is, of course, much more to be said of the depiction of police officers as post-war investigators, only some of which can be touched on here. In most if not all instances, authors create explicit connections between their present-day investigators and the war years. It may be, as is the case with *commissaire* Méribeau in Baumier's *Les Apôtres du néant* (2002), that the investigating officer quite simply harbours an (in this case unexplained) ethical and intellectual interest in the period: 'La Seconde Guerre mondiale, l'extermination des juifs d'Europe, ce n'était pas un point de détail, pour le commissaire. Une obsession plutôt' (103) ['The Second World War, the extermination of the European Jews, these weren't minor details as far as the police superintendent was concerned. More of an obsession']. Heading on a different tack, Fajardie, by including a black police officer, dubbed 'the black Devil' by some of the inhabitants of the small Normandy village at the centre of the investigation in *La Théorie du 1%* (1981), generates comparisons between wartime prejudice and present-day racism and raises the ethical spectre of France's colonial excesses. The fact that the investigating officer in Konop's *Pas de Kaddish pour Sylberstein* (1993) is a *pied-noir* and an observant Sephardic Jew has serious implications for his supposed neutrality in a case involving nazi atrocities.[3]

Although in these instances the link between post-war police investigators and the past is not a familial one, it is in fact the family connection which is most commonly exploited, and this in the case of all types of investigator. The principal police protagonists in Amoz's *L'Ancien crime* (1999) and Wagneur's *Homicide à bon marché* (1996), for example, are respectively the son of a French communist betrayed to the *milice* and the son of a former French POW who also bore the child of a young German woman (see below). In Jonquet's *Les Orpailleurs* (1993) it is an investigating magistrate who must live with the knowledge that her father sold the property of Jews during the war, whilst a lawyer on the case in Cayre's *Toiles de maître* (2005) confronts the problematic legacy of his Jewish father. The reader learns that the mother of private investigator Joe Dickman in Fajardie's *Après la pluie* (1998) was killed by the *milice* and that the father of Joly's investigator in *La Rage* (2002) was deported. It is a niece who seeks to piece together the facts of her aunt's wartime story in Couturier's *Sarah* (1997) and the grandson of a combatant who seeks out the truth concerning racism and black soldiers in the US army in Martin's *Jusqu'à ce que mort s'ensuive* (2008). Unsurprisingly given that

---

[3]   David Fraser discusses the case of Konop's police investigator Benamou in his 'Polarcauste: law, justice and the Shoah in French detective fiction', *International Journal of Law in Context*, 1.3 (2005): 253–6.

many of the texts are set some considerable years after the war, the investigators most often represent the second or third generation, though there are exceptions: Coulvin, a party apparatchik and one of the investigators in Jonquet's *Du passé faisons table rase* (1982), for instance, is a former deportee, as is the elderly investigator in Bialot's *La Nuit du souvenir* (1990).

Police officers and private investigators constitute two of the most common investigative avatars. With a variety to choose from, I have selected three other recurring figures which each represent different connections between the war years and the present: journalists; historians; investigating sons.

From *fait divers* to the Mediatization of History: Journalists and / as Investigators

In the context of French crime fiction the designation of a journalist as principal investigator goes back at least as far as Gaston Leroux and his master of deductive reasoning, Joseph Rouletabille. Occupying a position between the private and the public sphere journalists are useful devices for crime writers. Unlike ordinary members of the public, they may be granted access to crime scenes and privileged information, often entering into a symbiotic – if at times paradoxically also antagonistic – relationship with the police. Although they do not represent the State, journalists may well act as an interface between it and the private citizen, with some investigative journalists setting out precisely to reveal that which the State would prefer to keep concealed. In this respect, as Gorrara points out, they are not unlike a certain type of crime writer: 'Like an investigative journalist the *roman noir* writer seeks to uncover the "insider story" of social exclusion and deprivation and to expose the activities of powerful economic and political interest groups'.[4] Gorrara's comment indirectly foregrounds a critical facet of the journalist as investigator: unlike private eyes, police officers, or indeed most other investigator figures, journalists are also composers of a specific type of written narrative; they must construct or reconstruct a tale – whether of recent or past events – that will interest as well as inform the reading public. This is a brief which, as will emerge, has ethical as well as epistemological implications.

Before moving on to consider specific texts, a brief review demonstrates the range of roles and functions which journalists and the discourses of journalese more generally can assume. Journalists may play the lead investigative role: Laurent Laugier (aka 'Rouletabille' to his colleagues) in Merle's *Treize reste raide* (1997), for example, gets entangled in an investigation which has its roots in Marseille's wartime gangster culture; in d'Estienne d'Orves's *Les Orphelins du mal* (2007) Anaïs, recently out of journalism college, works with a mysterious stranger to unravel a baroque plot relating to the nazi *Lebensborn* programme. Tabachnik's Sandra Khan, a recurring investigator, uncovers links between the 'disappeared'

---

4   Gorrara, *Le Roman noir in Post-War French Culture* (Oxford UP, 2003), p. 78.

children of Argentina and a group of former nazis in *Tango des assassins* (2000). Chloé, a doctoral student of history and part-time freelance journalist, leads the way in Chaboud's tale of free-masonry and art theft, *Le Tronc de la veuve* (2003). A group of journalists seek out the truth of former nazi groups operating in collusion with various government agencies in Renaud's *Morts à l'appel* (1995). The journalist may assume the (usually mutually rewarding) role of 'helper', as typified by Malet's recurring character Marc Covet, working in tandem with P.I. Nestor Burma.[5] The range of cases in which journalism more broadly defined plays a part can easily be expanded. Redonnet's minimalist *Nevermore* (1994) includes successive unscrupulous newspaper editors and their publications (named generically 'La Gazette' and 'La Bataille'). Krivine's *Un souvenir de Berlin* (1990) opens with news of a missing journalist working for French television station *Antenne 2*, whilst police inspector Cadin in Daeninckx's *Meurtres pour mémoire* (1984) tries to locate film footage of the infamous 1961 Algerian demonstration in Paris shot by a Belgian TV magazine programme. Finally, texts may represent journalists from the war years: Dard's *Une gueule comme la mienne* (1958) traces the vicissitudes of a former collaborationist journalist's return to public life under a false identity in the late 1950s; Modiano's *Les Boulevards de la ceinture* (1972) sees the narrator (an aspiring author) invited to contribute to collaborationist magazine *C'est la vie*; Simenon's *Les Autres* (1962), as discussed in a previous chapter, represents cousins – one of whom is responsible for the deportation of the other – working together on news magazines published both during and after the war.

There is an abundance of material to be tapped here, but a further selection has inevitably had to be made. The texts chosen for closer analysis cover a publication span of over 50 years, allowing for the identification of both constants and variants in the functions of the journalist-investigator. Introduced in the previous chapter, Blond's *L'Ange de la rivière morte* (1946) features a young journalist coerced into reporting on a triple murder. A 40-year publication gap takes us to the next two texts: Daeninckx's *La Mort n'oublie personne* (1989), also touched on in Chapter 3, and Delteil's *KZ Retour vers l'enfer* (1987), set predominantly in a concentration camp, both framed narratives comprising narrative reconstructions of the past orchestrated by a journalist-investigator. Finally, Abécassis's *L'or et la cendre* (1997), something of a compendium of French war-related events and figures with the Holocaust at its core, represents a journalist in a key investigative role as well as alluding to the mediatization of war-related 'affairs' in 1990s France.

Discussed solely from the point of view of perpetration in the previous chapter, Blond's *L'Ange de la rivière morte* includes three murders, two of women killed for their black-market hoards, and one of a certain Pierre Marglat, a former resistant whose death and disfigurement are conceived as part of an attempt to

---

[5]   For a discussion of the Burma / Covet relationship see Emmanuel, *From Surrealism to Less-Exquisite Cadavers* (Rodopi, 2006), pp. 103–12. In Malet's *Du rebecca rue des rosiers* (1957), a different journalist, Jacques Ditvrai, features first as a suspect then as a victim.

frame him as the killer of the other two victims. But what of the investigators' role in this case? First-person narrator Robert Norrey, a sports journalist, is bullied by his editor into departing from his normal sphere of activity and reporting on the murder cases. It is with some reluctance (he professes a complete lack of interest in crime) that Norrey initially follows the rather lacklustre police team, then private investigator Pierre Bertrix, whose help the police elicit when the case founders. Norrey, Bertrix, and a third character, newspaper editor Combes, can be regarded as figures occupying varying ethical and epistemological positions in relation to the acts of investigation and narrative (re)construction.

It is Norrey's editor, Combes, whose rubric-oriented categorization of the murders raises the first point of interest. For the editor the killings constitute a welcome distraction for his newspaper's readers who, as he puts it, are sick to the back teeth of politics (17). Explicitly contrasted to and excluded from the realm of the political, which is exemplified by the editor as endless assassinations by men wielding machine-guns (17), the murders are to feature under the 'faits divers' rubric – indeed Norrey is instructed to take up the reportage because his 'camarades des faits divers' ['colleagues working on the "news in brief" column'] are busy working on other stories. The implied distinction between the 'fait divers' and 'la politique' cannot but bring to mind Barthes's essay 'Structure du fait divers' in which he differentiates between those killings which are to be classified as 'faits divers' and the 'assassinat politique', contrastively defined as 'une information' or (serious) news item.[6] According to Barthes, killings which can be designated as 'faits divers' are those which are severed from pre-existing narratives; unlike the 'information' or news item, they fit into neither 'un horizon nommé' ['a specific context'] nor 'un temps antérieur' ['a prior temporal framework'].[7]

Combes's categorizing act interrogates both our perception of wartime events and Barthes's essay: when, how (if at all) might the murder of a black marketeer become 'une information'; when and how would it cease to be, as Walker defines the 'fait divers', 'inédit'?[8] As for the unspecified machine-gun killings – unofficial purges of suspected collaborators? – Blond's incorporation of Combes's classification seems to suggest that these had already established themselves as part of a familiar narrative in the months following the Liberation, when the text is set. What, one wonders, would it mean to state that such 'political' shootings were part of a Barthean 'horizon nommé' or 'temps antérieur' in 1944? Perhaps such incidents featured as lead stories in the press; but which press, and under what rubric? Perhaps the rather vague Barthean 'horizon nommé' might

---

6   Barthes, 'Structure du fait divers', *Essais critiques* (Seuil, 1964), pp. 188–97 [188].

7   Barthes, 'Structure du fait divers', pp. 188–9.

8   David Walker, 'Writing between *fait divers* and *procès-verbal*', *French Cultural Studies*, 12 (2001): 237–51: 'One might propose that the *fait divers* and the *procès-verbal* are two avenues whereby the *inédit* enters the world of discourse. The term *inédit* suits my purpose since it signifies, as well as that which has not yet been subjected to the process of publication, something which is new, somewhat surprising and unsettling', p. 240.

be understood to include less tangible inscriptions of events into public memory. And what are we to make of the fictional framing and murder of resistant hero Pierre Marglat, a character whom we learn listened to Russian radio, favoured the poetry of Louis Aragon, and, just maybe, travelled to Russia as well as England in 1943 and early 1944? Although he is the murderer's intended scapegoat, little if any political capital is made of this in Blond's 1946 narrative (a year in which the French Communist Party still enjoyed huge popularity, though their days on the public scene were numbered). As we will see below, in subsequent decades the killing of such a potentially politically charged character would without doubt have found its place in a Barthean 'horizon nommé' as France began to question the credentials of its one-time unimpeachable Resistance heroes.

Combes's standpoint gives us pause for thought concerning which wartime events qualified as news(worthy) when, and in the eyes of which readership. As Rousso reminds us – though he does not pursue the issue of potentially competing or conflictual inscriptions of the war into different narratives – the press stands alongside history books, public commemorative events, novels, and film as a powerful 'vector of memory.'[9] Beyond this, the fictional editor's behaviour also highlights the inevitable imbrication of the ethical and the epistemological. Combes is, we might say, an anti-investigator. Where the investigator seeks truth and closure, the newspaper editor desires the endless renewal of the unusual and the deferral of closure. For him, the imperative lies not with the reconstruction of the (recent) past of the crimes but with the 'now' of the new. Norrey is duly dispatched to write pieces that can be readily consumed and leave the audience wanting more; indeed Combes's unethical stance extends to suggesting that his junior journalist produce an 'article posthume', just in case he is killed on the job (160). Nothing, not even death, stands in the way of a good story. Barthes describes the 'fait divers' as 'une information *monstrueuse*',[10] a qualification which is echoed in *L'Ange de la rivière morte* where it is linked synecdochically to the perpetrator and his crimes – 'le monstre a continué' (80) ['The monster continued']; 'crimes monstrueux' (101) ['Monstrous crimes'] – but also, significantly, to Combes: 'ce monstre, ce génie de la littérature journalistique' (49) ['that monster, that genius of journalistic prose']; 'Le monstre savait tout' (198) ['The monster knew everything'].

Where Combes's search for a narrative can be read as morally tainted, P.I. Bertrix's questing stands at the opposite end of the ethical scale. Of particular note is the description of his set-piece explanation of the crimes and designation of the perpetrator (the local landlord) at the close of the text: 'l'impitoyable et rigoureuse *démonstration* du détective faisait apparaître les faits dans leur horreur morale avec une objectivité absolue' (302, my emphasis) ['the detective's merciless, rigorous demonstration made the facts appear in all their moral horror

---

    9   Rousso, *Le Syndrome de Vichy* (Seuil, 1990; first edition 1987), 'Les vecteurs du syndrome', pp. 251–308.
    10   Barthes, 'Structure du fait divers', p. 188.

with absolute objectivity']. The 'dé-monstration' or undoing of the monstrous is here associated with the emergence of truth and the closure which comes of a reconstituted narrative. The reconstruction of the past, the 'discovery' of facts and the possibility of absolute objectivity are taken as givens and linked to justice: Bertrix's revelation of the criminal's motives and methods concludes with the latter's assumed removal from the community: '"Emmenez-le", dit le commissaire' (307) ['Take him away, said the police superintendant']. But where does Norrey stand? A crime journalist *malgré lui*, he can be positioned between Combes's unethical disregard for the past and Bertrix's ethical yet implausible (*invraisemblable*) cerebral detachment. Blond's text is, I would suggest, typical of crime fiction in its depiction of love or desire as a trope figuring the inevitable epistemological obstacles faced by those who attempt to reconstruct the past. Norrey's inability to match the P.I.'s objectivity is manifested when he falls for *femme fatale* Lydie and withholds evidence from Bertrix in the mistaken belief that the object of his affections might be compromised. The journalist's impetus to seek out the truth is there – Norrey berates himself repeatedly for his unethical behaviour – but human frailty cannot be denied. Norrey is also a character with an apparently divided nature. That part of himself dubbed 'Le bibliothécaire Norrey' ['Norrey the librarian'], which is drawn to 'le classement et les archives' (218) ['classificatory and archival work'] is complemented by a Norrey who is 'furieusement engagé dans l'action' (280) ['frantically caught up in the action']. Bertrix may represent the impossible purity of mind, the Poirot-esque little grey cells of ratiocination, but it is the journalist, – whose dual nature we will encounter again – who symbolizes the necessarily flawed, because embodied, reality of the tasks of investigation and reconstruction.

Journalists have often been cast in the role of helper and scribe for the main investigator,[11] and though Norrey is actively involved in the investigation ('Norrey agissant'), he is also a writer of narratives. For Combes a good story is one which pulls in the paying customer; for Bertrix it is a scrupulous chronicle of past events, but what of the journalist's tale? In fact, Norrey produces several written narratives. We are told that one (or indeed several) accounts appear under a pseudonym in the 'faits divers' rubric of Combes's newspaper, there to entertain those (intradiegetic) readers weary of 'political' items. We are left to imagine the precise nature of these texts. A longer piece describing the vicissitudes of the case but excluding Norrey's part in it, described in passing by the journalist as 'mon récit – vu de l'extérieur' ['my story – as seen from an outside point of view'], is also published in the paper.

---

[11]   For a discussion of the role of journalists in turn of the century US crime fiction see Leroy Panek, *The Origins of the American Detective Story* (McFarland & Co. Inc., 2006), 'Journalists and Journalism', pp. 111–31. Panek concludes his chapter: 'As appropriate as they seemed for the role, reporters never really made the grade as heroes in turn of the century detective fiction. They did pretty well playing second fiddle, acting as Watsons [...]', p. 130. In a self-conscious gesture to the genre Blond's Bertrix informs Norrey that he does not intend to play at Sherlock Holmes, adding 'et d'ailleurs, vous n'êtes pas ce idiot de Watson' (143) ['and besides, you're not that idiot Watson'].

Norrey, finally, is the writer of the first-person account we read, which as well as describing his involvement in the cases reads as a confession of his love.[12] Alluding to their capacity to fit into a pre-existing narrative, Barthes describes those news items such as political crimes which are explicitly contrasted to the 'fait divers' in the following manner: 'littérairement ce sont des fragments de roman' ['In literary terms they are fragments of a novel'].[13] Norrey's account is, of course, also the crime novel we read, as summed up paratextually on the back cover: 'Trois crimes affreux. Le suspense policier est remarquablement conduit, attachant jusqu'à la dernière page' ['Three terrible crimes. The suspense of the crime story is handled with remarkable skill, gripping the reader to the very last page']. *L'Ange de la rivière morte* stages the constructed nature of categories and the force of discursive contextualization as wartime figures and phenomena – in this case the resistant, the black market – are inserted into various narratives, from apolitical 'fait divers' to love story to – by the time of our reading – re-politicized crime fiction. This intradiegetic inscription of potentially reified wartime figures into different narrative contexts – for instance the written press and other media, fiction of various genres, historical works – which may complement or compete with each other, is, as will emerge below and in the following chapter, a feature of the corpus.

Daeninckx's *La Mort n'oublie personne* (1989) and Delteil's *KZ Retour vers l'enfer* (1987) have in common not only with each other but with Blond's *L'Ange de la rivière morte* the device of the journalist as first-person narrator, and the uncovering and subsequent narration of wartime events relating to the establishment of the guilt or innocence of a former member of the Resistance. There are also significant differences between the later and earlier texts, not least that of temporal distance: the near-contemporaneity of crime, investigation, and reconstruction in Blond's work dilates to an interlude of over four decades in the case of the later texts, which though set in the late 1980s both stage the reconstruction of events dating back to 1944. The 40-year gap in publication separating *L'Ange de la rivière morte* from *KZ Retour vers l'enfer* and *La Mort n'oublie personne* also marks significant changes in attitudes towards 'the Resistance' in France. By the late 1980s this mythified and mythical collective had endured various travails – Rousso refers to systematic attacks which were sometimes justified and fair and sometimes not[14] – and had been rewritten into a series of disparate narratives: from

---

[12]   In Gérard Delteil's *Mort d'un satrape rouge*, set in the 1990s and centring on the murder of a Communist mayor suspected of having sold out to the far right, journalist and editor of the municipal paper Daniel Bachelet not only acts as investigator but subsequently writes a work of crime fiction (or is it?) modelled on the case and published, like Delteil's work, by Métailié.

[13]   Barthes, 'Structure du fait divers', p. 189.

[14]   Rousso, *Le Syndrome de Vichy*, p. 245. In *Vichy, un passé qui ne passe pas* (Gallimard, 1996) Rousso and Conan describe changing attitudes towards the Resistance as a difficult transition from an epic to a historical narrative, p. 312.

the advocation of the 'parti aux 75,000 fusillés'[15] to Cold War hostilities; from the transfer of the ashes of Jean Moulin to the Pantheon in 1964 to Henri Frenay's accusing Moulin of crypto-communism in 1977. Delteil and Daeninckx's texts, for their part, were written in the shadow of Klaus Barbie's trial of 1987, an event which was to inflame debates relative to the integrity – in all sense of the word – of the Resistance.

In my reading of Blond's crime fiction cynical newspaper editor Combes and journalist Norrey's passion-induced withholding of evidence introduced an ethical dimension to the search for and construction of stories: the epistemological and the ethical were seen necessarily to be bound together. Unlike Norrey, Daeninckx's and Delteil's journalists do not fall in love, but their investigations too are vitiated by personal involvement; certainly neither can live up to a Bertrix-like dispassion. When Delteil's journalist – who is never named – makes the chance acquaintance of former deportee Paul Liebman, he decides to publish an account of the factional strife and political duplicities the latter encountered when deported to a concentration camp in Poland as a political prisoner. By his own admission the journalist's investigative drive is based on self-interest: he pursues his project in the hope of making money and to prove his authorial credentials. What some would regard as a worthier ethical motivation, such as countering the ignorance of younger generations or the need to keep memories alive (22), are dismissed, at least intradiegetically, as trite. War can be exploited both commercially and aesthetically. Daeninckx's investigator, Marc Blingel, who sets out researching a book on the liberation of the Pas-de-Calais, denies that he is a journalist ('Je ne suis pas journaliste … J'écris une sorte de petit bouquin' (28) ['I'm not a journalist … I'm writing a sort of short book']) though he is so designated both intratextually – 'Allons! Les journalistes ne sont pas aussi innocents …' (27) ['Come on! Journalists aren't as innocent as that …']; 'Il est encore là ton journaliste?' (168) ['Is your journalist still there?'] – and paratextually (specifically, on the back cover of the Folio edition). Blingel's denial and Delteil's character's writerly aspirations may reinforce the truism that all journalists are *auteurs manqués* but they also once again indirectly raise the issue of the timeliness of narrative context. Blond's fictional editor decreed his audience to be disenchanted by news stories of political assassinations. The decision made by these two fictional journalists to publish outwith the press seems to suggest that the events they investigate and subsequently narrate – conflict in a concentration camp full of political deportees; a resistant accused of murder – were not, in the late 1980s, deemed appropriate, that is relevant, commercially viable, material for substantive press coverage.

Where *L'Ange de la rivière morte*'s journalist-investigator brings to our attention different narratives into which wartime events and figures can be inscribed, these later texts add an implicit epistemological commentary: how do the two journalists arrive at 'the facts of the past', and how do they subsequently choose to present

---

[15] Literally meaning the 75,000 executed (shot), the name was given to the Communist Party to reflect the significance of the role its followers played in the Resistance.

the reconstructed narrative? Having identified a potential story worth telling, both Daeninckx's and Delteil's journalists rely primarily on an eye-witness account, recording the oral testimony of former Resistance protagonists Jean Ricouart and Paul Liebman respectively. Delteil's more self-reflective text uses the figure of the journalist as writer explicitly to reference some of the choices faced when moving from oral testimony as a primary source to a written narrative. In the words of his journalist: 'J'avais pensé à l'origine à présenter ce livre sous la forme d'une série d'entretiens, ou d'un récit autobiographique, rédigé à la première ou à la troisième personne' (235) ['I'd originally thought of presenting the book in the form of a series of interviews, or as an autobiographical account, written in the first or third person']. In the event Liebman's testimony is transposed into the third person, exposure to the wartime tale having apparently inculcated some ethical scruples in the journalist at the point of narrative reconstruction: 'ça m'aurait gêné de parler au nom du vieux, de me mettre dans sa peau, moi qui n'avait pas vécu tout ça' (235) ['I'd have felt awkward speaking for the old man, putting myself in his place; I hadn't lived through any of that']. Authorship does not equate to authority, which rests, it would seem, with the participant and witness. Strikingly, neither text questions the reliability of these eye-witness accounts, though the temporal framing of both novels inevitably throws into relief the artifice of the reconstructed narratives of the past. Ricouart's first-person account of his life in the Resistance in 1944 and subsequent deportation and trial, for instance, are narrated dramatically in a mixture of past historic and historic present tenses, complete with extended passages of dialogue. Sudden cuts back to the present of the 1980s effectively (if unimaginatively on the part of the author) break the narrative spell.

Norrey identified within himself a double persona: the archivist or librarian in search of knowledge and the embodied, interventionist 'Norrey agissant', a man very much 'on the case'. *La Mort n'oublie personne* and *KZ retour vers l'enfer* also represent journalists who gather 'evidence' from / of the past – albeit in the form of oral testimony rather than archival documents – complementing this symbolically static, cerebral investigation with a more physical, peripatetic mode of inquiry. In so doing, like Norrey in love, they end up interposing themselves in, and thereby affecting the course of, the story they seek to reconstruct. Towards the close of the text Daeninckx's Blingel temporarily abandons the task of transcribing his subject's oral account and sets out to locate survivors from Ricouart's wartime drama, thereby uncovering a tale of family grudges and a corrupt judge. Delteil's journalist, lured by a false tale of buried treasure, heads off for Germany and Poland, finally digging up – literally – not diamonds but documents revealing how SS concentration camp officials had tried to blackmail Liebman into betraying his fellow deportees.

What are we to make of these similar investigatory trajectories? By seeking out information 'on the ground', both journalists precipitate further crimes in the present. Blingel's discoveries prompt Ricouart to kill the judge who had handed down a verdict of murder on the innocent resistant four decades previously. Delteil's journalist takes matters into his own hands, locating a surviving senior

SS camp officer in Vienna and shooting him dead. In both cases, it is the second generation, represented by the journalists, who precipitate a form of belated rough justice. Investigation into the past is, however, represented as a hazardous enterprise, at least for the first generation: *La Mort n'oublie personne* closes with the arrest of the originally innocent Ricouart; Delteil's murderous journalist walks away, but discovers that Liebman has committed suicide in his absence. Written 40 years after Blond's *L'Ange de la rivière morte*, both texts also display greater ambivalence in their representation of the Resistance. Ricouart may be innocent, but one of his fellow resistants was not, and he in turn becomes a killer; it is never revealed whether or not Liebman betrayed his fellow deportees in the jungle of the concentration camp. Delteil's journalist's act of murder is reported in the text's epilogue via an intercalated clipping from the *Österreichische Zeitung* which outlines what is interpreted as a gratuitous act of violence. This and the headline – 'ODIEUX ASSASSINAT D'UN RETRAITÉ' (284) ['HORRIFIC OAP MURDER'] – suggests that this narrative may well feature in the *fait divers* rubric: call in Norrey and Combes.

Approximately one decade separates Delteil's and Daeninckx's texts from Abécassis's *L'Or et la cendre* (1997) which charts journalist Félix Werner's investigation into the present-day murder of Carl Rudolf Schiller, a German politician, media figure, and theologian with a particular interest in the Holocaust. As well as featuring a journalist as investigator, Abécassis's text represents aspects of the mediatization of the war prevalent in 1990s France, including one particular episode which came to be known as the 'Aubrac affair'. Raymond and Lucie Aubrac have been the subject of an array of narratives, one of the more hostile of which was authored by Klaus Barbie's defence lawyer, Jacques Vergès, who in 1984 revived a claim made several decades earlier, namely that the arrest of Jean Moulin and fellow resistants at Caluire in June 1943 was the consequence of an act of betrayal perpetrated by Raymond Aubrac.[16] As Suleiman has noted, Vergès's claims precipitated not merely a outcry in the press but a succession of further narratives, notably Lucie Aubrac's own *Ils partiront dans l'ivresse* (1984), a fictionalized memoir of her and Raymond's Resistance exploits which effectively elevated the couple to heroic status in France, and Claude Berri's 'hero-worshipping film' *Lucie Aubrac* (1997).[17] The same week as the film's release Raymond Aubrac was once again labelled a traitor, this time by a journalist, Gérard Chauvy, who published his *Aubrac: Lyon 1943* shortly thereafter.[18] The 'Aubrac affair' took off. Lucie and Raymond Aubrac were determined to absolve themselves once and for all and set about doing so by requesting a debate with historians. A round-table was organized by *Libération*, taking place at the newspaper's offices on 17 May 1997; the proceedings were published on 9 July in special sections of

---

[16]   See Susan Suleiman, *Crises of Memory* (Harvard UP, 2006), 'The "Aubrac Affair" and National Memory of the French Resistance', pp. 36–61.

[17]   The term is Suleiman's, *Crisis of Memory*, p. 43.

[18]   Gérard Chauvy, *Aubrac: Lyon 1943* (Albin Michel, 1997).

the paper. As historian Antoine Prost remarked (somewhat ironically in *Le Monde*): 'Il est curieux [...] que l'on se mette à traiter les controverses historiques dans les salles de rédaction des quotidiens' ['It is odd that historical controversies are being discussed in newspaper offices'].[19]

Contemporaneous with Chauvy's book and Berri's film, two narratives situated at opposite ends of the spectrum vis-à-vis representations of the Aubrac couple, Abécassis's crime narrative also represents – or arguably mis-represents – the troubled relationship between the couple and the press: Raymond and Lucie Aubrac appear in *L'Or et la cendre* in the barely disguised form of characters Jacques and Geneviève Talment. In this narrative version it is murder victim Karl Schiller who precipitates events by publishing a book which challenges the integrity of the Talment couple and accuses Jacques of being an agent of the Gestapo: 'il les accusait d'avoir trahi la Résistance et d'en avoir faussé l'histoire pour leur gloire personnelle' (188) ['he accused them of having betrayed the Resistance and of having distorted its history to guild their own reputation']. A press furore, described by one of the characters as 'l'affaire Talment', ensues, as does a meeting with historians. Precisely the same charges – relating to the supposed confusion or conflation of narratives and genres – are directed at the Talment couple by Abécassis's fictitious historians as were aimed at Raymond and Lucie Aubrac: 'Nous, historiens, nous nous devons d'intervenir pour empêcher que la Résistance devienne un sujet de légende, de fable romantique' (189) ['We historians are duty bound to intervene to stop the Resistance from becoming a subject of legend, a romantic fable']; 'Ils avaient confondu le récit historique et le récit de fiction' (190) ['They had mixed up historical and fictional accounts'].[20] But *L'Or et la cendre* offers a different take on these events. Although the exchanges did not turn out as they had intended or hoped, the Aubrac couple had initially requested a debate with historians. In the Abécassis narrative, their literary equivalents are quite simply the victims of aggressors whose intervention is at no point solicited:

> Le scandale avait éclaté dans la presse et les Talment furent contraints de répondre aux questions des historiens qui, sans autorité légale, s'étaient érigés en juges, les soumettant à la question, les sommant à répondre [...] (188)
>
> [The scandal had hit the press and the Talments were forced to respond to questions put to them by the historians who, with no legal authority, had set themselves up as judges, putting them to the question and ordering them to reply.]

---

[19] Antoine Prost, 'Les historiens et les Aubrac: une question de trop', *Le Monde*, 12 juillet 1997. For a discussion of the Aubrac 'affair' and its links to the controversy surrounding Papon, see Hanna Diamond and Claire Gorrara, 'The Aubrac Controversy', *History Today*, 51.3 (2001), p. 26.

[20] The foreword to Lucie Aubrac's *Ils partiront dans l'ivresse* (Seuil, 1984) informs the reader that although she could not keep an actual diary during the war, the account which follows is as accurate as possible, put together using her own memories, those of her husband, and some of their friends' accounts of the past (13).

Further skewing the facts, Abécassis sets the historians' inquisition of the Talment couple in 1994, making it contemporaneous with the trial of Maurice Crétel (against whom they are called to testify), a character loosely based on René Bousquet. Crétel, in Abécassis's narrative, arrested Jacques Talment and other resistants in 1943 (making of him at this point more of a Barbie figure than a Bousquet) but also delivered Geneviève Talment to the *milice* and thence the Germans, at whose hands she was tortured then deported to Auschwitz (none of which applied to Aubrac). Although it is hard to know quite what to make of this imbroglio of fact and fiction, what is quite clear is that Abécassis defends her fictitious Talment couple in relation to both their status as eye-witnesses and as members of the Resistance. Not only is their role as victims intensified; their fictional literary aggressor Schiller withdraws his claims and the historians who speak against them are, in various ways, discredited.

The 'Aubrac affair' constituted not just a conflict between eye-witnesses and historians and their respective claims to write history; it also emphasized the competing narrative interests of historians and journalists (as indeed did the trial of Maurice Papon, which began later the same year). Suleiman notes that 'critics deplored the use of a daily newspaper [*Libération*] for an attempt to arrive at historical truth'.[21] Jeanneney, in his *Le passé dans le prétoire. L'historien, le juge et le journaliste*, suggests that whilst journalists and historians are superficially engaged in a similar process – both seek the truth and both investigate – journalists depart from the epistemology of the historians in their tendency to focus on individuals, their affective approach to their material, and their greater susceptibility to anachronism.[22] The risk of the demands of the present on journalists (Blond's editor Combes comes to mind) is indeed a recurring argument in critiques of their position as writers of history, the latter apparently being all too easily distorted to fit the needs of the present.[23] Journalists are further charged with deficient working methods. Reid points out that journalist Chauvy's attempt to write history was disparagingly described by historian Jean-Pierre Azéma as the work of a '*historiant*' rather than a '*historien*': locating and reproducing archival documents is not enough; these must be assessed and analyzed, and their presence complemented by hypothesis and argumentation.[24] Finally, investigative

---

[21] Suleiman, *Crises of Memory*, p. 50.

[22] Jean-Noël Jeanneney, *Le passé dans le prétoire. L'historien, le juge et le journaliste* (Seuil, 1998), p. 75. For a review of several works which stemmed from and commented on the Papon trial, and in some cases the Aubrac affair, including Jeanneney's *Le passé dans le prétoire*, Marc Olivier Baruch's *Servir l'État français* (1997), Rousso's *La Hantise du passé* (1998), Éric Conan's *Le Procès Papon. Un journal d'audience* (1998), and Bertrand Poirot-Delpech's *Papon: un crime de bureau* (1998), see Richard Golsan, 'Papon: The Good, the Bad and the Ugly', *SubStance*, 91 (2000): 139–52.

[23] Béatrice Fleury and Jacques Walter, 'Le Procès Papon. Médias, témoin-expert et contre-expertise historiographique', *Vingtième siècle*, 88 (2005): 63–76.

[24] Donald Reid, 'Resistance and Its Discontents: Affairs, Archives, Avowals, and the Aubracs', *The Journal of Modern History*, 77 (2005): 97–137 [115]. The term 'historiant'

journalists are criticized for acting out: as enquirers claiming 'to uncover the history ignored or repressed by academic historians', they allegedly assume the subject position of resistants.[25]

This well-documented conflict between the ethics and epistemologies of the journalist vis-à-vis that of the historian plays out in *L'Or et la cendre* not merely in the rewriting of the Aubrac affair but via Abécassis's representation of the relationship between investigative journalist Félix Werner and the text's first-person narrator Raphael Simmer, a historian specializing in the Second World War. In this fictional narrative historian and journalist work closely together: a Henry Rousso and Eric Conan partnership, one might suggest.[26] Simmer describes himself as 'un coéquipier, un limier et un informateur pour son enquête' (39) ['team mate, sleuth (bloodhound), and source for his investigation'], whilst Werner lays claims to an even closer working relationship: 'Je suis journaliste; je mène mes enquêtes comme un historien. L'historien et le journaliste ne peuvent se quitter, savez-vous ...' (288) ['I'm a journalist; I carry out my investigations like a historian. The historian and the journalist are inseparable, you know ...']. This proclaimed symbiosis does not preclude the acknowledgement of differences. Fictional historian Simmer echoes some of the comments noted above when he points to the present-oriented nature of the journalist's task as one of crafting a story 'dans l'urgence' (38) ['as a matter of urgency']. We may be reminded here of 'Norrey agissant' (*L'Ange de la rivière morte*, 218). The historian, by contrast, takes time to master his material and write it up; where the journalist is in love with the present, the historian is the man of the past (64). Simmer also points to the journalist's affective investment in his investigations: 'Les choses avaient en lui une résonance infinie. [...] Il les [choses] vivait dans sa chair, dans son corps, de tout son être' (20) ['Things always affected him deeply. (...) He lived them in his very flesh, in his body, with all his being']. Werner, it would seem, represents the figure of the embodied and inevitably personally implicated investigator which we have already encountered.

But *L'Or et la cendre* lays a trap for its reader. In the final pages of the text it emerges that Werner and Simmer are one and the same; the first-person narration is unreliable, Werner a figure of Simmer's imagination. Such a doubling has already emerged in mitigated manner in Blond's text in the form of journalist Norrey's self-confessed dual nature. A similar trace can be found in Daeninckx's *La Mort n'oublie personne* when Ricouart fleetingly ascribes a different role to his interlocutor, journalist Marc Blindel: 'Malheureusement je ne possède aucune preuve, aucun document ... Vous êtes historien, vous pourrez certainement vérifier ce que j'avance' (170) ['Unfortunately I've got no proof, no documents ... You're a historian, you'll certainly be able to verify what I'm claiming'].

---

is modelled on Barthes's 'écrivain' / 'écrivant' distinction. See *Essais critiques*, 'Écrivains et écrivants', pp. 147–54.

  25   Reid, 'Resistance and Its Discontents', p. 115.

  26   Journalist Éric Conan and historian Henry Rousso joint authored *Vichy, un passé qui ne passe pas* (Gallimard, 1996).

Abécassis takes the process further. Not only does her act of fictional doubling unravel any suggestion that historians are more dispassionate and less at risk from the potentially damaging demands of the present than journalists: Raphael Simmer is revealed to be the murderer he had ostensibly been seeking. Both the historian and the journalist, two halves of a composite investigative figure, are thus discredited in a text which ultimately favours the first generation eye-witness above any attempt to reconstruct a 'second-hand' narrative of the past.

One final observation can be made regarding *L'Or et la cendre*: in spite of the author's allusions to an extensive array of war-related figures, events, and incidents, the book's point of focus is the Holocaust, and in this it differs markedly from the three other texts discussed in this section. Blond's *L'Ange de la rivière morte* includes a single mention of Jews, which lapses into atypically (it is tempting to say symptomatically) telegraphic style: 'Elle [la villa] paraît fermée depuis longtemps. Je me demande d'ailleurs comment on l'a laissée vide ... / – Propriétaire israélite déporté, histoire compliquée' (226) ['The house seems as though it's been closed up for a long time. I wonder how it came to be left empty like that ... / – Deported Jewish owner, complicated story']. Jewish characters are absent from *La Mort n'oublie personne*, and though Delteil's resistant Paul Liebman is a Jew who first meets his journalist interlocutor during an anti-semitic incident, this is not the primary thrust of the text. *L'Or et la cendre* is an investigation into the killing of one man, but beyond that it is arguably also about the mystery of evil: 'Le but de mes recherches', states Simmer, 'c'était de saisir, à travers la Shoah, l'origine du mal absolu' (63) ['The aim of my research was to grasp, through the Shoah, the origin of absolute evil']. It may be that all crime fiction which touches on the Holocaust is implicated in such a double investigation, making criminal enquiries in such texts either secondary to, or metonymically tied to, the search for the solution to the Final Solution.[27] If that is indeed the case, a theologian might be a more capable investigator than a journalist or a historian.[28]

Investigating Historians

Historians may lack the necessary theodicean competence to 'solve' the crime that was the Holocaust, but what role might they play in crime fiction? Parallels have certainly been drawn between criminal investigators and historians, as witnessed by such complementarily titled collections as *The Historian as Detective* and

---

[27] Michael's Chabon's *The Final Solution. A Story of Detection* (Fourth Estate, 2004), with its punning title, can be read in this light. Fraser suggests that crime fiction is ideally suited to such explorations, precisely because it is linked to evil: 'Law and crime, theology and sin, evil in its human and eschatological manifestations, are all inextricably linked in the detective novel', 'Polarcauste', p. 242.

[28] G.K. Chesterton's Father Brown found that his knowledge of the priesthood and hearing of confession taught him much about human evil, though even he might have been challenged by the extremes of the Holocaust.

The Detective as Historian.[29] More relevant to the crime fiction texts under consideration here is the critical impetus generated by two authors – Daeninckx and Modiano – whose work has been regarded as representative of a historical turn in French crime fiction dating back to the 1980s. Critical inquiries into this trend orbit around two variants. First, criminal investigators are likened to historians to the extent that both are involved in the task of 'recuperating stories of the past', or 'unearthing the past'.[30] Gorrara, for instance, uses the term 'detective-historian' when discussing Daeninckx's and Modiano's investigators,[31] suggesting at one point that police inspector Cadin's investigation in Daeninckx's *Meurtres pour mémoire* 'takes on the appearance of a historical research project'.[32] Forsdick, who compares Cadin's methodology to that of 'an investigative historian',[33] lays emphasis on the second, related line of approach, which posits these works of crime fiction as examples of a counter- or alternative history; a '*polar* history', to adopt Ross's terminology.[34] For some critics, this attempt to rewrite 'official' history is not altogether successful: Golsan, for example, objects to what he regards as an injudicious tracing of parallels between the Algerian and Second World wars in Daeninckx's work.[35] Coming at the question from a different discipline (that of law) and drawing on a larger, and later corpus, Fraser refers to 'a genre in which "fiction" writes and rewrites history and memory in search for an impossible justice'.[36]

Critical focus on criminal investigators' metaphorical or actual affinity to historians in French crime fiction has opened up some important avenues, but it has for the most part been based on a rather restricted set of texts. It is perhaps for this reason that discussion has not tended to extend to the representation of actual historians. Forsdick observes that Daeninckx's police inspector Cadin was 'destin[é] [...] à l'enseignement de l'histoire' ['destined to be a history teacher'],[37]

---

[29]   Robin Winks (ed.) *The Historian as Detective. Essays on Evidence* (Harper & Row, 1968); Ray B. Browne and Lawrence Kreiser Jr. (eds), *The Detective as Historian. History and Art in Historical Crime Fiction* (Bowling Green State U Popular P, 2000).

[30]   Claire Gorrara, *The Roman noir in post-war French culture*, Chapter 4, 'Historical Investigations: Didier Daeninckx, *Meurtres pour mémoire*', p. 81. Charles Forsdick, '"Direction les oubliettes de l'histoire": witnessing the past in the contemporary French *polar*', *French Cultural Studies*, 12 (2001): 333–50 [338].

[31]   Gorrara, 'Tracking down the Past: The Detective as Historian in Texts by Patrick Modiano and Didier Daeninckx', in Anne Mullen and Emer O'Beirne (eds) *Crime Scenes: Detective Narratives in European Culture since 1945* (Rodopi, 2000), pp. 281–90 [282].

[32]   Gorrara, 'Historical Investigations', p. 86.

[33]   Forsdick, 'Direction les oubliettes de l'histoire', p. 341.

[34]   Gorrara, 'Tracking down the Past', p. 287. Kristin Ross, 'Parisian Noir', *New Literary History*, 41.1 (2010): 95–109 [97].

[35]   Richard Golsan, 'Memory's bombes à retardement: Maurice Papon, crimes against humanity, and 17 October 1961', *Journal of European Studies* 28.1–2 (1998): 153–72.

[36]   David Fraser, 'Polarcauste', p. 237.

[37]   Forsdick, 'Direction les oubliettes de l'histoire', p. 341, citing Daeninckx's *Mort au premier tour* (Paris: Denoël, 1997; first published 1982), p. 88.

and as the corpus reveals, many investigators have, or claim to have, similar qualifications. When not flashing a fake press card, the 'Poulpe' may be found adopting the role of advisor to the Ministry of Education on the content of history textbooks (*La Route du Rom*, p. 126). The principal investigator in Perrin's *Chiens et louves* (1999) is encouraged to assume a false persona in order to assuage local inhabitants' curiosity: 'Faites-leur croire plutôt que vous êtes venu ici pour ... tenez, pour écrire un bouquin. Prétendez que vous êtes historien' ['Let them think you've come here to ... let's see, to write a book. Say that you're a historian'] (49). In many cases actual (fictional) historians play a key investigative role: doctoral student of history Chloé in the *Polarchives* series has already been mentioned; a former French soldier and resistant turned history teacher is the protagonist of Auclair's *Un Amour allemand* (1950); Jonquet's *Du passé faisons table rase* includes police officer Guilon, another historian by training. Historians both advance and hinder investigations; they may be victims or perpetrators. A father and son, both historians, are killed in Daeninckx's *Meurtres pour mémoire* when they look too closely into the past; an archivist – another recurring figure – proves to be a killer. Both good and bad historians and archivists feature in Daeninckx's later *Éthique en toc* (2000), whilst Benson's *Biblio-quête* (2001) and Busino's *Au nom du piètre qui a l'essieu* (1998) both favour the presence of good, but soon dead, historians.

As well as representing historians in various guises, a significant proportion of texts display a degree of self-reflexivity when it comes to categories of enquiry and enquirers. In Kââ's *Trois chiens morts* (1992), for instance, the first-person narrator, another history teacher, has two exchanges with a police investigator. On the first occasion, it is the similarities between criminal and historical enquiries which are stressed:

> De toute façon, dans cette affaire, il s'agit plus d'une enquête historique que d'une enquête policière, n'est-ce pas?
> Ce n'est pas un peu la même chose, parfois? Ce n'est pas un peu le même état d'esprit? (162)
>
> [In any case, as far as this business is concerned, it's more of a historical investigation than a criminal investigation, isn't it?
> Isn't it sometimes pretty much the same thing? Doesn't it involve pretty much the same state of mind?]

By the close of the text variance has come to the fore:

> Une enquête historique, même aussi bien menée que la vôtre, n'est pas en fin de compte un enquête policière: l'histoire finit par tout engloutir dans les souvenirs oubliés, elle ne fournit pas les coupables d'aujourd'hui, ceux-là seuls qui comptent pour les policiers. (208)
>
> [When all's said and done a historical investigation, even one as well conducted as yours, isn't a criminal investigation: history ends up engulfing everything in forgotten memories, it doesn't come up with today's guilty parties, the only ones that matter as far as the police are concerned.]

Or, as a character in Krivine's *Un souvenir de Berlin* frames it: 'Vous faites de la police et nous, nous faisons de l'histoire, vous me suivez?' (114) ['You "do" police work and we "do" history, got it?'].[38] It is not just fictitious historians who are quick to point out that their working methods should not be too readily compared to that of the criminal investigator. In Rousso's opinion 'Historians conduct inquiries and seek the truth just like the detectives you mention. In my opinion, the comparison stops there'.[39] Historian Annette Wieviorka, meanwhile, laments the dramatization of press enquiries into the Resistance. As the title of one of her pieces puts it: 'Jean Moulin ou l'Histoire comme énigme policière.'[40]

The extracts just cited already indicate how works of crime fiction may explicitly and self-reflexively differentiate between criminal and historical investigators. In what follows the focus will fall on matters epistemological and juridical, and on the question of closure, with the aim of charting the representation of criminal and historical enquiry in a sample of fictional texts. Abécassis's *L'Or et la cendre*, as discussed above, features a historian in an investigative role, as does Vargas's *Un peu plus loin sur la droite*, in the form of investigator Louis Kehlweiler's primary assistant, medieval historian Marc Vandoosler. Neither Modiano's *Dora Bruder* (1997) nor Rio's *Leçon d'abîme* (2003) represent actual historians, though the investigators in both texts explicitly raise issues of epistemological and juridical concern with regard to investigating the past.[41] Historians and court cases, France's 'obsessive' relationship to the Vichy years, archives, crimes against humanity: these are all issues which have been addressed by historian Henry Rousso, former director of the *Institut de l'histoire du temps présent* and author (or co-author) of some of the best-known works on Vichy France. For this reason, Rousso's work will be placed into an intermittent dialogue with the crime fiction sample.

It is a perceived common concern with uncovering 'the facts of the past' that is the usual starting point for comparisons between the criminal investigator and

---

[38]   An explicit distinction is also drawn in Notin's *Nom de code: La Murène* which stages a struggling historian's inquiries into the wartime (and 1958 Algerian) activities of Charles de Gaulle 'Mais bon, vous êtes historien, pas policier. Vous traquez les archives, pas les individus' (32) ['Ok, so you're a historian, not a police officer. You hunt down archival material, not individuals']. In fact, Notin's historian (egged on by an unscrupulous editor) displays the same duality of action and stasis we have witnessed before as he both investigates archives and travels the world in search of witnesses.

[39]   Rousso, *The Haunting Past. History, Memory, and Justice in Contemporary France* (U of Pennsylvania P, 2002), pp. 52–3.

[40]   Annette Wieviorka, 'Jean Moulin ou l'Histoire comme énigme policière', *Le Monde*, 18 November 1998.

[41]   Modiano's *Dora Bruder* can usefully be read alongside Michel del Castillo's *Les Portes du sang* (2003), another text with an autobiographical element (the central character, Clara del Monte, is at least partly modelled on the author's mother) which explores epistemological and ethical issues relating to the reconstruction of the past, especially the war years, and which makes use of and includes authentic period documents.

the historian, and it is not unusual for this sort of casual connection to be made by either fictional party: 'J'étais […] le détective qui mène son enquête après le crime, qui traque la vérité enfouie sous le mensonge des années, des passions et des intérêts humains' ['I was (…) the detective who carries out his investigation after the crime, who tracks down the truth which lies buried under the lies of passing years, human passions and self interest'] (64). These are the words of Abécassis's historian. The implication that a truth is there to be found, albeit one which is potentially obfuscated by two factors – time and human affectivity – typifies Simmer's epistemological model which is – or aspires to be; one should bear in mind that Simmer turns out to be a psychotic killer – one of 'scientific' rationality and objectivity. In a disquisition on his craft Simmer advances a list of potential means of access to the past, including: 'lois et décrets'; 'annonces et proclamations'; 'permis, passes, passeports'; 'lettres'; 'journaux'; 'documents personnels'; 'listes' ['laws and decrees'; 'announcements and proclamations'; 'permits, passes, passports'; 'letters'; 'newspapers'; 'personal documents'; 'lists']; but also '[p]aroles de rescapés, de survivants, de témoins'; 'phrases hachées, pleurs, peurs, hésitations' (64–5) ['the words of those who came back, survivors, witnesses; disjointed phrases, tears, fears, hesitations']. As an 'historien du temps présent', Simmer ostensibly recognizes two categories of primary source, that of written documents and that of oral testimony, but clearly favours the former over the latter: shortly after this passage Abécassis's historian notes disparagingly that eye-witnesses can only ever offer a subjective truth (71).

Simmer shares some of the working methods of Modiano's first-person narrator, who though not a historian nonetheless seeks to reconstruct the past of a young Jewish girl, Dora Bruder, who went missing during the Occupation. To achieve this he follows a variety of 'traces' (the same word is employed several times by Simmer); indeed he uses precisely the type of written documents enumerated by Abécassis's historian, including archived newspapers – it is a 1941 copy of *Paris-Soir* which triggers the investigation into the eponymous Dora Bruder's fate – maps and directories, birth and marriage certificates, legal documents of various sorts, lists of deportation convoys, and personal letters. But there are epistemological differences too. Although Simmer acknowledges that documents may be dispersed, even half destroyed or burnt (65), this is not a matter on which he dwells. Modiano's investigator, by contrast, not only alludes to the active suppression of documents (charged to the State-sanctioned 'sentinelles de l'oubli', p. 16) ['guardians of memory'] but also intersperses his attempted reconstruction of the missing Dora Bruder's past with expressions of hesitation and hypothesis in an attempt to compensate for a lack of 'hard fact': 'il semble que'; 'peut-être'; 'je devine'; 'j'ignore'; 'je suppose' ['it seems that'; 'maybe'; 'I'm guessing'; 'I don't know'; 'I assume']. Morris, who has studied the revisions made by the author in the move from the original 1997 text of *Dora Bruder* to the 1999 Folio edition, notes that factual errors were amended and newly unearthed information substituted 'for an earlier "Je ne sais pas" or

"J'ignore"', such alterations apparently being driven by 'the need to increase the accuracy, objectivity and reliability of information'.[42] Morris seems oddly piqued to discover that Modiano did not effect other changes, even though the information was known to have been available to him. He concludes with what sounds almost like disapproval, or at least disappointment, that Modiano was after all not aiming 'to produce a sort of history', as further demonstrated by the presence of 'metatextual interjections' – a procedure 'which official historians tend to scorn'– and those obtrusive expressions of conjecture.[43]

Morris's reaction to Modiano's text may well stem from what appears to be a conflation of author and narrator, an inadmissible gesture since, as he concedes, this is a text of indeterminate genre. Indeed *Dora Bruder* both partakes of, and self-reflexively reveals, some of the mechanisms of the writing of history, crime fiction, and (auto)biography. Whilst it is of course Modiano who altered (or in some cases chose not to alter) the later edition of *Dora Bruder*, it is his first-person investigator narrator – a narrative device like any other – who employs the expressions of doubt and hypothesis and engages in metatextual comment, thereby allowing the author to expose the necessary artifice at the heart of historical discourse: documents can take the historian only so far; from and around them a plausible narrative must still be constructed. Modiano's narrator is no '*historiant*' (above, p. 131), but neither is his self-consciously lacunae-ridden narrative that of the 'historien'. Both *Dora Bruder* and *L'Or et la cendre* expose the limitations of an epistemology premised exclusively on the existence of objective 'fact' or 'truth' about the past, Modiano by interspersing the text with his investigating narrator's self-confessedly subjective input; Abécassis by creating as first-person narrator who is an avowed – but unreliable – historian of the 'scientific' school. Epistemological limitations relating to historical enquiry are flagged by both texts, but what of the investigators' success or failure as criminal enquirers? The murder case is solved and guilty party identified in *L'Or et la cendre*, though not by the murderous historian investigator, who singularly fails to find himself, ending the text under arrest and secure psychiatric surveillance. In his *The Historian as Detective*, Winks notes that 'the full truth about the past can never be recovered. One of the reasons this is so, of course, is that we can never know the full truth about ourselves, the investigators'. Winks goes on to

---

[42]   Alan Morris, '"Avec Klarsfeld contre l'oubli": Patrick Modiano's *Dora Bruder*', *Journal of European Studies*, 36.3 (2006): 269–93 [272–3]. The relationship between Modiano and Klarsfeld – the two men exchanged letters from 1978 onwards – and Klarsfeld's contribution to the conception and completion of *Dora Bruder*, has been the source of considerable interest. See Morris's 'Avec Klarsfeld contre l'oubli' pp. 279–93 and 'Patrick Modiano / Serge Klarsfeld: Correspondance', in R. Guidée and M. Heck, *Modiano* (Éds de L'Herne, 2012). For an analysis of changes made in the English translation of *Dora Bruder*, including the reproduction of photographs and maps, see Jennifer Howell, 'In defiance of genre: the languages of Patrick Modiano's Dora Bruder project', *Journal of European Studies*, 40.1 (2010): 59–72.

[43]   Morris, 'Avec Klarsfeld contre l'oubli', p. 275.

state that 'most [historians] recognize the need for tracing the missing person within themselves'.[44] Modiano's *Dora Bruder* is as much 'the case of the missing narrator' as it is that of a missing girl. The investigating narrator fails to solve the individual mystery of Dora Bruder's past story: her thoughts and motives, the precise details of her flight and subsequent arrest and deportation either cannot be, or are not, recovered. The performative act of enquiry into Bruder's past does go some way towards illuminating the narrator's own story or 'missing person within himself'.

Amongst Morris's mildly disapprobatory reflections on Modiano's (in fact his first-person narrator's) methodology vis-à-vis the reconstruction of the past is the latter's recourse to 'vicarious experience', especially his own, as a means of filling in information gaps in the Dora Bruder case.[45] As a historical method empathy is more likely to appear in a set of instructions for a high school history curriculum (of the 'imagine you were a soldier in the trenches' variety) than in a work of serious historiography, though the concept has made something of a reappearance in the context of writing the history of the Holocaust.[46] Strikingly, variants on the notion of 'putting yourself in the place of' can be found in *L'Or et la cendre*, *Dora Bruder*, and Rio's *Leçon d'abîme*, each potentially raising further questions relating to investigative methodology and potential epistemological perils. Modiano's narrator puts himself in the place of Dora Bruder via an act of retrospective comparison with his own lived experience: 'Qu'est-ce qui nous décide à faire une fugue? Je me souviens de la mienne [...]' (57) ['What makes us decide to run away? I remember when I ran away']; 'Je me souviens de l'impression forte que j'ai éprouvé lors de ma fugue de janvier 1960' (77) ['I remember when I ran away in January 1960, the powerful impression it made on me']. The narrator's recalling of his own experience as a means of understanding approaches what Dean criticizes as a largely self-centered form of empathy. As she puts it: 'identification with the victim and repression of his or her difference – or unconscious presumptions about the centrality of our own experience – go together, and empathy turns out to be a [...] form of hegemony'.[47] According to LaCapra in order for empathy to function as an epistemological tool 'heteropathic identification' or 'empathic unsettlement' is required, that is, 'virtual not vicarious experience [...] experience in which one puts oneself in the other's position without taking the place of – or speaking

---

[44] Winks, *The Historian as Detective*, p. 60.

[45] Morris, 'Avec Klarsfeld': '[...] the trouble with this procedure is glaring – the vicarious experience could very well be similar to Dora's, but it cannot be guaranteed to be identical, so it remains far from unquestionable', p. 275.

[46] See Dominick LaCapra *History in Transit: Experience, Identity, Critical Theory* (Cornell UP, 2004), especially Chapter 3, 'Trauma Studies: Its Critics and Vicissitudes', pp. 106–43; William V. Harris, 'History, Empathy and Emotions', *Antike und Abendland*, 56 (2010): 1–23; Samuel Moyn, 'Empathy in History, Empathizing with Humanity', *History and Theory*, 45 (2006): 397–415.

[47] Carolyn Dean, *The Fragility of Empathy after the Holocaust* (Cornell UP, 2004), p. 11.

for – the other'.[48] Modiano's investigator's empathic methodology based on the recalling of his own experience, which is extended by invitation to the reader via the first-person pronoun ('Qu'est-ce qui nous décide à faire une fugue?'), is complemented by the literal, physical act of putting himself in the young girl's place by walking the streets of Paris, visiting locations where she and her parents once lived, following routes she is likely to have followed. As a means of acquiring precise information about Bruder's case the narrator's Chandleresque taking to the mean streets yields little beyond a replaying of personal memories, though the elegiac peripateticism does inscribe Paris and a fantasmagoric trace of all those deportees whom the missing girl represents in a commemorative narrative.[49]

A variant on the 'vicarious experience' methodology appears in *L'Or et la cendre* in a section of the text with the italicized incipit '*Qu'aurais-je fait?*' (152) [*'What would I have done?'*]. Historian Simmer goes on to pose close to one hundred questions in quick succession, from the more general 'Qu'aurais-je fait sous la tourmente nazie?' (153) ['What would I have done faced with the upheaval of the nazi occupation?'] to 'Aurais-je été un type un peu paumé embauché par la milice?' (153) ['Would I have been a pretty hapless kind of individual taken on by the milice?'], and 'Aurais-été un collaborationiste forcené, soutenant Pétain avec entrain?' (154) ['Would I have been a fanatical collaborationist, an enthusiastic supporter of Pétain?']. The self-reflexively uncertain narrator of *Dora Bruder* seeks to fill epistemological lacunae by drawing on the known-ness of his own past experience (marked by the relative certainty of the present tense of memory and the perfect of recalled actuality: 'je me souviens'; 'l'impression forte que j'ai éprouvée' ['I remember'; 'the strong impression I had']). Simmer the man of scientific certainty, by contrast, yields to the unknown of the conditional perfect. Seeking knowledge in his case is an ethically charged affair, and one question, 'Aurais-je dénoncé des juifs?' (154) ['Would I have denounced Jews?'], triggers a palpable crisis ('Des voix hurlaient dans ma tête, des voix tonitruantes à la faire éclater' ['Voices screamed in my head, thunderous voices threatening to blow it apart'], p. 155) as what appears to have been a disavowed or repressed memory bubbles briefly to the surface: 'Les aurais-je dénoncés comme mes parents? *Oh Dieu!*' (155) ['Would I have denounced them like my parents did? *Oh God!*']. 'Putting oneself in the place of' in Simmer's case results in the evanescent perception of a traumatic legacy of guilt, and, perhaps, a foreshadowing of his own. Simmer is no disinterested investigator.

Simmer's largely unacknowledged personal implication in his case makes of him more of a typical *noir* criminal investigator than a so-called objective historian. Obversely, it seems at least initially that in Rio's inspector Malone

---

[48] LaCapra, *History in Transit*, p. 135.

[49] For a reading of the text which focuses on the ethically necessary trans-generational transmission of the trauma of the victims see Judith Greenberg, 'Trauma and transmission: echoes of the missing past in *Dora Bruder*', *Studies in Twentieth and Twenty-First Century Literature*, vol. 31 (2007): 351–449.

we have a criminal investigator with all the detached analytic know-how of the historian which Simmer purports to be: Malone qualifies his role as 'enquêteur' as that of 'une sorte de machine neutre dénuée d'affect' (21) ['A sort of neutral machine devoid of affect']. *Leçon d'abîme* confronts its investigator with a knotty problem: in brief, Malone must ascertain whether the man he questions is Hans Uzler, a former nazi wanted for crimes against humanity, or the Jewish David Klein, whose sister Judith was tortured and sexually exploited by Uzler in Dachau. A DNA sample would solve the mystery, but Uzler / Klein refuses to provide one. Unlike Modiano's investigator and Abécassis's Simmer, Malone has no material sources to work with: 'tous leurs [the Klein siblings'] papiers, documents, souvenirs et objets personnels identifiables détruits. Une véritable éradication des traces matérielles de leur existence' (22) ['all their papers, documents, mementos, and identifiable private possessions destroyed. A veritable eradication of all material traces of their existence']. Rio, it might be said, sets up an epistemological experiment: can the truth about the past be found by rational enquiry alone, when the only source is a potentially highly unreliable eye-witness and participant? Malone, rather like Simmer, starts out confident in his ratiocinative powers and investigative detachment, but he too is soon personally implicated in the case, at one point finding himself hiding in a secret vault watching sado-masochistic (if apparently consensual) sexual acts unfold between two of Uzler's / Klein's employees. In so doing Malone assumes the subject position formerly held by David Klein in Dachau, who looked on helplessly as his sister was abused. As I have argued elsewhere, Malone plays out what LaCapra would describe as the not atypical situation of a historian of the Holocaust, unwittingly caught up in transferential relation to his material and acting out certain subject positions.[50] Rio's investigator is unaware of the precise nature of his acting out (such indeed is the nature of the latter), but does recognize that his 'scientific' methodology has somehow failed (him): 'Il sentait qu'il avait abandonné, en dépit de sa volonté [...] sa fonction critique contre celle d'acteur, que lui aussi jouait un rôle' (85) ['He felt that against his will, he had abandoned (...) his critical faculties for those of an actor, that he too was playing a role']. Malone is obliged to face the fact that his investigation into the past 'n'avait plus ce caractère de jeu d'échecs objectif qui lui garantissait une sorte d'invulnérabilité affective' (85) ['was no

---

[50] For a discussion of Rio's text see my 'Is France Post Post-War? Judging the Nazi Past in Recent Novels by Maud Tabachnik, Michel Rio and Sylvie Germain', in *Narratives of French Modernity*, Lorna Milne and Mary Orr (eds), (Peter Lang, 2011), pp. 301–16. See Dominick LaCapra, *History and Memory after Auschwitz* (Cornell UP, 1998), Chapter 1, 'History and Memory: In the Shadow of the Holocaust' and Chapter 6, 'Conclusion: Psychoanalysis, Memory and the Ethical Turn'; and *History, Theory, Trauma: Representing the Holocaust* (Cornell UP, 1994), especially the concluding 'Acting out and Working Through'. For a reading of Rio's work, especially his Malone texts, as reactionary in both their politics and their representation of women, see Ralph Schoolcraft and Richard Golsan, 'Paradoxes of the postmodern reactionary. Michel Rio and Michel Houellebecq', *Journal of European Studies*, 37 (2007): 349–71.

longer characterized by the chess-like objectivity which guaranteed him a sort of affective invulnerability']. It is not insignificant that both Simmer and Malone, like Norrey the journalist in Blond's *L'Ange de la rivière morte*, become involved with women whose presence can again be read as symbolic of impediments to investigative attempts to reconstruct the past.

Finally, Vargas's *Un peu plus loin sur la droite*, which takes its title from the lead investigator's credo that reconstructing a narrative of the past is most likely to succeed when logic and reason are if not abandoned, then at least complemented by an epistemological model which is rather less grounded in certainty:

> Main gauche, annonçait Louis en levant les bras et en étendant les doigts, imparfaite, malhabile, hésitante, et donc productrice salutaire du cafouillis et du doute. Main droite, assurée, ferme, détentrice du savoir-faire, conductrice du génie humain. Avec elle, la maîtrise, la méthode et la logique. (21)

> [Left hand, announced Louis, lifting his hand up and spreading his fingers out, imperfect, clumsy, hesitant, and thus salutary producer of disarray and doubt. Right hand, assured, steady, keeper of *savoir-faire*, facilitator of human genius. With it comes mastery, method, and logic.]

A move further to the right equates to an increase in 'la rigueur et la certitude' of the type a Simmer might appreciate. Further still – 'un peu plus loin sur la droite' – comes 'la bascule tragique dans la perfection, dans l'impeccable, et puis dans l'infaillible et l'impitoyable' ['a tragic toppling over into perfection, into faultlessness, then into infallibility and ruthlessness'], casting the investigator in the role of 'cruel imbécile fermé aux vertus du doute' (21) ['a cruel imbecile impervious to the virtues of doubt']. It should by now be apparent that all the texts discussed in this section, by different means, undermine the concept of objective enquiry as an achievable, or even desirable, epistemological tenet. Historians in these texts may aspire to an objective detachment and analytic methodology which can be likened to that of the ratiocinative investigator of the whodunnit – a Holmes or Poirot – but end up closer to a *noir* investigator paradigm. 'Unearthing the past', these texts seems to suggest, is more likely to succeed when analysis and so-called hard evidence are complemented by a measure of affective investment and subjective involvement in the case, ideally accompanied by a healthy dose of self-awareness.

So much for how to access the past; what is the investigator to do with, to make of, the excavated knowledge? Perorating upon his status as historian Simmer asserts that his one and only ethical obligation is to the truth: 'la vérité, toute la vérité, rien que la vérité ...' (51) ['The truth, the whole truth, and nothing but the truth ...'].[51] There is a certain irony to this use of the courtroom paradigm given

---

    [51]   This distancing of the historian's professional conduct from any further moral imperative, coupled with what we have already seen of Simmer's epistemological pretensions to a 'scientific' objectivity, finds an echo in Rousso's appraisal of the current state of history and historians: 'D'une manière générale, les historiens d'aujourd'hui s'inscrivent plus volontiers

the character's disregard for eye-witness testimony and later disparaging reference to 'les historiens nouveaux juges' (368) ['the new judges, the historians']. The latter allusion is a timely one. Since the late 1980s historians have been increasingly – and in many cases reluctantly – implicated in the juridical process. Rousso, who has written extensively on the subject, famously refused to appear as a so-called expert witness at the trial of Maurice Papon;[52] Richard Evans, called to the witness stand in his professional capacity on more than one occasion, stresses the differences between the juridical and the historical, insisting that

> in criminal trials the central issue is that of guilt or innocence, concepts which are not only far from central to the historian's enterprise but also, some would argue, entirely alien to it; for what historians are, or should be, engaged in, is explanation and interpretation, not moral judgment.[53]

It is here that historian and criminal investigator most obviously part company. Both seek to reconstruct a narrative about the past, but for the historian this enterprise is an end in itself. For the criminal investigator, it is precisely 'guilt or innocence' and the rendition of justice which matters.

Simmer, as noted in the preceding section, insists on the differing relations to time which set him and his journalist 'colleague' apart: where the latter is in love with the present, he, as a historian, is the man of the past (64). In his discussion of some of the fundamental incompatibilities between historical and juridical enterprises, Rousso points to the crucial part played by statutory limitations, or more specifically, imprescriptibility, in the blurring of temporal priorities: 'Cette notion [...] signifie concrètement que le temps de la justice et le temps de l'histoire ne sont plus séparés. [...] "Le régime d'imprescriptibilité rend chacun contemporain des crimes passés dont les coupables sont en vie"' ['this notion means in practical terms that juridical time and historical time are no longer separate. (...) "The system of imprescriptibility makes everyone contemporary with those past crimes whose perpetrators are still alive"'].[54] Imprescriptible in France since 1964, crimes against humanity have long been linked to high-profile media events, with legislation and definitions evolving and mutating through the trials of Klaus Barbie, Paul Touvier, and Maurice Papon. All four of the sample

---

dans une démarche critique, scientifique, professionnelle qu'ils ne se reconnaissent dans une posture morale, même s'ils ne peuvent évacuer cette dimension' ['Broadly speaking, historians today are more likely to embrace a critical, scientific, professional approach to their subject than to adopt an ethical stance, though this dimension cannot be entirely eliminated'], Rousso, *Vichy. L'Événement, la mémoire, l'histoire*, p. 679.

[52]   Rousso's letter of refusal is reproduced in Richard Golsan (ed.), *The Papon Affair. Memory and Justice on Trial* (Routledge, 2000), pp. 193–4.

[53]   Evans, 'History, Memory, and the Law: the Historian as Expert Witness', *History and Theory*, 41 (2001): 326–45 [330].

[54]   Rousso, *Vichy. L'Événement, la mémoire, l'histoire*, p. 683. (Rousso is citing Yan Thomas, 'La vérité, le temps, le juge et l'historien', *Le Débat*, no. 102 (1998), p. 29.

texts focus, to varying degrees and in different ways, on the deportation and murder of Jews, and for that reason all are concerned, if only implicitly, with the temporally transcendent crime against humanity. *Un peu plus loin sur la droite* and *Leçon d'abîme*, more specifically, represent investigations into individual perpetrators and thus highlight the ethical agenda of the criminal investigator, driven in both texts to bring the guilty party to book. A closer look at just one of these texts reveals something of the potential ethics-related tensions between criminal and historical enquiry which crime fiction can illustrate.

When Vargas's investigator locates a former *milicien* responsible for the murder of Jews and resistants in 1944, he threatens him with the full force of the law: 'je te fais plonger au trou pour crime contre l'humanité' (226) ['I'll have you banged up for crimes against humanity'].[55] In fact, threat apart, Kehlweiler eschews recourse to due legal process, opting instead to force the guilty party to step down from his public duties, provide the names and addresses of other former *miliciens* as well as the contact details of those of his contemporaries who are of extreme right-wing persuasion. In his rendering of a pragmatic, future-oriented justice, Kehlweiler seems to achieve a balance between past and present; as he puts it: 'je ne suis pas passéiste, crois pas, on va aussi s'occuper de l'actuel' (225) ['There's no way I'm a slave to the past, we're going to deal with the present as well']. Vargas's investigator would probably find a measure of favour with a historian like Rousso, for whom dwelling on the past can itself precipitate injustice. As he famously states in the final paragraph of *Vichy, un passé qui ne passe pas*: 'l'obsession du passé [...] n'est qu'un substitut aux urgences du présent. Ou, pis encore, un refus de l'avenir' ['this obsession with the past (...) is just a substitute for the urgent needs of the present. Or, even worse, a refusal to look to the future'].[56]

Kehlweiler's historian assistant, meanwhile, follows a significant trajectory. Initially – like a Rousso or an Evans – Vandoosler distances himself from a judgmental stance: 'l'enquête criminelle, ça m'emmerde, je ne sais pas soupçonner. Comprendre, étudier, déduire, oui, mais soupçonner des vivants, incapable' (107) ['criminal investigations piss me off, suspicion's not my thing. Understanding, studying, deducing, yes, but suspecting living people, no can do']. It is only when he breaches the gap between past and present by realizing that justice is not just a contemporary affair – 'Ce n'était pas rien, la justice, en 1245. Et en fait, oui, ils s'en seraient occupés, s'ils avaient su que c'était de l'os humain' (68) ['Justice in 1245 wasn't a mere nothing. And in fact, yes, they would have dealt with it,

---

[55] In Rio's *Leçon d'abîme* when Uzler / Klein tells Malone that the worst that can happen is that he spend the rest of his life in jail, Malone replies with a clear allusion to Papon's trial and subsequent release on the grounds of ill health: 'Je sais. Et même peut-être moins. Vous envoyez des enfants à la mort, on vous colle dix ans et vous sortez aussitôt parce que vous avez attrapé un rhume. Mais ça ne se passera pas comme ça, Uzler' (81) ['I know. Maybe less than life in fact. You send children to their deaths, you get put away for ten years and you're out straight away because you've caught a cold. But that's not how it's going to happen, Uzler'].

[56] Rousso, *Vichy, un passé qui ne passe pas*, p. 423.

if they'd known that it was a human bone'] – that he leaves his static supporting role working in Kehlweiler's archives and gets on a train (another symbolic act of physical displacement) to join the criminal investigator in his hunt for the guilty party. Archives in France had a bad press in the 1990s. Various media-fuelled 'affairs' led to accusations that documents were being deliberately withheld or hidden, though for Rousso, the notion of 'secret' or 'forbidden' archival material was little more than a fantasy symptomatic of the famous Vichy syndrome.[57] As Derrida reminds us, archives have links to the givers of law: the term itself comes from the Greek *arkheion*, 'initially a house, a domicile, an address, the residence of the superior magistrates, the *archons*, those who commanded'.[58] Simmer, it is worth noting, is a self-confessed lover of archives, referring to them in etymologically telling manner as 'ma deuxième maison' (37) ['my second home']. It is significant that in the corpus archivists or those who frequent archives too assiduously are often cast in the role of villain, tending to represent an extreme form of historian; a sclerotic or 'State historian', to employ the term used by Sonia Combe, author of the polemical *Archives interdites*.[59]

Historians and criminal investigators cannot too readily be likened or assimilated as 'historian-detectives': many works of crime fiction, which represent *both* historians and detectives, reveal epistemological and juridical differences between what are often two distinct modalities of 'unearthing' the past. One final concept merits brief discussion, and that is closure, flagged up by Rousso as inimical to historical enquiry:

> La justice au sens large du terme est un processus qui vise à clore un événement (accident, délit, crime etc.) qui est venu rompre la continuité: elle classe, elle absout, elle condamne, et ce faisant, elle répare partiellement le dommage. [...] L'analyse historique se confronte, elle, à de l'"inachevé" [...] elle n'a jamais clos un dossier qui peut toujours être rouvert, révisé, et plus encore complété'.[60]

> [Justice in the broad sense of the term is a process which aims to bring to a close an event (accident, misdemeanour, crime etc.) which has disrupted continuity: it classifies, it absolves, it condemns, and in so doing it partly repairs the damage. (...) Historical analysis, by contrast, confronts the 'unfinished' (...) it has never closed a case which can always be reopened, reviewed, and further added to.]

If historical investigation remains open-ended and criminal investigation demands justice which in turn implies closure, where does this leave works which represent investigations into historical(ly real) crimes? Let us return to where this section began and consider what critics have to say about closure in Daeninckx's *Meurtres pour mémoire*, featuring 'historian-detective' Cadin, a text which ends

57   Ibid., 'Les archives: on nous cache tout, on nous dit rien', pp. 97–156 [121].

58   Derrida, *Archive Fever: A Freudian Impression* (U of Chicago P, 1996).

59   Sonia Combe, *Archives interdites. Les peurs françaises face à l'histoire contemporaine* (Albin Michel, 1994).

60   Rousso, *Vichy. L'événement, la mémoire, l'histoire*, pp. 707–8.

with the murder of the principal criminal (a thinly disguised Maurice Papon) and the suggestion that the case will be officially hushed up. Forsdick stresses the novel's critical function in revealing 'the mechanisms that prevent elements of the past from being exposed', describing this process as 'disrupting the mechanisms of the *roman policier* and refusing closure'.[61] Gorrara suggests that although '[I]n one sense, *Meurtres pour mémoire* provides a satisfying sense of closure for the reader' (the guilty party is dead), to the extent that there will be a cover-up the text 'undermines a wider sense of resolution'. Or as she puts it elsewhere, although 'a form of justice has been meted out', inasmuch as it is neither public nor exemplary, it 'falls far short of what Cadin and the reader would have wished'.[62]

Comments such as these indicate a need for greater specificity when it comes to discussion of closure: are we talking about ethical closure or aesthetic closure and how are these defined and related? After all, a reader of crime fiction would not expect the text they are reading to end with a representation of official or exemplary justice: the whodunnit traditionally closes with the public identification of the criminal, avoiding the representation of due legal process; *noir* versions typically bypass the law, which they tend to critique, in favour of poetic (rough? natural?) justice. It all comes down, of course, to readerly expectations, these being both genre-driven *and* extra-textual. Both *Leçon d'abîme* and *Un peu plus loin sur la droite* close with a bypassing of the official justice system: neither criminal (or potential criminal, in the case of Rio's text) will stand trial for crimes against humanity. For those readers who may balk at such endings – who may feel, like Gorrara, that they 'fall short' of what 'they would have wished' – a firm reminder that this is not real life but crime fiction is provided by the final line of each text, which in each case underlines common *noir* investigator traits (liking a drink and being easily distracted by women): '– Je veux une bière, dit-il' (Kehlweiler's words, p. 254) ['I want a beer, he said']; '"Aimez-moi, Malone! Aimez-moi!" / Il lui caressa doucement la tête. / "Bien sûr", dit-il' (87) ['"Love me, Malone! Love me!" He gently stroked her head. Of course, he said'].

Dora Bruder and *L'or et la cendre* also invoke readerly expectations in their closing lines, though they do so quite differently, by gesturing more to the extra-textual (the ethical?) than to genre convention (the aesthetic?). Modiano's narrator closes his investigation by making a virtue of necessity. Dora Bruder's story can never be told in full; everything that remains unknown about her 'case' is redefined as her 'precious secret', kept safe from perpetrators, laws, camps, History, and time; that is, 'tout ce qui *vous* souille et vous détruit' (145, my emphasis) ['Everything that sullies and destroys you']. *L'Or et la cendre* ends with the narrator (in a psychiatric unit, and thus likely to avoid the justice system) invoking a demonic force, presumed responsible for the crime – or the evil – of the Holocaust. His last words are ambiguous in terms of their addressee, with both his journalist double or (and) the reader potentially filling the role: 'J'ai toujours su que *vous* et moi

---

61   Forsdick, 'Direction les oubliettes de l'histoire', p. 349.

62   Gorrara, 'Historical Investigations', p. 87.

étions faits pour *nous* entendre' (379, my emphases) ['I always knew that you and I were made to get along']. With their introduction of the first and second person pronouns Abécassis's and Modiano's texts indirectly address us, and thereby also remind us of the real stuff of historical time, our time. The message is that these texts are about real issues in the real world. Rio's and Vargas's texts, by contrast, underline the fact that we are reading crime fiction, where criminals are dealt with according to quite different rules. It is perhaps telling that the genre-focused endings come in the texts marketed as works of crime fiction, whilst those which seek to involve us in the real, do not.

'I tell you these things as a stranger':[63] Investigating Fathers and Sons

Motifs and narrative patterns which might be dubbed 'oedipal' have already come to light in previous chapters, for instance in Simenon's *La neige était sale* (allusions to Frank's masculinity, problematic father figures, recurring references to blindness and enucleation), and Troye's *Meurtre dans un Oflag* (an investigator seeking himself as a possible guilty party, ocular-themed hallucinations). To these might be added Modiano's *Dora Bruder*, which also stages a search for both the self and the father, the latter recalled with ambivalence by the investigator-narrator. None of this would come as a surprise to critics of crime fiction, many of whom recognize the 'oedipal' (defined with varying degrees of precision) as a common characteristic of the genre. Links to the Sophoclean or Freudian version, or both, typically extend to several areas. First, a plot-centred version: crime fiction and Sophocles's *Oedipus The King* share 'the inevitable linearity of a plot in which murder will out, and the murderer be revealed'; 'la tragédie est structurée comme une enquête' ['the tragedy is structured like an inquiry'].[64] Factoring in the psychoanalytic yields up the notion that every detective, like every man (*pace* Freud) is a would-be killer, and that 'in the detective novel, the perpetrator is reassuringly revealed to be another, not the detective himself, not the reader, but someone quite different'.[65] Or, a claim which would strike a chord

---

[63] Sophocles, *Oedipus Tyrannus*, trans. Peter Meineck and Paul Woodruff (Hackett Publishing Company, Inc., 2000), lines 218–19.

[64] Page Dubois, 'Oedipus as Detective: Sophocles, Simenon, Robbe-Grillet', *Yale French Studies*, 108 (2005): 102–15; Jacques Dubois, *Le Roman policier ou la modernité*, p. 208 (see Chapter 7, 'Le genre où Oedipe est roi' for fuller discussion, pp. 205–18). Michael Holquist (whose take on detective fiction as kitsch reveals its age) suggests that 'it has long been a favorite trick of classicists to teach *Oedipus Rex* as a detective story', a point of view one suspects many classicists might contest, 'Whodunit and Other Questions: Metaphysical Detective Stories in Post-War Fiction', *New Literary History*, 3 (1971–72): 135–56 [139].

[65] Page Dubois, 'Oedipus as Detective', p. 111. Dubois's analysis of the oedipal motif in detective fiction as a means whereby the reader may, if only temporarily, master guilt, draws on the work of Geraldine Pederson-Krag (pp. 114–15); see Pederson-Krag's

with *noir* readers, 'the investigator's identity ultimately comes to be confused with the criminal's, so that the story being investigated slowly begins to overlap with the investigator's own story'.[66] Focus may fall on various aspects of the crime genre's exploration of identity, which binds it to both its Sophoclean and Freudian predecessors,[67] or on a paternal theme, here a little clumsily conflated with the uncovering of the past:

> La nécessité de renouer avec le passé, avec l'origine, apparaît dans la prédilection accordée au thème du père. Il semble que le retour au père vienne du désir assumé de désenfouir le passé en refusant la faculté d'aveuglement de notre civilisation.[68]
>
> [The need to re-establish contact with the past and with one's origins manifests itself in the genre's predilection for the paternal theme. It would seem that the return to the father stems from an avowed desire to disinter the past whilst repudiating our civilization's capacity for blindness.]

The fact that connections, albeit tenuous ones, can be made between almost any work of crime fiction and Sophocles's tragedy seems self-evident, if only to the extent that both involve the commission of crime and the reading of signs (Barthes, indeed, goes so far as to suggest that 'every story' leads back to 'the Oedipus story').[69] My concern here is to explore those aspects of the tragedy which can best be accommodated (modified, transposed) by texts representing the legacy of the war years in France. The following discussion is based on a cluster of five texts published within a very short time-span (1992–99), all of them featuring investigations into the past which centre on father-son relations. These familial representations will not be interpreted solely, or even primarily, in terms of character-centred complexes or parricidal pathologies (though these have their place in some of the texts), but rather in terms of transgenerational relations, with a specific focus on guilt and atonement, the keeping of family secrets, and the significance of mixed national parentage. Much has been written on the subject of second- and indeed third-generation German-language representations of the war centring on familial and transgenerational dynamics: specifically, the *Väterliteratur* (fathers' literature) of the late 1970s and what has been identified

---

'Detective Stories and the Primal Scene', in Glenn Most and William Stowe (eds), *The Poetics of Murder* (Harcourt Brace Jovanovich, 1983), pp. 13–20. For another Freudian approach focusing primarily on *The Moonstone*, see Hanna Charney, 'Oedipal Patterns in the Detective Story', in *Psychoanalytic Approaches to Literature and Film*, ed. Maurice Charney and Joseph Reppen (Associated UP, 1987), pp. 238–48.

[66]   Richard E. Goodkin, 'Killing Order(s): Iphigenia and the Detection of Tragic Intertextuality', *Yale French Studies*, 76 (1989): 81–107 [95–6].

[67]   Dubois, *Le roman policier ou la modernité*, pp. 211–14.

[68]   Evrard, *Lire le roman policier* (Dunod, 1996), pp. 126–7.

[69]   Barthes, *Le Plaisir du texte* (Seuil, 1973), p. 75.

as its much more recent variant.[70] The discussion which follows is intended as a step towards an equivalent analysis of the representation of France's post-war generations' wartime legacy.[71]

On the basis that it includes no explicit references to the Oedipus story Vargas's *Un peu plus loin sur la droite* can serve as a useful base-line for the detection of Sophoclean (or Freudian) influences. Investigator Louis Kehlweiler's unearthing of a *milicien* guilty of crimes against humanity was noted in the previous section, but one additional detail was omitted: amongst those members of the Resistance subjected to rape (and narrowly escaping murder) was Kehlweiler's French mother-to-be. The reader also learns that the investigator's father was German, more specifically, that he deserted from the Wehrmacht and joined the French Resistance. Two aspects of this parental representation merit further comment. First, as will emerge, this is only one of a significant proportion of the works under consideration which feature a protagonist of mixed French / German parentage. Secondly, the text foregrounds French criminality, in the form of the *milice*, whilst omitting the representation of nazis: the only German is a good German. I have written elsewhere of a pattern in recent French fiction in which Germans are represented as victims of the war, and I would suggest that Vargas's text and others like it (representing good Germans who are nonetheless not victims) may be related to such a trend.[72] Vargas's creation of an investigator of mixed parentage is, furthermore, used to short-circuit simplistic national and perpetrator / victim binaries: 'il pensa pour la millième fois que ça faisait cinquante ans qu'il vivait en France et cinquante ans qu'on l'appelait "l'Allemand". Les gens n'oubliaient pas, et lui non plus' (105) ['for the umpteenth time he reflected on the fact that he'd been living in France for 50 years and that for 50 years he'd been referred to as "the German". People didn't forget, and neither did he']. The implication may be that as a second generation German, Kehlweiler, and by extension all second generation Germans, should be forgiven;[73] as a second generation Frenchman, the responsibility for bringing the previous French generation to justice is his.

Un peu plus loin sur la droite represents a son who seeks justice for an as yet un-investigated crime committed against one of his parents (-to-be). Is this

---

[70] See Anne Fuchs, *Phantoms of War in Contemporary German Literature, Films and Discourse* (Palgrave Macmillan, 2008).

[71] For a complementary discussion of what Morris refers to as the 'missing heritage' of the children of collaborators (and some resistants) see his *Collaboration and Resistance Reviewed* (Berg, 1992), pp. 81–118.

[72] Hutton, 'Is France Post Post-War'.

[73] In Dantec's *Les racines du mal* the half-German, half-Alsacien Schaltzmann is held responsible for the crimes of French killers: 'Un demi-Teuton. Un Boche. Un M le Maudit de la fin du siècle' (247) ['Half-Deutsch. A Fritz. A turn of the century M for Murderer']; he is, the narrator states, the ideal scapegoat. Set in post-war Berlin Robbe-Grillet's *La Reprise* (2001), which might best be described as a meta-crime-novel complete with *Die Sphinx* cabaret, dreams of giant eyes and accursed Theban families, also represents family members of mixed French and German nationalities.

sufficient to make of Vargas's crime story an 'oedipal' text? Perhaps, although a
key factor – the investigator-son is himself innocent of all crimes – weakens such
a reading. Further motifs common to both texts can, however, be identified. More,
for instance, might be made of the notion of foreignness: Louis remains known
as 'l'Allemand'; Oedipus believes himself to be a foreigner in Thebes, a putative
stranger in his own land. The dispensing and withholding of knowledge is also
key to both texts: Oedipus' tragedy (Fate aside) stems in large part from the lies
he is told about his origins. Polybus and Merope conceal from him the truth of
his 'adoption', and according to some critics at least, Jocasta is well aware of the
incestuous conflation of generations in which she participates (Oedipus as both
husband and son to the woman who bore him). Seen in this light perhaps *Un peu
plus loin sur la droite* is more of an anti-oedipal text. Unlike Oedipus Kehlweiler
is aware of his origins; his maternal legacy is precisely that of revelation. As he
puts it, 'J'avais vingt ans quand ma mère me l'a refilée, l'histoire' (225) ['I was 20
when my mother passed the story on to me']. In this text handing down the truth
about the past to the second generation leads to a successful, and tragedy-free,
investigation.[74]

Unlike *Un peu plus loin sur la droite* Amoz's *L'Ancien crime* explicitly
references Sophocles, with an epigraph relocating the title in its original context:
'Mais comment retrouver à présent la trace presque effacée de l'ancien crime?',
Sophocle, *Oedipe Roi*, v. 109' ['Where can the faint / Track of this old blood-crime
be found?'].[75] Just in case we are left in any doubt, the investigator, police officer
Hopenot (in fact his case is less hopeless than that of his Sophoclean precursor)
also confesses to an intense childhood dislike of his father: 'Il y a de quoi se crever
les yeux, comme l'autre […] Oedipe!' (241) ['It's enough to make you put your
own eyes out, like that Oedipus character']. Without going into plot detail, we
learn that a chain of individuals were responsible for the death of Hopenot's father,
a communist: a French collaborator named Soublayrolles, who handed him over
to the *milice*, but also the six-year-old Hopenot, who first betrayed his father's
whereabouts to the collaborator. Amoz, like Vargas, stresses French and not German
criminality; unlike Vargas, he places a burden of guilt on his second generation
character. In *Un peu plus loin* Kehlweiler tells the apprehended criminal 'Ça fait
vingt-cinq ans que je sillonne le pays au cul de meurtriers' (225) ['For 25 years
now I've been the length and breadth of the country hot on the trail of murderers'].
Hopenot's has been a very similar trajectory, but with almost the opposite outcome:
'Il a passé sa vie à faire des enquêtes, à chercher la vérité d'autrui, et il a manqué
sa vérité, à lui' (240) ['He's spent his life investigating, seeking out the truth about
other people, and he's failed to find out the truth about himself'].

---

[74] As Charles Segal, referencing Aristotle's *Poetics*, notes, 'the best action for tragedy
occurs in ignorance followed by knowledge or recognition as in the *Tyrannus*'. (Aristotle
also mentions the importance of events occurring within the family.) *Sophocles' Tragic
World* (Harvard UP, 1998), p. 143.

[75] *Oedipus Tyrannus.*

In *Un peu plus loin sur la droite* Kehlweiler locates the first generation criminal and justice is done. At the close of Amoz's text we discover that the former collaborator Soublayrolles, after a very brief period in jail post-Liberation, has been living out his life in happy anonymity. Again, the key to a successful investigation lies with family secrets. In Vargas's text the investigator's mother informed him about the family's past; quite the opposite is the case in *L'Ancien crime*: 'Le silence et l'oubli. C'était la volonté maternelle' (239) ['Silence and forgetting. Such was the maternal will']. Only when forced to confront the war years via the Soublayrolles case does Hopenot face his childhood act of parricide by proxy, realizing in a moment of revelation that he has been acting out: his moustache is identical to that of Soublayrolles; like the collaborator, he has become an expert interrogator. Interpreting this and other similar texts, we can suggest that working through for France's 'children' (i.e., the second or post-war generation) means acknowledging and accepting both 'good' (resistance) and 'bad' (collaborator) fathers. France's second generation will not stop investigating (searching for its own identity) until and unless it comes to terms with what is both hatred and guilt directed towards the fathers of the first generation. Hatred, perhaps because war accentuated the power of the fathers, metaphorically castrating those who came after and could never 'prove' their masculinity; guilt arising both from that hatred but also, perhaps, as an expression of shame, the guilt which collaborators should have experienced, but did not.

A variant on the representation of second generation guilt can be found in Klotz's *Kobar* (1992) which adds another factor to the familial dynamic. Zoltan Kobar is approached by an organization claiming to know who denounced his Jewish father, who was deported and died in Maidanek in 1943. The offer is a trap: relatives of the dead are being misinformed and used to kill former resistants. What appears to be a Kehlweiler-like second generation search for justice, however, is turned on its head by a revelation towards the close of the text: it was the 15-year-old Zoltan who denounced his own father. The oedipal allusions are if not explicit, then at least pointed: Zoltan is afflicted with a limp: 'son pied blessé' (72) ['his injured foot']; 'la cheville gonfle' (154) ['his ankle was swelling up']. 'Pourquoi un enfant tue son père ...' (152) ['Why a child kills his father ...'], he ponders, and '"Parricide", ce mot que je n'ai jamais prononcé' (154) ['"Parricide". The word I've never uttered']. Although Zoltan claims to feel no sadness at his father's death and to despise all things Jewish, like Amoz's investigator-son, he cannot fully repress the war years: images from the concentration camps haunt his imagination; he practises holding his breath, wondering how long a man could hold out against the asphyxiating gas (45). Klotz's text differs in one respect from that of Amoz: this guilt-ridden son seeks to atone for his crime. By the close of the text Zoltan is dead, but not before he has killed every member of the organization which sought to trap him and others like him: 'je vous ai détruits. C'était mon rachat' (152) ['I've destroyed you. This is my atonement']. The notion of redemption in this context is an interesting one, especially if we read the text in terms of trauma, and consider once more the question of textual closure. Amoz's *L'Ancien crime* eschews closure at the level of justice: arguably, the collaborator and denouncer Soublayrolles is inadequately punished. Investigator Hopenot's recognition of his hitherto unconscious symptoms, however, does suggest a degree of closure if the text is read as a tale of self-investigation and trauma (where the investigator represents an entire generation). Klotz's text, by comparison, stages what LaCapra might refer to as an impossible closure:

> [...] there is a sense in which, while we may work on its symptoms, trauma, once it occurs, is a cause that we cannot directly change or heal. And any notion of full redemption or salvation with respect to it, however this-wordly or deferred, is dubious.[76]

Seen in this light Klotz's *Kobar* could only ever end with death of the protagonist.

The texts considered so far have emphasized Franco-French relations: criminality has been displaced from an external foe (the nazis) to an internal perpetrator-traitor. The next group of texts emphasize German criminality but, as in the case of *Un peu plus loin sur la droite*, represent second generation investigators of mixed parentage (for which read also heritage) and / or nationality. Aubert's *La Rose de fer* (1993) features French protagonist and first-person narrator Georges Lyons, who discovers that his father was Lucas von Klaussen, a nazi, and his mother an Austrian Jew. He also learns that his twin brother, Grégory von Klaussen, killed his father in order to secure a list of former high ranking nazis still involved in right-wing activities. Aubert's text manifests a dual splitting or doubling process: between perpetrator (nazi) and victim (Jew), but also French and German (via the siblings' names and chosen nationalities). As with Vargas's second generation investigator (still dubbed 'L'Allemand'), Georges is held accountable (here by a nazi hunter) for the misdeeds of the previous generation:

> Tu sais, parfois, j'ai l'impression que nous avons entretenu une réelle obsession de la vengeance, mais si tant d'hommes comme Lucas von Klaussen n'avaient pas été acquittés par les tribunaux d'après guerre! Et toi, tu es son fils! (254)

> [You know, I sometimes think we've been completely obsessed with revenge – but so many men like Lucas von Klaussen were acquitted by the courts after the war! And you, you're his son!]

A pattern becomes evident if we turn to Fonteneau's *Otto* (1997). Like Georges Lyons (and Amoz's Hopenot), Fonteneau's second generation protagonist, Jean Ménard, initially lacks information about his parentage and metaphorical heritage – we are told that a mystery hangs over his origins (113). As with Aubert's protagonist, Ménard discovers that he has a dual national identity: his father is the German Franz Sauer, and his mother the French Hélène Ménard. Just like Kehlweiler and Georges Lyons, Ménard is charged with the sins of his father: when only a young child his (French) uncle snapped out a nazi salute over his bedside.

---

[76]   LaCapra, *History in Transit*, p. 119.

Where Georges Lyons discovers his father was a nazi, Jean Ménard learns that the Sauer family supplied the nazi camps with crematoria. A successful investigation in these texts equates to the re-integration of split or doubled identities. Aubert's investigator discovers that his twin Grégory von Klaussen does not exist, that he is schizophrenic, and the true parricide. Closure is marked by the integration of the French and German aspects of the self into one: the protagonist signs off under his newly assumed name: 'G. Lyons-von Klausen'. Fonteneau's Jean Ménard, killed whilst hunting down a white supremacist group, atones for the sins of his (German) fathers: 'il aurait a racheter l'honneur perdu de la famille Sauer' (176) ['He would have to atone for the lost honour of the Sauer family']. Closure means integrating both his German and French heritage. Like Georges Lyons, Ménard alters his name, declaring, on the final page of the text: 'Je suis Jean Otto Ménard Sauer' (206).

Each of these five works of crime fiction stages a son's investigation into matters linked to his parents', and especially his father's, involvement in the war. More than just investigators, all of these sons, who are born during or shortly before the war years, can be read as symbolic of a second generation which must work through the legacy of the war, and this whether they are the offspring of French Resistance fighters, Wehrmacht deserters, Jewish deportees, or nazis. The present-day crimes represented in these works of fiction act primarily as triggers for investigations into the wartime past and transgenerational relations. Only acceptance of the role of the father – the first generation – whatever that role may have been, and the bringing to light of family secrets, provides closure. Simplistic binaries designating wartime Germans as bad and the French as good are unpicked in these texts, which represent *miliciens* and deserting Wehrmacht soldiers and, much more strikingly, also offer us second generation protagonists of mixed national heritage.

Closing Statement

Between crimes and the investigation into their perpetration lies a temporal and thus an epistemological gap. The attempt to breach this gap – which may in its temporal form span a few hours or several decades – has been at the centre of this chapter. Analysis of three investigating figures found in a significant proportion of works of crime fiction representing World War II – the journalist, the historian, the son inquiring into his father's past – reveals not just the epistemological, but also the ethical implications which arise when the attempt is made to reach back into the past and reconstruct a tale fit for the present.

Discussion of the journalist as investigator in texts published from the 1940s to the 1990s gave rise to some notable constants and variants. First, in their staging of what is, or is not, newsworthy, all four texts served to remind us of the waxing and waning interest of present generations vis-à-vis different aspects of the war years. In this case the works showed marked changes in their representation of members of the Resistance, from not particularly newsworthy scapegoat and murder victim (Blond) to protagonists of at best ambiguous morality (Daeninckx and Delteil) to media headline-making purported mythomaniacs who are nonetheless ultimately exonerated of all ill-doing (Abécassis). As well as exploring key issues such as the reliability of eye-witness testimony, the texts underlined the journalist-investigator's status as *writer*: into what different narrative forms can the past be inscribed?; (how) might these forms skew the 'facts' of 'the past'?; how best can the needs of the present and today's readers be met? All four texts, finally, revealed a splitting process at work: the investigator was represented by stasis, archival work, and emotional disengagement, but also by affective involvement and a degree of active participation impinging on, and in some cases directly influencing, the course and outcome of events.

Texts with historians as detectives, or works which invited a comparison between historical and criminal investigations, were likewise seen to undermine the notion of the 'scientific' i.e., objective and detached investigator, with the figure of the archivist coming to represent an undesirable extreme whose closest criminal counterpart can be found in the ratiocinative detective. Whilst criminal and historical investigators were seen to share epistemological and methodological difficulties involved in attempts to reconstruct the past, the texts also highlighted differences which have often been overlooked by critics writing on historian / detective affinities: concepts of, and attitudes to, judgment, justice, and closure were seen to have a very different place in historical and criminal investigations. Epistemological and ethical issues were explicitly flagged up in these texts, introducing a self-reflexive note with regard to both criminal investigation (and thus, by extension, crime fiction) and historical investigation (and thus the writing of the history of, in this instance, World War II).

Commenting on *Oedipus* MacIntosh states that 'Sophocles' tragedy clearly spoke to the audiences of Europe in the immediate post-war period because it showed an exemplary hero embattled and yet ennobled by his suffering at the hands of seemingly arbitrary fate'.[77] Analysis of a small group of texts published some 50 years after the war points to a rather different process of reception. In a reworking of the oedipal motif these works represent a post-war generation (sons) seeking with some difficulty and varying degrees of success to come to terms with the acts of the war generation (fathers), with the latter occupying a range of roles (nazi, French *milicien*, deported Jew, economic collaborator, resistant etc.). The decision to represent both 'good' and 'bad' fathers, and the representation in a significant proportion of texts of second generation protagonists of mixed French / German parentage, indicates a move towards the breaking down of simplistic ethical categories. Analysis of these texts can be regarded as a contribution to a fuller theory of a French version of *Väterliteratur*. Further work in this area would reveal that the representation of transgenerational tensions and conflicts extends to what is now the third generation.[78]

---

[77] Fiona MacIntosh, *Sophocles. Oedipus Tyrannus* (Cambridge UP, 2009), p. 148.

[78] See, for instance, Wagneur's *Homicide à bon marché* (1996).

Where the texts analyzed in Chapter 3 emphasized the historical inflection of the categories 'crime', 'criminals', and enforcers of 'law and order', the texts in this chapter have revealed the extent to which investigators too are more than genre-bound figures constructed only in accordance with aesthetic norms; they and the nature of their investigations are also inevitably molded by the historical context(s) represented. Equally, we are reminded that history exists only in narrative form; that World War II is written into different discourses (media, historical, psychoanalytic / mythical) with different audiences in mind. All, of course, wrapped up within another discourse – that of crime fiction itself.

Chapter 5
Criminal Continuities

Time has fallen asleep in the afternoon sunshine.

—Bradbury[1]

Reflection requires that you watch out for occurrences, that you don't already know what's happening. It leaves open the question: *Is it happening*? [*Arrive-t-il?*] It tries to keep up with the now [...].

—Lyotard[2]

For some time now critical perspectives on the war years have gravitated towards what might be referred to as a 'memory turn'. Andreas Huyssen, typically, suggests that 'since the 1980s [...] the focus has shifted from present futures to present pasts'; we are, it would appear, a culture obsessed with memory, archives, and musealization.[3] As emerged in the previous chapter, for commentators on the specifically French historical context such as Henry Rousso, the wartime past has become overly intrusive: indigestible, it refuses to pass as it should ('un passé qui ne passe pas');[4] Vichy is a 'syndrome' redolent of repression and denial. It may well be time, figures such as Rousso seem to suggest, for the ethical obligation of a 'duty to remember' to cede to the enough-already pragmatism of a 'right to forget'. From the digestive to the neurotic, discourses relating to the war court metaphors. Consider, for instance, the future-oriented notion of learning lessons from the past and its vicissitudes, or the war years as a (usually burdensome) legacy, with implications of both continuity, in the form of the next generation, and the rupture marked by the real or symbolic death of the legator. The past and its conflicts may be conceptualized as a mode of haunting, complete with uncanny revenants and the correlative collapse of discrete temporalities as figures from the past stalk the present.

---

[1] Ray Bradbury, *Fahrenheit 451* (HarperCollins, 2008), p. 51.

[2] Jean-François Lyotard, *The Differend. Phrases in Dispute* (U of Minnesota P, 1988), p. xv.

[3] Andreas Huyssen, *Present Pasts. Urban Palimpsests and the Politics of Memory* (Stanford UP, 2003), p. 11 and p. 6.

[4] In fact, as Pierre Nora points out (though he does not name Nolte), Rousso and Conan's title is taken from an article that was to trigger the *Historikerstreit* (historians' debate): Ernst Nolte's highly controversial piece 'Vergangenheit, die nicht vergehen will. Eine Rede, die geschrieben, aber nicht gehalten werden konnte', *Frankfurter Allgemeine Zeitung*, 6 June 1986. See Nora, 'Le Syndrome, son passé, son avenir', *French Historical Studies*, 19.2 (1995): 487–93 [491].

As was the case with Chapter 4, this final chapter treats texts whose criminal plots hinge on events relating to the French experience of World War II and do so in a post-war setting. However the focus, this time, is especially on time; more specifically, on the manner in which representations of the war are linked to the past, the present, and the future. As Currie points out in his *About Time*, with their capacity to explore the theme both constatively and performatively, works of fiction have a great deal to tell us about time (and, it might be said, its metaphors).[5] This seems all the more likely to be true of works of crime fiction which are set in one period but look back to another, which frequently represent crimes perpetrated in two at least apparently distinct eras of 'then' and 'now', and which tend to be structured in such a way as to promote suspense, which is future-oriented, and / or curiosity, which can be both future- and past-oriented. These are, furthermore, works which represent characters living with both acute and chronic emotions such as guilt, regret, fear, the desire for revenge, all of which key into various temporalities. As the ensuing discussion makes clear, the works of crime fiction examined in this chapter seem to bear out the Rousso-esque claims that French society remains focused on its wartime past; but two crucial caveats must be sounded. First, a very simple yet powerful fact: as works of fiction peopled with a range of characters, these texts humanize the issue of the past's incursions into the present, revealing *why* it may be that the past cannot be so readily set aside, and this in a variety of contexts. Secondly, the past's presence in the present is, in many cases, future-oriented. These texts often strike an admonitory note; they may well express grounded concern rather than obsession or neurosis. This is not always the case of a self-indulgent dwelling in the past.

In what follows a first, classificatory, section offers readings of representative texts which have been chosen to demonstrate something of the range of time-related approaches to the war and, equally, war-related perceptions, or constructions, of time. The second section deepens the focus, examining a small group of novels which expose and denounce the dangers represented by the extreme political right and Holocaust deniers in contemporary France.

That Was Now; This Is Then: Variants on the Theme of Continuity

Texts deemed to be set 'after the war' must, by implication, manifest a gap or break – some manner of discontinuity – between the events of World War II and a later diegetic context, but what is this break and how is it constituted? Set in 1944 Dard's *La Crève* (1946) serves as a useful borderline case. Is the war over in this diegetic world? Is it – has it become – 'then' in relation to some newly constituted 'now', and if so, how has this come about? Dard's text features the Lhargne family, consisting of Louis, a *milicien*, his sister Hélène, who has consorted with a German lover, and their parents, all effectively in hiding as triumphant French

---

[5]   Mark Currie, *About Time. Narrative, Fiction and the Philosophy of Time* (Edinburgh UP, 2007), p. 90.

Forces of the Interior (FFI) take to the streets. Normative historical periodization, broadly speaking, may posit 1945 as a point of temporal rupture between 'war' and 'post-war', but for these characters the war is already over, a new era signalled by the now criminal status of the siblings: by the close of the text Louis will have been shot and Hélène's head shaved. For the original 1946 reader for whom the often unregulated purges were a recent event, this diegetic future would in all probability have been expected – we might say that as far as the text's ending was concerned it would have been only a matter of time. For later generations of readers it is possible, indeed likely, that both suspense and curiosity generated by an as-yet-unknown textual future would have been sustained. With this is mind it is worth noting that *La Crève* was only published and marketed as a work of crime fiction in its 1989 *Fleuve noir* edition.

In the case of the characters Louis and Hélène the socio-political discontinuity which heralds a new era is imposed upon them by external agents; their own views do not change, indeed Louis defiantly insists that he is as much a representative of France as any other man (92). The break or gap between 'then' and 'now' may, however, be marked out by an interiorized moment of changed perspective. When the father, who like the majority of French citizens had merely kept his head down during the Occupation, first glimpses the victorious troops, his point of view changes abruptly: 'Il imaginait les maquisards à travers les récits de son fils. […] des dévoyés, de la racaille […] et voilà qu'il tombe sur l'armée française' (90) ['He used to picture the *maquisards* in the light of his son's stories. (…) delinquents, a rabble (…) and lo and behold, he'd stumbled across the French army']. This sort of personal paradigm shift, underscored here by both a change of tense from the imperfect to the present and by the revelatory deictic 'voilà', need not be quite so dramatic. In Dard's *Batailles sur la route* (1949), which reads as a sequel to *La Crève*, Hélène has been rescued from the grasp of FFI troops threatening to rape her and here, some time later, explains the sensation she has of having entered a new (personal) era:

> Tu comprends, un cycle de souvenirs ne s'achève pas à une date, à une heure fixe. Lorsqu'il finit, on ne s'en aperçoit pas tout de suite; on continue à exister, et puis tout à coup on s'arrête; on écoute et on s'aperçoit que ça y est, qu'on est engagé dans une autre période. (100)
>
> [You see, a cycle of memories doesn't come to a close on a certain date, at a fixed time. When it's over, you don't realize straight away; you carry on existing, and then suddenly you stop; you listen and you realize that that's it, you're engaged in a new period of your life.]

Both of Dard's novels offer insight into the difference between subjective and historical periodization; the discrepancy between tranches of time as they are lived and as they are officially recorded or, perhaps more accurately, retrospectively constructed. *La Crève* also demonstrates how biological time in the form of generational periodization may be subverted. Horrified by his son's affiliations Lhargne senior states that he feels like a brother to the youthful FFI troops whilst his son Louis and his generation seem to belong to an earlier era (94), indeed to represent an external threat to the nation: 'D'autres hommes sont venus: nos enfants, et nous ont envahis bien avant les Allemands' (119) ['Other men came: our children, and invaded us long before the Germans']. Generations may, we are reminded, be conceived in terms other than the biological and chronologically successive.

La Crève and *Batailles sur la route* illustrate how for the individual a new era can be born, a personal page turned, and the wartime past can pass. Many more works demonstrate the various and varied ways in which the war may be deemed *not* to be over, showing rather how it seeps or thrusts its way into the present or lived 'now', years, even decades, 'after the event'. The first of what will be presented as different categories of such texts – though there are overlaps and echoes amongst all of these – involves the representation of trauma, and can be illustrated by two differently accented works: Garnier's *L'A26* (1999) and Japp's *Le Silence des survivants* (2000).

The Temporal Textures of Trauma

Set in the 1990s *L'A26* takes its title from the highway on which serial killer Bernard picks up his young female victims. Bernard's criminal acts of rape and murder, it is suggested, are generated by the resentment born of his having to devote his life to the care of his sister Yolande, with whom he lives. The spatial displacement implied in the text's title is contrasted with the depiction of Yolande, who has not left the house since the day her head was shaved during the purges of 1944 as a punishment for her 'crime' of horizontal collaboration.[6] The past, *L'A26* would seem to suggest, takes its toll on the present, and not just with regard to the primary victim of trauma: Yolande's crime – or the crime committed against her, depending on one's perspective, for she can be constructed as both a victim of the 'liberators' and the perpetrator of low grade treason – apparently precipitates criminal acts carried out by a third party half a century later. Garnier, however, keeps his ethical distance: the narrative remains locked in the subjective point of view of its protagonists, thereby avoiding a simplistic blaming of the ills of the present on the past. And if the author eschews determinism with respect to his criminal, Bernard, he also introduces temporal texture into what is perhaps the typical portrayal of a trauma victim as one who is passively subjected to influxes of the past into the present.

True, Yolande is depicted as trapped, held as if in amber in a condition of both spatial and temporal stasis: 'Elle ne devient plus depuis près de cinquante ans' (16) ['She stopped becoming nearly 50 years ago'], we are told. Figurative language

---

6   Other works of crime fiction which centre on the perceived injustices of the 'épuration sauvage' (unregulated or unofficial post-war purges) include Claude Courchay's *Retour à Malaveil* (1982), Frédéric Fajardie's *La Théorie du 1%* (1981), Robert Deleuse's *Retour de femme* (1991), Jean-Pierre Perrin's *Chiens et louves* (1999), Maurice Gouiran's *Sous les pavés, la rage* (2005) and Philippe Huet's *Bunker* (2008).

also binds the character to the past: Yolande is like a 'vieille photo' (7) ['an old photo'], a 'bouquet fané' (85) ['a faded bouquet']. Composed of 'une matière inaltérable' ['immutable matter'], she is compared to a statue on which moss will spread and pigeons defecate (85). From her perspective, the present is at times occluded by a narrative from the past: she believes that her brother's excursions from the house are Resistance missions; that he is killing German soldiers. (This constitutes a neat subversion of wartime stereotypes: the Resistance hero as serial killer; we may be reminded of Dantec's killer, Schaltzmann.) But Garnier's representation does more than bind Yolande to the past; she occupies several temporal dimensions. 'Yolande peut avoir entre vingt et soixante-dix ans' (7) ['Yolande could be anything between 20 and 70 years old'], we learn on the opening page. Statue-like she may be, but she is also compared to the sea into which anything and everything can be thrown, 'et la surface redeviendra intacte, comme si de rien n'était' (85) ['And the surface would just close over them as if nothing had happened']: apparent unchange is only an illusion; the ocean, it might be said, represents a present whose constant flux cannot necessarily be detected. Yolande, finally, is also described as 'the great witness', a figure whose reach at least by implication extends over three temporal dimensions: witnessing the past in the present tense of memory, for a future generation.

Where the past is associated with trauma for Yolande – let us say, with what was but should not have been – for the killer, Bernard, it signals regret, or what was not but should have been: were it not for his sister, he might be with Jacqueline, an unhappily married woman with whom he meets regularly but for whom he will not abandon Yolande. In a short but noteworthy dialogue, Bernard and Jacqueline exchange views about time. For Jacqueline, when it comes to retrospection, remorse trumps regret: 'Je me demande si je ne préférerais pas. Au moins, on aurait fait des choses' (20) ['I wonder if I wouldn't prefer that. At least we'd have done something']. The exchange continues:

> – Des choses? ... pour ce qu'il en reste des choses!
> – Ben quoi, tu voulais laisser des pyramides derrière toi? ... Les choses c'est pas que des trucs en pierre [...] des monuments! C'est que des petits riens, comme quand on allait pêcher les grenouilles dans les trous des bombes, la première P4 en fumée en cachette, tout ce qu'on se disait qu'on allait faire même si on savait déjà qu'on ne le ferait jamais ... (20–21)

> [Done something? ... as if there's anything left of 'things'! What, so you'd like to leave behind a few pyramids? ... Things aren't just lumps of carved stone, (...) monuments! They're just tiny scraps of nothing at all, like when we used to go looking for frogs in bomb craters, or smoking that first cigarette on the sly, everything we told each other we'd do even if we already knew we never would ...]

Lived temporality in the form of wartime memories of unremarkable quotidian activities is positively contrasted here to official records which in their marking of the past in the present commemorate death rather than life (the pharaoh's pyramid, the monument to the fallen). The future-in-the-past ('ce qu'on se disait qu'on allait faire') also has value even if was always-already never to be. We are a long way here from a wholesale dismissal of 'un passé qui ne passe pas'.

At the close of *L'A26* it is revealed that Yolande's head was shaved by André, the father of Jacqueline's husband Roland, and a big figure in the wartime black market. The final page sees a justice of sorts meted out via the conflation, or confusion, of generations: living in the past but acting in the present, Yolande shoots Roland, mistaking him for his father. It might be said that Garnier's text undercuts a victim / criminal binary through time, using time: the wartime victim becomes a killer whilst the present day serial killer is, if only up to a point, represented as a victim of past events. Japp's *Le Silence des survivants* also presents its reader with a potentially uncomfortable probing of victim / perpetrator boundaries, and it too represents victims of trauma and a serial killer operating out of a family unit.[7] Isabel, a French-Cambodian victim of the *Khmer rouge* by whom she was tortured and raped, is married to Isaac, whose father, Simon, was deported to Auschwitz as a child. The text opens with the brutal murder of Isabel's daughter, followed by that of Isaac. (There have been other victims, unrelated to the family.) As with *L'A26*, Japp's text offers a nuanced temporal representation of how crimes committed in the past affect the present. The following passage is narrated from Isabel's point of view:

> d'une certaine façon, Simon et elle étaient déjà morts depuis bien longtemps dans les camps [...] même si parfois ils parvenaient eux-mêmes à l'oublier. Ils étaient des survivants, des sursitaires en attente de quelque chose, peut-être [...] d'une explication. (43)
>
> [in a way, she and Simon had died a long time ago in the camps (...) even if they themselves sometimes managed to forget the fact. They were survivors, living on borrowed time whilst waiting for something, maybe an explanation.][8]

In metaphorical terms these victims of war crimes are revenants, belonging to the past but inhabiting the present. As 'sursitaires' – those who are reprieved, whose sentence is suspended – they still await death, looking to a future which remains open (as it does for the reader, who also awaits the textual end). Operating simultaneously in three temporal dimensions the two characters are by no means represented as determined or paralyzed by the forces of the past, indeed it is a conflation of past and present which provides a dual motive for future action: Isabel determines to kill her daughter's murderer, knowing that to do so will be also symbolically to kill the *Khmer rouge* criminals who tortured her ('Elle tuerait

---

[7]   For another work of crime fiction which explores the effects of wartime trauma within a family unit see Hélène Couturier's *Sarah* (1997).

[8]   See Richard Rechtman, 'Produire du témoignage', in Catherine Coquio (ed.), *L'Histoire trouée: négation et témoignage* (L'Atalante, 2003), pp. 613–24, for a discussion of the links between past and present and life and death experienced by the survivors of the Cambodian genocide.

du même coup Ta Mok, "le boucher", et Nam Nay, l'homme de main spécialiste des décharges électriques et de l'arrachage des ongles' (42) ['By the same token she would be killing Ta Mok, "the butcher", and Nam Nay, the henchman who specialized in administering electric shocks and ripping out finger-nails']. Isabel's is represented as a self-conscious agency. The character reflects on the potential impact of her actions in a future that she realizes may well become an officially recorded past: 'Jusqu'où est-on capable d'aller pour modifier la course des choses, ce qui, un jour peut-être, deviendra l'Histoire' (42) ['Just how far is someone willing to go in order to change the course of events, events which might, one day, become History'].

In Garnier's *L'A26* we saw the present generation stand in for that which preceded it when a son was killed in the place of his father, whilst Dard's *La Crève* revealed how different generations need not imply a simple succession in chronological time. For its part *Le Silence des survivants* offers insight into the question of generational transmission via a series of biological metaphors. First, in a time-collapsing image which edges towards the conflation of two genocides occurring a generation apart – that of Pol Pot's Cambodia and the Shoah – and positions History, or the war, the past, in the role of grotesque mother, trauma victims Simon and Isabel are described as twins born of a monstrous pregnancy (83). When it is revealed that it is Thomas, Isabel's son, who is the serial killer, his mother holds firm to her resolution to kill the killer: 'Je ne permettrai pas que le nom de Thomas s'ajoute à ceux de Ta Mok, Cham Daravuth et des autres' (173) ['I will not allow Thomas's name to be added to those of Ta Mok, Cham Daravuth, and others']. Isabel seeks to disrupt criminal continuity, but Simon's rejoinder, which recasts the trauma victims as dangerous metaphorical parents, suggests that bad blood will out: '– Ni de Hitler, Mengele et Eichmann. Il sort aussi de moi' (173) ['Nor that of Hitler, Mengele, and Eichmann. He's my descendant too']. Japp, like Garnier, is treading potentially controversial ground, at the very least gesturing towards a determinism that would construct a killer from the trauma of others; the metaphorical genes, or blood, of two victims combining to produce a perpetrator of multiple crimes.

From Phantasy to the Fantastic: Nazis Who Transcend Time

Characters who have been traumatized by past events are represented as both enduring and fearing a repetition of those events. Shuttling between the past-in-the-present of memory and a future present fuelled by fear, Japp's Simon endlessly recalls his experiences in Auschwitz and also conceptualizes Thomas as a future avatar of Hitler; Garnier's Yolande similarly lives in the past whilst anticipating its return: 'Les Allemands reviendront. Elle ne les attend pas particulièrement, mais elle sait qu'ils reviendront' (24) ['The Germans will come back. She's not especially waiting for them, but she knows they'll come back']. In such instances the notion of return is an individual's phantasy. Some texts, however, untroubled by the demands of verisimilitude, make it real: the nazis really do come back; indeed strictly speaking, they have never gone away.

A romping spy thriller set in the late 1980s, Fajardie's *Le Loup d'écume* (1986) centres on the activities of the titular U-Boat, which roams the oceans torpedoing enemy ships, crewed by three generations of nazis. The vessel is dubbed the 'phantom submarine' on the cover blurb, but this is no metaphorical haunting. As Admiral Dönitz himself explains in one of several analepses set in 1945, the original crew of the U-boat will be dispatched to set up the Nibelungen (what else?), a secret nazi base in the Amazon:

> Pour ceux-là, à des milliers de kilomètres de la Patrie, la guerre continuera. [...] je sais que dans dix, vingt ou peut-être trente ans, l'élite de la marine de guerre allemande, augmentée de deux générations, pourra [...] reprendre le combat pour l'Idée allemande. (28)

> [For them, thousands of kilometres from the Fatherland, the war will continue. (...) I know that in 10, 20, maybe 30 years, the elite of the German navy, strengthened by two generations, will (...) once again take up arms in the name of the German Idea.]

Fajardie's use of twin temporalities allows him to represent the realization of Dönitz's (almost) impossible dream. The trauma-induced phantasy of returning nazis experienced by characters such as Simon and Yolande transmutes into a text which, in its actualization of the figurative – the haunting past – flirts with the fantastic as a literary mode. How seriously should we take this? As the text comes to a close a young American checking video footage of the destroyed U-Boat on the ocean bed reflects: 'Les voilà tranquilles jusqu'à la fin des temps. Faut jamais jouer avec l'Histoire. Oh non!' (247) ['That's them at peace until the end of time. It never does to play with History. For sure!']. Read as a self-conscious authorial quip, the remark casts *Le Loup d'écume* in the role of a ludic, parodic take on both the spy thriller and fantastic tales of lurking and returning nazis. Not all texts of this type adopt a light-hearted approach to their subject matter, though all are obliged to relinquish at least some measure of realism.

Time and its passing ensure that the continued existence of the 'original' nazis – what Darnaud refers to as 'vieux gammés' (from the 'croix gammé' or swastika) in his *Le Crépuscule des vieux* (1997) – becomes increasingly unlikely in any text with a contemporary setting (Fajardie's first generation nazi submariners are already in their sixties and seventies). Authors wishing to represent non-*ersatz* nazis – and the return, or uncanny continued presence, of the real thing is that much more powerful than an imitation in terms of fantasy fodder – are forced to veer increasingly further away from the realm of realism. This is certainly the case for Darnaud's *Le Crépuscule des vieux* (another Wagnerian echo) and d'Estienne d'Orves *Les orphelins du mal* (2007), both of which begin with the apparently unexceptional investigation of murders in the contemporary diegesis before plunging ever deeper into the frankly bizarre. It is at once impracticable and unnecessary to outline plots here (not least because *Les orphelins*, coming in at over 500 pages, hops between multiple temporalities and secondary narratives) but worth noting that the texts display striking similarities. Both authors have found inspiration in the *Ahnenerbe*, a research group set up in the 1930s by Himmler, amongst others, to investigate the ancestry of the 'Aryan race', and in the historically real figure of Otto Rahn, a medievalist and SS officer with interests in the Holy Grail and *Nibelungenlied*. Where the nazis sought to trace their supposed racial lineage backwards in time, however, d'Estienne d'Orves and Darnaud project the race issue forwards into the future. Both texts feature elixirs of eternal life quaffed by first-generation nazis alongside clones and 'l'Élu', a time-transcending *Ur*-nazi who will ensure the perpetuation of the Master Race. Although both of these texts display self-reflexive elements – *Les orphelins* features an intradiegetic author who writes popular fiction of questionable merit; in its final pages *Le Crépuscule* introduces a note of uncertainty as to whether the events really took place before confirming that they did – there is nothing to indicate that they are intended to be read as out-and-out parodies. Of course the very existence of texts which represent timeless nazis, whether these be parodic, humorous, or intended as works to be read 'straight', speaks to some degree of persistent anxiety on the part of their intended readership.

Handing Down the Past: Problematic Legacies

Both ph/fantasies of returning nazis and the representations of trauma discussed so far can be conceived of in terms of metaphorical legacies: the psychological remnants of wartime events are unwittingly passed on and disrupt the present. Other texts deal with literal legacies. (Boileau-Narcejac's *Maldonne*, discussed in Chapter 2, can be regarded as a pseudo literal legacy narrative, in which a tale of inheritance is deliberately deployed in an attempt to foil a gang of nazi hunters.) I have written elsewhere on the subject of those works of crime fiction which represent the problematic handing on of Jewish property which was plundered and spoliated during the war.[9] A rather different version of a Jewish inheritance crime

---

[9] Margaret-Anne Hutton, 'Legacies of the Second World War: Representations of the Theft of Jewish Property in Recent French Crime Fiction', *French Studies*, 66.4 (2012): 493–509. The article focuses on Geffray, *Les teutons flingueurs* (1999); G.-J. Arnaud, *Spoliation* (2000); Chaboud, *Le Tronc de la veuve* (2003); Simsolo, *Wazemmes* (2005); and Cayre, *Toiles de maître* (2005). Zufferey, *L'Étoile d'or* (1998) also centres on the topic of Jewish material legacy, whilst G. Arnaud's *Maudit blood* (1985) represents four generations of the Savetan family, whose 'evil' – the murder and spoliation of Jews during the war – is symbolized by a hereditary haemophilia. For key works on the nature of the spoliation of Jewish goods, especially art works, see Avi Becker (ed.), *The Plunder of Jewish Property During the Holocaust* (Palgrave, 2001); Hector Feliciano, *Le musée disparu* (Éditions Austral, 1995); Jean Mattéoli, *Mission d'étude sur la spoliation des juifs de France*, and Lynn Nicholas, *The Rape of Europa* (Vintage, 1995). For a discussion of post-war justice (or a lack of it) and reparation see Michael Bazyler and Roger P. Alford (eds), *Holocaust Restitution. Perspectives on the Litigation and its Legacy* (New York UP, 2006); Stuart

narrative can be identified in Monteilhet's *Le Retour des cendres* (1961).[10] First (some of) the decidedly baroque plot in brief: Jewish doctor Elisabeth Pilgrin, née Wolf, returns from a concentration camp to discover that she has inherited great wealth from her extended family, all of whom have died in the camps. Although she initially delays a reunion with her husband, Stan, in order to recuperate physically, the couple meet up by chance. Stan, who has taken up with Fabienne, Wolf's daughter by a former partner, singularly fails to recognize his wife, and persuades her to play the role of herself, so that her legacy, which has been frozen in the absence of physical proof of her death, can be claimed by her legatee, Fabienne. After much to-ing and fro-ing, during which Stan rejects Fabienne in favour of Elisabeth, the latter is murdered.

Montelheit's text is both ahead of its time and of its time. Ahead, because it deals with the matter of war-related Jewish inheritance – it even mentions Swiss bank accounts – some 35 years before these became highly mediatized global issues. Of its time, because unlike works of crime fiction published in the late 1990s and early twenty-first century, *Le Retour des cendres* is not concerned with the spoliation or plunder of Jewish wealth by agents of Vichy or the Nazis: this is a tale of personal – and as it turns out, exclusively Jewish – jealousy and greed. Monteilhet's plot device of a material legacy is, I suggest, inextricably linked yet secondary to the author's not particularly philosemitic representation of Jewish identity. One of the female protagonist's first ventures upon her return from the camps is to consult a plastic surgeon and request a remodelled 'Jewish nose' (19) in a move to reaffirm her Jewishness. Quite apart from the preposterous physical stereotyping involved in his episode,[11] as historians have noted, the majority of Jews returning to France from the camps were in fact keen to assimilate and to play down their status as Jews, for the most part remaining silent about their ordeal.[12] Elisabeth, however, is set up by the author to facilitate an exploration and exposition of Jewishness. Late in the text Stan, in a *coup de théâtre*, reveals to her that his parents, or at least his mother, was a Jew, adding with considerable vehemence that he is not. Elisabeth's observation that Stan was not circumcised is

---

Eizenstat, *Imperfect Justice. Looted Assets, Slave Labor, and the Unfinished Business of World War II* (Public Affairs, 2003); Jon Elster, *Closing the Books: Transitional Justice in Historical Perspective* (Cambridge UP, 2004); and Michael Marrus, *Some Measure of Justice. The Holocaust Era Restitution Campaign of the 1990s* (U of Wisconsin P, 2009).

[10] For a reading of Montelheit's text as an example of anamnestic French texts which represent the wartime persecution of the Jews see Gorrara, 'Forgotten crimes? Representing Jewish experience of the Second World War in French crime fiction', *South Central Review*, 27.1–2 (2010): 3–20. Jean Amila's *La Lune d'Omaha* (1964) also centres on a disputed inheritance as well as issues relating to commemoration.

[11] The stereotyping of Jewish characters is discussed in my 'From Christ-Killers to Christ-Figures: Representations of Jews in Post-1980 French Occupation Fiction', *French Cultural Studies*, 18.1 (2007): 107–24.

[12] See Annette Wieviorka, *Déportation et génocide* (Paris: Plon, 1992), 'L'Impact du génocide sur la communauté', pp. 337–68.

met by a feeble pun: 'J'y ai coupé' (190).[13] For Elisabeth, however, Jewish identity is a matter of inheritance: 'Tes parents étaient juifs, tu auras beau faire: tu resteras juif!' (190) ['Your parents were Jews; say what you like, you'll still be a Jew'].

Elisabeth's belief in a familial (matrilineal) handing down of Jewish identity is countered by Stan's claim that it is 'false Jews' like her – this would appear to signify secular Jews – who perpetuate the myth of the Jew as victim. This, of course, is nothing more than the point of view of one character. But the text's conclusion is discomfiting. When she learns of her material legacy Elisabeth reflects on the irony of the situation: 'le massacre m'a rendue riche: j'hérite à perdre haleine' (12) ['The massacre's made me rich: all this money's taken my breath away']. Given the author's predilection for puns, this can surely only be read as deliberately infelicitous: in a repetition of the crime of the Holocaust, transmuted here into common murder, Elisabeth is to be literally deprived of breath, dying of gas inhalation in her flat. Denied her material legacy the character may be, but a metaphorical legacy casting her in the role of Jew-as-victim is inexorably played out. And if *Le Retour des cendres* seems to posit a certain determinism – the past, and / as race, will out – then this is further reinforced at a performative level.

The text consists of Elisabeth's first-person diary entries, which run from 29 June 1945 to 29 October 1945. In temporal terms the diary as a narrative mode records the past for posterity, and indeed Elisabeth's final entry is marked by a triple gesture to the future as she comments of her journal: 'Un jour, je le relirai, il me fera sourire, et je le jetterai au feu' (192) ['One day I'll read it again and it will make me smile and I'll throw it on the fire']. From the perspective of the reader the diary is a form which holds the future open, and is thus in keeping with the creation of suspense. Monteilhet's text, however, is framed. The first-person diary entries are preceded by a letter dated 1 November 1945 and addressed to Elisabeth's daughter Fabienne. Written by an investigating magistrate the letter both informs the reader of Elisabeth's murder, and expresses the firm conviction that Fabienne will confess to the crime the same day. The frame makes of Elisabeth – like trauma victims Simon and Isabel in Japp's *Le Silence des survivants* – a 'sursitaire'; one who is only temporarily reprieved: the reader knows that she will die. There is a tension in this text which is comparable to Garnier's representation of his trauma victim Yolande as both statue (fixity) and sea (flux). Elisabeth's diary represents her as fighter who refuses to extend her past suffering into the present (hers is an individual claim to a right to forget): although a literal revenant – she has come back from the camps – she herself rejects the metaphorical status of living dead. The text's opening frame, however, reinforces the thematic determinism, setting her fate in stone, or at least in type. And the closing frame is yet more disturbing. In a final, unattributed, line, we read: 'N.B. Mademoiselle Wolf s'est donné la mort par le gaz dans la nuit du 1er au 2 novembre 1945' (192) ['Nb. Miss Wolf died at her own hand by gas inhalation on the night of 1 to 2 November 1945'].

---

[13] Meaning 'I got away with it' this also functions as a pun, since 'couper' means to cut.

Two generations of Jews die by gas in Monteilhet's textual world: the end that awaited so many in the camps can, apparently, only be postponed.

Unfinished Business: Justice and Revenge

The crime works which I have categorized here as legacy texts tend to open with the actual or presumed wartime death of the legator, before going on to play out the contemporary consequences of that rupture or discontinuity. The next grouping of texts, which is one of the most common, generally stages a death in the form of a murder or murders in the present perpetrated as a response to crimes which were committed during the war years and which are deemed to be unresolved. These can be called justice, or revenge texts, though the two terms need to be unpicked. As to what form the original crime which calls forth justice or revenge takes, or the identity of the present day seeker of closure, this answer is perhaps best summed up by Carraud's *Les Poulets du cristobal* (1998), whose title alone, with its referencing of Steiner's *The Portage to San Cristobal*, gestures to the notion of belated or delayed justice.[14] Set on board a ship on the Caribbean Sea in the 1950s this zany whodunnit opens with the murder of former collaborator Eric le Manant, (pseudo) baron de Tartifume. As the text unfolds it becomes clear that everyone-dunnit (Christie's *Murder on the Orient Express* comes to mind): all of the passengers and some of the crew are revealed as having a motive to kill le Manant, and as having attempted to do so, from Jewish nazi hunters,[15] to the son of French resistants, a priest, and a swindled art dealer, to name but some protagonists. Whether or not Carraud set out to parody crime revenge narratives – it turns out that it was not murder but suicide – *Les Poulets du Cristobal* serves to make the point that this category of text can accommodate a wide range of motives and erstwhile avengers.

Carraud includes 'nazi hunters' in his hyperbolic cohort of potential murderers, and these are not uncommon figures, though their metaphorical prey is as often the French collaborator as it is the German nazi. Thus, whilst Tabachnik's *Tango des assassins* (2000), for instance, includes Mossad agents seeking out a former German SS officer in Argentina, in Laveau's *La Trace du diable* (1996) Israeli agents are passed information about French collaborators guilty of crimes against humanity. In many cases these 'nazi hunters' are at least semi-official figures whose aim is not to kill those labelled war criminals but rather to bring them to trial. In such instances it is official or state justice which provides a thread of continuity between past, present, and future. Crime authors seeking to maintain a degree of verisimilitude are obliged to tailor their plots to fit the law. If the past crime represented is imprescriptible (i.e., crimes against humanity) and thus the criminal still a criminal in the diegetic present, then official justice may be sought.

---

[14]   George Steiner, *The Portage to San Cristobal* (Faber & Faber, 1981).

[15]   Jewish stereotyping is sadly once more in evidence, with the Jewish Aaron described as of short stature, with thick lips, dark eyes, and a hooked nose (32).

In the case of, say, collaborators falling under the French amnesty laws of 1951 and 1953, whose crimes have been officially relegated to the past, the legal pursuit of justice has to cede to a criminal act of vengeance. In the latter case a personal motive is required, and the present-day killer is in nearly all instances represented as a close relative of what is perceived as the victim of a past wrong.

These distinctions are brought out clearly in Bellanti and Vacher's *Le Manuscrit de la mémère morte* (1998) which represents two contrastive, indeed conflicting, figures, each concerned with criminal continuity, each bridging past and present, but with very different concepts of what the future should hold. Bernard Kost, an American lawyer working for an organization which seeks out war criminals, is determined to bring to trial a group of former French actresses guilty of crimes against humanity. Florence, an ex-resistant whose brother was tortured and murdered by the same actresses, opts for a more expedient solution and begins to kill them one by one. For her only the radical discontinuity of death, the closing off of all futurity, will provide closure. A conditional perfect tense, by contrast, underlines the lawyer's thwarted desire to pursue the case: 'Quelqu'un est venu leur coller une balle de revolver en pleine tête, j'ai échoué ... Elles [les comédiennes] auraient dû comparaître en justice, avoir un procès public, j'ai échoué ...' (115) ['Someone came and just shot them in the head, I've failed ... They should have appeared in court, should have had a public trial, I've failed ...']. Writers of revenge narratives in which past wrongs are righted years, or in this case decades, after the perpetration of the original crime have to devise a convincing motive for the delay. This may take the form of, for instance, new information coming to light, or the ageing – running out of time – of those agents in question. In this case, paradigmatically, it is the very appearance of the lawyer which triggers the perpetration of criminal acts. Florence kills because she fears a repetition of the unjust past should Kost take his case to court: 'je suis sûre qu'elles s'en seraient encore sorties, comme à la Libération ...' (130) ['I'm sure they'd have got away with it again, just like they did during the Liberation ...']. For the privately motivated avenger, state justice is all too often no justice at all. Paradoxically, only a second crime, committed in the present, can expunge the debt incurred by the original, wartime transgression.

Whereas *Le Manuscrit de la mémère morte* pits justice against revenge via the explicitly competing interests of two characters and sees revenge prevail, Tabachnik's *La Honte leur appartient* (2002) merges the two figures into one in the form of a Jewish lawyer who returns to the village of his youth where those responsible for the deportation of his family still live. The distinction between revenge and justice is, in this case, articulated by the protagonist:

> Mais que voulait-il pour eux [sa famille], la justice or la vengeance? Et est-ce tellement important de le savoir? La justice est fille de la civilisation. Mais trop souvent, c'est une fille ingrate qui ne se donne qu'aux puissants. Tandis que la vengeance ... la vengeance est un sentiment qui exalte celui qui s'en sert; lui rend sa dignité. (224)

[But what did he want for them, justice or revenge? And is it really important to know? Justice is the daughter of civilization. But all too often she is an ungrateful child who gives herself only to the powerful. Whilst revenge ... revenge is a feeling which brings elation to those who wield it, which gives them back their dignity.]

In Tabachnik's variation on a theme, neither official justice nor private revenge prevails. The former collaborators die according to the laws of poetic justice – the mechanism matters little; it is the pattern which holds – but it is not the protagonist lawyer who kills them. Tabachnik's putative righter of wrongs is no criminal. He does, though, return to the scene of the original crime(s). Beyond its exploration of justice and revenge, this text, set in a small provincial town in the east of France, also serves to remind us of the importance of space, communities in place, and the inseparability of these from time.

The opening sentence of *La Honte leur appartient* underscores its protagonist's status as an insider: 'En remontant dans sa mémoire il se revoyait, petit garçon, venir avec son chien Toby chercher son père les lundis après-midis' (9) ['Trawling back through his memories he saw himself as a young boy with his dog Toby, coming to fetch his father on Monday afternoons']. Walter's return to the town where he grew up is also a figurative return to his past. But like all revenants in justice / revenge texts, Walter is out of sync, seeking out traces of a past which those who have remained behind wish only to forget. His departure and return – the wandering Jew turned prodigal son – can be contrasted to the temporal and spatial stasis of one of the wartime perpetrators, tellingly described as 'planté plutôt que posé sur cette bonne terre de ses ancêtres' (12) ['Planted rather than just standing on the good ancestral soil']. For this 'true' Frenchman and others like him time is measured in the slow continuity of centuries of belonging which no war can disrupt. Operating in a different relation to time has consequences. Walter the anachronistic revenant, rendered alien by his asynchronicity as much as by his Jewishness, is confirmed as an outsider. This is less the case of the past as a foreign country than that of the individual who lives time differently becoming a foreign body.[16]

Writing specifically about the Holocaust, Huyssen points out that 'local and national memory practices contest the myths of cyber-capitalism and globalization and their denial of time, space and place'.[17] Tabachnik's text (and others like it) stages precisely this issue via its representation of the out-of-sync revenant, reminding us that even at the level of individuals from a small community the (wartime) past can resonate in the present differently. The text's provincial setting is also worthy of comment. Whilst a significant proportion of the works of crime fiction under consideration here are set in Paris or other major cities such as Lyon

---

[16] A similar basic pattern, though one which plays out variants, can be found in Fajardie's *La Théorie du 1%* and Courchay's *Retour à Malaveil*.

[17] Andreas Huyssen 'Present Pasts: Media, Politics, Amnesia', *Public Culture*, 12.1 (2000): 21–38 [37].

and Marseille, the corpus in fact bears witness to an extremely wide geographical spread, from the Alps in Baumier's *Les Apôtres du néant* (2002) to the Pas de Calais in Daeninckx's *Les Figurants* (1995); from the Lorraine region in Kolaire's *Sur la ligne marginaux* (1999) to Brittany in Ouvard's *Le plongeon du frère Boileau* (1964); the Camargue in Harlay's *Le Sel de la guerre* (2008); to the Côte d'Azur in Tanugi's *Les grottes de crésus* (1974), to single out just some. The war casts its general shadow over all of these texts, but every named region or town is inflected by the particular nature of its own wartime past. Authors can thus choose to bring geographically specific modalities into play. To give just two examples: The nostalgia and guilt of the wartime generation competes with a future-oriented pragmatism in Huet's Normandy-based *Bunker* (2008) as the second and third generation opt for commercial exploitation of the region's experience of the war years: good money can be made from the sale of German and American militaria and by guided tours of local fortifications. Luraghi's *Pour cigogne le glas* (1999), by contrast, works with its Strasbourg past by tracing a line of continuity from the *Malgré nous* to a contemporary fascist organization which meets on the site of the Struthof concentration camp, forming 'une lignée d'ignominieux kapos intemporels' (172) ['a lineage of timeless ignominious kapos'].[18] The war was a local as well as a national affair, and each work of fiction contributes to the elaboration of a spatial as well as temporal fictional map of France.

Regimes Continuous and Discontinuous

So far this typology of criminal continuities has included trauma and legacy texts, those featuring improbable returning or ever-present nazis, and revenge or justice texts. Before leaving the last of these categories brief mention should be made of what might be termed non-justice continuity texts. These works, typified by Daeninckx's *Itinéraire d'un salaud ordinaire* (see above, pp. 110–12), represent a character with some degree of public or official status and his (it is always his) more or less unimpeded progress through time, from the Vichy regime to a contemporary diegetic setting. Jonquet's *Du passé faisons table rase* (1982), whose protagonist René Castel is a thinly disguised stand-in for Georges Marchais, leader of the French Communist Party from 1972 to 1994, falls into the same category, showing how an individual who volunteers to work in Germany during the war might end up at the head of a political party which had prided itself on its Resistance credentials. Texts such as these eschew a diegetic seeker of justice, leaving it to the reader to register the incongruity and injustice of career continuity in the context of at least apparent legal, ideological, and political discontinuity. Where in the case of justice / revenge texts the finger of blame tends

---

[18] The *Malgré nous* (literally 'in spite of us' or 'against our wishes') was the name given to those inhabitants of the Alsace-Lorraine region forcibly conscripted into the Wehrmacht and Waffen SS. The Natzweiler concentration camp was set up by the Nazis in 1941 near the village of Struthof in the annexed region of Alsace.

to be directed at representative characters who were in some way complicit with the Vichy regime – usually French collaborators of some hue – these 'non-justice' texts extend judgment and condemnation to both the protagonists and the post-war regimes that have accepted them in their midst.

In both *Itinéraire d'un salaud ordinaire* and *Du passé faisons table rase* the Algerian War features as a significant stage along the historical-political temporal trajectory tracking from the Vichy years through to the present day. Involvement in Algeria earns Daeninckx's opportunistic protagonist official plaudits and hastens his career ascension; we are specifically informed that two characters in Jonquet's text, the agents Guilon and Dartier, met during military operations in Algeria. Such references are far from uncommon. The plot of what is doubtless the best-known text representing continuities between Vichy and the Algerian War, Daeninckx's *Meurtres pour mémoire* (1984), hinges on the activities of the Maurice Papon-like character's involvement in both the deportation of Jews in 1942–43 and the brutal suppression of the demonstration held by Algerians in Paris in October 1961. This issue of criminal continuity was to re-emerge in a juridical context during Papon's trial (October 1997–April 1998), giving rise to considerable resistance in some official circles. David Fraser cites Henry Rousso's dismissive disclaimer: 'Is it possible to make an equivalency between the round up of Jews between 1942–44 and the massacre of Algerians in 1961, and thus between Pétain and de Gaulle! Absurd!'[19] Parallels had been drawn before, notably during the 1987 trial of Klaus Barbie, when Jacques Vergès, Barbie's lawyer, compared what he described as French colonialist excesses in Algeria to nazi torture in Lyon (a not so different line was sketched out in the famous anti-war *Manifeste des 121* of 1960).[20] One articulation of criminal continuity thus centred on the actions of a French collaborator (Papon) operating under two supposedly discontinuous political regimes (Vichy and the Fifth Republic), and the other on that of a German SS officer (Barbie) whose activities under Vichy were likened to those of French soldiers operating in the name of the Republic. Both approaches condemn French double standards by undermining the notion of discontinuity at the level of socio-political regime.

---

[19]   Fraser, *Law after Auschwitz* (Carolina Academic P, 2005), p. 210, his translation (from Rousso's *La Hantise du passé*, p. 121).

[20]   Fraser, *op. cit.*, p. 190. The *Manifeste des 121* which supported those who did not wish to fight in Algeria, represented the Algerians as victims of colonialism, and attacked what were perceived as anti-democratic military means: '[...] quinze ans après la destruction de l'ordre hitlérien, le militarisme français [...] est parvenu à restaurer la torture et à en faire à nouveau comme une institution en Europe' ['(...) 15 years after the destruction of Hitler's regime, French militarism has succeeded in reinstating torture and making of it once again an institution in Europe'], *Vérité-Liberté* no. 4, 6 Sept. 1960. For a discussion of the emerging, overlapping memories of the Holocaust and decolonization, see Michael Rothberg's 'Between Auschwitz and Algeria: Multidirectional Memory and the Counterpublic Witness', *Critical Inquiry*, 33 (2006): 158–84.

Fraser, who indeed argues that 'the forces of continuity between the Vichy period and subsequent Republican regimes are stronger than official legal, collective memory would have us believe',[21] picks out *Meurtres pour mémoire* specifically as the source of an important alternative construction of the past:

> Whilst novelist Didier Daeninckx can use a fictionalized Papon-like character to make the deeply resonant point about continuity between Vichy and Algeria in French popular culture, attempts to raise similar concerns in the context of the actual trial of Papon for crimes against humanity are dismissed as absurd.[22]

Although Daeninckx's text was unique in its proactive targeting of a real participant who had taken part in both conflicts, his is of course not the only work of crime fiction to establish links between Vichy and the Algerian War. We have already encountered an earlier example in the form of Boileau-Narcejac's *La Lèpre* (1976) in which a son fighting in Algeria disposes of a troublesome Vichy revenant for his father. Frequent representations of, or allusions to, Vichy-Algeria continuities in more recent works of crime fiction suggest that the genre continues to probe this particular tender spot.[23] Several texts, including Pavloff's *Le Vent des fous* (1993) and Tabachnik's *La Honte leur appartient* (2002), for instance, trace a line of political and ideological continuity from Vichy through Algeria and thence into the present via the depiction of characters – usually cast in the role of principal criminal or helper to the latter – whose pasts include collaboration, membership of the OAS (*Organisation armée secrète*), the SAC (*Service d'action civique*), and finally, a contemporary far right movement or party, usually the *Front national*.[24] Links between the two wars may be both understated and light-hearted: alluding to the 1962 Évian Agreements which brought the Algerian War to an official close, Pavloff's narrator, for instance, merely quips of Evian and Vichy that spa towns in France appear to meet with most unusual of fates (135). This is just to touch on an area which merits further investigation. Two texts, Joly's *La Rage* (2002) and Gouiran's *Les vrais durs meurent aussi* (2008) will provide

---

[21]   Fraser, *op. cit.*, p. 207.

[22]   Ibid., p. 211. Stephen Steele recognizes the importance of *Meurtres* as a text which brought Papon's crimes to a wide audience, but questions its historical accuracy, describing the representation of the Occupation and the Algerian crisis as somewhat caricatural, warped by the demands of the crime genre, 'Daeninckx, quand le roman policier part en guerre', *French Studies Bulletin*, 71 (1999): 9–10 [10].

[23]   Although Francis Zamponi's *Le Boucher de Guelma* (2007) focuses primarily on Algeria (notably the Sétif and Guelma massacres of 8 May 1945) and the charge of crimes against humanity brought against the protagonist, Maurice Fabre, we also learn of the role played by the latter in Algeria during the war years.

[24]   The OAS was a far right underground movement which engaged in armed combat in its attempts to prevent Algerian independence. Set up in 1960 as a pro de Gaulle association, the SAS had something of a checkered anti-left history, gaining a reputation as a parallel police. It was disbanded in 1981 by Mitterrand.

some idea of further ways in which continuities and discontinuities between and amongst French conflicts and the political contexts in which they take place can be mapped out through time.

Going back some three decades, Boileau-Narcejac's take on the relationship between Vichy and the Algerian War in *La Lèpre* is ultimately ambiguous: father and son have contrastive views and both perspectives are filtered through the politician-protagonist's self-justificatory first-person narrative. As is typical of later texts Joly's and Gouiran's crime novels are more obviously condemnatory of France's role in Algeria, though they too have their ambiguities. An easily missed detail from *La Lèpre* is worth noting as a point of departure. On one of several occasions on which the narrator likens his wartime Resistance activities to those of his son's travails in Algeria, we learn more of the son's status: 'à Saint-Maixent, on t'a préparé au combat [...] Moi, je me sentais comme un lapin un jour d'ouverture' (65) ['You were prepared for combat at Saint-Maixent (...) I felt like a rabbit on the opening day of the hunting season']. Boileau-Narcejac's Algerian combatant is a career officer. Both Joly and Gouiran focus on altogether different types of soldier. Gouiran's narrator expresses sympathy for conscripts cut down in their prime in Algeria because of the political ambitions of those in power (64). The narrator of *La Rage*, himself a former conscript, insists on his opposition to the war in Algeria and the pro-independence stance he embraced in 1960, complaining that 'presque tous étaient d'accord pour nous envoyer jouer les cons au nom de l'intégrité de la Patrie en danger' (73) ['nearly everyone agreed that we should be sent out there to play silly buggers to safeguard the integrity of the French Nation'].[25] Literary works representing the views of conscripts sent to Algeria are by no means unique to the contemporary period,[26] but Gouiran and Joly's texts introduce new elements. Gouiran muddies the waters by using the figure of the legionnaire as a key player in his tale of multiple wars. Both authors raise the issue of civilian rapes carried out by French soldiers during the Algerian war, an aspect of the conflict which entered the public arena late.[27] Finally, the arc of continuity is extended beyond Vichy-Algeria to include the Franco-Indochinese conflict of 1946–54, the post-1991 Algerian civil war, and the presence of the extreme right in contemporary France.

Gouiran's text opens with the present day murder of former members of the foreign legion. As the plot unfolds, the reader is offered two explanations for these crimes and two corresponding back stories. One, this is a revenge narrative: the legionnaires are being killed by the son of an Algerian woman who was raped

---

[25]   Referring to the 'myth' of *L'Algérie française* Philip Dine notes of the French State's justification for conscription that 'French citizens were being sent to Algeria to fight for the integrity of the nation', *Images of the Algerian War* (Clarendon P, 1994), p. 110.

[26]   See Dine, *Images of the Algerian War*, especially Chapter 5 '"La Quille, bordel!": Recalling *Le Rappel*'.

[27]   See Raphaëlle Branche, 'Des viols pendant la guerre d'Algérie' in *Vingtième Siècle. Revue d'histoire*, 75 (2002): 123–32.

by members of the legionnaires' battalion during the Algerian War. Two, this is a tale of hidden nazi treasure, and the killers are disposing of all those who might know where the loot is located. Revenge or greed, rape in Algeria or nazi plunder: at the stripped back level of plot *Les vrais durs* constructs the two wars as interchangeable, and thus in effect, timeless; the text dehistoricizes both conflicts. A similarly dehistoricizing stance is expressed by one of the legionnaires when he insists that the rape of Algerian civilians was – or perhaps we should say is – comparable to that of German women and children raped by the advancing Russian army in 1945, just as torture carried out by French forces in Algeria can be likened to the vicissitudes of nazi concentration camps or to the horrors of the 're-education' policies of the Vietminh during the Indochinese conflict (226). The choice of a legionnaire as combatant does open up new perspectives on the issue of continuity, not least by bracketing the question of national belonging. Gouiran's legionnaires are not Frenchmen but former SS officers who were subsequently captured at Dien Bien Phu. If there is continuity here it is that of the soldier who finds himself on the losing side on three occasions. Readers are of course unlikely to take Gouiran's character's views at face value, but his first-person narrator also proffers a largely dehistoricized message. In an extended passage on rape which opens with the statement that the violations perpetrated by French soldiers during the Algerian War remain a taboo subject, he restates the case against the Russian army in 1945, adding to it examples drawn from the conflicts in Bosnia, Chechnya, the Congo, and Rwanda. Civilian rape in the context of war is condemned, but historical specificities are minimized.

Where *Les vrais durs meurent aussi* ultimately posits the evils of war, or perhaps of human nature, as the principal element of continuity, Joly's *La Rage* might be read as a journey through its protagonist-narrator's changing perception of both continuity and discontinuity. Initially, a self-exculpatory stance is espoused: the narrator opposed the war in Algeria and he actively prevented the rape of young Algerian girls by fellow French soldiers. From the perspective of the reluctant recruit, establishing continuity between Vichy and Algeria amounts to blaming successive governments:

> Il avait fallu un demi-siècle pour condamner Papon et s'apercevoir que l'extrême droite puisait ses forces dans les restes camouflés de Vichy et beaucoup moins pour oublier le napalm balancé par ordre de Mitterrand sur la gueule des Kabyles. (15)
>
> [It had taken half a century for Papon to be found guilty and for people to realize that the far-right was drawing its resources from the disguised remnants of Vichy and much less time to forget the napalm dumped on the Kabyles on Mitterrand's instructions.]

This abjuration of individual responsibility is later transformed. In the course of a series of exchanges with a second generation Algerian, the narrator acknowledges that unlike his father, a World War II deportee, he was no heroic soldier. The Algerian conflict, indeed, is described as an implant in his body that will not take, and a deadly sin which cannot be expiated (105). The representation of the ambivalence of the recruit as both victim of the State and responsible perpetrator is not exceptional, but *La Rage* takes matters further. When a local family's farmhouse cellar is discovered to contain compromising documents detailing acts of torture carried out some 60 years before by local *miliciens* and the family refuses to move, they find themselves under siege by right-wing gendarmes, backed by the local politician, also of far right persuasion. The narrator duly takes up arms and dies fighting what are pointedly referred to as 'les nazis du coin' (176) ['the local nazis']. To right the wrong and re-establish the continuity of pro-Republican values, to expunge the inglorious Algerian interlude, Joly must have his protagonist fight the good fight as his father did before him. This is a tale of redemption. As such, like Gouiran's dehistoricizing narrative, it has something of the atemporal about it: the text closes with the first-person narrator's death, establishing an impossible narrative perspective from beyond the grave.

Nazis, French collaborators, and present day supporters of the far right are not the only anti-democratic forces represented in these texts, both of which also focus their attention on the civil war which took hold in Algeria at the start of the 1990s: 'Avoir autant lutté pour aboutir à une dictature!', states a second generation Algerian in *Les vrais durs meurent aussi*' (59) ['To have fought so hard just to end up with a dictatorship!']; 'Vous nous avez mis dehors de l'Algérie au nom de la démocratie et vous vous comportez en fachos', echoes Joly's narrator (76) ['You threw us out of Algeria in the name of democracy and you behave like fascists']. The colonized Algerians of the 1950s and 60s have become the oppressive masters of the 1990s. Continuities are problematized in both Joly's and Gouiran's works. On the negative side, both texts reveal a dehistorizing tendency which locates continuity in an essentialized human nature. On the plus side, both authors remind us that fascist and democratic regimes are not the preserve of any one nation state, any more than are the roles of victim and perpetrator.

This section has sought to show something of the range, and nature, of the relationships between past, present, and future represented in works of crime fiction. Tales of trauma, legacy (actual or metaphorical), revenants (real or phantastical), justice and revenge, all establish particular temporal ties between the war and the present day, these in some cases extending into a putative future. Texts which point to continuities between the war years and the present day do so primarily via the representation of individual characters and their emotions (fear, anger, guilt etc.), though they may also point to, and critique, aspects of regime continuity. The emphasis on range in this section has inevitably precluded extensive discussion of any one category of text. The next section redresses this balance by focusing on a small group of works which mobilize the wartime past in their representation of the present with the aim of protecting the future.

Holocaust Denial and the Far Right: Cautionary Tales

In the introduction to his study of the far right in France Jean-Paul Gautier states that although the country has been affected at various stages of its history by the 'fascist virus', fascist and neo-fascist movements have in fact with one exception remained relatively insignificant in terms of scale, that exception being Jacques Doriot's *Parti populaire français* (PPF).[28] Gauthier's tone is rather less sanguine in a chapter entitled 'Les nostalgiques du 3ᵉ Reich', in which he acknowledges that the last 30 years have witnessed a proliferation of far right groups which attest to the vigour of neo-fascist tendencies in France.[29] Viruses, as is well-known, can both mutate and lie dormant for many years. Gauthier's referencing of Doriot and his wartime PPF serves as an example of what the present day manifestations of the far right might become. A more explicitly admonitory message can be found in a cluster of crime novels published between 1996 and 2001, a significant date span with respect to the political context in France: the municipal elections of 1995 saw the *Front national* (FN) secure control of the town halls of Toulon, Orange, Vitrolles, and Marignane, with the FN leader, Jean-Marie Le Pen, securing 15 percent of the vote in the first round of the presidential elections.[30] As a Jewish character states on the closing page of Arnaud's *L'Antizyklon des atroces* (1998), referring to the apparent rise of the far right: 'Après cinquante ans de sérénité j'ai peur à nouveau' (95) ['After 50 years of peace of mind I'm scared again'].[31] But what extreme right are we talking about? Gauthier identifies the principal neo-*nazi* movements in post-war France as the FANE ('Fédération d'action nationaliste europénne'), which was wound down in the 1980s, the PNFE ('Parti nationaliste français et européen'), which succeeded it, and various groups of 'skins'.[32] The works of crime fiction discussed below are less precise in their nomenclature. Although a distinction is drawn between the returning, cloned, or otherwise temporally transcendent nazis discussed above (the 'vieux gammés') and that of a new *French* generation situated on the far right, the precise affiliation of the latter is usually generalized. Terms such as 'nazillon' are commonly employed to designate any character with far right inclinations, with members of the *Front national* often simply equated to nazis. In the words

---

[28] J.-P. Gautier, *Les Êxtremes droites en France. De la traversée du désert à l'ascension du Front national (1945–2008)*, (Éditions Syllepse, 2009), p. 8.

[29] Gautier, *Les Êxtremes droites*, p. 282.

[30] Written collectively by members of the anti-extreme-right group Orange amère, *L'Ordure, hein!* (Baleine, 2000), a roman à clé set in a fictional Orange, satirizes the policies and internal conflicts of the FN.

[31] See also Fajardie's *Sous le regard des élégantes*. Though published in the same period (1997) the text is set in 1962 (the end of the Algerian War) and 1967 (the Six Day War) and stages the opposition between two race-horse owners, the English Lord Bates, fascist follower of Oswald Mosley, and Jewish Jean Sternberg.

[32] Gautier, *Les Êxtremes droites*, p. 277. Martin's *Le G.A.L., l'égout* (Éditions Baleine, 1996) provides a short factual footnote explaining the acronyms FANE and PNFE, p. 30.

of an anti-FN demonstrator in Martin's *Le G.A.L., l'égout*: 'F comme fasciste, N comme nazi! A bas le Front National!' (48) ['N for nazi, F for fascist. Down with the National Front!'].

The works of crime fiction analyzed below display a common interest not only in the representation of the far right, but also of Holocaust denial or what the French call 'négationnisme' (a term I will adopt on occasion in its adjectival form),[33] which in accordance with the terminology of the Gayssot Act of 1990 will be taken to designate the calling into question of the existence or scope of crimes against humanity.[34] The representation of Holocaust denial in crime fiction is of particular interest not just because Holocaust denial is itself a crime in France – in fact, as will emerge, it is very rarely the principal crime under investigation in such works – but because it is an ideology whose representation mobilizes a range of epistemological, ontological, and – important in this chapter – temporal issues. The epistemological implications are obvious enough: how can it be 'proven' that gas chambers existed and why should anyone feel the need to argue what is in any event a closed case? For Bernard-Henri Lévy, epistemological and ethical issues relating to Holocaust denial in fact yield to the realm of the ontological. The main question we should be posing, he suggests, is what kind of world do we live in where people feel that they can, or need to, ask if things exist or not and if reality is real?[35] One partial answer might be provided by a doomed hitchhiker in Garnier's serial killer tale, *L'A26*, commenting here on the Second World War as a whole from the perspective of the third generation:

> Nous on en a toujours entendu parler, à la télé, partout dans le monde, mais on ne l'a jamais vue en vraie. On est pas sûr que ça existe. […] On doute de tout, même de nous. On sait jamais si on est pas dans un jeu Nintendo. (30)

> [We've always heard about it, on the TV, all over the world, but we've never seen it in real life. We're not sure it exists. We question everything, even ourselves. You never know if you're not part of some Nintendo game.]

When not just seeing, but existing, is no longer believing, the ontological status of the past – all of it – becomes fragile indeed. This is all the more troubling since Holocaust denial represents for some the paradigmatic reason for which the past must be remembered. Those who propound the right to forget and a purging of the

---

[33]   Noting that the term 'révisionnisme' designates acceptable historical procedure, Rousso adopted what he termed the 'barbaric' (i.e., not very euphonic) but more appropriate term 'négationnisme', *Le Syndrome de Vichy* (Seuil, 1987), p. 176.

[34]   For a comprehensive account of Holocaust denial in France see Valérie Igounet, *Histoire du négationnisme en France* (Seuil, 2000). On the Gayssot Act and the intricacies of the term 'contestation', see Sévane Garibian, 'La Loi Gayssot ou le droit désaccordé' in Catherine Coquio (ed.) *L'Histoire trouée*, pp. 223–46.

[35]   Bernard-Henri Lévy, *Le Point* 13 juillet 1996.

past which will not pass, suggest their critics, run the risk of seeing a repetition of the horrors of that past.[36]

Issues such as these as well as a consideration of whether crime fiction's aesthetic engagement with Holocaust denial and the far right 'works' – and what 'working' might mean in this context[37] – will be pursued and developed in the analysis of the following texts: Daeninckx's *Nazis dans le métro* (1996) and *Éthique en toc* (2000); Arnaud's *L'Antizyklon des atroces* (1998); Busino's *Au nom du piètre qui a l'essieu* (1998) and Benson's *Biblio-quête* (2001). With the exception of Benson's novel, all of these texts form part of the explicitly left-leaning 'Poulpe' series launched in 1995 by Jean-Bernard Pouy, and featuring Gabriel Lecouvreur aka 'le Poulpe' as the recurring amateur investigator. Written in the context of alarming political gains for the *Front national*, these works also engage with a number of 'affairs' or high-profile stories surrounding Holocaust denial, all of which made their way into the French media in the early to mid-1990s.[38] In order better to grasp the fictional reworkings of these mediatized events, there follows a brief review of four cases.

Holocaust Denial in the Media

The most highly mediatized Holocaust denial incident of the 1990s involved two established public figures: Roger Garaudy, philosopher, author, former Communist MP, and subsequent convert to Islam, and *l'abbé Pierre*, popularity-poll-topping Catholic priest, former member of the Resistance, and founder of Emmaüs, a now international charitable movement set up in 1949 to support the homeless.[39] In December 1995 Garaudy published his *Les Mythes fondateurs de*

---

[36]   'En érigeant l'amnésie au rang de vertu, ils ouvrent toute grande la voie aux falsificateurs du passé et nous condamnent à risquer d'en revivre, un jour, les horreurs' ['By making a virtue of amnesia they are throwing open the doors for the falsifiers of history and condemning us to one day reliving its horrors']: Alain Bihr, 'Du passé ne faisons pas table rase!', in Alain Bihr, Guido Calderon et al., *Négationnistes: les chiffonniers de l'histoire* (Éditions Golias et Éditions Syllepse, 1997), pp. 17–34 [32–3].

[37]   Though he does not pursue the matter, Jean Pons states that the extreme right and negationism are natural targets for the *roman noir* and its engagement with society, noting, in a phrase that gestures to both the past and the present/future, that 'le roman noir est alors garantie de mémoire parce qu'il oblige à l'éveil', 'Le Roman noir, littérature réelle', *Les Temps modernes*, 595 (1997): 13. Although E. Müller and A. Ruoff suggest that history is often used in works of French crime fiction to elucidate the present, they do not discuss the representation of neo-nazism or Holocaust denial, noting rather than although nazism often serves as a backdrop, it is rarely key to plot development, *Le Polar français. Crime et histoire* (La Fabrique, 2002).

[38]   See Sylvie Lindeperg, 'Scénarisation du négationnisme par la télévision française: les temps et logiques d'un média', *French Cultural Studies*, 13 (2002): 259–80. Lindeperg's statistics reveal that the mediatization of Holocaust denial in France reached a peak in 1996.

[39]   See Igounet, 'L'affaire Garaudy', *Histoire du négationnisme*, pp. 472–83.

la politique israélienne with *La Vieille Taupe*, a publishing house known for its anti-semitic and negationist publications, following this up with a second edition in early 1996. The publication was widely reported in the press, but media hype was to increase exponentially when *l'abbé Pierre* weighed in to help his long-time friend.[40] His supportive letter of 15 April 1996, deliberately exposed to the media by Garaudy and his lawyer, runs from praise of Garaudy's astonishing and scrupulous erudition (*sic*) to insistence that labelling him a Holocaust denier is a calumny perpetrated by the ignorant. Amidst a further deluge of media coverage *l'abbé Pierre* was excluded from the *Ligue internationale contre le racisme et l'antisémitisme* (LICRA) on 1 May 1996 and withdrew from the public eye. In late February 1998 Garaudy was found guilty of Holocaust denial under the Gayssot Act,[41] a verdict confirmed on appeal some 10 months later. Although no single work of crime fiction under discussion here focuses exclusively on Garaudy and the *abbé Pierre*, Busino's *Au nom du piètre qui a l'essieu* has Emmaüs at its centre, whilst the views of both Garaudy and the *abbé* are mentioned in several texts.[42]

Crime writer Didier Daeninckx was at the centre of the second mediatized affair which was, in fact, instigated by a sustained campaign on his part to raise awareness of a 'rouge-brun' alliance in France. This association of the far (Communist) left and the far right, engaged, amongst other things, in the publication of anti-semitic and negationist material, was typified by, though by no means limited to, journals such *L'Idiot international*, (re)launched in 1989 and headed by the controversial Jean-Edern Hallier. The case was soon taken up by the national press with *Le Monde* running a piece in June 1993, followed up in July with another long article titled 'La tentation national-communiste, *L'Idiot*, laboratoire rouge-brun'.[43] The 'rouge-brun' affair returned to the public eye a few years later following further revelations by Daeninckx, this time of an unholy alliance between the extreme far left ('l'ultra gauche') and the far right. The *Le Monde* headline of 8 June 1996 this time reads 'La querelle du négationnisme rebondit à l'ultra gauche'.[44] It was not just the political ramifications which made for a good media story. Daeninckx singled out for criticism figures such as Serge Quadruppani and Gilles Dauvé, both crime fiction authors, and threatened to withdraw one of his own works if his publisher

---

[40]   See Philippe Videlier, 'Nouvelle affaire négationniste. Zones d'ombre et coup monté', *Le Monde diplomatique*, June 1996.

[41]   A. Pereira, 'Le philosophe Roger Garaudy est condamné pour contestation de crimes contre l'humanité', *Le Monde*, 2 March 1998.

[42]   For an earlier satire of *l'abbé Pierre* and charitable associations such as Emmaüs which predates the Garaudy scandal, see Thierry Jonquet's *Le pauvre nouveau est arrivé!* (Manya, 1990).

[43]   Plenel, Edwy, and Olivier Biffaud, 'La tentation national-communiste. En France comme en Russie, des anciens staliniens et des intellectuels d'extrême gauche rêvent d'une "troisième voie" rouge et brune', *Le Monde* 26 juin, 1993; Edwy Plenel and Olivier Biffaud, 'La tentation national-communiste. *L'Idiot*, laboratoire rouge-brun', *Le Monde*, 1 July 1993.

[44]   Ariane Chemin, 'Interview. Didier Daeninckx, écrivain et éditeur. Ils veulent faire sauter le verrou d'une "mythe" génocidaire' *Le Monde*, 8 June 1996.

accepted a novel by Dauvé in the same 'Poulpe' series.[45] In the words of Louis Janover, 1996 thus also witnessed 'la guerre picrocholine entre auteurs de polars' ['petty wrangling between crime writers']; 'l'intrigue policière de l'été' ['the crime story of the summer'].[46] Daeninckx's *Nazis dans le métro* – the text he threatened to withdraw from publication – centres on the 'rouge-brun' alliance, which features, as we will see, barely disguised references to real public figures and publications.

The third mediatized affair was the longest-running, arguably dating back to December 1978 when Holocaust denier Robert Faurisson's by now infamous piece 'Le problème des chambres à gaz ou la rumeur d'Auschwitz' was published in *Le Monde*.[47] Faurisson, who taught at the University of Lyon II, was just the first in a series of members of academic staff to be involved in far right and Holocaust denial scandals at the Universities of Lyon II and, especially, III. In June 1985 Henri Roques defended his *'Confessions' de Kurt Gerstein. Étude comparative des différentes versions. Édition critique* at Nantes University. Two members of the academic jury which passed the work, subsequently recognized as negationist in nature, were based at Lyon II and III. There were to be several other cases, but the one which concerns us most directly in what follows is that of Jean Plantin. In June 1990 Plantin defended his *maîtrise* thesis, *Paul Rassinier (1906–67), socialiste, pacifiste et révisionniste*, at the University of Lyon III, going on to defend a second piece of work, *Les Epidémies de typhus exanthématique dans les camps de concentration nazis, 1933–1945*, for his advanced diploma (DEA) a year later, this time at Lyon II. His supervisor on that occasion was Yves Lequin, director of a research centre, the Centre Pierre Léon. Both of Plantin's pieces of work were negationist in nature. The 'affaire Plantin' emerged in the media in 1999 when he was found guilty of publishing a negationist journal.[48] Bad press surrounding the University of Lyon kept on coming – would its authorities strip Plantin of his qualifications, for instance?[49] – and in November 2001 the then Minister for Education, Jack Lang, set up a commission led by Henry Rousso to look into racism and Holocaust denial at the University of Lyon III. The resulting *Rapport de la commission sur le racisme et le négationnisme à l'université Jean-Moulin Lyon III* was published in 2004.[50]

---

[45] This episode is discussed in *Négationnistes: les chiffonniers de l'histoire*, pp. 99–127.

[46] Janover, *Nuit et brouillard du révisionnisme* (Paris-Méditerranée, 1996), p. 23 and p. 34. Similar tensions between crime writers (with Daeninckx at the centre of the row) were still making the press five years later. See Dominique Simonnot, 'Le conflit vire à la bagarre entre les auteurs de polars', *Libération*, 3 juillet 2001.

[47] *Le Monde*, 29 December 1978.

[48] First reported in *Le Monde* on 29 May 1999: Claude Francillon, 'Un éditeur lyonnais condamné pour publicité en faveur d'œuvres révisionniste'.

[49] See, for instance, Olivier Bertrand, 'Lyon-II nie la faute négationniste. Le président de l'université refuse d'annuler le DEA d'un étudiant condamné', *Libération*, 2 October 2000.

[50] Henry Rousso, *Le dossier Lyon III. Le Rapport sur le racisme et le négationnisme à l'université Jean-Moulin* (Fayard, 2004). The report includes comprehensive chapters on

Daeninckx's *Éthique en toc* (2000), based on the 'affaire Plantin', preceded Rousso's report by four years; Benson's *Biblio-quête* (2001) is dedicated to Daeninckx.

The final case to make it into the French media was to be the inspiration for Arnaud's *L'Antizyklon des atroces*, a tale of two generations of far right ideologues and hidden canisters of Zyklon B gas. On 11 October 1996 *Le Monde* picked up on the story of historian Annie Lecroix-Riz who complained that her work on economic collaboration under Vichy had been rejected by the periodical *Études et documents*, published under the aegis of the Ministry of Finance, and further informed the press that she had been receiving threats from Holocaust deniers. Dealing with a controversial topic, Lecroix-Riz's article included details of a French-based company which had manufactured Zyklon B gas and shipped it to Germany between 1941 and 1943. On 9 October 1996 *Le Monde* ran a story under the title 'Le groupe Ugine a-t-il produit du gaz Zyklon B durant les années 40?', following this up with a longer piece two days later.[51] Although the uses to which the exported product was to be put were never established with any degree of certainty, the Zyklon B tag was to propel the story across the Channel: 'French Chemical firm is linked to Holocaust gas' was the chosen wording of *The Times* of October 1996; 'French "made B Gas for Holocaust"', with its fig-leaf quotation marks, that of the *Observer*.[52] It is worth noting that Lacroix-Riz devotes some five pages of her 650-page monograph on economic collaboration to the Zyklon B case.[53]

Ethics and Aesthetics: Good Holocaust Denial Crime Fiction

In his *Les Assassins de la mémoire* historian Pierre Vidal-Naquet insists that although it is important to analyze their writings, one should not engage in debate with Holocaust deniers: 'A dialogue between two parties, even if they are adversaries, presupposes a common ground, a common respect – in this case for truth. But with the "revisionists", such ground does not exist.'[54] Others have approached the issue with rather less faith in the concept of 'truth' (Stanley Fish's

Faurisson and Roques (Chapter IV), Notin (Chapter V), and Plantin (Chapter VII), as well as an overall 'verdict' on these cases in the 'Conclusions générales', pp. 271–90.

[51] Jean-Luc Douin and Patrick Kechichian, 'Le groupe Ugine a-t-il produit du gaz Zyklon B durant les années 40? La revue Études et documents refuse l'article d'une historienne', *Le Monde*, 9 October 1996; Nicolas Weill, 'Des entreprises françaises au service de l'Allemagne nazie', *Le Monde*, 11 October 1996.

[52] Ben MacIntyre, *The Times*, 9 October 1996; Alex Duval Smith, *The Observer*, 13 October 1996.

[53] Annie Lacroix-Riz, *Industriels et banquiers sous l'Occupation. La collaboration économique avec le Reich et Vichy* (Armand Colin, 1999), pp. 162–6.

[54] Pierre Vidal-Naquet, *Assassins of Memory. Essays on the Denial of the Holocaust*, trans. Jeffrey Mehlman (Columbia UP, 1992), p. xxiv. First published as *Les Assassins de la mémoire* (Éditions de la Découverte, 1987).

views, for instance, are mentioned below), but what of aesthetic engagement: how might crime fiction take issue if not directly with the deniers, then at least with their ideas? Holocaust denial is a slippery subject to write fiction about. Authors setting out to expose its fallacious nature and the dangers it represents need to avoid the pitfalls of legitimation. They should seek to represent in one sense without representing in the other; must speak *of* without speaking up *for*. Ambiguity or moral uncertainty, which are key to so much *noir* fiction, may create hostages to fortune: for the Holocaust denier any suggestion that the truth may be hard to pin down; any blurring of victim and perpetrator boundaries, is grist to the mill. How then, do these works of crime fiction go about representing negationist issues which, in these particular instances, were based on specific events?

Nazis dans le métro opens with an assault on a writer, André Sloga, a character modelled according to Daeninckx on crime fiction author Jean Amila.[55] The motive behind the assault is revealed in *mise en abyme* manner to be Sloga's uncovering of a *rouge-brun* alliance responsible for the publication of anti-semitic and negationist materials. Sloga's part is a minor one (the writer as imperilled unveiler of criminal truths) but it gestures towards the status of *Nazis dans le métro* as a *roman à clé*. Several of Daeninckx's characters are stand-ins, including, to name just some, the fictional Ivan Astrapov for Edward Limonov (one-time leader of the National Bolshevik Party), Kevin Kervan for Jean-Edern Hallier (editor of *L'Idiot international*), and Pierre Jumel for Patrick Besson (author and contributor to *L'Idiot*). As well as these thinly disguised references to the real, the text quotes extracts from actual publications, in most cases providing precise sources: Sloga's recovered database includes a negationist extract from *La Guerre sociale* of 1979 headed 'Qui est le Juif' (57) and a piece from *L'Imbécile de Paris* of 1991 celebrating *l'Übermensch* and the Aryan race (57–8).[56] Two further extracts are attributed to a fictitious journal, *Fureur continentale*, the first headed 'La Lâcheté juive à l'Élysée' (56), dated 8 november 1989, the second, an anti-semitic attack on Bernard-Henri Lévy, undated (66). A little investigative work on the part of the reader reveals that the material cited in fact comes from *L'Idiot international* (the correct date is given in the first instance; the second extract can be traced to *L'Idiot* of 3 mai 1991).

What does Daeninckx make of – in the sense of use, transform – this incorporation of the real into his criminal fictional world? The short answer is

---

[55] See 'Rencontre avec Didier Daeninckx', <http://www.bibliosurf.com/Rencontre-avec-Didier-Daeninckx>. Accessed 25 July 2010. Platten also comments on the Sloga / Amila link, noting that Amila was beaten up in 1974 'in what appeared to be a politically motivated assault', possibly in response to his *La Vierge et le taureau* in which he criticized the French (military) presence in Tahiti. Platten, 'The Impact of the Contemporary *Roman noir*: Pennac, Daeninckx, and the Question of a Cultural Evolution', in M. Bishop and C. Elson, *French Prose in 2000* (Rodopi, 2002): 155–64 [164].

[56] *La Guerre sociale* was an extreme ('ultra') left magazine published between 1977 and 1984; *L'Imbécile de Paris* appeared briefly in 1991, describing itself as a monthly magazine which expressed views which journalists could not.

not a great deal since he seems above all to have set himself an expositionary and explanatory task. When Gabriel ('le Poulpe') discovers Sloga's database, the nature of the *rouge-brun* alliance it reveals is thus duly, and somewhat laboriously, explained to him – and thereby to the reader – on two occasions; first over several pages (60–63) by Pedro, another recurring figure in the Poulpe series, then again at even greater length by a professor of philosophy (pp. 72–6). As far as the identities of the disguised characters are concerned, little can be said beyond the fact that the reader in the know will know already. Those who fail to identify the real personalities may, perhaps more worryingly, assume that this is a work of 'pure fiction'; in the sense, that is, of having little or no factual basis. It may be that *L'Idiot international* remained unidentified for legal reasons, but one cannot help feeling some disquiet about the combination of real and fictional titles in this case, given the ease with which Holocaust deniers will point to 'lies' (though all fiction, of course, 'lies' …).

Daeninckx's characters do express anti-semitic and negationist views in various passages of direct speech, but on the whole the author eschews the hyperbole often associated with the satirical intentions of the *roman à clé*, perhaps because extremist views already tend to the caricatural in their very irrationality. In *Nazis dans le métro* Astrapov (Limonov) airs his fascist, nationalist, and anti-semitic views at a meeting covertly attended by Gabriel; an anonymous bookseller working at the 'Vieille Gaufre' – for which read 'Vieille Taupe' – includes in his exposition to Gabriel his belief in the 'myth' of the gas chambers, which he describes as the greatest lie of our time (87). Views such as these are never met with counter-arguments. Like Vidal-Naquet, Gabriel does not engage in dialogue with Holocaust deniers. The bookseller's remarks are dismissed with a peremptory 'Ton discours est vraiment puant' (88) ['What you're saying really stinks'], followed by a swift act of violence involving a monkey wrench and a jab to the kidneys. The material on Sloga's database is similarly dismissed by Gabriel as nauseating, ignominious rubbish (57), the reading of which brings a foul taste to the investigator's mouth (58). For one critic of the Poulpe series this approach is both typical and unsatisfactory: reproducing extremist views and saying that they are wrong, states Lomnitz, serves little purpose if there is no political engagement.[57] This is, I think, to underplay the function of genre. As a recurring hero in a much loved and hugely successful series, freelance investigator Gabriel 'le Poulpe' carries considerable moral weight; in this context dismissive revulsion speaks more than discursive debate, and is certainly more aesthetically appropriate: readers would no more expect Gabriel to launch into extended political or historical debate than to drink red wine.

---

[57]   Sacha Lomnitz, 'Le Poulpe, le Pen et le roman populaire', *Critique*, 55.624 (1999): 445–56: 'Les aventures du Poulpe ne sont ni des pamphlets ni des textes à thèses. Elles baignent dans une atmosphère anarchisante ou libertaire sans que le débat politique soit vraiment présent' ['The Poulpe's adventures are neither satirical tracts nor novels which convey a specific socio-political message. They are imbued with some sort of anarchistic or libertarian ethos but devoid of real political debate'], p. 450.

Gabriel's ethical status as the good guy also facilitates the expression of strong views. In an exchange about the *abbé Pierre* in *Au nom du piètre qui a l'essieu* the investigator declares bluntly: 'J'aime pas les gens qui font savoir qu'ils font quelque chose de bien. J'aime pas les abbés, j'aime pas les donneurs de leçons' (58) ['I don't like people who let it be known that they do good deeds. I don't like priests, I don't like people who sermonize'].[58] In a subsequent discussion with Gérard, another recurring character in the Poulpe series, Gabriel states that the *abbé Pierre* has effectively legitimized anti-Semitism and suggests that he think more carefully about what he writes and says in the future.[59] The ensuing exchange sticks the knife into both the *abbé Pierre* and Roger Garaudy with libel-free humour: '– Bah, c'est pas juste de dire ça, c'est un vieil homme, il a même pas lu le livre d'Hitler. / – Garaudy, pas Hitler, c'est toi qui exagères' (124) ['Come on that's not fair, he's an old man and he didn't even read Hitler's book. / Steady on; Garaudy, not Hitler'.][60] Daeninckx's seizing of what is presented as the uncontested moral high ground has had its effect. Patrick Besson, represented by the character Pierre Jumel in *Nazis dans le métro*, responded to Daeninckx's attacks by writing his own crime fiction *roman à clé*, *Didier dénonce* (2002), whose Daeninckx-like protagonist revels in his rectitude: 'Je suis un antifasciste, moi. Je parle du Bien, et donc tout ce que je dis est bien, et devient donc vrai. Je peux dire n'importe quoi sur n'importe qui: c'est vrai. Magique, hein?' (46) ['Me I'm an anti-fascist. I speak about Good, so everything I say is good, and so it becomes true. I can say anything I like about anyone at all: it's true. Magic, eh?'].[61]

The focus so far has been primarily on the author's manipulation of characters, but what of plot? Whereas Daeninckx made little – in the sense of adapting the facts to fit the aesthetic norms of crime fiction – of the *rouge-brun* alliance at the centre of *Nazis dans le métro*, in his *Éthique à toc* he does rather more. Based on the Plantin scandal at Lyon University, the text represents Jean Plantin in the guise of historian and archivist André Béraud, with Plantin's supervisor Yves Lequin appearing as the fictitious Hubert Hynkel, head of the Centre Gabriel-Roux (for which read the real Centre Pierre Léon). But Daeninckx adds arson, murder, and pornography to the mix. Other authors, too, make more of what we might call the

---

[58] The punning title *Au nom du piètre qui a l'essieu*, which plays on the words 'prêtre' [priest] and 'piètre' [a pathetic figure] and opens with the religious phrasing 'au nom du' (in the name of; as in 'in the name of the Father'), itself represent a none too subtle dig at the *abbé*. (The reference to 'l'essieu' [an axle] alludes to Gabriel's long-term project of rebuilding an aircraft.)

[59] The fictional Gabriel's words echo those expressed by historian Pierre Vidal-Naquet: 'Je crains que la prise de position de l'abbé Pierre ouvre les vannes d'une poussée antisémite', interview by François Bonnet and Nicolas Weill, 'Pierre Vidal-Naquet analyse les relais dont disposent les négationnistes', *Le Monde*, 4 May 1996.

[60] Busino's *Au nom du piètre qui a l'essieu* cites part of the *abbé Pierre*'s letter of support for Roger Garaudy (53); Daeninckx's *Éthique en toc* includes Garaudy's response to the scandal – *Réponse au lynchage médiatique* – amongst a list of negationist publications (112).

[61] Patrick Besson, *Didier dénonce* (Fayard, 2002).

raw materials of fact. Arnaud's *L'Antizyklon des atroces* starts out with Gabriel's reading of a genuine article from *Libération* on Annie Lacroix-Riz's work on the production of Zyklon B gas in France (12) and situates the action in Villers-Saint-Sépulcre, site of the actual Zyklon B producing factory. The author, however, adds to this factual scaffolding a character with extreme far right views who has not only stashed away a wartime shipment of Zyklon B canisters but has built and used his own gas chamber. Busino's *Au nom du piètre qui a l'essieu* takes as its factual starting point the scandal associated with the *abbé Pierre* and makes of the latter's beloved Emmaüs organization a front for the buying and selling of Jewish goods plundered during the war years and run by an anti-semitic network of extremists.[62] One issue which arises from all of these texts is how and whether the aesthetic, specifically in the form of generic crime fiction traits, and the ethical, which I shall take as a contestation of Holocaust denial, function together harmoniously.

In investigator mode, Daeninckx seems to have seized upon a number of enigmas when writing his *Éthique en toc*: why would Plantin's supervisor, who (as Rousso was to record some three years later in his official report) had no known record as a Holocaust denier or far right extremist, allow Plantin to write the thesis he did? What became of Plantin's second thesis, *Les Épidémies de typhus exanthématique dans les camps de concentration nazis, 1933–1945*, which has never been located? What, or who, caused the fire which, on 12–13 June 1999, partly destroyed the library of the University of Lyon? In Daeninckx's reworking of the facts, the missing thesis is borrowed from the library by historian Pierre Floric, who is on the trail of negationist elements in the University. Floric, like Béraud's (Plantin's) supervisor, Hubert Hynkel (Lequin), is subsequently blackmailed by Béraud (the former over an extra-marital affair, the latter for his taste for pornographic films) and commits suicide. The library fire is planned by Béraud when he realizes that the stacks of negationist material it holds may soon be discovered. All of which makes for good crime fiction, not least when Hynkel takes his revenge on the final page by shooting Béraud dead,[63] but does (and should) this manipulation of the facts engage usefully with Holocaust denial? For historian Rousso, Daeninckx's acts of conflation and invention were worthy of explicit condemnation. His *Rapport de la commission sur le racisme et le négationnisme à l'université Jean-Moulin Lyon III* implicitly acknowledges the aesthetic potential of a missing thesis and a fire of unknown origin: 'Sans qu'il y ait de liens connus entre cet événement [the fire]

---

[62]   Busino is careful to avoid libel, backing off intratextually when the integrity of those in charge of the Emmaüs movement is explicitly challenged. The question 'Ils sont au courant, les dirigeants d'Emmaüs?' ['Do the people running Emmaüs know about it?'] is thus answered in the negative (88).

[63]   Passing mention is made of Hynkel as the killer of André Béraut in Benson's *Biblio-quête*, which serves as an unofficial sequel to *Éthique en toc*: 'L'affaire [the suicide of Floric and murder of Béraut] a été rapidement classée, le meurtrier jugé irresponsable de ses actes et interné en milieu psychiatrique. Il s'est suicidé deux mois plus tard', p. 157 ['the case was quickly closed, the killer was judged not to be responsible for his actions and was interned in a psychiatric hospital. He killed himself two months later'].

et l'affaire Plantin, la concomitance des faits dramatise la situation' ['Although there is no known link between this event and the Plantin affair, the concomitance of the facts dramatizes the situation']. A terse footnote adds: 'Ces événements ont fait l'objet d'un roman: Didier Daeninckx, *Éthique en toc*, Paris, Éd. Baleine / Le Poulpe, 1998. L'écrivain est membre du cercle Videlier' ['These events have become the subject matter of a novel. (…) The author is a member of the Videlier circle'].[64] Rousso's condemnatory stance emerges rather more clearly a few pages later when he points out that whereas the missing facts or so-called mysteries should have elicited caution in commentators, they led instead to wild supposition and accusations, including the suggestion that the library had been set ablaze in order to destroy the missing thesis.[65]

Rousso's objections are clearly inapposite: as he himself records, *Éthique en toc* is a work of fiction; Daeninckx does not purport to present us with facts. There is, however, perhaps a case to be made against the text, albeit on different grounds. The filling in of the gaps in the facts of the real Plantin case via the addition of the crime fiction staples of murder, blackmail, and arson makes this a decent work of crime fiction, but it could be argued that Daeninckx's fictionalized version of events, the *poesis* exercised in the specific context of Holocaust denial, might invite the wrong sort of attention. Holocaust deniers, who themselves lack or choose to ignore facts, often act like perverse investigators, thriving on the detection of apparent error: witnesses who (inevitably) make mistakes in their testimonial accounts, or historians who disagree with one another, are automatically deemed to be unreliable. Denial of the facts of the Holocaust, it might be said, can only be supported in negative mode, by seeking to undermine those who deny the deniers. It will come as no surprise then to learn that Daeninckx's mixing of fact and fiction was immediately commented on by Holocaust denier Robert Faurisson, who remarked in his blog that Daeninckx's version of the library fire as a criminal act was wholly unsubstantiated (going on in a later post to suggest that Jewish arsonists are more likely to have set the fire …).[66] Views such as these are of course ludicrous, and I am by no means suggesting that these are grounds for saying that Daeninckx was wrong to make what he did of the Plantin affair: I merely note that the risks, and stakes, may be higher when the subject matter involves Holocaust denial. The second, perhaps more crucial point to be made, is that Holocaust denial is not the only crime in any these texts, or even the most conspicuous. Béraud in *Éthique en toc* is also a murderer, as are the anti-semitic

---

[64]   Henry Rousso, *Rapport*, p. 218, and footnote 1 (p. 218). Historian Philippe Videlier (then working at Lyon II) accused a coworker of having had negationist links in his youth, thereby setting off another long-running and acrimonious 'affaire'. See Rousso, *Rapport*, 'Le Cas Videlier à Lyon II', pp. 172–9. The 'Cercle Videlier' consists of a group of Videlier's supporters.

[65]   Henry Rousso, *Rapport*, p. 230.

[66]   I prefer not to facilitate further dissemination of such material by providing the website address.

negationist characters in *Au nom du piètre qui a l'essieu*. The aesthetic decision to include murder, which lies at the centre of so much crime fiction, is understandable, but also potentially problematic. Whilst making murderers of Holocaust deniers adds to their moral turpitude and designates them as unambiguously bad, it also shifts the focus away from the crime of denial itself: these are assassins before and above being assassins of memory.

Layering further crimes upon that of Holocaust denial is not the strategy adopted in all of the texts being considered here: Arnaud opts for a rather different approach to the tricky balancing of aesthetic and ethical considerations in his *L'Antizyklon des atroces*. Like the protagonists of *Éthique en toc* and *Au nom du piètre* his Philippe Brichet is a far right extremist and a murderer, but unlike those characters he is no Holocaust denier. In fact, Brichet's victims die in the gas chamber he has constructed on his own property. As Lyotard points out in *The Differend*, referring here to views expressed by Faurisson: 'To have "really seen with his own eyes" a gas chamber would be the condition which gives one the authority to say that it exists and to persuade the unbeliever.'[67] The following direct speech is that of a potential collaborator in Brichet's extremist projects who has come to inspect the installation:

> Je suis convaincu mais très ennuyé car depuis pas mal de temps j'appartiens à ce que nos ennemis appellent les ignobles révisionnistes ou négationnistes. Je ne voulais pas y croire. Non parce qu'un ridicule sentiment m'agitait mais cette performance technique me paraissait inconcevable. [...] Mais elle [cette réalité] a existé. (9)

> [I'm convinced but I'm extremely put out because for quite a while I've been part of what our enemies call the despicable revisionists or negationists. I didn't want to believe it. Not because of some silly sentimentality but because for me this sort of technical feat was inconceivable. (...) But it really existed.]

In this case, seeing is believing.[68] Whilst this is admittedly a rather clunky and unconvincing device (not to mention one which for some readers might be deemed to be in rather poor taste), it has the merit of foregrounding the issue of denial. The present-day gas chamber also raises temporal issues with respect to the so-called repetition of the past. Firstly, it brings into relief the paradox of Holocaust deniers' position: those who refute the existence of the gas chambers may well, in the very extremity of their ideology, be those most likely to precipitate, or at the very least welcome, its 'repetition' in the future. Secondly, Arnaud's text acts a reminder that the notion of the repetition of the past can only be approximate or metaphorical.

---

[67]   Lyotard, *The Differend*, p. 3.

[68]   For Faurisson only the impossible eye-witness – one who had passed through the gas chamber – would be truly convincing: 'The only acceptable proof that it was used to kill is that one died from it. But if one is dead, one cannot testify that it is on account of the gas chamber', *The Differend*, p. 3 (Lyotard is paraphrasing Faurisson's view here as well as expressing his own).

A new historical context inevitably means change: as we will see, Brichet's intended victims are not Jews but illegal immigrants. *L'Antizyklon*, in other words, focuses on the socio-political context of its readers at the time of the work's publication.[69] It is not all about the present, though. Whilst focusing on the contemporary, Arnaud and his fellow crime writers also look to the past for a situation which readers will recognize and superimpose upon the present; a familiar cognitive framework which will stress that 'this might happen because something like it already has'. France's World War II experience provides the ideal narrative.

Nazis dans le métro invokes the 'evidence' of the past crimes of the Vichy years in various ways, most obviously via its punning title,[70] but also by means of chapter titles such as 'Pedro et les nazis de gauche' ['Pedro and the left wing nazis'] or 'Un alphabet vert-de-gris' ['A verdigris A-Z'].[71] Daeninckx makes full use of the moral authority of the Poulpe series' recurring characters to establish links between wartime fascists and their present day avatars. Pedro points out to Gabriel that the far right in France has already shown what it was capable of, stressing the similarities between past and present by comparing the new *rouge-brun* alliance and anti-semitic writings to what he perceives as their 1930s' version: Doriot, he remarks, was a leading figure in the French Communist Party before espousing fascism; Laval was once a socialist (61); some of the anti-semitic material recorded by Sloga on his database echoes precisely texts written by Léon Daudet (60). If today's extremists are likened to wartime French fascists then the good guys are situated on the side of the Resistance. Sloga, the writer who uncovers the *rouge-brun* alliance, and himself a former resistant, is described by Gabriel as having rejoined the *maquis* (58), as are immigrants in *L'Antizyklon des atroces* (55). In *Éthique en toc* historian Pierre Floric commits suicide at Caluire with a copy of Jean Moulin's *Premier combat* in his pocket. The Holocaust denying Béraut, by contrast, works in the very room in which Klaus Barbie tortured prisoners. In some cases the metaphor of the repetition of the past combines with a narrative of familial legacy: we learn that Béraud's father was a *gestapiste* who wrote for the pro-Nazi anti-semitic publication *Gringoire* and was condemned to death for his wartime activities (*Éthique*, 63; 107). Philippe Brichet's father was a member of Doriot's PPF and, having signed up for the *Légion des Volontaires Français*, was incorporated into the Waffen SS in 1945 (*L'Antizyklon*, 6). As one of the characters in *L'Antizyklon* puts it, 'La saloperie doit se perpétuer en famille' (28) ['Disgusting behaviour must run in families'].

---

[69] Ann Rigney discusses the importance of relevance, and how it might be balanced with accuracy in historical novels' treatment of past, in her 'Fiction as a Mediator in National Remembrance', in S. Berger, L. Eriksonas, A. Mycock (eds), *Narrating the Nation* (Berghahn Books, 2008): 79–96.

[70] Translating as 'Nazis in the métro', Daeninckx's title is a punning allusion to Raymond Queneau's novel *Zazie dans le métro* (1959).

[71] 'Vert-de-gris' would be recognized by a French readership (of a certain age, at least) as the colour of the German soldiers' uniforms during World War II.

The Vichy past is invoked in *L'Antizyklon* to underline the possible reality, or real possibility, of fascism taking over in France, this narrative of the past combining with the present socio-political context in order to hint at a dystopic future. Protagonist Philippe Brichet plans to construct an extermination camp once the far right has come to power in France. In the character's words the gas chambers of the 'camp de Séricourt-Jacques-Doriot' which he will run will constitute the 'final solution' to the immigrant problem in a way that charter flights never could (55). Both past and present allusions would have struck a chord with Arnaud's readers. In the context of what was already a bitter public debate surrounding the implementation of new immigration laws, on 27 February 1997, 77 illegal immigrants were forcibly deported from France to Mali by charter flight during the course of which some 20 police officers were injured when violence broke out. Arnaud's dystopic vision of a repetition of deportation and murder may seem extreme, but links between past and present are not restricted to the fictional world. As Daeninckx has pointed out, the *Front national* slogan '3 millions de chômeurs, 3 million d'immigrés' echoes a Nazi propaganda poster of the 1930s which read '500,000 chômeurs, 500,000 juifs'.[72] David Fraser traces an element of legal continuity from the principles which allowed Jews to be stripped of their citizenship during the Vichy years to contemporary legislation on illegal immigration in France.[73] More telling yet is an article flagged up by Valérie Igounet in her study of Holocaust denial. Written in 1998 by Martin Peltier the piece came out in *National Hebdo*, the weekly publication of the *Front national* and expresses Peltier's opinion that illegal immigrants have no excuse for failing to obey the law. Ramping up the provocation, he suggests that the matter could be sorted out readily enough:

> Le reste n'est qu'une question d'organisation, il y a des fonctionnaires pour cela. Des négociations, ça se mène. Des transports, ça se trouve. Et s'il faut des rafles et des camps de concentration pour le transit, ce n'est pas un problème.[74]
>
> [After that it's just a matter or organization, and there are civil servants to do that. Negotiations can be had. Transportation can be sorted out. And if raids and transit concentration camps are needed, it's not a problem.]

The texts considered so far look to the wartime past to reinforce the notion of future dangers arising from a present socio-political situation. In all cases the present of the diegesis is contemporary to the texts' date of publication. The last of the crime fiction texts to be discussed here, Benson's *Biblio-quête*, provides a twist on this pattern: written as a sequel to Daeninck's *Éthique en toc*, the text is

---

[72]   Daeninckx 'Ce n'est pas tout que de ne pas brûler les gens ...' in *Paroles à la bouche du présent. Le négationnisme: histoire ou politique?*', ed. Natacha Michel (Éditions Al Dante, 1997), p. 47.

[73]   Fraser, *Law after Auschwitz*, p. 157.

[74]   Igounet, *Histoire du négationnisme*, p. 600, citing Martin Peltier, 'Ma Semaine', *National Hebdo*, 6–12 August (1998), pp. 1–2.

set in 2021. Representing cross-diegetic familial continuity as well as literary continuity with Daeninckx's text, *Biblio-quête* features Marc Floric, son of *Éthique en toc*'s Pierre Floric, a history teacher like his father, who is completing a monograph on Holocaust denial. Guillaume Béraut, represented as the brother of Daeninckx's Plantin figure, André Béraut, runs the rebuilt Lyon library which sits at the centre of Benson's plot. The story begins when a 69-year-old historian of World War II, Gabriel Joesandi, is murdered as he sets fire to books in the library. Shortly after, Marc Floric and his partner, a policewoman on the case, are also killed. When the matter is hushed up by the authorities, EPICUR, a European team of investigators, takes over.

Above all, Benson's text foregrounds the evolving role of memory. In *Nazis dans le métro* Pedro bemoans the apparent historical amnesia suffered by those now voting for the *Front national* (61), whilst the philosopher consulted by Gabriel points out that whilst time may go by immeasurably slowly for victims of the war, where many others are concerned the past is soon forgotten (73). In the case of former deportee Samuel Carinas in *L'Antizyklon des atroces*, the horrors of the past were witnessed at first hand. Benson's futuristic 2021 setting, however, ensures that few, if any, eye-witnesses to France's Vichy past remain alive. This is less a case of the metaphorical assassination of memory by Holocaust deniers than its dying a natural death. And the repercussions are immense. Once the eye-witnesses have gone, the baton is passed to the historians and their publications. The oft-cited tensions between memory and history begin to blur, even to lose their relevance. Historian Joesandi, murdered in the library, a repository later described as the symbol *par excellence* of memory (115), is known by his students as the professor with the exceptional memory, the expert who could direct them to the precise page of a periodical or monograph to discover information on the war years, and, especially, the Holocaust. As one of his graduate students puts it, memory was the main tool with which he worked (114). Memory in Benson's text is, however, not only associated with historians and their hard copy. It is also the stuff of bytes and disks: when a computer's hard drive is found to have been wiped clean, its saved files or electronic memory deleted, we are told that 'ordinateur [...] est devenu parfaitement amnésique' (116) ['the computer (...) was struck with total amnesia']. A later reference to 'le virus de l'oubli' (157) ['the forgetting virus'] relates to both human agents and software.

In a world in which information is increasingly stored in media other than print, new threats and vulnerabilities arise. As Huyssen asks, 'how reliable are our digitalized archives?'[75] Benson's futuristic world suggests that the answer is not at all. As the EPICUR team discover, the historians' murders are carried out by members of a group of fascists (including Béraut, the library director) who have the European Presidency in their sights. The aim of the group is to implement a new approach to Holocaust denial: all primary and secondary source documents relating to the war, books and periodicals alike, are being altered in the process of

---

[75] Andreas Huyssen, 'Present Pasts: Media, Politics, Amnesia', p. 26.

their digitization so as to expunge all references to the Shoah. Once it has bought global copyright, Booktech will be free to rewrite history. In a reversal of the trope of book burning carried out at the instigation of totalitarian regimes, historian Joesandi's fire-setting is revealed as a last desperate bid to draw attention to his discovery of the corruption of the truth which lies at the heart of the library.[76]

Focusing as it does on the loss of eye-witnesses and the potential corruption of primary and secondary historical sources via digitization *Biblio-quête* engages further with epistemological concerns than the other works of crime fiction dealing with the subject of Holocaust denial. All of the texts, however, whether implicitly or explicitly, raise issues relating to truth and the facts of the matter, a suitable topic on which to bring this chapter to a close.

In Chapter 4, in the context of a series of texts featuring historians as investigators, we saw that the question of whether or not these works demonstrated closure could be approached from an ethical or an aesthetic perspective (above pp. 145–7). The Holocaust denial texts being considered here, which represent their historian characters as villains and victims rather than primarily as investigators, also generate epistemological questions relating to 'truth' and the 'facts' of 'the past' which need to be addressed on two different, but I will suggest, related levels. On the one hand we have crime fiction texts which are driven, as the base-line norms of the genre dictate, by an element of mystery which requires investigation, and which feature victims and criminals, where the latter's acts are underpinned by identifiable motives. In the case of all five texts the truth emerges and the facts are established via a reconstruction of past events (Sloga was assaulted because he discovered the truth about the *rouge-brun* alliance; Béraut was responsible for the library fire, and so forth). This epistemological certainty is coupled with a moral unambiguity which is uncommon in much crime fiction, as previous chapters have revealed. Unlike the police officers or common criminals discussed in Chapter 3, for instance, far right political extremists and Holocaust deniers are not represented in shades of grey: there is no hint of the victim about them, and no mitigating circumstances are proffered, however subtly. But the question of truth runs deeper than this. Murders may be solved and the facts of 'what happened' in the recent past of the diegesis established, but what of the extermination camps of World War II and the truth of genocide? Where – if anywhere – do these texts

---

[76]   Joesandi might be said to represent a failed version of the characters in Bradbury's *Fahrenheit 451* who memorize books in an attempt to preserve them from oblivion. One of those individuals, Granger, addresses former fireman and book-burner Montag on the subject of war in terms which Joesandi might appreciate: 'But even when we had the books on hand, a long time ago, we didn't use what we got out of them. We went right on insulting the dead. We went right on spitting in the graves of all the poor ones who died before us. We're going to meet a lot of lonely people in the next week and the next month and the next year. And when they ask us what we're doing, you can say, We're remembering. That's where we'll win out in the long run. And some day we'll remember so much that we'll build the biggest goddam steam-shovel in history and dig the biggest grave of all time and shove war in and cover it up', p. 209.

stand on epistemological questions relating specifically to the Holocaust denial which is also their subject matter?

As already noted, all four authors tend to eschew epistemological debate on the subject of the Holocaust in the form of exchanges between characters. The inclusion of references to history and historical truth, and the presence of historians cast in key roles, however, is such that an epistemology does emerge, if only implicitly, and that epistemology, I suggest, is rather less sure of its facts than that which drives the texts as works of crime fiction. First, we are reminded that Holocaust deniers and other falsifiers of history believe that they have access to the truth of the past. In *Biblio-quête* the phrase '*real* history' (Benson's emphasis) is used ironically to designate the teaching of history associated with Chinese reeducation programmes, the Russian Gulag, or Hitler Youth (117). In *Nazis dans le métro* it is a Holocaust denier who speaks of 'La véritable Histoire', contrasting this to the 'lies' perpetuated by a 'Jewish lobby' (67). One might add to this the *abbé Pierre*'s letter of support for Holocaust denier Garaudy, with its appeals to 'true' history and historiography: 'Il faut tout faire, et je m'y emploie, pour que bientôt des historiens vrais, de la même passion du vrai qui est la tienne, s'attachent à en débattre avec toi' ['Everything must be done, and I'm doing what I can to make it happen, to ensure that real historians, who have the same passion for the truth as you do, endeavour to debate the matter with you in the near future']. Secondly, these are texts which represent historians in both a positive and a negative light. Gabriel may stress the importance of historical analysis in *Au nom du piètre qui a l'essieu*, for instance, but in the same breath he bemoans the penetration of the university sector by inadequate and unscrupulous teaching staff (120). Daeninckx's *Éthique en toc* features the good historian Pierre Floric, but the latter's presence is countered by the immoral Béraut and his pusillanimous boss, Hynkel. *Biblio-quête* includes good historians Gabriel Joesandi and Marc Floric, but also shows how everything they represent can be threatened by the ideological deployment of new technologies.

Strikingly, these works of popular crime fiction play out some of issues at the centre of a debate on Holocaust denial which took place between literary theorist Stanley Fish and historian Richard Weisberg at around the same time the novels were published.[77] Fish, like Vidal-Naquet though for different reasons (the latter because he believes Holocaust deniers refute the truth; the former because he is not convinced that there is a truth to be found) believes that debate – specifically epistemological debate – with Holocaust deniers should be avoided. Above all, to posit the irrefutable existence of facts or truths is, he claims, to set the bar too high: 'If the standard of validation is the establishment of a truth that is

---

[77] Stanley Fish, 'Holocaust denial and academic freedom', *Valparaiso University Law Review*, 35 (2001): 499–524. Richard H Weisberg's 'Fish Takes the Bait: Holocaust Denial and Post-Modernist Theory', *Law and Literature*, 14 (2002): 131–42. See also Nick Spearing '"Don't go changing": on Richard Weisberg's critique of Stanley Fish and Holocaust Denial', *Law and Literature*, 20 (2008): 318–42.

invulnerable to challenge, no one [...] could meet it.'[78] For Fish, '[t]hose fighting against Holocaust deniers are in the same business as their enemy, not in some cleaner, less interpretive, less interested business'.[79] Fish's solution is to appeal to the established authority of the collective or 'guild' of professional historians, a group which would and should quite simply exclude Holocaust deniers. He sums up his advice to historians as follows:

> [F]orget the theory, forget the epistemology, forget the meta-history – they are
> the preferred games of the opponent – and just go with the privileged position
> you already enjoy by belonging to a pre-eminent and powerful guild.[80]

In his critique (which he bases on a topic which has been mentioned at several points in this book, namely the implication of lawyers under Vichy in the implementation of anti-semitic measures) Weisberg points out that professional guilds can both change and do the wrong thing. He asks Fish if 'a believer in his theory might not *accept Holocaust denial* if things changed enough and if Irving's disciples had grabbed power in the history departments'.[81] This is precisely the situation alluded to in *Au nom du piètre qui a l'essieu* and depicted in texts such as *Éthique en toc*, with its negationist historians ensconced in a university setting, or *Biblio-quête*, which shows that and how the historians' guild can be subverted. As a character in Benson's novel points out, if digitized sources are corrupted and students in large enough numbers are deliberately misled by Holocaust denying lecturers and supervisors, then history can be rewritten (158).

In his reply to Weisberg Fish finds himself obliged to agree that should the guild of historians evolve towards Holocaust denial, then he would have to recommend that it be rejected. As Weisberg points out, in so responding Fish has slipped back into the espousal of a normative view: something outside the guild (or interpretive community, to use another of Fish's terms from his earlier work) is guiding his choices.[82] It is precisely such a given – that the Holocaust took place – which lies at the centre of the crime fiction texts, manifested not via epistemological debate, but in the epistemological certainty which underpins the crime story plots (the truth of the past emerges) and which manifests itself also, and especially, in a moral unambiguity which dismisses fascists and Holocaust deniers alike out of hand. Epistemological uncertainty may be implicitly acknowledged in the representation of unreliable historians and Holocaust deniers' belief in the truth of their position, but all that is trumped by ethical certainty. As Lyotard might put it, a 'differend' (i.e., 'a case of conflict [...] that cannot be resolved for lack of a rule of judgment applicable to both of the arguments') might arise between a

---

78   Fish, 'Holocaust denial', p. 504.

79   Ibid., p. 509.

80   Fish, 'Holocaust denial', p. 511.

81   Weisberg, 'Fish Takes the Bait', p. 138.

82   Ibid., p. 140.

Holocaust denier and a historian who believed in the facts of the Holocaust, but the bottom line is that killing is unjust: 'Absolute injustice would occur if [...] the possibility of continuing to play the game of the just were excluded.'[83] Perhaps the decision of the crime fiction authors discussed here to represent Holocaust deniers as murderers makes both aesthetic and ethical sense.

Closing Statement

This final chapter has analyzed some of the ways in which works of crime fiction set after the war represent links between that wartime past and the present of the diegesis (which usually, though not always, unfolds within approximately a year of the date of publication). This has meant looking again at the notion that the past will not readily pass, but doing so by paying specific attention to the human dimension of lived temporality and the reasons for which forgetting the past may be no easy task: when is the war really over?; why and how are the war years invoked?; by whom, with what, if any, intention and consequence?

In the first section a number of text types or categories were constructed according to the varying temporal resonances of World War II: trauma texts; legacy (real and metaporical) texts; tales of returning or ever-present nazis; revenge and justice texts featuring the asynchronous returnee; works which stressed criminal continuity under apparently discontinuous socio-political regimes; those which suggested a direct line of criminal descent from World War II to the Algerian War and other conflicts. With Borgesian taxonomy once again in mind I would not wish to suggest that these are impermeable categories (any one work of crime fiction may 'fit' into several), nor that the temporal variants I have identified are by any means comprehensive. What I do hope to have demonstrated is the manner in which these fictional representations bring out the very human, and by no means always neurotic, or wilful, or irrational, reasons which may lie behind the slow passing of the wartime past. By choosing to focus especially on textual temporal relations, as one might do with any epithet-free text, my intention has also been to show how works of crime fiction may be read with a critical eye which sees beyond the genre label.

Where the first section provided a synoptic view of the corpus based on a selection of representative texts, in the second section, which can be regarded as methodologically complementary to the first, I narrowed the analytic focus to a small group of works representing the threat of the political far right and Holocaust denial. These are quick-response texts which pick up on, and by fictionalizing the real, probe events which have made their way into the mainstream French press. Past, present, and future form a particular weave in what can be described as cautionary tales in which fears for the future precipitated by events unfolding in the present are underscored by the admonitory presence of World War II.

---

[83]   Lyotard, with Jean-Loup Thébaud, *Just Gaming* (U of Minnesota P, 1985).

Whilst the past cannot literally be repeated, these texts tell us, its ills and traumas can certainly play out in contemporary form.

Finally, and a suitably paradoxical point at which to end a book about fictional inscriptions of World War II: the representation of those who seek to unwrite the past. Having explored the complexities involved in representing Holocaust deniers in works of crime fiction – the need to balance the aesthetic demands of genre with the ethical requirement to deny the deniers – I pointed to some potential vulnerabilities in the texts. I further observed that the latter combine the representation of epistemological uncertainty – extremist right-wing historians, the death of witnesses, digitally stored data which is vulnerable to erasure and corruption – with absolute ethical certainty (the unambiguously villainous deniers who get their come-uppance). There is, I feel, something eminently pleasing in this. Representing the assassins of memory as assassins, writing those who seek to rewrite, or unwrite, the past into a crime narrative in which poetic justice prevails, is ethically satisfactory in the very real time of the reader. And if we recall that in thus representing Holocaust deniers and historians these texts are playing out debates taking place amongst historians, literary critics, and philosophers, I think we can also say that these works of crime fiction merit the same degree of attention as other discursive representations of World War II.

Bibliography

Primary Texts

(All works are published in Paris unless stated otherwise. The publication details of the edition I have used are followed by the original publication details where these differ.)

Abécassis, Éliette, *L'Or et la cendre* (Livre de Poche, 2006; Éd. Ramsay, 1997).
Amila, Jean [published under the name Jean Meckert], *Nous avons les mains rouges* (Gallimard, 1947).
Amila, Jean [published under the name Jean Meckert], *Nous sommes tous des assassins*. (Éd. Joëlle Losfield, 2008; Gallimard, 1952).
Amila, Jean, *Au balcon d'Hiroshima* (Gallimard, 1985).
Amila, Jean, *La Lune d'Omaha* (Folio policier, 2004; Gallimard, 1964).
Amoz, Claude, *L'Ancien crime* (Payot & Rivages, 1999).
Arnaud, Georges J., *Maudit blood* (Éd. du Rocher, 1998; Encre, 1985).
Arnaud, Georges J., *L'Antizyklon des atroces* (Librio, 2003; Baleine, 1998).
Arnaud, Georges J., *Spoliation* (Fleuve noir, 2000).
Aubert, Brigitte, *La Rose de fer* (Seuil, 1993).
Auclair, Georges, *Un Amour allemand* (Gallimard, 1950).
Baumier, Matthieu, *Les Apôtres du néant* (Flammarion, 2002).
Bellanti, Louis and Frédérique Vacher, *Le Manuscrit de la mémère morte* (Baleine, 1998).
Benson, Stéphanie, *Biblio-quête* (Seuil, 2001).
Berenboom, Alain, *Périls en ce royaume* (B. Pacuito, 2006).
Bialot, Joseph, *Babel-ville* (Folio, 2002; Gallimard, 1979).
Bialot, Joseph, *La Nuit du souvenir* (Gallimard, 1990).
Blond, Georges, *L'Ange de la rivière morte* (Livre de Poche, 1978; C. Bourgeois, 1946).
Boileau-Narcejac, *Les Louves* (Folio, 2005; Denoël, 1955).
Boileau-Narcejac, *Maldonne* (Denoël, 1962).
Boileau-Narcejac, *La Lèpre* (Denoël, 1976).
Brussolo, Serge, *La Fille aux cheveux rouges* (J'ai lu, 2006).
Busino, Jean-Jacques, *Au nom du piètre qui a l'essieu* (Baleine, 1998).
Carraud, Jypé, *Les poulets du Cristobal* (Payot & Rivages, 1998).
Castillo, Michel del, *Les portes du sang* (Seuil, 2003).
Cayre, Hannelore, *Toiles de maîtres* (Métailié, 2005).
Chaboud, Jack, *Le Tronc de la veuve* (Le Passage, 2003).
Coatmeur, Jean-François, *On l'appelait Johnny* (Denoël, 1979).
Courchay, Claude, *Retour à Malaveil* (P. Belfond, 1982).

Couturier, Sarah, *Sarah* (Payot & Rivages, 1997).

Daeninckx, Didier, *Meurtres pour mémoire* (Folio, 2002; Gallimard, 1984).

Daeninckx, Didier, *La Mort n'oublie personne* (Folio, 2003; Denoël, 1989).

Daeninckx, Didier, *Les Figurants* (Librio, 1998; Verdier, 1995).

Daeninckx, Didier, *Nazis dans le métro* (Librio, 2001; Baleine, 1996).

Daeninckx, Didier, *Éthique en toc* (Librio, 2004; Baleine, 2000).

Daeninckx, Didier, *La route du Rom* (Folio, 2005; Baleine, 2003).

Daeninckx, Didier, *Itinéraire d'un salaud ordinaire* (Folio, 2008; Gallimard, 2006).

Dantec, Maurice, *Les racines du mal* (Folio, 2004; Gallimard, 1995).

Dard, Frédéric, *Équipe de l'ombre* (Fayard, 2003; Éd. Lugdumum, 1941).

Dard, Frédéric, *La Crève* (Fleuve noir, 1989; Confluences: 1946).

Dard, Frédéric, *Batailles sur la route* (Fayard, 2004; Saint-Étienne: Éd. Dumas, 1949).

Dard, Frédéric, *Une gueule comme la mienne* (Fleuve noir, 1998; Fleuve noir, 1958).

Darnaud, Guillaume, *Le Crépuscule des vieux* (Baleine, 1997).

Deleuse, Robert, *Retour de femme* (Denoël, 1991).

Del Pappas, Gilles, *Bleu sur la peau* (Marseille: Jigal, 1998).

Delteil, Gérard, *KZ Retour vers l'enfer* (Métailié, 1998; Vertiges du Nord/Carrère, 1987).

Delteil, Gérard, *Mort d'un satrape rouge* (Métailié, 1995).

Demouzon, Alain, *Agence Melchior* (Fayard, 2006).

d'Estienne d'Orves, Nicholas, *Les orphelins du mal* (XO éditions, 2007).

Exbrayat, Charles, *Avanti la musica!* (Le Masque, 1961).

Fajardie, Frédéric, *La Théorie du 1%* (Table ronde, 1995; Néo, 1981).

Fajardie, Frédéric, *Querelleur* (Denoël, 1983).

Fajardie, Frédéric, *Le Loup d'écume* (Livre de Poche, 2005; Albin Michel, 1986).

Fajardie, Frédéric, *Sous le regard des élégantes* (Folio, 2005; Table ronde, 1997).

Fajardie, Frédéric, *Après la pluie* (Folio, 2000; Table ronde, 1998).

Fajardie, Frédéric, *Ciao, bella, ciao* (Table ronde, 1999).

Fonteneau, Pascale, *Otto* (Gallimard, 1997).

Frachet, Pierre, *Comme dit ma grand-mère* (Presses de la Cité, 1966).

Garnier, Pascal, *L'A26* (Zulma, 1999).

Geffray, Stéphane, *Les teutons flingueurs* (Baleine, 1999).

Giovanni, José, *Mon ami le traître* (Gallimard, 1977).

Gouiran, Maurice, *La nuit des bras cassés* (Marseille: Jigal, 2000).

Gouiran, Maurice, *Sous les pavés, la rage* (Marseille: Jigal, 2005).

Gouiran, Maurice, *Train bleu, train noir* (Marseille: Jigal, 2007).

Gouiran, Maurice, *Les vrais durs meurent aussi* (Marseille: Jigal, 2008).

Guimard, Paul, *L'Ironie du sort* (Folio, 2007; Denoël, 1961).

Harlay, Jérôme, *Le Sel de la guerre* (Belfond, 2008).

Héléna, André, *Les salauds ont la vie dure* (e-dite, 2001; World Press: 1949).

Héléna, André, *Le Festival des macchabées* (e-dite, 2001; A. Fleury: 1951).

Héléna, André, *Le Goût du sang* (e-dite, 2004; Lyon: E. Vinay, 1953).

Héléna, André, *Les Clients du Central Hôtel* (e-dite, 2000; SEPFR: 1959).

Huet, Philippe, *Bunker* (Payot & Rivages, 2008).

Japp, Andrea, *Le Silence des survivants* (Livre de Poche, 2005; Éd. du Masque, 2000).

Joly, François, *La Rage* (Gallimard, 2002).

Joly, François, *Les fans sans balance* (La Branche, 2006).

Jonquet, Thierry, *Du passé faisons table rase* (Folio, 2006; Albin Michel, 1982).

Jonquet, Thierry, *Le pauvre nouveau est arrivé* (Manya, 1990).

Jonquet, Thierry, *Les Orpailleurs* (Folio, 2006; Gallimard, 1993).

Kââ, *Trois chiens morts* (Fleuve noir, 1992).

Kolaire, Pierre, *Sur la ligne marginaux* (Baleine, 1999).

Klotz, Claude, *Kobar* (Livre de Poche, 1994; Albin Michel, 1992).

Krivine, Frédéric, *Un souvenir de Berlin* (Denoël, 1990).

Konop, *Pas de Kaddish pour Sylberstein* (Gallimard, 1997; Gallimard, 1993).

Las Vergnas, Raymond, *Le Mystère Niagara* (Albin Michel, 1956).

Laveau, Gérard, *La Trace du diable* (Éd. Du Choucas, 1996).

Luraghi, Cyprien, *Pour cigogne le glas* (Baleine, 1999).

Magnan, Pierre, *Un grison d'Arcadie* (Folio, 2000; Denoël, 1998).

Malet, Léo, *120, rue de la gare* (Fleuve noir, 1983; SEPE, 1943).

Malet, Léo, *Nestor Burma contre CQFD* (Éd. de la butte aux cailles, 1981; SEPE, 1945).

Malet, Léo, *Des kilomètres de linceuls* (R. Laffont, 1955).

Malet, Léo, *Du rebecca rue des Rosiers* (Fleuve noir, 1984; R. Laffont, 1958).

Manchette, Jean-Patrick, *Que d'os* (Folio, 2005; Gallimard, 1976).

Manotti, Dominique, *Nos fantastiques années fric* (Payot & Rivages, 2003; Payot & Rivages, 2001).

Manotti, Dominique, *Le Corps noir* (Seuil, 2006; Seuil, 2004).

Martin, Roger, *Le G.A.L., l'égout* (Baleine, 1996).

Martin, Roger, *Jusqu'à ce que mort s'ensuive* (le Cherche Midi, 2008).

Mazarin, Jean, *Collabo-Song* (Zulma, 1998; Fleuve noir, 1981).

Merle, Robert, *Treize reste raide* (Gallimard, 1997).

Modiano, Patrick *La ronde de nuit* (Folio, 1983; Gallimard, 1969).

Modiano, Patrick, *Les boulevards de la ceinture* (Gallimard, 1972)

Modiano, Patrick, *Dora Bruder* (Folio, 2000; Gallimard, 1997).

Monsour, Jean, *Le Renard de la Forêt-Noire* (Éd. du Masque, 2002).

Monteilhet, Hubert, *Le Retour des cendres* (Livre de Poche, 1967; Denoël, 1961).

Morris, Gilles-Demoulin, *Assassin, mon frère* (Presses de la Cité, 1954).

Nord, Pierre, *Double crime sur la ligne Maginot* (Éd. du Masque, 1936).

Nord, Pierre, *Peloton d'exécution* (Livre de Poche, 1970; Fayard, 1952).

Notin, Jean-Christophe, *Nom de code: La Murène* (Seuil, 2008).

Orange amère (collectif), *L'Ordure, hein!* (Baleine, 2000).

Ouvard, Jacques, *Le plongeon du frère Boileau* (Le Masque, 1964).

Pavloff, Franck, *Le Vent des fous* (Gallimard, 1993).

Pécherot, Patrick, *Boulevard des branques* (Gallimard, 2005).

Pennac, Daniel, *Au Bonheur des ogres* (Gallimard, 1988).

Perrin, Jean-Pierre, *Chiens et louves* (Gallimard, 1999).

Piljean, André, *Passons la monnaie!* (Gallimard, 1951).

Redonnet, Marie, *Nevermore* (POL, 1994).

Renaud, Dominique, *Morts à l'appel* (Éd. Canaille, 1995).

Rio, Michel, *Leçon d'abîme* (Seuil, 2003).

Robbe-Grillet, Alain, *La Reprise* (Minuit, 2001).

San-Antonio, *Règlez-lui son compte* (Fleuve noir, 2006; Fleuve noir, 1949).

San-Antonio, *Laissez tomber la fille* (Fleuve noir, 1975; Fleuve noir, 1950).

San-Antonio, *Les souris ont la peau tendre* (Fleuve noir, 1975; Fleuve noir, 1951).

San-Antonio, *Mes hommages à la donzelle* (Fleuve noir, 1973; Fleuve noir, 1952).

San-Antonio, *Descendez-le à la prochaine* (Fleuve noir, 1953).

San-Antonio, *Du plomb dans les tripes* (Fleuve noir, 1998; Fleuve Noir, 1953).

San-Antonio, *Les doigts dans le nez* (Fleuve noir, 1956).

San-Antonio, *La Tombola des voyous* (Fleuve noir, 1957).

San-Antonio, *San Antonio renvoie la balle* (Fleuve noir, 1960).

Simenon, Georges, *Le Clan des Ostendais* (Folio policier, 2009; Gallimard, 1947).

Simenon, Georges, *La neige était sale* (Livre de poche, 2008; Presses de la Cité, 1948).

Simenon, Georges, *Le Train* (Livre de Poche, 2008; Presses de la Cité, 1961).

Simenon, Georges, *Les Autres* (Livre de Poche, 2008; Presses de la Cité, 1962).

Simsolo, Noël, *Wazemmes* (L'Écailler du Sud, 2005).

Simsolo, Noël, *Exterminateurs* (Seuil, 2001).

Siniac, Pierre, *Les Morfalous* (Gallimard, 1968).

Siniac, Pierre, *Les sauveurs suprêmes* (Gallimard, 1971).

Siniac, Pierre, *Sous l'aile noire des rapaces* (Payot & Rivages, 1995; J.-C. Lattès, 1975).

Siniac, Pierre, *Le Tourbillon* (Payot & Rivages, 1996; J.-C. Lattès, 1976).

Siniac, Pierre, *L'Orchestre d'acier* (Payot & Rivages, 1998; J.-C. Lattès, 1977).

Siniac, Pierre, *Aime le maudit* (1981; Éd. Jean Goujon, 1980).

Siniac, Pierre, *Les mal lunés* (Payot & Rivages, 1995).

Siniac, Pierre, *Ferdinaud Céline* (Payot & Rivages, 2002; Payot & Rivages, 1997).

Slocombe, Romain, *Sake des brumes* (Baleine, 2002).

Soulas, Antoinette, *Café sans tickets...* (Bordeaux: Delmas, 1949).

Tabachnik, Maud, *Tango des assassins* (Livre de Poche, 2003; Éd. du Masque, 2000).

Tabachnik, Maud, *La Honte leur appartient* (Éd. du Masque, 2002).

Tanugi, Gilbert, *Les grottes de Crésus* (Le Masque, 1981; Le Masque, 1974).

Troye, Raymond, *Meurtre dans un oflag* (Brussels: Éd. Labor, 2006; Brussels: Dessart, 1946).

Vargas, Fred, *Un peu plus loin sur la droite* (J'ai lu, 2008; V. Hamy, 1996).

Villemot, Jean-Marie, *L'œil mort* (Gallimard, 1999).

Wagneur, Alain, *Homicide à bon marché* (Gallimard, 1996).

Zamponi, Francis, *Le Boucher de Guelma* (Seuil, 2007).

Zufferey, Daniel, *L'Étoile d'or* (Éd. du Masque, 1998).

Critical Works Cited

Alavoine, Bernard, 'Roman populaire, roman policier et roman psychologique chez Georges Simenon: les trois facettes d'un auteur en quête de légitimation', in Jacques Migozzi, *Le Roman populaire en question(s)* (Limoges: Presses universitaires de Limoges, 1997): 433–53.

Amouroux, Henri, *La grande histoire des Français sous l'Occupation*, Tome VIII (Paris: Robert Laffont, 1988).

Arendt, Hannah, *Eichmann in Jerusalem. A Report on the Banality of Evil* (London: Penguin Books, 1994; first published Viking P, New York, 1963).

Ascari, Maurizio, *A Counter-History of Crime Fiction* (Houndsmills, Basingstoke: Palgrave Macmillan, 2007).

Assouline, Pierre, *Simenon* (Paris: Gallimard 1996).

Atack, Margaret, *Literature and the French Resistance: Cultural Politics and Narrative Forms 1940–1950* (Manchester and New York: Manchester UP, 1989).

Atack, Margaret, 'Crime and Punishment. Narratives of order and disorder', *French Cultural Studies*, 12 (2001): 233–50.

Atack, Margaret, 'Representing the Occupation in the Novels of the 1950s: *Ne Jugez pas*', *Cincinnati Romance Review*, 29 (2010): 76–88.

Atack, Margaret, 'Introduction', *French Cultural Studies*, 22 (2011): 183–5.

Aubrac, Lucie, *Ils partiront dans l'ivresse* (Paris: Seuil, 1984).

Auda, Grégory, *Les belles années du "milieu" 1940–1944* (Paris: Éditions Michalon, 2002).

Auden, W.H., 'The Guilty Vicarage', *Harpers*, May 1948, <http://harpers.org/archive/1948/05/0033206>.

Aziza, Claude, *La littérature policière* (Paris: Pocket, 2003).

Balzac, Honoré de, *Le Colonel Chabert* (Paris: Gallimard, 1974; first published 1832).

Baronian, Jean-Baptiste, *Simenon ou le roman gris. Neuf études sentimentales* (Paris: Textuel, 2002).

Barthes, Roland, 'Structure du fait divers', *Essais critiques* (Paris: Seuil, 1964).

Barthes, Roland, 'L'Effet de réel', *Communications*, 11 (1968): 84–9.

Barthes, Roland, *Le Plaisir du texte* (Paris: Seuil, 1973).

Bazyler, Michael J. and Roger P. Alford (eds), *Holocaust Restitution. Perspectives on the Litigation and its Legacy* (New York and London: New York UP, 2006).

Becker, Avi, (ed.), *The Plunder of Jewish Property During the Holocaust* (Houndmills, Basingstoke: Palgrave, 2001).

Becker, Lucille, *Georges Simenon Revisited* (New York: Twayne Publishers, 1999).

Bell, Ian A. and G. Daldry (eds), *Watching the Detectives: Essays on Crime Fiction* (Basingstoke: Palgrave Macmillan, 1990).

Benvenuti, Stefano, Gianni Rizzoni, and Michel Lebrun, *Le Roman criminel* (Nantes: L'Atalante, 1979).

Berlière, Jean-Marc, *Policiers français sous l'Occupation* (Paris: Perrin, 2001).

Bertrand, Olivier, 'Lyon-II nie la faute négationniste', *Le Monde*, 2 October 2000, accessed via Nexis UK.

Besson, Patrick, *Didier dénonce* (Paris: Fayard 2002; first published 1997).

Bihr, Alain, 'Du passé ne faisons pas table rase!', in Alain Bihr, Gido Calderon et al., *Négationnistes: les chiffonniers de l'histoire* (Paris: Éditions Golias et Éditions Syllepse, 1997): 17–34.

Bishop, Michael and Christopher Elson, *French Prose in 2000* (Amsterdam: Rodopi, 2002).

Bloom, Clive, (ed.), *Twentieth-Century Suspense: The Thriller Comes of Age* (Basingstoke: Palgrave Macmillan, 1990).

Boileau-Narcejac, *Le Roman policier* (Paris: PUF, 1975).

Bonnet, François and Nicolas Weill, 'Pierre Vidal-Naquet analyse les relais dont disposent les négationnistes', *Le Monde*, May 4 1996, accessed via Nexis UK.

Bonny, Jacques, *Mon père, l'inspecteur Bonny* (Paris: Laffont, 1975)

Borniche, Roger, *Le Gang* (Paris: Arthème Fayard, 1975).

Botta, Anna, 'Detecting Identity in Time and Space. Modiano's *Rue des boutiques obscures* and Tabucchi's *Il Filo dell'orizzonte*', in Merivale, P. and S.E. Sweeney (eds), *Detecting Texts: The Metaphysical Detective Story from Poe to Postmodernism* (Philadelphia: U Pennsylvania P, 1999).

Boudard, Alphonse, *L'Étrange Monsieur Joseph* (Paris: Robert Laffont: 1998).

Bourdier, Jean, *Histoire du roman policier* (Paris: Éditions de Fallois, 1996).

Bourdrel, Philippe, *L'Épuration sauvage* (Paris: Perrin, 2002).

Branche, Raphaëlle, 'Des viols pendant la guerre d'Algérie', *Vingtième Siècle. Revue d'histoire*, 75 (2002): 123–32.

Bradbury, Ray, *Fahrenheit 451* (London: HarperCollins, 2008; first published 1954).

Breton, Jacques, *Les collections policières en France* (Paris: Éditions du Cercle de la Librairie, 1992).

Breton, Auguste le, *2 sous d'amour* (Paris: Vertiges du Nord, 1986).

Browne, Ray B. and Lawrence A. Kreiser Jr, *The Detective as Historian: History and Art in Historical Crime Fiction* (Bowling Green, OH: Bowling Green State U Popular P, 2000).

Camus, Albert, *L'Étranger* (Paris, Folio, 1978; first published 1942).

Camus, Albert, *La Peste* (Paris: Gallimard, 1947).

Cathelin, Jean and Gabrielle Gray, *Crimes et trafics de la Gestapo française* tomes 1 and 2 (Paris: Historama, 1972).

Cawelti, John G., *Adventure, Mystery and Romance* (London and Chicago: U Chicago P, 1976).

Chabon, Michael, *The Final Solution: A Story of Detection* (London: Fourth Estate, 2005).

Charney, Hanna, 'Oedipal Patterns in the Detective Story', *Psychoanalytic Approaches to Literature and Film*, eds Maurice Charney and Joseph Reppen (London and Toronto Associated UP, 1987): pp. 238–48.

Chauvy, Gérard, *Aubrac: Lyon 1943* (Paris, Albin Michel, 1997).

Chemin, Ariane, 'La querelle du négationnisme rebondit à l'ultra gauche', *Le Monde*, 8 June 1996, accessed via Nexis UK.

Cima, Denise, *Étude sur La Ronde de nuit, Modiano* (Paris: Ellipses, 2000).

Cheyney, Peter, *Your deal my lovely* (London: Collins, 1941).

Cheyney, Peter, *A toi de faire, ma mignonne*, trans. by Marcel Duhamel (Paris: Gallimard, 1949).

Chernaik, Warren, Martin Swales, and Robert Vilain, *The Art of Detective Fiction* (Basingstoke: Macmillan P, 2000).

Cloonan, William, *The Writing of War. French and German Fiction about World War II* (Gainesville: UP of Florida, 1999).

Collins, Wilkie, *The Moonstone* (Oxford: Oxford UP, 1999; first published 1868).

Collovald, Annie and Éric Neveu, *Lire le noir: enquête sur les lecteurs de romans policiers* (Paris: Centre Pompidou, 2004).

Combe, Sonia, Archives interdites. Les peurs françaises face à l'Histoire contemporaine (Paris: Albin Michel, 1994).

Comentale, Edward P., Stephen Watt and Skip Willman (eds), *Ian Fleming and James Bond. The Cultural Politics of 007* (Bloomingdale and Indianapolis: Indiana UP, 2005).

Coquio, Catherine (ed.), *L'Histoire trouée: négation et témoignage* (Nantes: L'Atalante, 2003).

Corcuff, Philippe and Lison Fleury, 'Profondeurs du social et critique politique: hypothèses comparatives sur Maigret et le néo-polar', *Mouvements*, 15/16 (2001): 28–34.

Couégnas, Daniel, *Introduction à la paralittérature* (Paris: Seuil, 1992).

Currie, Mark, *About Time. Narrative, Fiction and the Philosophy of Time* (Edinburgh: Edinburgh UP, 2007).

Daeninckx, Didier, *Mort au premier tour* (Paris: Denoël, 1997; Le Masque, 1982).

Daeninckx, Didier, 'Ce n'est pas tout que de ne pas brûler les gens ...' in *Paroles à la bouche du présent. Le négationnisme: histoire ou politique?*', ed. Natacha Michel (Marseille: Éditions Al Dante, 1997): 45–56.

Dantec, Maurice, 'La fiction comme laboratoire anthropologique expérimentale', *Les Temps modernes*, 595 (1997): 263–81.

Dean, Carolyn, *The Fragility of Empathy after the Holocaust* (Ithaca, NY: Cornell UP, 2004).

Deighton, Len, *SS-GB* (London: Cape, 1978).

Derrida, Jacques, 'Force de loi: le "fondement mystique de l'autorité"', *Cardozo Law Review*, 11 (1989–90), in parallel text, trans. Mary Quaintance: 920–1045.

Derrida, Jacques, *Archive Fever: A Freudian Impression* (Chicago and London: U Chicago P, 1996), trans. Eric Preenowitz; *Mal d'Archive: une impression freudienne* (Paris: Éditions Galilée, 1995).

Descartes, René, *Discours de la méthode* (Paris: Bordas, 1984; first published 1637).

Diamond, Hannah and Claire Gorrara, 'The Aubrac Controversy', *History Today*, 51.3 (2001): 26–7.

Dick, Philip, *The Man in the High Castle* (London: Penguin Books 1965; first published 1962).

Dine, Philip, *Images of the Algerian War* (Oxford: Clarendon P, 1994).

Douin Jean-Luc and Patrick Kechichian, 'Le groupe Ugine a-t-il produit du gaz Zyklon B durant les années 40? La revue Études et documents refuse l'article d'une historienne', *Le Monde*, 9 October 1996, accessed via Nexis UK.

Doucey, Bruno, *La ronde de nuit de Patrick Modiano* (Paris: Hatier, 2001).

Dubois, Jacques, 'Simenon à la Pléiade', <http://laguinguette.com/lejournal/2003/07cult/>.

Dubois, Jacques, *Le Roman policier ou la modernité* (Paris: Armand Collin, 2006).

Dubois, Page, 'Oedipus as Detective: Sophocles, Simenon, Robbe-Grillet', *Yale French Studies*, 108 (2005): 102–15.

Duff, David, *Modern Genre Theory* (Harlow, Essex: Longman, 2000).

Durand, Alain-Philippe and Naomi Mandel (eds), *Novels of the Contemporary Extreme* (London: Continuum, 2006).

Eco, Umberto, 'Narrative Structures in Fleming', in Christopher Lindner (ed.) *The James Bond Phenomenon* (Manchester and New York: Manchester UP, 2003): 34–55.

Eizenstat, Stuart E., *Imperfect Justice. Looted Assets, Slave Labor, and the Unfinished Business of World War II* (New York: Public Affairs, 2003).

Eisenzweig, Uri, *Autopsies du roman policier* (Paris: UGE, 1983).

Eisenzweig, Uri, *Le récit impossible: forme et sens du roman policier* (Paris: Christian Bourgois, 1986).

Eismann, G., 'L'escalade d'une répression à visage légale. Les pratiques judiciaires des tribunaux du Militärbefehlshaber in Frankreich, 1940–1944', in *Occupation et répression militaire allemandes: 1939–1945. La Politique du 'maintien de l'ordre' en Europe occupée* dir. G Eismann and S. Martens, (Paris: Éditions Autrement, 2007): 127–68.

Elster, Jon, *Closing the Books: Transitional Justice in Historical Perspective* (Cambridge: Cambridge UP, 2004).

Emmanuel, Michelle, *From Surrealism to Less Exquisite Cadavers. Léo Malet and the Evolution of the French Roman Noir* (Amsterdam, New York: Rodopi, 2006).

Evans, Richard, 'History, Memory, and the Law: the Historian as Expert Witness', *History and Theory*, 41 (2001): 326–45.

Evrard, Franck, *Lire le roman policier* (Paris: Dunod, 1996).

Ewert, Jeanne, 'Lost in the Hermeneutic Funhouse: Patrick Modiano's Postmodern Detective', in Walker, R.G. and J.M. Frazer, *The Cunning Craft: Original Essays on Detective Fiction and Contemporary Literary Theory* (Macomb: Western Illinois UP, 1990): 166–73.

Fabre, Jean, *Enquête sur un enquêteur: Maigret. Un essai de sociocritique* (Montpellier: CERS, 1981).

Faurisson, Robert, 'Le problème des chambres à gaz ou la rumeur d'Auschwitz', *Le Monde*, 29 December 1978, accessed via Nexis UK.

Feliciano, Hector, *Le Musée disparu. Enquête sur le pillage d'œuvres d'art en France par les nazis* (Paris: Éditions Austral, 1995).

Fish, Stanley, 'Holocaust Denial and Academic Freedom', *Valparaiso University Law Review*, 35 (2001): 499–524.

Fleury, Béatrice and Jacques Walter, 'Le Procès Papon. Médias, témoin-expert et contre-expertise historiographique', *Vingtième siècle*, 88 (2005): 63–76.

Fondanèche, Daniel, *Le Roman policier* (Paris: Ellipses, 2000).

Forsdick, C., '"Directions les oubliettes de l'histoire": witnessing the past in the contemporary French *polar*', *French Cultural Studies*, 12 (2001): 333–50.

Francillon, Claude, 'Un éditeur lyonnais condamné pour publicité en faveur d'œuvres révisionnistes', *Le Monde*, 29 May 1999, accessed via Nexis UK.

Fraser, David, *Law after Auschwitz: Towards a Jurisprudence of the Holocaust* (Durham, NC: Carolina Academic P, 2005).

Fraser, David, 'Polarcauste: law, justice and the Shoah in French detective fiction', *International Journal of Law in Context*, 1.3 (2005): 237–59.

Frommer, Franck and Marco Oberti, 'Dominique Manotti: du militantisme à l'écriture tout en parlant politique: entretien', *Mouvements*, 15–16 (2001): 41–7.

Frow, John, *Genre* (London and New York: Routledge, 2006).

Fry, Stephen, *Making History* (London: Hutchinson, 1996).

Fuchs, Anne, *Phantoms of War in Contemporary German Literature, Films and Discourse* (Houndmills, Basingstoke: Palgrave Macmillan, 2008).

Garibian, Sévane, 'La Loi Gayssot ou le droit désaccordé' in Catherine Coquio (ed.) *L'Histoire trouée*: 223–46.

Gascoigne, David, (ed.), *Violent Histories. Violence, Culture and Identity in France from Surrealism to the Néo-polar* (Oxford, Bern: Peter Lang, 2007).

Gaston-Breton, Tristan, *Sauvez l'or de la Banque de France* (Paris: le cherche midi, 2002).

Gaudin, Nicolas, 'Interventions digressives du narrateur, ou l'élaboration de San-Antonio', *French Review*, 58 (1984): 58–67.

Gautier, Jean-Paul, *Les Êxtremes droites en France. De la traversée du désert à l'ascension du Front national (1945–2008)* (Paris: Éditions Syllepse, 2009).

Genette, Gérard, *Paratexts: Thresholds of Interpretation*, trans. Jane E. Lewin (Cambridge: Cambridge UP, 1997; first published as *Seuils*, Paris, Seuil, 1987).

Gerin, Pierre-M., 'San-Antonio fou de sa langue. Création lexicale dans un argot littéraire', *Initiales/initials*, 5 (1985): 11–20.

Ginzburg, Carlo, *Clues, Myths and the Historical Method* (Baltimore, MD: Johns Hopkins UP, 1989).

Golsan, Richard, 'Memory's bombes à retardement: Maurice Papon, crimes against humanity, and 17 October 1961', *Journal of European Studies*, 28.1–2 (1998): 153–72.

Golsan, Richard, *The Papon Affair. Memory and Justice on Trial* (New York and London: Routledge, 2000).

Golsan, Richard, 'Papon: The Good, the Bad, and the Ugly', *SubStance*, 91 (2000): 139–52.

Golsan, Richard, 'L'Affaire Karski: Fiction, History, Memory Unreconciled', *L'Esprit créateur*, 50.4 (2010): 81–96.

Goodkin, Richard E., 'Killing Order(s): Iphigenia and the Detection of Tragic Intertextuality', *Yale French Studies*, 76 (1989): 81–107.

Gorrara, Claire, 'Narratives of Protest and the Roman Noir in Post-1968 France', *French Studies*, 54.3 (2000): 313–25.

Gorrara, Claire, 'Tracking down the past: the detective as historian in texts by Patrick Modiano and Didier Daeninckx', in Mullen, Anne and Emer O'Beirne, *Crime Scenes. Detective Narratives in European Culture since 1945*: 281–90.

Gorrara, Claire, 'Malheurs et ténèbres: Narratives of Social Disorder in Léo Malet's *120, rue de la gare, French Cultural Studies*, 12.3 (2001): 271–83.

Gorrara, Claire, *The Roman noir in Post-War French Culture* (Oxford: Oxford UP, 2003).

Gorrara, Claire, 'Reflections on Crime and Punishment: Memories of the Holocaust in Recent French Crime Fiction', *Yale French Studies*, 108 (2005): 131–45.

Gorrara, Claire, 'French Crime Fiction: from *genre mineur* to *patrimoine culturel*', *French Studies* 61.2 (2007): 209–14.

Gorrara, Claire, *French Crime Fiction and the Second World War. Past Crimes, Present Memories* (Manchester: Manchester UP, 2012).

Gorrara, Claire (ed.), *French Crime Fiction* (Cardiff: U of Wales P, 2009).

Gorrara, Claire, 'Dramatic and traumatic: French crime fiction and the Reconstruction of France', in Louise Hardwick (ed.) *New Approaches to Crime* (Oxford, Bern: Peter Lang, 2009): 121–36.

Gorrara, 'Forgotten crimes? Representing Jewish experience of the Second World War in French crime fiction', *South Central Review*, 27.1–2 (2010): 3–20.

Greenberg, Judith, 'Trauma and transmission: echoes of the missing past in *Dora Bruder*', *Studies in Twentieth and Twenty-First Century Literature*, 31 (2007): 351–449.

Grenard, Fabrice, *La France du marché noir (1940–1949)* (Paris: Payot, 2008).

Guidée, Raphaëlle and Maryline Heck (eds), *Cahier de l'Herne. Modiano* (Paris : Éditions de l'Herne, 2012).

Guyot-Bender, Martine. *Mémoire en dérive: poétique et politique de l'ambiguïté chez Patrick Modiano* (Paris: Minard, 1999).

Hardwick, Louise (ed.), *New Approaches to Crime* (Oxford, Bern: Peter Lang, 2009).

Harris, Frederick J., *Encounters with Darkness. French and German Writers on World War II* (Oxford and New York: Oxford UP, 1983).

Harris, Robert, *Fatherland* (London: Hutchinson, 1992).

Harris, William V., 'History, Empathy and Emotions', *Antike unr Abendland*, 56 (2010): 1–23.

Holquist, Michael, 'Whodunit and Other Questions: Metaphysical Detective Stories in Post-War Fiction', *New Literary History*, 3.1 (1971): 135–56.

Horsley, Lee, *The Noir Thriller* (Basingstoke: Palgrave, 2001).

Horsley, Lee, *Twentieth-Century Crime Fiction* (Oxford: Oxford UP, 2005).

Howell, Jennifer, 'In defiance of genre: the languages of Patrick Modiano's Dora Bruder project', *Journal of European Studies*, 40.1 (2010): 59–72.

Hutton, Margaret-Anne, 'From Christ-Killers to Christ-Figures: Representations of Jews in Post-1980 French Occupation Fiction', *French Cultural Studies*, 18.1 (2007): 107–24.

Hutton, Margaret-Anne, 'Jonathan Littell's *Les Bienveillantes*: Ethics, Aesthetics and the Subject of Judgment', *Modern and Contemporary France*, 18.1 (2010): 1–15.

Hutton, Margaret-Anne, 'Is France Post Post-War? Judging the Nazi Past in Recent Novels by Maud Tabachnik, Michel Rio and Sylvie Germain', in *Narratives of French Modernity*, Lorna Milne and Mary Orr (eds) (Oxford, Bern: Peter Lang, 2011): 301–16.

Hutton, Margaret-Anne, 'Legacies of the Second World War: Representations of the Theft of Jewish Property in Recent French Crime Fiction', *French Studies*, 66.4 (2012): 493–509.

Huyssen, Andreas, 'Present Pasts: Media, Politics, Amnesia', *Public Culture*, 12.1 (2000): 21–38.

Huyssen, Andreas, *Present Pasts. Urban Palimspests and the Politics of Memory* (Stanford, CA: Stanford UP, 2003).

Igounet, Valérie, *Histoire du négationnisme en France* (Paris: Seuil, 2000).

Jameson, Fredric, 'Magical Narratives: On the Dialectical use of Genre Criticism', in David Duff (ed.), *Modern Genre Theory* (Harlow, Essex: Longman, 2000): 167–92.

Jacquemard, Serge, *La bande Bonny-Lafont* (Paris: Fleuve noire, 1992).

Janover, Louis, *Nuit et brouillard du révisionnisme* (Paris: Paris-Méditerranée, 1996).

Jeanneney, Jean-Noël, *Le Passé dans le prétoire* (Paris: Seuil: 1998).

Jeannerod, Dominique, *San-Antonio et son double* (Paris: Presses Universitaires de France, 2010).

Jones, Kathryn N., *Journeys of Remembrance. Memories of the Second World War in French and German Literature, 1960–1980* (Oxford: Legenda, 2007).

Jouanneau, Virgile and Sandra Gabbai, 'Entretien avec Maurice G. Dantec', March 1996: <http://www.les-ours.com/novel/dantec/dantec1.htm>.

Jouvin, Emmanuel, and Laurence Ducousso, *La Guerre dans le roman noir français* (Fontenay-sous-Bois: Médiatèque Louis Aragon, 1994).

Kawakami, Akane, *A Self-Conscious Art. Patrick Modiano's Postmodern Fictions* (Liverpool: Liverpool UP, 2000).

Kawakami, Akane, 'Patrick Modiano's Unreliable Detectives', in Anne Mullen and Emer O'Beirne *Crime Scenes* (Amsterdam: Rodopi, 2000): 195–204.

Kemp, Simon, *Defective Inspectors. Crime Fiction Pastiche in Late-Twentieth-Century French Literature* (Oxford: Legenda, 2006).

Kitson, Simon, *The Hunt for Nazi Spies* (Chicago and London: U Chicago P, 2008; first published as *Vichy et la chasse aux espions nazis* (Éditions Autrement, 2005).

Klein, Holger, (ed. with J. Flower and E. Homberger), *The Second World War in Fiction* (London: Macmillan, 1984).

Knight, Stephen, *Form and Ideology in Crime Fiction* (London: Macmillan Press, 1980).

Knight, Stephen, *Crime Fiction 1800–2000: Detection, Death, Diversity* (Basingstoke: Palgrave Macmillan, 2004).

Kritz, Neil J. (ed.), *Transitional Justice. How Emerging Democracies Reckon with Former Regimes*, vol. II. (Washington, DC: United States Institute of Peace P, 1995).

LaCapra, Dominick, *History, Theory, Trauma: Representing the Holocaust* (Ithaca, NY: Cornell UP, 1994).

LaCapra, Dominick, *History and Memory after Auschwitz* (Ithaca, NY: Cornell UP, 1998).

LaCapra, Dominick, *History in Transit: Experience, Identity and Critical Theory* (Ithaca, NY: Cornell UP, 2004).

Lacassin, Francis, *Mythologie du roman policier* (Paris: UGE, 1974).

Lacroix-Riz, Annie, *Industriels et banquiers sous l'Occupation. La collaboration économique avec le Reich et Vichy* (Paris: Armand Colin, 1999).

Le Breton, Auguste, *2 sous d'amour. Une biographie du Milieu français sous l'occupation allemande* (Paris: Vertiges du Nord/Carrère, 1986).

Lebrun, Michel and Jean-Paul Schweighaeuser, *Le guide du polar: histoire du roman policier français* (Paris: Syros, 1987).

Leroux, Gaston, *Le Mystère de la chambre jaune* (Paris: Livre de Poche 1960; first published 1908).

Lévy, Bernard-Henri, 'Le Bloc-notes de Bernard-Henri Lévy', *Le Point*, 13 July 1996, accessed Nexis UK.

Lindeperg, Sylvie, 'Scénarisation du négationnisme par la télévision française: les temps et logiques d'un média', *French Cultural Studies*, 13 (2002): 259–80.

Lindner, Christopher (ed.), *The James Bond Phenomenon* (Manchester and New York: Manchester UP, 2003).

Lits, Marc, *Le roman policier* (Liège: Éditions du Céfal, 1993).

Lomnitz, Sacha, 'Le poulpe, Le Pen et le roman populaire', *Critique*, 55 (1999): 445–56.

Longuechaud, Henri, *Conformément aux ordres de nos chefs* (Paris: Plon, 1985).

Lloyd, Christopher, *Collaboration and Resistance in Occupied France* (Houndmills, Basingstoke: Palgrave Macmillan, 2003).

Lloyd, Christopher, 'In the Service of the Enemy: The Traitor in French Occupation Narratives', *French Cultural Studies*, 22 (2011): 239–49.

Lyotard, Jean-François with Jean-Loup Thébaud, *Just Gaming*, trans. Wlad Godzich (Minneapolis: U Minnesota P, 1985; first published as *Au Juste*, Paris: Christian Bourgeois, 1979).

Lyotard, Jean-François, *The Differend. Phrases in Dispute* (Minneapolis: U Minnesota P, 1988); translation George Van Den Abbeele; first published as *Le Différend*, Paris: Éditions de Minuit, 1983.

Macintosh, Fiona, *Sophocles. Oedipus Tyrannus* (Cambridge: Cambridge UP, 2009).

MacIntyre, Ben, 'French Chemical firm is linked to Holocaust gas' *The Times*, 9 October 1996, accessed via Nexis UK.

Malmgren, Carl, *Anatomy of Murder* (Bowling Green, OH: Bowling Green U Popular P, 2001).

Mandel, Ernest, *Delightful Murder: A Social History of the Crime Story* (London: Pluto Press, 1984).

Manifeste des 121, *Vérité-Liberté*, 4, 6 septembre (1960).

Marrus, Michael, *Some Measure of Justice. The Holocaust Era Restitution Campaign of the 1990s* (London and Madison: U Wisconsin P, 2009).

Mattéoli, Jean, *Mission d'étude sur la spoliation des juifs de France*, <http://www.ladocumentationfrancaise.fr/rapports-publics/984000110/index.shtml>.

McHale, Brian, *Constructing Postmodernism* (London and New York, Routledge: 1992).

McLoughlin, Kate, *Authoring War. The Literary Representation of War from the Iliad to Iraq* (Cambridge: Cambridge UP, 2011).

Merivale, P. and S.E. Sweeney (eds), *Detecting Texts: The Metaphysical Detective Story from Poe to Postmodernism* (Philadelphia, U Pennsylvania P, 1999).

Mertens, Thomas, 'Continuity or Discontinuity of Law? – David Fraser's *Law after Auschwitz: Towards a Jurisprudence of the Holocaust*', *German Law Journal*, 8.05 (2005): 533–46.

Mertens, Thomas, 'But was it Law?', *German Law Journal*, 7. 02 (2006): 191–8.

Messac, Régis, *Le "Detective Novel" et l'influence de la pensée scientifique* (Paris: H. Champion, 1929).

Migozzi, Jacques, *Le roman populaire en question(s)* (Limoges: PULIM, 1997).

Million, Clément, *Occupation allemande et justice française: les droits de la puissance occupante sur la justice judiciaire 1940–1944* (Paris: Dalloz, 2011).

Milne, Lorna and Mary Orr (eds), *Narratives of French Modernity* (Oxford, Bern: Peter Lang, 2011).

Morris, Alan, 'Attacks on the Gaullist "Myth" in French Literature since 1969', *Forum for Modern Language Studies*, 21.1 (1986): 71–83.

Morris, Alan, *Collaboration and Resistance Reviewed. Writers and the Mode Rétro in Post-Gaullist France* (New York and Oxford: Berg, 1992).

Morris, Alan, *Patrick Modiano* (New York: Berg, 1996).

Morris, Alan, '"Avec Klarsfeld contre l'oubli": Patrick Modiano's *Dora Bruder*', *Journal of European Studies*, 36.3 (2006): 269–93.

Morris, Alan, '*Roman noir, années noires*: the French *néo-polar* and the Occupation's Legacy of Violence', in David Gascoigne (ed.), *Violent Histories* (Oxford, Bern: Peter Lang, 2007): 131–54.

Morris, Alan, 'From Social Outcasts to Stars of the Mainstream: the Combatants of the Collaboration in Postwar France', *Journal of War and Culture Studies*, 2.2 (2009): 167–79.

Most, Glenn and William Stowe (eds), *The Poetics of Murder* (San Diego, New York, and London: Harcourt Brace Jovanovich, 1983).

Motte, Warren, 'Introduction to San Antonio', *French Forum*, 4 (1979): 195–205.

Mouvements, 15–16 mai-août (2001), special edition on the 'roman noir'.

Moyn, Samuel, 'Empathy in History, Empathizing with Humanity', *History and Theory*, 45 (2006): 397–415.

Müller, Elfriede, and Alexander Ruoff, *Le polar français. Crime et histoire*, trans. Jean-François Poirier (Paris: La Fabrique, 2002).

Mullen, Anne and Emer O'Beirne, *Crime Scenes. Detective Narratives in European Culture since 1945* (Amsterdam: Rodopi, 2000).

Narcejac, Thomas, *The Art of Simenon*, trans. C. Rowland, (London and New York: Routledge & Kegan Paul, 1952; originally published as *Le Cas Simenon*, Paris, Presses de la Cité, 1950).

Nicholas, Lynn, *The Rape of Europa* (London: Vintage, 1995).

Novick, Peter, *The Resistance Versus Vichy: The Purge of Collaborators in Liberated France* (New York: Columbia UP, 1968).

Nora, Pierre, 'Le Syndrome, son passé, son avenir', *French Historical Studies*, 19.2 (1995): 487–93.

Norden, Eric, *The Ultimate Solution* (New York: Warner Paperback Library, 1973).

Nothomb, Amélie, *Acide sulphurique* (Paris: Albin Michel, 2005).

Palmer, Jerry, *Thrillers. Genesis and Structure of a Popular Genre* (London: Edward Arnold, 1978).

Panek, Leroy, *The Origins of the American Detective Story* (Jefferson, NC and London: McFarland & Co. Inc., 2006).

Pederson-Krag, Geraldine, 'Detective Stories and the Primal Scene', in Most Glen and William Stowe (eds), *The Poetics of Murder* (San Diego, New York, and London: Harcourt Brace Jovanovich, 1983): 13–20.

Peitsch, Helmut, Charles Burdett, and Claire Gorrara, *European Memories of the Second World War* (New York and Oxford: Berghahn Books, 1999).

Pereira, Acaio, 'Le philosophe Roger Garaudy est condamné pour contestation de crimes contre l'humanité', *Le Monde*, 2 March 1998, accessed via Nexis UK.

Platten, David, 'The Geist in the machine: nazism in Tournier's *Le Roi des Aulnes*', *Romanic Review*, 84.2 (1993): 181–94.

Platten, David, 'Reading-Glasses, Guns and Robots: A History of Science in French Crime Fiction', *French Cultural Studies*, 12 (2001): 253–70.

Platten, David, 'The Impact of the contemporary *roman noir*: Pennac, Daeninckx, and the question of a cultural evolution', in M. Bishop and C. Elson (eds) *French Prose in 2000* (Amsterdam: Rodopi, 2002).

Platten, David, '"Ceci n'est pas une pipe": shades of *noir* in Simenon', *Australian Journal of French Studies*, 43.1 (2006): 19–34.

Platten, David, 'Origins and Beginnings: the Emergence of Detective Fiction in France', in Claire Gorrara (ed.), *French Crime Fiction* (Cardiff: U Wales P, 2009).

Platten, David, *The Pleasures of Crime. Reading Modern French Crime Fiction* (Amsterdam: Rodopi, 2011).

Plenel, Edwy and Olivier Biffaud, 'La tentation national-communiste. En France comme en Russie, des anciens staliniens et des intellectuels d'extrême gauche rêvent d'une "troisième voie" rouge et brune', *Le Monde*, 26 June, 1993, accessed via Nexis UK.

Plenel, Edwy and Olivier Biffaud, 'La tentation national-communiste. *L'Idiot, laboratoire rouge-brun'*, *Le Monde*, 1 July 1993, accessed via Nexis UK.

Pons, Jean, 'Le roman noir, littérature réelle', *Les Temps modernes*, 595 (1997): 5–14.

Porch, Douglas, *The French Secret Services* (Oxford: Oxford UP, 1997).

Porter, Dennis, *The Pursuit of Crime. Art and Ideology in Detective Fiction* (New Haven: Yale UP, 1982).

Priestman, Martin, *Detective Fiction and Literature: the Figure on the Carpet* (New York: St. Martin's P, 1991).

Priestman, Martin, *Crime Fiction: From Poe to the Present* (Cambridge: Cambridge UP, 1998).

Prost, Antoine, 'Les historiens et les Aubrac: une question de trop', *Le Monde*, 12 July 1997, accessed via Nexis UK.

Proust, Marcel, *Le temps retrouvé* (Paris: Gallimard, 1954; first published 1927).

Radbruch, Gustav, 'Statutory Lawlessness and Supra-Statutory Law', trans. B. Litschewski and S.L. Paulson, *Oxford Journal of Legal Studies*, 26.1, 1–11; first published as 'Gesetzliches Unrecht und übergesetzliches Recht', *Süddeutsche Juristen-Zeitung*, 1 (1946): 105–8.

Rajsfus, Maurice, *La Police de Vichy* (Paris: le cherche midi, 1995).

Rechtman, Richard, 'Produire du témoignage', in Catherine Coquio (ed.), *L'Histoire trouée: négation et témoignage* (Nantes: L'Atalante, 2003): 613–24.

Reid, Donald, 'Resistance and Its Discontents: Affairs, Archives, Avowals, and the Aubracs', *The Journal of Modern History*, 77 (2005): 97–137.

Reuter, Yves, *Le Roman policier* (Paris: Armand Colin, 2005).

Rezpka, Charles, *Detective Fiction* (Cambridge: Polity, 2005).

Rigney, Ann, 'Fiction as a Mediator in National Remembrance', S. Berger, L. Eriksonas, A. Mycock (eds) *Narrating the Nation* (New York and Oxford: Berghahn Books, 2008).

Rolland, Michel, 'Construction et métamorphose d'un type populaire dans la culture médiatique: le mauvais garçon', in Jacques Migozzi (ed.) *Le Roman populaire en question(s)* (Limoges: PULIM, 1997): 37–45.

Ross, Kristin, 'Parisian Noir', *New Literary History*, 41. 1 (2010): 95–109.

Roth, Marty, *Foul and Fair Play. Reading Genre in Classic Detective Fiction* (Athens: U Georgia P, 1995).

Rothberg, Michael, 'Between Auschwitz and Algeria: Multidirectional Memory and the Counterpublic Witness', *Critical Inquiry*, 33 (2006): 158–84.

Rousset, David, *L'Univers concentrationnaire* (Paris: Éditions du Pavois, 1946).

Rousso, Henry, *Le Syndrome de Vichy de 1944 à nos jours* (Paris: Seuil, 1990; first edition 1987).

Rousso, Henry, and Eric Conan, *Vichy, un passé qui ne passe pas* (Paris: Gallimard, 1996).

Rousso, Henry, *The Haunting Past. History, Memory, and Justice in Contemporary France*, transl. Ralph Schoolcraft (Philadelphia: U Pennsylvania P, 2002; originally published as *La Hantise du passé: entretien avec Philippe Petit* (Paris: Textuel, 1998).

Rousso, Henry, Vichy. *L'Événement, la mémoire, l'histoire* (Paris: Gallimard, 2001).

Rousso, Henry, *Le Dossier Lyon III. Le Rapport sur le racisme et le négationnisme à l'université Jean-Moulin* (Paris: Fayard, 2004).

Sanders, Paul, *Histoire du marché noir 1940–1946* (Paris: Perrin, 2001).

Sartre, 'La République du silence', *Situations III* (Paris: Gallimard, 1949).

Sartre, 'Qu'est-ce qu'un collaborateur?' *Situations III* (Paris: Gallimard, 1949).

Scaggs, John, *Crime Fiction* (London and New York: Routledge, 2005).

Schehr, Lawrence, 'Dantec's Inferno', in A.-P. Durand and N. Mandel (eds) *Novels of the Contemporary Extreme* (London: Continuum, 2006).

Schoolcraft, Ralph and Richard Golsan, 'Paradoxes of the postmodern reactionary: Michel Rio and Michel Houellebecq', *Journal of European Studies*, 37.4 (2007): 349–71.

Schweighaeuser, Jean-Paul, *Le roman noir français* (Paris: PUF, 1984).

Segal, Charles, *Sophocles's Tragic World. Divinity, Nature, Society* (Cambridge, MA: Harvard UP, 1998).

Simenon, Georges, *L'Age du roman* (Bruxelles: Complexe, 1988).

Simonnot, Dominique, 'Le conflit vire à la bagarre entre les auteurs de polars', *Libération*, 3 July 2001, accessed via Nexis UK.

Smith, Alex, Duval, 'French "made B Gas for Holocaust"' *The Observer*, 13 October 1996, accessed via Nexis UK.

Sophocles, *Antigone, Oedipus the King, Electra*, trans. H.D.F. Kitto (Oxford: Oxford UP, 1994).

Sophocles, *Oedipus Tyrannus*, trans. Peter Meineck and Paul Woodruff (Indianapolis: Hackett Publishing Co., Inc., 2000).

Spearing, Nick, '"Don't go changing": on Richard Weisberg's critique of Stanley Fish and Holocaust Denial', *Law and Literature*, 20 (2008): 318–42.

Steiner, George, *The Portage to San Cristobal* (London: Faber & Faber, 1981).

Steele, Stephen, 'Daeninckx, quand le roman policier part en guerre', *French Studies Bulletin*, 71 (1999): 9–10.

Strong, Jeremy, *Genre Matters: Essays in Theory and Criticism* (Bristol: Intellect Books, 2005).

Suleiman, Susan, *Crises of Memory and the Second World War* (Cambridge, MA. and London: Harvard UP, 2006).

Sutherland, Nina, 'Trois continents, une guerre, un empire: Francophone Narratives of War and Occupation in the French Empire', *French Cultural Studies*, 22.3 (2011): 187–96.

Swirski, Peter, *From Lowbrow to Nobrow* (Montreal: McGill-Queen's University Press, 2005).

Symons, Julian, *Bloody Murder. From the Detective Story to the Crime Novel: A History* (London: Pan Book, 1994; first published Faber and Faber 1972).

Les Temps modernes, 595 (1997), 'Pas d'orchidées pour les temps modernes', special edition.

Todorov, Tzvetan, *Poétique de la prose* (Paris: Seuil, 1971).

Tournier, Michel, *Le Roi des Aulnes* (Paris: Gallimard, 1970).

Tournier, Michel, *Le Vent paraclet* (Paris: Gallimard, 1977).

Van Dine, S.S. 'Twenty Rules for Writing Detective Stories', in H. Haycraft (ed.), *The Art of the Mystery Story: A Collection of Critical Essays* (New York: Carroll & Graf): 189–93.

Vanoncini, André, *Le roman policier* (Paris: PUF, 2003).

Veldman, Hendrik, *La Tentation de l'inaccessible* (Amsterdam: Rodopi, 1981).

Verdaguer, Pierre, 'Le héros national et ses dédoublements dans *San Antonio* et *Astérix*', *The French Review*, 61.4 (1988): 605–16.

Vergaduer, Pierre, *La séduction policière* (Birmingham, AL: Summa Publications, 1999).

Vernant, Jean-Pierre and Pierre Vidal-Naquet, *Myth and Tragedy in Ancient Greece* (New York: Zone Books, 1990).

Viala, Fabienne, *Le roman noir à l'encre de l'histoire. Vásquez Montalbán et Didier Daeninckx* (Paris: L'Harmattan, 2006).

Vidal-Naquet, Pierre, *Assassins of Memory. Essays on the Denial of the Holocaust*, trans. Jeffrey Mehlman (New York: Columbia UP, 1992; first published as *Les Assassins de la mémoire*, Paris: Éditions de la Découverte, 1987).

Videlier, Philippe, 'Nouvelle affaire négationniste. Zones d'ombre et coup monté', *Le Monde diplomatique*, 507, 1 June 1996, accessed via Nexis UK.

Walker, 'David, Writing between *fait divers* and *procès-verbal*', *French Cultural Studies*, 12 (2001): 237–51.

Walker, R.G. and J.M. Frazer (1990) *The Cunning Craft: Original Essays on Detective Fiction and Contemporary Literary Theory* (Macomb: Western Illinois UP).

Weill, Nicolas, 'Des entreprises françaises au service de l'Allemagne nazie', *Le Monde*, 11 October 1996, accessed via Nexis UK.

Weisberg, Richard, *Vichy Law and the Holocaust in France* (New York: New York UP, 1996)

Weisberg, Richard, 'Fish Takes the Bait: Holocaust Denial and Post-Modernist Theory', *Law and Literature*, 14 (2002): 131–42.

Wieviorka, Annette, *Déportation et génocide* (Paris: Plon, 1992).

Wieviorka, Annette, 'Jean Moulin ou l'Histoire comme énigme policière', *Le Monde*, 18 November 1998, accessed via Nexis UK.

Winks, Robin (ed.), *Detective Fiction: A Collection of Critical Essays* (Englewood Cliffs, NJ: Prentice-Hall, 1980).

Winks, Robin (ed.), *The Historian as Detective: Essays on Evidence* (New York: Harper & Row, 1968).

Yale French Studies, 108 (2005), special edition, 'Crime Fiction', ed. Andrea Goulet and Susanna Lee.

Index

abbé Pierre 179–80, 185n58, 185n59,
185n60, 185–6, 193
Abécassis, *L'Or et la cendre* 9, 109, 122,
129–33, 136–41, 146–7, 154
Alavoine, Bernard 11, 14, 16
Algerian War
as continuity theme 5, 110, 134,
171–6, 195
in *La Lèpre* (Boileau-Narcejac) 72,
79, 174
Amila, Jean 5
Au balcon d'Hiroshima 6, 46, 94, 97,
98, 101, 115
La Lune d'Omaha 166n10
La Vierge et le taureau 183n55
amnesia 50–53, 69–70, 179n36, 191
Amouroux, Henri 91n29
Amoz, Claude, *L'Ancien crime* 120,
150–52
anamnesia 71
anti-Semitism
and Holocaust denial 177–94
and Malet 93, 93n34
and police relations 120
and San-Antonio 57–8, 58n38
archives and archivists 125, 128, 131, 135,
136, 145, 154, 158, 185, 191
Arnaud, Georges J.
L'Antizyklon des atroces 177, 179, 182,
186, 188–90
Maudit blood 165n9
Spoliation 165n9
Ascari, Maurizio 8
Assouline, Pierre 20, 23n53, 26
Atack, Margaret 2, 3, 5, 26
Aubert, Brigitte 5
La Rose de fer 152–3
Aubrac affair 129–32, 130n20
Auclair, Georges, *Un Amour allemand*
47, 135
Auda, Grégory 100, 102–4, 105n57, 106

Auden, W.H. 11, 25
Azéma, Jean-Pierre 131

Balzac, Honoré de 71–2, 72n65
bande Bonny-Lafont (*Carlingue*) 101–5,
105n57, 112–15
Barbie, Klaus 75, 127, 129, 131, 143–4,
172, 189
Baronian, Jean-Baptiste 15
Barthes, Roland 49, 123–4, 126, 131n24, 148
Baumier, Matthieu, *Les Apôtres du néant*
120, 171
Belgian literature 4–5, 4n14, 49n12,
53n22, 95n40, 165n9: *see also*
Simenon; Troye
Bellanti, Louis and Frédérique Vacher, *Le
Manuscrit de la mémère morte* 169
Benson, Stéphanie, *Biblio-quête* 4, 135, 179,
181–2, 186n63, 190–94, 192n76
Berenboom, Alain, *Périls en ce royaume*
4n14, 49n12, 53n22, 95n40
Berlière, Jean-Marc 88n20, 107–8, 112
Berri, Claude 129, 130
Bialot, Joseph
Babel-ville 109
La Nuit du souvenir 47, 121
black marketeering 5, 78, 162
and discursive contexts 123, 126
and legal system 21–2, 84–5, 87,
90–93, 100–106
and occupying forces 85
as patriotic 90n25
Blond, Georges, *L'Ange de la rivière morte*
90–91, 93, 122–9, 133, 142
Boileau-Narcejac 5
La Lèpre 45, 66, 70–74, 78–9, 173–4
Les Louves 45, 66, 66n53, 69–73, 78, 79
Maldonne 45, 47, 66, 69–74, 78, 79, 165
Bonny, Pierre 101, 101n49, 113: *see also*
bande Bonny-Lafont
Borges, Jorge Luis 6–7, 195

Borniche, Roger 103, 104
Boudard, Alphonse 81, 81n3, 103, 104
Bourdrel, Philippe 89
Bousquet, René 107n60, 108, 109, 111,
    112, 131
Bradbury, Ray 157, 192n76
Breton, Auguste le 101n50
Breton, Jacques 14, 59
Busino, Jean-Jacques, *Au nom du piètre qui
    a l'essieu* 135, 179–80, 185n58,
    185n60, 186, 188, 193–4

camps
    and father-son relations 151
    and Holocaust denial 192–3
    and immigrants today 190
    light-hearted treatment in San Antonio
        58n38, 64, 79
    phantasy of in *Les Racines du mal*
        (Dantec) 75
    repression of in *Maldonne* (Boileau-
        Narjecak) 70
    return from in *Le Retour des cendres*
        (Monteilhet) 166–7
    as setting for crime fiction 46–7
        Acide sulphurique (Nothomb) 77
        Meurtre dans un Oflag (Troye)
            46–53
    and trauma 162
Camus, Albert 20, 25, 43n71
Carlingue (bande bonny-Lafont) 101–3,
    105–6, 112–15
Carraud, Jypé, *Les poulets du Cristobal*
    46n5, 168, 168n15
Castillo, Michel del, *Les portes du
    sang* 136n41
Cawelti, John G. 14
Cayre, Hannelore, *Toiles de maîtres*
    120, 165n9
Chabon, Michael, *The Final Solution. A
    Story of Detection* 133n27
Chaboud, Jack, *Le Tronc de la veuve*
    122, 165n9
Chandler, Raymond 15, 83, 140
Chauvy, Gérard 129–31
Chesterton, G.K. 133n28
Cheyney, Peter 56n31, 56n33, 56–7,
    59, 59n42
Cloonan, William 2

closure 124, 145–7, 152
clues, 33–4, 48–9, 50–52, 53, 78
Coatmeur, Jean-François, *On l'appelait
    Johnny* 46n5
collaboration and collaborators
    and 'bad' criminals 100–106, 114,
        116–17
    and black marketeering 22, 91
    'horizontal' 27, 29, 40, 63, 158–9
    in justice and revenge texts 168–70
    played down in San-Antonio 63–5
    and return of repressed 71–2
Collins, Wilkie 45, 50n14, 53n21
colonialism 72, 120
Combe, Sonia 145
coming-of-age novels 19, 24, 24n55, 26
communists 46, 110, 120, 124, 126n12,
    127, 150, 179, 180, 189
Conan, Éric 126n14, 132, 144, 157, 157n4
concentration camps: *see* camps
continuity themes 157–8
    and Algerian War 171–6
    and Holocaust denial 177–96
    justice and revenge 168–71
    and legacies 165–8
    and periodisation 158–60
    revenant nazis 163–5
    trauma 160–63
Courchay, Claude, *Retour à Malaveil* 9,
    160n6, 170n16
Couturier, Hélène, *Sarah* 6, 120, 162n7
crime: *see also* criminals
    committed by the State 92–5
    common and / or political 84–95
    and historical context 81–4
crime fiction
    categorisation of 6–8
    devaluation of 16–17, 17n29
    and fiction 8–10, 16–19, 43n71, 112–13
    legitimization of 17, 17n30
crimes against humanity 70, 136, 141,
    143–4, 146, 149, 168–9, 173, 178
criminals
    'bad' criminals 100–106, 114, 116–17
    'good' criminals 95–100, 116–17
    in roman noir 82–3
    in whodunnit 82
Currie, Mark 158
cyber-*noir* 73

Daeninckx, Didier 5
  Éthique en toc 135, 179, 181–2,
    185n60, 185–91, 193–4
  Itinéraire d'un salaud ordinaire 9,
    110n64, 110–12, 171–2
  La Mort n'oublie personne 6, 88, 89,
    122, 126–9, 132–3
  La route du Rom 135
  Les Figurants 171
  Meurtres pour mémoire 5, 122, 134–5,
    145–6, 172–3, 173n22
  Nazis dans le métro 179, 181, 183–5,
    189, 193
Dantec, Maurice G.
  Les racines du mal 4, 73–7, 78–9,
    149n73, 161
Dard, Frédéric (San-Antonio)
  Batailles sur la route 65, 159–60
  Descendez-le à la prochaine 54n25
  Du plomb dans les tripes (PT) 45, 54,
    60–62, 64–5
  Équipe de l'ombre 65
  La Crève 65, 158–60, 163
  La Tombola des voyous 54n25
  Laissez tomber la fille (LTF) 45, 54,
    55, 57, 60–62, 64, 107
  Les souris ont la peau tendre (SPT) 45,
    54–8, 61–4
  Mes hommages à la donzelle
    54n25, 58n38
  Réglez-lui son compte 54n25, 58
  San Antonio renvoie la balle 54n25
  Une gueule comme la mienne 65, 122
Darnaud, Guillaume, *Le Crépuscule des*
  vieux 164, 165
de Gaulle, Charles 53, 62, 62n47, 91, 97,
  136n38, 172, 173n24
Dean, Carolyn 139
Del Pappas, Gilles, *Bleu sur la peau* 47, 101
Deleuse, Robert, *Retour de femme* 160n6
Delteil, Gérard
  KZ Retour vers l'enfer 46, 122, 126–9,
    133, 153–4
  Mort d'un satrape rouge 126n12
Demouzon, Alain, *Agence Melchior* 89n21
denunciation 29, 35–6, 37, 92, 140
deportees 47, 162, 165–8
  David Rousset 64
  light-hearted treatment in San Antonio 64

Derrida, Jacques 1, 81, 145
Descartes, René 51, 51n17
D'Estienne d'Orves, Nicholas, *Les*
  orphelins du mal 6, 121, 164–5
detective fiction, and crime fiction 6–7, 8
Dick, Philip K. 45, 76
Dine, Philip 174n25
Doriot, Jacques, 177, 189, 190
doubling or splitting in protagonist, 50,
  52–3, 53n22, 77, 153: *see also*
  Abécassis, *L'Or et la Cendre*
Dubois, Jacques 13, 14, 17–19, 48–9, 52
Ducousso, Laurence 3
Duhamel, Marcel 59

Eichmann, Adolf 70, 79, 112
Eisenzweig, Uri 8n22
Emmanuel, Michelle 14–15, 19,
  93n34, 122n5
empathy, as investigative mode 139–40
épuration sauvage (unregulated purges) 6,
  40, 65, 89, 123, 159, 160n6
euthanasia 93–4
Evans, Richard 143, 144
Evrard, Franck 14, 17, 34, 58, 83
Exbrayat, Charles *Avanti la musica!* 4
extermination camps: *see* camps

Fabre, Jean 11, 12, 15, 19
fait divers 86, 119, 123–6, 123n8, 129
Fajardie, Frédéric 5
  Après la pluie 97n42, 106, 120
  La Théorie du 1% 120, 160n6, 170n16
  Le Loup d'écume 164
  Querelleur 102
  Sous le regard des élégantes
    91n29, 177n31
far right (political) 126n12, 176–82, 184,
  188–90, 192–3, 195–6: *see also*
  Holocaust denial; anti-Semitism
father-son relationship: *see* generational
  relations; oedipal themes;
  investigators, sons and fathers
Faurisson, Robert 181, 187, 188, 188n68:
  see also Holocaust denial
femme fatale as symbol 125, 142
Fish, Stanley 182–3, 193–4
Fleming, Ian 56, 57
Fonteneau, Pascale, *Otto* 47, 152–3

Forsdick, Charles 134, 146
Frachet, Pierre, *Comme dit ma
     grand-mère* 59–60
Fraser, David 92, 93n34, 95n39, 120n3,
     133n27, 134, 172n20, 172–3
freedom / imprisonment theme 66–9, 71,
     73, 78, 79
French and German mixed parentage
     149, 152–3
Front national 173, 177–8, 179, 190, 191:
     see also far right

Garaudy, Roger 179–80, 185, 185n60, 193
Garnier, Pascal, *L'A26* 160–63, 167, 178
Gautier, Jean-Paul 177
Geffray, Stéphane, *Les teutons
     flingueurs* 165n9
generational relations: *see also* legacies;
     investigators, sons and fathers
     blurring generations 159–60, 162, 163
     second generation coming to terms
          with first 147–54, 175–6
     second generation revenge 72, 129,
          162, 169–70
     third generation 121, 148, 154, 171, 178
Genette, Gérard 16
German and French mixed parentage
     149, 152–3
Gestapistes 92, 100–106, 108, 111,
     113–14, 117: *see also* bande
     Bonny-Lafont
Giovanni, José, *Mon ami le traître* 3n10,
     81n3, 81–2, 92
Golsan, Richard 2n4, 134, 141n50
Gorrara, Claire 2n6, 3, 7, 17, 47n6, 61n43,
     84–5, 85n13, 95, 121, 134,
     146, 166n10
Gothic 51–2, 54, 77
Gouiran, Maurice
     Les vrais durs meurent aussi 173–6
     Sous les pavés, la rage 160n6
Guimard, Paul, *L'Ironie du sort* 9, 43n71

Hallier, Jean-Edern 180, 183
Hammett, Dashiell 15, 61n44
Harlay, Jérôme, *Le Sel de la guerre*
     107n60, 171
Harris, Frederick J. 2

Héléna, André
     Le Festival des macchabées (FM) 87,
          96, 98–100, 101, 107
     Le Goût du sang 89, 95n40
     Les Clients du Central Hôtel 88, 114–15
     Les Salauds ont la vie dure (SVD) 6,
          86, 88–9, 96–8, 101, 109, 113, 114
historians: *see also* investigators, historians
     as; investigators, journalists as
     and Holocaust denial 185–6, 189, 191–5
historiant 131, 131n24, 138
Hitler 38, 64, 85, 163, 172n20, 185, 193
Holocaust
     and common crime 70
     light-hearted treatment in San Antonio
          57–8, 58n38
     in *L'Or et la cendre* (Abécassis) 133,
          133n28, 146
     role-play in *Les racines du mal*
          (Dantec) 74–7, 79
Holocaust denial 47, 74, 74n69, 177–96
Horsley, Lee 8, 20, 27, 77
Huet, Philippe, *Bunker* 160n6, 171
Huyssen, Andreas 157, 170, 191

internment camps, *see* camps
investigators
     in classic whodunnit 31
     compromised powers under
          Occupation 24–5, 31–2, 106–13
     historians as 133–47, 192
     journalists as 121–33
     police as 24–5, 31, 86, 106–13, 120
     range of 119–21
     ratiocinative 31, 51, 51n16, 78, 125,
          141, 142, 154
     in *roman noir* 31
     and secret services 62, 129
     in series
          Nestor Burma 13, 84–5, 93–4,
               109, 122
          Poulpe 135
          San Antonio 55–8
     sons and fathers 147–53

Jacquemard, Serge 103, 104
Jameson, Fredric 12–13
Japp, Andrea, *Le Silence des survivants*
     160, 162–3, 167

Jeanneney, Jean-Noël 131
Jews: *see also* anti-Semitism; Holocaust;
    Holocaust denial
  identity of 166–7, 167n13
  police relations with 109
  and spoliation 46–7, 165n9, 166
  and statutory lawlessness 94–5
  stereotyping of 166, 168n15
  as symbols 79
Joanovici, Joseph 81n3, 101, 103
Joly, François, *La Rage* 120, 173–6
Jones, Kathryn N. 2
Jonquet, Thierry
  Du passé faisons table rase 121,
    135, 171–2
  Le pauvre nouveau est arrivé 180n42
  Les Orpailleurs 46–7, 120
journalists: *see* investigators, journalists as
Jouvin, Emmanuel 3
justice
  and closure 146, 152, 154
  in conflict with law 94
  as continuity theme 168–70
  and historians 142–5, 154
  and non-justice texts 171–2
  poetic (or rough) 49, 84, 91, 93, 129,
    162, 196
  post-war 89, 91–3, 116, 165n9

Kââ, *Trois chiens morts* 135
Kitson, Simon 62–3
Klein, Holger 2
Klotz, Claude, *Kobar* 47, 151–2
Knight, Stephen 8
Kolaire, Pierre, *Sur la ligne marginaux*
    60, 171
Konop, *Pas de Kaddish pour
    Sylberstein* 120
Krivine, Frédéric, *Un souvenir de Berlin*
    122, 136

LaCapra, Dominick 139–40, 141, 152
Lafont, Henri (Henri Chamberlin; Henri
    Normand) 101n50, 101–5, 105n57,
    112–15
Las Vergnas, Raymond *Le Mystère
    Niagara* 6
Laveau, Gérard, *La Trace du diable* 168
Lecroix-Riz, Annie 182

legacies 33, 35, 66, 165–8: *see also*
    generational relations;
    investigators, sons and fathers
Leroux, Gaston 51, 119, 121
Lindeperg, Sylvie 179n38
linguistically ludic works 45, 58–61,
    59n42, 61, 61n43, 61n44, 64
Lits, Marc 9, 17n29
Lloyd, Christopher 2–3, 3n10
Luraghi, Cyprien, *Pour cigogne le glas* 171
Lyotard, Jean-François 157, 188,
    188n68, 194–5

Malet, Léo 5, 14
  Du rebecca rue des Rosiers 101, 122n5
  Nestor Burma contre CQFD 94n36
  120, rue de la gare 6, 84–5, 93–5, 106
Malle, Louis, *Lacombe Lucien* 21, 23n54
Malmgren, Carl 16
Manchette, Jean-Patrick, *Que d'os* 101
Mandel, Ernest 15, 83, 99–100
Manotti, Dominique
  Le Corps noir 6, 91n29, 91–3, 96, 105,
    109–11, 112
  Nos fantastiques années fric 111n65
Martin, Roger
  Jusqu'à ce que mort s'ensuive 120
  Le G.A.L., l'égout 177n32, 178
Mazarin, Jean, *Collabo-Song* 92–3, 104,
    112, 113, 115
McHale, Brian 45, 74
McLoughlin, Kate 3
Meckert, Jean: *see also* Amila, Jean
  Nous avons les mains rouges 85
  Nous sommes tous des assassins 92
media and mediatisation
  controlling society 76, 77
  and Holocaust denial 179–82
  and journalists 121–33
memory
  collective 1–2, 20, 76, 124, 170–71, 173
  and Holocaust denial 191–2
  Jewish 109
  and repression 69, 71, 140: *see also*
    Rousso, *Le Syndrome de Vichy*
  and technology 74, 191–2
  turn to 157
Merle, Robert, *Treize reste raide* 60, 101, 121
Messac, Régis 7

milice 65, 71, 82, 88–90, 108–9, 120,
131, 140, 144, 149–50, 153–4,
158–9, 176
Modiano, Patrick
Dora Bruder 9, 113, 134, 136–41,
146–7
La Ronde de nuit 5, 9, 113–16
Les boulevards de la ceinture 122
Monsour, Jean, *Le Renard de la forêt
noire* 4
Monteilhet, Hubert, *Le Retour des cendres*
47, 166–8
Morris, Alan 2–3, 47n6, 115n69,
137–9, 149n71
Morris, Gilles-Demoulin, *Assassin, mon
frère* 46, 89, 114
Moulin, Jean 127, 129, 136, 181, 186, 190
Müller, Elfriede 3, 179n37
murder
as common or political crime 86–9,
92, 116
and death penalty 92

Narcejac, Thomas 13, 15, 65: *see also*
Boileau-Narcejac
nazis
and common or political crime 84–8
and fathers and sons 149–53
omission of reference to 149, 152
revenant 5, 163–5
and role play 74–6, 77, 79
and San Antonio 62–5, 78–9
and statutory lawlessness 94
symbolic role of 77
victim / perpetrator doubling 141, 152
nazi hunters 5, 47, 66, 152, 165, 168
negationism: *see* Holocaust denial
neo-nazis 54, 74n69, 177, 179n37
néo-polar, as crime fiction category 7
neuro-polar 73
Nora, Pierre 157n4
Nord, Pierre, *Double crime sur la ligne
Maginot* 46
Norden, Eric 76
Nothomb, Amélie, *Acide sulphurique* 77
Notin, Jean-Christophe, *Nom de code: La
Murène* 136n38
Novick, Peter 92–3

oedipal themes 6, 23–6, 30, 39, 40, 50–51,
69, 119, 147–53, 154
Orange amère, *L'Ordure, hein!* 177n30
Ouvard, Jacques, *Le plongeon du frère
Boileau* 88, 171

Papon, Maurice 130n19, 131, 134, 143,
144n55, 146, 172–3, 175
paratext 9, 16, 18, 27, 30, 37, 43n71, 48,
112, 115, 127
past links to present: *see* continuity themes
Pavloff, Franck, *Le Vent des fous* 173
Pécherot, Patrick, *Boulevard des branques*
6, 60, 93–4, 104–6, 108–9, 120
Peitsch, Helmut 2, 3
Pennac, Daniel, *Au Bonheur des ogres* 51n16
Perrin, Jean-Pierre, *Chiens et louves*
135, 160n6
Pétain 53, 62, 81n3, 95n40, 140, 172
Piljean, André, *Passons la monnaie!* 58n38
Plantin, Jean 181–2, 185–6, 187, 191
Platten, David, 13, 15, 19–20, 26, 39, 41,
42n70, 51, 61, 86n15, 183n55
polar, as crime fiction category 7
police: *see also* investigators, police as
and Occupation 24–5, 31, 86, 106–13
and Jews 109
police procedural 7, 77
Porch, Douglas 55n28, 62n47
Porter, Dennis 8, 9, 22, 24, 61n44,
82n5, 83
Pouy, Jean-Bernard 13n9, 179
POW (prisoner of war) 6, 46, 66–8, 70, 78,
79, 119, 120
present links to past: *see* continuity themes
Priestman, Martin 8, 9
proleptic intertextuality 40–42, 43
Proust, Marcel 23, 23n52

racism 57, 79, 93, 93n34, 120
Radbruch, Gustav 94–5
Rajsfus, Maurice 110n64
ratiocination 31, 51, 51n16, 78, 125, 141,
142, 154
Redonnet, Marie, *Nevermore* 122
Renaud, Dominique, *Morts à l'appel* 122
repression (of painful memories) 53, 69,
70–72, 132, 140, 151, 157

resistants and Resistance
changing public perception of 124–6,
153–4
as part of cognitive framework 189
and political or common crime 84–99,
113–15, 116
and recurring hero San-Antonio 56–7,
63, 65
serial killer and 75–7, 161
Reuter, Yves 9, 17n29, 19–20
revenge or justice texts 168–71
Rezpka, Charles 8
Rigney, Ann 189n69
Rio, Michel, *Leçon d'abîme* 136, 140–42,
141n50, 144n55, 146–7
Robbe-Grillet, Alain, *La Reprise*
149n73
Rolland, Michel 99
roman à clé 183, 185
roman à énigmes, as crime fiction
category 7
roman à suspense
as crime fiction category 7
Boileau-Narcejac 65–73, 78
roman jeu, as crime fiction category 7
roman noir
as crime fiction category 7
and *La neige était sale* 19–26
and language play 58–60
and *Le Clan des Ostendais* 27–8
and self-reflexivity 60, 61
and Simenon 14–16
roman noir engagé, as crime fiction
category 7
roman policier
crime fiction categories and 7–8,
13–17, 43
Roth, Marty 31–2, 50, 51–2
rouge-brun alliance 180–81, 183–5, 189,
192: *see also* Holocaust denial
Rousset, David 64
Rousso, Henry
The Haunting Past 1–2, 131n22, 136,
172n19
Holocaust denial commission and
181–2, 186–7
Le Syndrome de Vichy 1n3, 46, 53, 71,
78, 124, 126, 158, 178n33

*Vichy. L'Événement, la mémoire,
l'histoire* 142n51, 143, 145
Vichy, un passé qui ne passe pas
(Rousso and Conan) 126n14, 132,
144, 145, 157, 157n4
Ruoff, Alexander 3, 179n37

San-Antonio: *see* Dard, Frédéric
Sanders, Paul 90–91
Sartre, Jean Paul
'La République du silence', 67–9, 71,
73, 78
'Qu'est-ce qu'un collaborateur?' 70n64
representations of the war and 6
Schweighaeuser, Jean-Paul 58n40
sci-fi (science fiction) and crime fiction
integration 6, 73–9
screen narrative 36–7, 39–40
self-reflexivity 25, 42, 44, 45, 50, 60–61,
116, 138, 140, 154, 165
serial killers 6, 73–9, 160–63, 178
série noire 9, 19n43, 59
Simenon, Georges
categorizing his work 11–19
La neige était sale 15–18, 19–26, 27,
31, 35–7, 40, 42–4, 108, 147
Le Clan des Ostendais 16–19, 27–32,
35, 37, 42–4, 108
Le Train 16, 18, 19, 37–44
Les Autres 16–19, 32–7, 39–40, 42–4,
46, 51, 122
Simsolo, Noël
Exterminateurs 91n29
Wazemmes 165n9
Siniac, Pierre
Ferdinaud Céline 102
Le Tourbillon 102n52
Les mal lunés 101–2
Les Morfalous 96
Les sauveurs suprêmes 97
L'Orchestre d'acier 97, 98
Sous l'aile noire des rapaces 85, 96,
99, 101, 103–5, 108–9
Sophocles 119, 147n64, 147–8, 150, 154:
see also oedipal themes
Soulas, Antoinette, *Café sans tickets* … 46n5
statute of limitations 143, 168
statutory lawlessness 94–5

Steiner, George, *The Portage to San Cristobal* 168
Suleiman, Susan 68n60, 68n61, 129, 131
suspense novel (*roman à suspense*)
  Boileau-Narcejac 65–73, 78
  as crime fiction category 7
Swirski, Peter 9

Tabachnik, Maud
  La Honte leur appartient 169–70, 173
  Tango des assassins 6, 121–2, 168
Tanugi, Gilbert, *Les grottes de Crésus* 171
thriller 3n10, 66
  comic or parodic 6, 45, 53–65, 77–8, 164
  as crime fiction category 7, 8n24
  marketed as 18, 37, 41, 112
  pseudo- 27–32, 35, 43–4
  traits of 20, 27
Todorov, Tzvetan 8–9, 19–20, 27
Tournier, Michel
  Le Roi des Aulnes 40–42
  Le Vent paraclet 40n68
Touvier, Paul 75, 143–4
trauma 37, 39–40, 160–63, 167
Troye, Raymond, *Meurtre dans un Oflag* 4, 45, 46, 47–55, 60, 66, 77–8, 119–20, 147

Vacher, Frédérique and Louis Bellanti, *Le Manuscrit de la mémère morte* 169
Van Dine, S.S. 32

Vargas, Fred 5
  Un peu plus loin sur la droite 119, 136, 142–4, 149–52
Väterliteratur 148–9, 154
vector of memory 1–2, 1n3, 71, 124
Vichy régime and the law 21–2, 82n4, 85n13, 86–7, 90–92, 94–5, 107, 109, 111, 172–3
Vichy syndrome: *see* Rousso, *Le Syndrome de Vichy*
Vidal-Naquet, Pierre 182, 184, 185n59, 193
Videlier, Philippe 187, 187n64
Villemot, Jean-Marie, *L'œil mort* 94n35

Wagneur, Alain, *Homicide à bon marché* 47, 120
Walker, David 123n8
Weisberg, Richard 193–4
whodunnits:
  crime fiction categories and 7–8
  hybrid whodunnit 45–53, 78
  pseudo whodunnit 32–7, 39
Wieviorka, Annette 136, 166n12
Winks, Robin 133–4, 138–9
witness
  accounts produced by 128, 131, 133, 137, 141, 154, 187, 191, 196
  expert 142–3
  impossible 188n68

Zamponi, Francis, *Le Boucher de Guelma* 173n23
Zufferey, Daniel, *L'Étoile d'or* 4n14, 165n9